The Role of Police
in American Society

THE ROLE OF POLICE IN AMERICAN SOCIETY

A Documentary History

Edited by BRYAN VILA
and CYNTHIA MORRIS

Primary Documents in American History and Contemporary Issues

GREENWOOD PRESS
Westport, Connecticut • London

Library of Congress Cataloging-in-Publication Data

The role of police in American society : a documentary history /
    edited by Bryan Vila, Cynthia Morris.
        p.   cm.—(Primary documents in American history and
    contemporary issues, ISSN 1069–5605)
      Includes bibliographical references and index.
      ISBN 0–313–30164–6 (alk. paper)
        1. Police—United States—History—Sources.   2. Law enforcement—
    United States—History—Sources.   I. Vila, Bryan, 1947–   .
    II. Morris, Cynthia, 1961–   .   III. Series: Primary documents in
    American history and contemporary issues series.
    HV8138.R64   1999
    363.2'0973—dc21   98–41420

British Library Cataloguing in Publication Data is available.

Library of Congress Catalog Card Number: 98–41420
ISBN: 0–313–30164–6
ISSN: 1069–5605

First published in 1999

Greenwood Press, 88 Post Road West, Westport, CT 06881
An imprint of Greenwood Publishing Group, Inc.
www.greenwood.com

Printed in the United States of America
∞™

The paper used in this book complies with the
Permanent Paper Standard issued by the National
Information Standards Organization (Z39.48–1984).

10 9 8 7 6 5 4 3 2 1

Copyright Acknowledgments

Contents

Series Foreword

This series is designed to meet the research needs of students, scholars, and other interested readers by making available in one volume the key primary documents on a given historical event or contemporary issue. Documents include Supreme Court decisions, government reports, laws, speeches, conference proceedings, academic articles, biographical accounts, book excerpts, and news stories.

The purpose of the series is twofold: (1) to provide substantive and background material on an event or issue through the text of pivotal primary documents that shaped policy or law, raised controversy, or influenced the course of events; and (2) to trace the controversial aspects of the event or issue through documents that represent a variety of viewpoints. Documents for each volume have been selected by a recognized specialist in that subject with the advice of a board of other subject specialists, school librarians, and teachers.

To place the subject in historical perspective, the volume editor has prepared an introductory overview and a chronology of events. Documents are organized either chronologically or topically. The documents are full text or, if unusually long, have been excerpted by the volume editor. To facilitate understanding, each document is accompanied by an explanatory introduction. Suggestions for further reading follow the document or the chapter.

It is the hope of Greenwood Press that this series will enable students and other readers to use primary documents more easily in their research, to exercise critical thinking skills by examining the key documents in American history and public policy, and to critique the variety of viewpoints represented by this selection of documents.

Preface

We took on this book project for Greenwood Press because it provides a unique resource for scholars, students, police officers, policy makers, and others concerned with the criminal justice system. Many books on policing, including some excellent histories, discuss the development and role of police in the United States. But none of them tells the story in the words of the people who were involved in the struggle to enforce laws, uphold the Constitution, maintain safe and stable communities, and create efficient and effective police. The documentary history approach presents core excerpts from original documents in chronological order so that readers can see for themselves how the issues, concerns, and ideals of police officers, chiefs, reformers, judges, and researchers changed over time.

The Introduction provides a historical overview of the development of the role of police in the United States. Each of the book's seven parts opens with a discussion of the social, economic, demographic, and environmental forces that affected our need for people to enforce laws and maintain order—as well as whom we chose to fill the role of police officer, our expectations of them, and how they actually tended to behave. In addition, the comments preceding each document explain the historical context in which it was written and provide information about its author. Taken as a whole, the introductory material weaves together key themes regarding the police in each historical era and is designed to provide the reader with an unbiased and accurate picture of how the role of police has changed in American society from colonial times to the present.

Another unique aspect of this book is the editorial team. One of the editors, Bryan Vila, is a former police officer who had substantial experience as a patrol officer, supervisor, police chief, and policy maker before earning a Ph.D. and becoming a university professor and researcher. Cynthia Morris is a professional writer with more than ten years' experience excerpting the heart from a wide variety of scientific and technical topics and then interpreting them for everyday people. Based upon the response of readers to another Greenwood documentary history we wrote, *Capital Punishment in the United States* (1997), we think that you will find that this book provides the insights and information needed to develop your own opinions about the role of police, how they came to play it, and what changes need to be made if police in the future are to meet the needs of a rapidly changing and increasingly diverse society.

Thousands of books, articles, essays, memoirs, and court cases have been written about the role of police, but due to space limitations we could select fewer than a hundred documents. We used several criteria to choose which documents to include. First, because we wanted the documents to be representative historically, we tried to include items from as many time periods as possible, beginning with colonial settlements in the "New World." We also wanted to cover as many issues as possible—including riots, strikes, commission reports, innovations, ground-breaking studies, and major court cases—and cover them in a balanced manner.

In order to achieve these conflicting goals we excerpted all of the longer documents, attempting to present the most important and relevant material without changing an author's meaning. Because so many Supreme Court cases have affected policing, we had to limit ourselves to those that had the most fundamental impact on policing or made the strongest statements about the role and responsibilities of police officers. Rather than ignore a number of other well-known cases that substantially affected police conduct, we elected to discuss them in the introductions to Parts I–VII. We hope that those interested in learning more about the subjects covered in this book—or in obtaining the complete text of documents from which excerpts were taken—will make use of the Select Bibliography and Appendix A, which list all the materials that we found useful in editing this volume.

As the many citations throughout the book and the bibliography indicate, we are indebted to the research and writings of many scholars and authors. We would like to express our deep appreciation to them, and to the distinguished members of our advisory panel, Drs. Geoffrey P. Alpert, Gary Cordner, Jack R. Greene, Dennis Jay Kenney, and Otwin Marenin, whose comments and suggestions have been invaluable in editing this book. In addition, we thank the extremely helpful and knowledgeable staffs of the libraries at the University of Wyoming and the University of California, Irvine. Special thanks also are due to William H. Davis, an archivist in the Center for Legislative Archives at the National Archives in Washington, D.C., and Dorothea D. Newport, a reference librarian in the U.S. Department of Justice Library in Washington, D.C.; we always will remember their extraordinary assistance in tracking down rare historical documents—and the friendly, efficient, knowledge-able manner in which their agencies were run. Even farther afield, we thank Helen Krarup of the Cambridge University Institute of Criminology's Radzinowicz Library, who was extremely helpful in obtaining a full copy of the London Municipal Police Act of 1829. We also thank Carey Pearson, a graduate student in Political Science at the University of Wyoming, who provided meticulous assistance in researching connections between women's emancipation and the progressive movement.

This is our second book working with Emily Birch, acquisitions editor at Greenwood Press. Without her continuing support, advice, attentiveness, and friendship, this project would not have been possible.

Last, but far from least, we thank our families and friends, who have provided encouragement and understanding despite too many missed dinners, gatherings, and fishing trips. We especially thank Dwight and Siobhan Rowell and the staff of the Library Restaurant and Brewing Company and John and Jodi Guerin and the staff of Coal Creek Coffee Company, who provided sustenance, good cheer, and large tables to edit and proofread upon throughout the production process.

Introduction

How we define the role of police is much more than an interesting problem in government. Rather, it is a direct reflection of society's heart. Using primary source documents to trace the evolution of the role of police in American society from colonial times to the present gives us firsthand accounts of watchmen and constables, rangers and marshals, Pinkertons and G-men, as well as the officers, deputies, troopers, and patrolmen who handle contemporary police problems in the United States. But it also chronicles the attempts of political leaders, reformers, scholars, and police executives to deal with a range of social problems such as immigration, population growth, urbanization, racism, poverty, gender bias, and technological change as well as crime.

Policing addresses one of the most fundamental problems of social living—how to deal with those who violate group customs, norms, rules, and laws that enable cooperation. Cooperating together in large groups enables us to take advantage of one another's strengths and to compensate for individual weaknesses. The resulting sum can be much greater than the parts and, all else being equal, the larger the social group, the larger the potential benefit. But social living also provides opportunities for people to cheat. Instead of cooperating to produce a shared benefit, people can use force, fraud, or stealth to obtain valued resources. Once again, generally speaking, the larger the social group, the greater the opportunities for cheating. Cheaters weaken the cooperative bonds that enable productive social living and, like parasites in an animal, too many cheaters can kill or cripple a society.

FORMAL VS. INFORMAL SOCIAL CONTROL

The history of humanity is dominated by our struggle to maximize the benefits of social living and to control its liabilities. A great deal of social control is informal. Most often, children are taught and adults are sanctioned by a frown, a negative word, or the chilly response of others to undesirable behavior. But as misbehaviors become more serious, the potential consequences of being the person who provides sanctions increase as well. For example, shushing a child who is talking in a theater or speaking up when someone breaks a queue at the market is much less hazardous than trying to stop a bank robbery or intervening when a man is striking his wife. Larger societies, those with more than a few hundred people, develop cooperative solutions to this dilemma. Instead of individuals shouldering the burden for challenging more serious breaches of the social contract, the responsibility is delegated to people who specialize in formal social control. In most contemporary societies, these people include police, prosecutors, judges, and prison workers.

POLICING IN A FREE SOCIETY

To the extent that a society values individual liberty, formal social control is limited to behaviors that tangibly threaten productive social living—all productive societies must control interpersonal violence and protect property rights. But societies vary a great deal with regard to whether, and how much, they attempt to control more private behaviors such as prostitution, gambling, and drug use. There also is a great deal of variation in how tightly different societies attempt to control the behavior of social control agents themselves.

Because police specialize in, among other things, managing the most serious and dangerous breaches of social behavior, we provide them with the authority to use force, weapons, and other tools not available to the average citizen. The power we delegate to police—as well as the prestige that accompanies the special trust we place in them—enables them to fulfill their responsibilities, but it also makes it easier for corrupt officers to take advantage of people who possess less power and prestige. Thus, if providing formal social control is a fundamental problem of living in large productive social groups, so too is controlling the police. The manner in which we manage formal social control, and the extent to which we rely on formal rather than informal means of social control, says a great deal about how we perceive human beings and about our aspirations for social living—not just what we *say* about such things, but our actual beliefs.

In the preamble to the Constitution, the founders of the United States declared that the purpose of our nation was to "establish justice, insure domestic tranquillity, provide for the common defense, promote the general welfare, and secure the blessings of liberty to ourselves and our posterity." A careful look at how the gritty everyday problems of formal social control actually were being handled at different times in our history should tell us a great deal about how well those goals were being achieved. Examining efforts to change the role of police in American society over the years should speak volumes about how closely current values match those upon which the nation was founded.

SEVENTEENTH- AND EIGHTEENTH-CENTURY NIGHT WATCHMEN, CONSTABLES, AND SHERIFFS

Serious crimes were rare in the earliest American colonies, and there was little need for formal law enforcement. However, as the colonies rapidly grew and became more diverse, it became more difficult to maintain the peace and enforce laws. Internal pressure and outside threats from pirates, Indians, and foreign enemies soon led the colonies to adopt variants of the night watch, constabulary, and sheriffs of their European homelands.

These precursors to the police typically were ordinary citizens—usually drafted, sometimes elected or appointed—who had no training. In towns, citizen watches stood guard at night, often under the supervision of a full-time constable who also was responsible for maintaining order, enforcing the law, and administering punishments during the day. In rural areas, colonial governors appointed sheriffs to enforce laws, collect taxes, and apprehend criminals.

These citizen-police were well tuned to the problems of their counties, towns, and small cities. However, they also were untrained, ill-paid, and often held in low regard. As real cities with populations exceeding 50,000 began to emerge in the 1700s, the quality of life in them declined rapidly due to a lack of effective policing. Ineffective rural law enforcement, especially in the South, led to the establishment of extralegal "regulators." These bands of citizens were successful against outlaws, but without the control of law they often degenerated into bands of zealots who attacked virtually anyone of whom they disapproved.

One of the key problems that the new nation would face was how to delegate sufficient power to law enforcers so that they could "establish justice, insure domestic tranquillity, . . . [and] promote the general welfare" but still protect individual liberty.

NINETEENTH-CENTURY POLICE ON THE FRONTIER AND IN THE CITIES

In the explosive century following the Revolution, the population of the United States increased fifteenfold and its western boundary was pushed from the Appalachians to the Pacific. The role of police changed drastically as society attempted to maintain order during this period of incredible growth and upheaval.

Frontier Policing

Policing in sparsely settled, unorganized territories was delegated to U.S. marshals. As the territories organized and elected governments, county sheriffs and town marshals were established to keep the peace and enforce laws. Small frontier towns tended to follow policing models similar to those in eastern cities. But the vast distances and economic free-for-all that characterized most of the frontier required more novel approaches.

Railroads and huge livestock industries formed private police forces to look after their interests. Unfettered by jurisdictional boundaries, private police like the Pinkertons were effective at protecting property and tracking down outlaws and robbers who preyed upon their clients' far-flung enterprises. Later in the nineteenth century, they would become notorious for brutal strike-breaking activities in the increasingly industrialized nation's mines and factories.

In the least developed places, private citizens banded together during crises to dispense vigilante justice to bandits, rustlers, and murderers. When disturbances became more widespread, such as when a range war broke out between competing ranchers or between ranchers and farmers or sheep herders, the militia or military were brought in to restore order. Some areas, like Texas, organized Rangers to protect against bandits and Indian raids territory-wide.

Municipal Movement Toward "Modern" Policing

By the nineteenth century, American cities were bursting at the seams with immigrants from many cultures. As cities grew more crowded and disorganized, their problems compounded, quickly overwhelming the abilities of the night watch and constabulary. Initial aversions to a more capable standing police force—rooted in Revolutionary era suspicions of state power—finally were overcome in mid-century by widespread public disorder and fears of social disintegration. Several of the more disorderly cities established full-time police systems by adapting the successful "modern policing" model developed by the London Metropolitan Police to their own political realities. Soon, police services were accepted as yet another expected municipal service.

However, the American adaptation of modern policing lacked a number of key features that for years made the London Metropolitan Police, or "bobbies," a model for much of the world. Bobbies were career officers hired by the national government who served far from their homes and reported to a central headquarters. Officers in American cities like New York were appointed by the politician in charge of a local district in which they lived and worked. They reported to neighborhood precinct houses rather than citywide.

In comparison with London police, who fostered an air of fair and impartial authority, the American arrangement provided strong local control and police who were likely to rely on good neighborly relations to keep the peace. Of course, the downside to all this was political control, favoritism, and corruption.

Police Reform

In response to rampant post–Civil War corruption, the reform movement began to take on corruption in the nation's statehouses, legislatures, city halls, and police stations. Progressives such as Teddy Roosevelt instituted merit-based systems for hiring and promoting officers and managing police departments. Women's and religious groups fought for establishment of matrons in police departments to look after the needs of arrested women. And police chiefs began working together to improve their departments' integrity and efficiency.

In a single century, the young nation confronted first the need to increase the effectiveness of formal social control mechanisms, and then the need to improve control over those mechanisms. Some preliminary steps toward controlling the police were taken by the Supreme Court, which established ground rules limiting the tactics federal officers could use to obtain confessions. Political reformers and civic groups also played important roles, as did police executives who began to wrestle with what the scope of police duties should be as well as ideas for improving the quality of police officers, the equipment they used, and the administration of police departments.

ASPIRATIONS TO PROFESSIONALISM

During the first three decades of the twentieth century, "modern" police models had been adopted across the United States and were being refined under the influence of the progressive movement. By 1929, American policing had set the goals and ideals toward which it would strive for the rest of the century—the efficient administration of police services by officers who were honest, diligent, fair, well-trained, and capable of protecting the public from criminals, enforcing the law, and keeping the peace.

Over the years, progress toward these goals was erratic as the reform spirit waned periodically in the face of wars and economic troubles as well as social and technological change. In a system with thousands of independent policing agencies, the quality of different departments also varied dramatically. Overall, however, there was substantial progress as society and its institutions responded to scandals involving various types of police corruption and misconduct and as police executives and scholars strove to improve the efficiency and effectiveness of police organizations.

The striking contrast between policing in the 1920s and the 1980s highlights how much progress had been made. In most jurisdictions, the grossly underpaid, uneducated, untrained, bribe-taking white 1920s cop walking a beat and supervised by political cronies had been replaced by highly trained, and generally honest, officers who earned decent wages. In 1985, officers were driving patrol cars equipped in a manner that was inconceivable sixty years earlier, and their behavior was constrained by an array of rules, regulations, laws, and court decisions that probably would have been equally inconceivable. Although racial and ethnic minorities still were underrepresented in most American police agencies in 1985, their very presence would have shocked most of the old cops. So would the growing presence of women—not just as matrons, clerks, or juvenile officers, but as patrol officers, supervisors, and even chiefs of police.

Yet for all the legal, administrative, and technological improvements in the quality of policing, crime rates in the 1980s also were unimaginably high by 1920s standards. Part of the increase was due to population growth, urbanization, and social and technological changes that both had increased opportunities for crime and made it more difficult to prevent crime. But more and more, people began to recognize that something valuable had been lost along with the cop on the beat. For all the gains that had been made in crime-fighting ability, the police largely were unable to control crime or the production of criminals. Nor were they able to help people in many communities feel safe. In fact, many residents of minority communities sometimes felt threatened both by criminals who injured them and stole from them and by overzealous and discourteous police who subjected them to unwarranted harassment.

After decades of reforms that focused on who should be a police officer and how police organizations should be administered, attention returned to a fundamental question that had been largely ignored for decades: What should the police be expected to accomplish? Once again, the role of police was being recast in an effort to adapt to changing social needs and values.

THE RISE OF COMMUNITY POLICING

A new consensus began to emerge in the 1990s that police should play a major role in helping communities solve problems, especially problems related to crime. A major change in this approach was that, instead of just responding to crime, officers should work with others in their communities to identify and eliminate its underlying causes. Officers still needed to handle traditional police matters such as taking crime reports, making arrests, conducting investigations, and suppressing crime, but now their goals were broadened further. In deteriorating neighborhoods, this might mean discouraging panhandlers, prostitutes, addicts, and drunks from controlling public places—much as the neighborhood beat cop had done years previously. But the key to community policing was an emphasis on improving the quality of life in communities by helping residents deal with the problems that most concerned them.

The goals of community policing are laudable, but they also produce conflicting demands on police officers and police organizations. Some question whether it is possible for the same person to alternate freely between serving as a counselor, dispute mediator, community activist, and law enforcer because each task demands such different personal characteristics. Others have pointed out the irony of staffing many community policing assignments through the increased use of overtime. It is difficult for officers to develop stronger and more intimate bonds with the people within their communities when they are exhausted; tired cops get cranky just like the rest of us. The unusually high level of autonomy and initiative required of lower ranking officers under community policing also challenges traditional police organizations. Quasi-military police departments rely on a fairly rigid chain of command to direct departmental operations and to control employees. Higher ranking officers decide what needs to be done and how it should be done, and then delegate tasks to subordinates who report back after completing them. Commands flow downhill in this model, and reports flow back. Under community policing, officers and first-line supervisors work with community groups and organizations to decide what needs to be done, and then report on their decisions to higher-ups. This autonomy may make officers more effective, but it also weakens supervisory controls designed to inhibit corruption and misconduct. These are just a few examples of the kinds of problems that must be solved if community policing is to achieve its promise.

AMERICAN POLICING'S FUTURE

One of the insights that emerges from the type of historical review this volume provides is the dynamic tension between social order and individual rights. The police can be more efficient and effective agents of social control if we increase their power and capabilities. Increasing the power of the police can erode the freedom of criminals to injure people and take their property, but it also tends to diminish the liberty of law-abiding citizens. For example, having the police monitor remote televi-

[handwritten margin notes: what will be good for the to help the police.]

sion cameras that scan public parks can help cut down on crime, but it also intrudes on the privacy of law-abiding people as they walk, play, or perhaps sit on a bench and kiss. Requiring that parcels be mailed in person instead of allowing people to drop them in postboxes after hours might possibly make it more difficult for mail-bombers to escape detection, but it also steals the lunch hours from millions of innocent people.

A second, less well-discussed, dynamic that comes to light from reviewing the documents in this book is the tension between "modern" and community policing. On the one hand, the former emphasizes hierarchical control and fair and impartial authority. It enables administrators to monitor crime and to control crime-fighting activities efficiently, but has limited ability to deal with the day-to-day concerns of communities and neighborhoods. These concerns, as James Q. Wilson and George L. Kelling remind us in Document 78, can affect both the level of fear in a community and how vulnerable it is to crime problems. Community policing, on the other hand, improves the responsiveness of police to local problems and may be more effective at mobilizing community resources to address the root causes of crime and social disorder. But it also offers officers much more autonomy and provides more opportunities for misfeasance, corruption, and partiality.

It seems to us that the only way to manage these two sets of tensions—one between individual rights and social order, the other between local responsiveness and administrative efficiency—is through real professionalism. The challenges of community policing require high integrity, a mature sense of ethics, thoughtful problem-solving, people-dealing skills, and bureaucratic savvy in addition to the courage, determination, compassion, command presence, action orientation, and common sense that are needed for tactical police work. A great deal of progress has been made toward professionalizing the police since the last millennium. It will be exciting to see whether truly professional police officers emerge during the twenty-first century, the kinds of highly educated and skilled men and women August Vollmer argued for in 1919 (Document 33).

Significant Dates in the History of the Police in America

1631   The first night watch is established in Boston.

1704   The first slave patrol, a precursor to modern police forces, is established in the South. Slave patrols would continue until 1861.

1710   *The Constables Pocket-Book*, a guide for new constables, is published.

1737   Benjamin Franklin proposes establishing a paid watch in Philadelphia. However, his idea is not carried out for eight years.

1767   The Regulators, a vigilante group, emerge in the crime-ridden back country of South Carolina.

1789   The office of U.S. Marshal—the first federal law enforcement agency in the country—is established by the federal Judiciary Act of 1789.

1791   The Bill of Rights is adopted.

1823   The Texas Rangers are formed to protect American settlers from Indian attack in the Mexican territory of Texas.

1829   Sir Robert Peel establishes a centralized, "modern" police force in London. The London force eventually would serve as a model for the first modern police forces in America.

1845   America's first unified, prevention-oriented police force, patterned after the London Metropolitan Police, is established in New York City.

1853   The New York City police become the first police officers in America to wear uniforms.

1867   Allan Pinkerton publishes a manual on private policing for his agents titled *General Principles of Pinkerton's National Police Agency*.

1871   The first National Police Convention is held in St. Louis, Missouri.

1874   The first Indian Police force is established by John Clum on an Apache reservation in San Carlos, Arizona.

1878   Police matrons first begin to be employed by police departments.

1884   *Hopt v. Utah*: The Supreme Court establishes the first federal guidelines defining what would be considered an involuntary confession.

1887   Retired New York Police Chief George W. Walling publishes his *Recollections of a New York Chief of Police*.

1890   George M. Roe publishes *Our Police: A History of the Cincinnati Police Force from the Earliest Period Until the Present Day*.

1893   The first meeting of the National Chiefs of Police Union is held in Chicago.

        Marie Owens is hired as a "patrolman" with the Chicago Police Department after her police officer husband's death.

1894   A special investigative committee chaired by Republican Senator Clarence Lexow is formed to examine the nature and extent of corruption in the New York City Police Department. Its shocking revelations of police corruption lead to the downfall of Tammany control of the police.

1895   Future U.S. President Theodore Roosevelt is appointed head of a new, bipartisan New York City Police Commission established by anti-Tammany mayor William Strong.

1905   Lola Baldwin is hired by the Portland Police Department as an "operative" to provide protection and assistance for young women and children at the Lewis and Clark Centennial Exposition.

1908   The Louisville, Kentucky, police department becomes one of the first American police departments to use the automobile in police work.

1909   Noted police reformer Leonhard Felix Fuld publishes his influential book, *Police Administration*.

1910   Prominent police reformer Richard Sylvester, superintendent of the Washington, D.C., police department and president of the International Association of Chiefs of Police, delivers his well-known speech, "A History of the 'Sweat Box' and 'Third Degree,'" at the 1910 International Association of Chiefs of Police convention.

        Alice Stebbins Wells, the first official female police officer, is hired by the Los Angeles Police Department.

1911   Noted police reformer August Vollmer, known as the "father of modern professional policing in the United States," puts his entire police force in Berkeley, California, on bicycles.

1912   August Vollmer establishes motorcycle patrols within the Berkeley Police Department.

1913   August Vollmer establishes automobile patrols within the Berkeley Police Department.

1914   *Weeks v. United States*: The Supreme Court establishes the "exclusionary rule" disallowing the use of illegally obtained evidence in federal criminal trials.

1919   Former New York City Police Commissioner Arthur Woods publishes *Policeman and Public*, in which he advocates improved training for police officers.

        Dissatisfied with low wages and poor working conditions, nearly three-quarters of the Boston police force go on strike for three days. The Boston police strike is denounced by President Woodrow Wilson and Governor Calvin Coolidge of Massachusetts, and the striking officers are fired and replaced.

1920   Police critic and reformer Raymond B. Fosdick publishes *American Police Systems*, in which he harshly criticizes America's police departments for their political control, poor recruitment standards, and training, among other problems.

1921   Berkeley, California, police chief August Vollmer puts the first lie detector to use in a police laboratory.

        August Vollmer's Berkeley, California, police department is the first to install and use a radio in a police car.

1922   The Chicago Commission on Race Relations, established in the aftermath of a race riot that lasted for six days, releases its report, *The Negro in Chicago: A Study of Race Relations and a Race Riot*.

1923   The National Rifle Association assumes a leadership role in promoting and assisting police firearms and marksmanship training.

1924   John Edgar Hoover is appointed director of the Department of Justice's Bureau of Investigation, which in 1935 is renamed the Federal Bureau of Investigation (FBI).

1925   *Carroll et al. v. United States*: The Supreme Court establishes the right of the police to search a vehicle without a warrant if sufficient probable cause of illegal activity exists.

1928   The Detroit Police Department develops an improved police radio system. By the 1930s, radio will become a common feature in patrol cars.

1930   Congress passes legislation to enable the U.S. Department of Justice's Bureau of Identification to operate and manage the Uniform Crime Reporting system developed by noted police consultant Bruce Smith.

1931   The National Commission on Law Observance and Enforcement, also known as the Wickersham Commission, issues its *Report on Police*, prepared under the direction of August Vollmer, then professor of police administration at the University of Chicago.

        Ernest Jerome Hopkins publishes his popular book, *Our Lawless Police*, based in part on the findings of the National Commission on Law Observance and Enforcement's report, *Lawlessness in Law Enforcement*.

1933   Retired New York Police Captain Cornelius W. Willemse publishes his memoirs, *A Cop Remembers*.

1935   The Federal Bureau of Investigation establishes the National Police
        Academy to provide extensive instruction to exceptional officers from
        municipal, county, and state law enforcement agencies nationwide.

1936   *Brown et al. v. Mississippi*: The Supreme Court establishes the inadmis-
        sibility of involuntarily obtained confessions at state trials.

1937   The "FBI Pledge for Law Enforcement Officers" is published in the *FBI
        Law Enforcement Bulletin*.

1940   *Chambers et al. v. Florida*: The Supreme Court further defines what it
        considers to be coerced or involuntary confessions.

1944   In response to renewed efforts to unionize the police, the International
        Association of Chiefs of Police publishes a bulletin, *Police Unions and
        Other Organizations*, making clear its position against unionization.

1950   Influential police administrator and educator Orlando Winfield Wilson
        publishes a textbook, *Police Administration*, that eventually becomes
        known as the "bible" for U.S. police chiefs.

        In the wake of a corruption scandal, longtime Los Angeles police officer
        William H. Parker is appointed police chief for the LAPD.

1957   The International Association of Chiefs of Police adopts a "Law Enforce-
        ment Code of Ethics" as the standard for ethical police conduct.

1961   *Mapp v. Ohio*: The Supreme Court extends the federal exclusionary rule,
        established in the 1914 case of *Weeks v. United States*, to the states.

        Lois Lundell Higgins, director of the Crime Prevention Bureau of Illinois
        and president of the International Association of Women Police, pub-
        lishes the *Policewoman's Manual*, an instructional guide for female police
        officers.

1964   Juby E. Towler, captain and commanding officer of the detective bureau
        for the Danville, Virginia, police department, publishes *The Police Role
        in Racial Conflicts*, a guide intended to help police officers better under-
        stand their role, duties, and obligations when handling civil rights dem-
        onstrations.

1965   The Governor's Commission on the Los Angeles Riots, chaired by John
        A. McCone, issues its report on the Watts riots, *Violence in the City—An
        End or a Beginning?*

1966   *Miranda v. Arizona*: The Supreme Court rules that once a criminal sus-
        pect has been taken into police custody, he may not be interrogated
        without first being informed of his Fifth Amendment right against self-
        incrimination, his right to remain silent, and his Sixth Amendment right
        to an attorney.

1967   The President's Commission on Law Enforcement and Administration
        of Justice releases its general report, *The Challenge of Crime in a Free
        Society*, as well as several separate special reports, including *Task Force
        Report: The Police*.

1968   *Terry v. Ohio*: The Supreme Court establishes the legal right of the police to stop, question, and frisk a person who is behaving suspiciously, as long as the police officer has reasonable grounds for perceiving the person's behavior as suspicious.

The National Advisory Commission on Civil Disorders, also called the Kerner Commission after its chairman, Governor Otto Kerner of Illinois, issues its report on the causes of and solutions to the race riots of the 1960s, including a number of recommendations for improved police-citizen relations.

Congress passes the Omnibus Crime Control and Safe Streets Act. Title I of the act establishes the Law Enforcement Assistance Administration within the U.S. Department of Justice, and the Law Enforcement Education Program.

Noted expert on crime and public policy James Q. Wilson reports the findings of his in-depth study of police behavior in his book, *Varieties of Police Behavior*. Wilson's is the first study to explore the very different styles of policing that are implemented in different kinds of communities.

The Indianapolis Police Department is the first police department in the United States to assign women to routine patrol duty.

1969   Lawyer Paul Chevigny reports the findings of his two-year study of police abuses of power in New York City in his book, *Police Power*.

The police unionization movement gains momentum. By the 1970s, police unions are established nationwide.

1970   Patrick V. Murphy takes over as police commissioner of New York City after Howard R. Leary resigns amid a highly publicized corruption scandal.

Brandeis University professor Egon Bittner publishes his well-known monograph, *The Functions of the Police in Modern Society*, in which he argues that the capacity to use force is the core of the police role.

1972   The Commission to Investigate Allegations of Police Corruption, also called the Knapp Commission after its chairman, United States District Judge Whitman Knapp, releases its report detailing widespread police corruption in New York City.

The 1972 Equal Employment Opportunity Act and subsequent employment discrimination lawsuits lead to the establishment of affirmative action hiring programs within many police departments.

1974   George L. Kelling and his co-researchers publish the results of *The Kansas City Preventive Patrol Experiment*, which found that decreasing or increasing the level of police patrol in a given area had no significant impact on the level of crime, police response time, people's fear of crime, or their attitudes toward police service in that area.

Florida State University criminology professor George L. Kirkham publishes a widely read article, "A Professor's Street Lessons," about his experiences working as a police officer.

1978   The Washington, D.C.–based Police Foundation releases its report, *The Quality of Police Education*, prepared by the National Commission on Higher Education for Police Officers, a twelve-member group led by Lawrence W. Sherman, then assistant professor in the Graduate School of Criminal Justice at the State University of New York (SUNY) at Albany.

1979   University of Wisconsin, Madison law professor Herman Goldstein introduces the concept of problem-oriented policing in his 1979 article, "Improving Policing: A Problem-Oriented Approach."

1980   James J. Fyfe questions the wisdom of requiring or encouraging police officers to carry their weapons while off duty in his article, "Always Prepared: Police Off-Duty Guns."

        Harvard Law School professor Donald Black and his graduate student, M. P. Baumgartner, argue that gradually reducing police protection would lead people to take more responsibility for their own safety and conflict settlement, and make them more likely to help others in need, in Black's book, *The Manners and Customs of the Police*.

1982   In their well-received and influential article, "Broken Windows," James Q. Wilson, Shattuck Professor of Government at Harvard University, and George Kelling, a research fellow at Harvard's John F. Kennedy School of Government, argue that the police role should be expanded beyond law enforcement to include active participation in maintaining and/or improving the quality of community life through an increased focus on order maintenance activities.

1985   *Tennessee v. Garner et al.*: The Supreme Court establishes the "defense of life" standard for the police use of deadly force, meaning that if the suspect is armed and threatens police officers or others, or if there is probable cause to believe the suspect has committed a crime involving the infliction of serious physical harm, then the police may use deadly force if necessary to prevent his or her escape.

1988   Albert J. Reiss, Jr., publishes a study in which he examines the growing trend toward private policing in *Private Employment of Public Police*.

        David H. Bayley, a professor in the School of Criminal Justice at the State University of New York at Albany, points out twelve potential problems with community policing in his book chapter, "Community Policing: A Report from the Devil's Advocate."

1989   The 1957 "Law Enforcement Code of Ethics" is replaced by a new code by the International Association of Chiefs of Police. This decision is followed by widespread controversy.

1990   In his book *The Police Mystique*, retired Minneapolis Police Chief Anthony V. Bouza argues that the police officer's role should extend beyond fighting crime and violence to helping to solve the underlying social and economic causes of these problems.

1991   Following two years of controversy among the International Association of Chiefs of Police membership, the 1957 "Law Enforcement Code of Ethics" is revised slightly and reinstated. The 1989 code, which briefly replaced the 1957 code, is renamed "The Police Code of Conduct."

San Fernando Valley resident George Holliday videotapes Los Angeles police officers as they beat motorist Rodney King following a high-speed chase. The widely televised videotape causes the King beating to become perhaps the most widely publicized incident involving the use of excessive force by police officers in modern history.

The Independent Commission on the Los Angeles Police Department, also called the Christopher Commission after its chairman, Warren Christopher, delivers its report on the Los Angeles Police Department. The report recommends that the LAPD abandon the professional model of policing in favor of a community policing approach.

1992   After the four white police officers arrested and charged with excessive use of force in the Rodney King beating are acquitted by a mostly white jury, the city of Los Angeles erupts into a six-day riot reminiscent of the 1965 Watts riot.

1994   In his book, *Police for the Future*, David H. Bayley, a professor in the School of Criminal Justice at the State University of New York at Albany, recommends expanding and redefining the police role so that finding and implementing ways to prevent crime is one of the main responsibilities of the police.

1996   In his article, "A Theory of Excessive Force and Its Control," Carl B. Klockars, professor of sociology and criminal justice at the University of Delaware, proposes that excessive police force should be defined as "the use of more force than a highly skilled police officer would find necessary to use in that particular situation."

The Office of Community Oriented Policing Services and the National Institute of Justice sponsor a National Symposium on Police Integrity. During the symposium, keynote speaker Stephen J. Vicchio, professor of philosophy at the College of Notre Dame, presents a definition of police integrity.

1997   In her article, "The Thin Blue and Pink Line," Sgt. Lisa Shores of the Charlotte-Mecklenburg, North Carolina, police department argues that, with the exception of those who are pregnant or injured, women police should not be treated differently than their male counterparts.

In his article, "A Time to Remember," Darrell L. Sanders, chief of police in Frankfort, Illinois, pays tribute to police officers who have died in the line of duty.

Part I

Night Watchmen, Constables, and Sheriffs: The Role of Early "Police" in Seventeenth- and Eighteenth-Century America

From the time the first colonies were established in eastern North America until the United States became a separate nation, numerous social, political, economic, demographic, philosophical, and ideological changes took place that affected American attitudes toward crime and crime control. To understand how these changes helped create a demand for what we now think of as "police" services—and how the role of police changed over time—it is important to look first at the historical context in which the new nation emerged.

EUROPEAN COLONIZATION OF NORTH AMERICA

The colonies that later became the United States were established during a wave of English exploration and settlement that saw roughly

10 percent of England's population immigrate to the New World. Many of these people also were driven by diverse religious beliefs that had flowered during the Protestant Reformation. Although Spain, Portugal, and France initially dominated expansion into the Americas, England used its colonies as a safety valve to relieve itself of the pressure of rapid population growth and political and religious dissent. The English practice of sending entire families to establish new communities provided them with a substantial long-term advantage. By the mid-1700s, English dominion over the eastern seaboard of North America was complete. As is discussed further on, English dominance over the colonies strongly influenced the development of policing institutions.

INCREASING NEED FOR FORMAL SOCIAL CONTROL

During the eighteenth century, the colonies grew extremely rapidly. For example, in 1680, the population of Pennsylvania was only 4,000; within sixty years it had risen to 80,000 and still was growing rapidly. Overall, the population of the colonies was doubling every twenty-five years. High birth rates and lower mortality accounted for some of the colonies' growth, but most growth was a result of immigration.

The diversity and settlement patterns of immigrants coming to the colonies changed remarkably between 1700 and 1775. Although there had been substantial differences between the early settlements, each individual colony had tended to be quite homogeneous. However, later immigrants to the colonies were quite different. Unlike the middle- and working-class English who established most of the early settlements, many of the new immigrants were paupers and convicts, Scottish, Irish, and German refugees, and slaves from Africa.

Crime—particularly crimes like murder, robbery, rape, and burglary that preoccupy contemporary American society—was rare in the earliest colonies (see Walker 1998:17–18). This was largely due to the fact that they initially were settled by small and fairly homogeneous groups of people whose strong religious beliefs tended to provide the basis for social control. However, as the colonies grew and their populations became more diverse and less isolated, maintaining the peace and enforcing the laws became more difficult (Bridenbaugh 1938:63, 68). In addition to these difficulties were outside threats such as the Indian raids of the 1630s, pirate activities against the seacoast towns, and potential invasions by foreign enemies. As a result, it wasn't long before the vast majority of settlements established variants of the law enforcement and protection procedures that long had been in place in their

European homelands, such as the night watch, constabulary, and sheriff.

EARLY EUROPEAN PRECURSORS TO THE POLICE

In England, the active involvement of civilians in law enforcement began in about the tenth century. Each citizen was made responsible for aiding neighbors who were victimized by outlaws. This relatively informal voluntary model for policing villages became known as the "kin police." After the Norman Conquest of 1066, this community-based system was modified further into a *frankpledge* system that required adult male freeholders to form groups of ten called *tithings* which were responsible for helping to protect fellow citizens and for delivering up any of the tithing's own members who committed crimes. Each ten tithings were grouped into a *hundred*, which was directed by a constable appointed by a local nobleman (Peak 1997: 2–6). Ten of the hundreds constituted a *shire*. The enforcement of law within the shires was the responsibility of an agent of the king called a *shire reeve*—a term that eventually was modified into the modern "sheriff."

In the mid-seventeenth century, Oliver Cromwell modified the "constabulary" into a mounted cavalry force that was supposed to serve a quasi-police role. They eventually were replaced in 1663 by the restored King Charles II because of their merciless attacks on freemen. In their place, Charles instituted a night watch and day constable system composed primarily of elderly men, called "Old Charlies" by the citizenry, who were largely ineffective against outlaws (Astor 1971:10). Since Charles II reined in England's constables, the balance between police power and civil rights has shifted many times. This tension between the need to provide the police with sufficient power to protect public order and the need to prevent the abuse of police power is one of the most fundamental problems that free societies must confront. As such, it will be a recurring theme in this book.

THE ROLES OF EARLY COLONIAL POLICING ORGANIZATIONS

When colonial villages such as Boston, Charles Town, New York, and Philadelphia were first formed in the mid-seventeenth century, their articles of incorporation included provisions for night watches and constables whose duties included keeping the peace, ensuring public safety, and law enforcement (Documents 1, 2, 3, and 4). As rural counties were formed, colonial governors often appointed sheriffs whose duties were modeled after those of English shire reeves. Outside the cities, these sheriffs often became the most important law enforcement officials, as they apprehended criminals, served legal processes, and collected taxes.

Constables, who generally were unpaid and untrained elected officials, were expected to keep their communities peaceful and orderly, supervise the night watch, administer punishments, and provide at least minimal protection from criminals during the day. These time-consuming duties often imposed a significant financial hardship on early constables, who often were tradesmen or craftsmen. Their businesses suffered, and even though they were paid fees for many of the tasks they performed, they also were fined for failing at their duties. In addition to entailing financial hardship, a constable's duties often were unpleasant and/or dangerous; just like contemporary police officers, they sometimes were assaulted when making arrests. As a consequence of these hardships, there was little incentive for most people to serve as constable.

Constables remained the chief colonial law enforcement officers during the early eighteenth century. As colonial cities grew rapidly, so did their need for more constables, but the onerous and sometimes hazardous duties and low pay and status made it increasingly difficult to get solid citizens to accept this position. As a consequence, the job often was taken by people of dubious integrity who used the office to advance their personal interests and line their own pockets. This, of course, caused a further decline in the prestige of the position and made the job of constable even less attractive (see Document 4).

The decline in the quality of life cities experienced as a consequence of growing crime and less effective law enforcement was compounded by the fact that constables supervised night watches, often hiring disreputable drunks and ruffians for the watch who grossly neglected their duties (Document 5).

While northern towns grappled with problems associated with rapid urban growth, southern colonies had to deal with a different set of problems. In the South, the economy was dominated by labor-intensive crops such as tobacco, sugar, and rice. Southern planters had to maintain and control a large, cheap labor force consisting of indentured workers and slaves. As the slave population in these communities grew—by 1740, two-thirds of South Carolina's population was black, and most of them were slaves—whites became increasingly fearful of revolts (Reichel 1988:55). By the early eighteenth century, many southern cities and rural areas had established elaborate patrols to control the slave population. Especially in rural areas, where slaves often outnumbered whites, "slave patrols provided what was essentially a rural police" (Reichel 1992:4). Document 6 describes the development of these early forerunners to the police.

Sheriffs and slave patrols were not the only forms of law enforcement in rural southern colonies. When the colonial government failed to protect citizens in the rural areas of South Carolina from outlaws and highway robbers, groups composed of many leading citizens formed to take the law into their own hands. When first formed in 1767, these "Regulators" attacked outlaw groups that had been raping and pillaging across the rural countryside for several years. Unfortunately, as with Cromwell's constabulary a century earlier, the Regulators soon went astray. Once the outlaws were under control, they began a campaign to rid the back country of "lower people" that included corporal punishment of virtually anyone of whom they disapproved (Brown 1963: 46–51). Another citizen group, the Moderators, eventually was formed to counter the Regulators' abuses. By 1769 the Regulators were disbanded (Document 7).

CONSTITUTIONAL CONSTRAINTS ON POLICE POWER

Tensions between the colonies and England mounted from the 1760s onward. Driven primarily by disputes over taxation and the quartering of British soldiers, confrontations between colonists and British military and customs officials became increasingly violent. By the 1770s, riots and mob actions—often involving prominent citizens—had occurred in most major cities as the colonists resisted one Parliamentary act after another. Parliament responded with a series of Coercive Acts which increasingly undermined the authority of colonial legislative and judicial bodies. Attempts by England to enforce these and other acts finally led to open war in April 1775. By the time the Revolutionary War was over, many colonial leaders had experienced the criminal justice system firsthand after being charged with crimes by the British, tried, imprisoned and, on a few occasions, executed. It seems likely that these experiences made them particularly aware of the need to restrain state power.

When the U.S. Constitution was ratified in 1788, it contained a number of checks and balances designed to insure against the government becoming overly powerful. Soon after that, however, the framers recognized that there was insufficient protection of individual citizens against potential abuses by the new federal government. The first ten amendments to the Constitution, which became known as the Bill of Rights, were adopted in 1791. Three of these amendments, the Fourth,

Fifth, and Sixth Amendments, eventually would substantially affect the activities of the police (Document 8).

DOCUMENT 1: The Boston Night Watch (April 1631)

The first, and perhaps most famous, night watch in America was established in Boston on April 12, 1631 (Bopp and Schultz 1972a:17; Bridenbaugh 1938:65). Initially a military guard consisting of an officer and six men, it was changed on February 27, 1636, to a citizen-staffed watch in which every able-bodied man of the town was required to take a turn or hire a substitute (Bopp and Schultz 1972a:17–18; Bridenbaugh 1938:65). For many years the Boston night watch was maintained during the summer months only, but in 1653 the town leaders hired a "bellman" to make the rounds at night during the winter months (Bridenbaugh 1938:65).

Other colonial towns soon established night watches of their own. For example, in 1652 the Dutch town of Nieuw Amsterdam (New York) created a citizens' "rattel wacht," in which citizens assigned to specific watch posts would use rattles to communicate with each other and summon assistance if needed (Bopp and Schultz 1972a:19; Palmiotto 1997:14).[1]

The duties of these night watches, from Boston to New York to Philadelphia to Charles Town and beyond, basically were the same. In addition to being on the lookout for crime and external threats of all sorts, the watchmen were expected to keep the town peaceful and quiet throughout the night, make regular announcements of the time and weather conditions, and keep an eye out for fire. In some towns, such as Boston and Charles Town, watchmen also were expected to keep tabs on servants or slaves who were out on the streets after dark (Bridenbaugh 1938:219).

Although the night watch persisted in one form or another throughout many towns for nearly two hundred years, it was by no means an ideal system of protection and law enforcement. One of its main weaknesses was that in most cases watchmen were unpaid and had little or no interest or training in law enforcement. Those who could afford to pay a substitute usually did so, often hiring men of "questionable reputation," and those who could not afford to hire a substitute found the system unfair because of the burden it placed upon them (Greenberg 1976:157). Hence, without an adequate system of law enforcement, as the towns grew, so did their crime problems (Regoli and Hewitt 1996:217–219).

Following is an account of the establishment and duties of the Boston Watch by nineteenth-century police officer and historian Edward Hartwell Savage.

* * *

Although the inhabitants of Boston were at first quite numerous, yet not until 1631, (April 12), was it ordered "by Court" that ['] *Watches* be set at sunset, and if any person fire off a piece after the watch is set, he shall be fined forty shillings, or be whipped." And two days after, it was said, "we began a Court of Guard upon the *Neck*, between Roxburie and Boston, whereupon shall always be resident an officer and six men."

This was an organization of the first *Boston Watch*; and although it partook more of the character of a military guard than otherwise, it was well adapted to the wants of the people, as all Police arrangements should be; and was probably continued, with greater or less numbers, till the organization of a watch by the selectmen. . . .

Although a Watch had been established as early as 1631, it does not appear that the authorities of the town assumed the prerogatives of its appointment and control till the twenty-seventh day of February, 1636, when, at a Town Meeting, "upon pryvate warning, it was agreed yt there shalbe a watch taken up and gone around with from the first of the second month next for ye summertime from sunne sett an houre after ye beating of ye drumbe, upon penaltie for every one wanting therein twelve pence every night."

The organization of a Town Watch here established, under various names and hundreds of different modifications (with perhaps the exception of a brief period during the Revolution), has existed to the present time. The duties of the Watch, as appears by the order, were to be performed in turn by the inhabitants; they were not "citizen soldiers," but citizen Watchmen, and having an interest in their work, no doubt did it well. What their duties were is not laid down in the record, and can only be inferred from the condition of things at the time.

The dwellings of the inhabitants had mostly been thrown up in a hurry, with such material as was at hand, and were built of wood or mud walls, thatched roof and stick chimneys, plastered with clay; this left them particularly exposed to fire, and a fire in those days was a calamity indeed. There were numerous straggling Indians, who paid their nocturnal visits from the wilderness, and they were not over scrupulous in relation to etiquette or the ownership of property. There were also among the inhabitants (if we believe the report), a set of knaves, thieves, and burglars, of their own "kith and kin." Wolves and bears were also numerous, and came into Boston even, and carried off young kids and lambs. Nor was this all; *masters* were sorely annoyed by the frequent desertions of their *slaves*; for Boston men had slaves, and not only black slaves, but white ones. (At one time a ship-load of one hundred and fifty Scotch emigrants were sold in Boston to pay their passage;) and these, especially, were prone to take French leave of their masters the first opportunity, preferring a wild life and a wigwam with liberty, to civilization and bondage.

These and attending circumstances would plainly indicate what might be the nature of the duties required of the Town Watch at that time.

Source: Edward H. Savage, *Police Records and Recollections, or Boston by Daylight and Gaslight for Two Hundred and Forty Years* (Boston: John P. Dale & Co., 1873). [Montclair, N.J.: Patterson Smith, 1971, 11–14.]

DOCUMENT 2: The Duke of York's Laws (1675–1775)

The night watch was not the only law enforcement institution the early American colonists brought with them from their homelands. As local governments and laws were established, the leaders of the towns also made provisions for the selection of constables (or their equivalent in non-English colonies) to enforce the laws. In rural agricultural areas outside the towns, the principal law enforcement officer was the sheriff—a position dating back to England sometime between A.D. 700 and 800, when the *shire reeve*[2] was responsible for keeping the peace in the shire, or county (Bopp and Schultz 1972a:15–16; Palmiotto 1997:13, 44).

In the early Dutch colonial settlement of New Netherlands, the *schout fiscal* (sheriff attorney) was the equivalent of the English constable. When the English took over New Netherlands in 1664 (renaming it New York in honor of the English Duke of York, who was "granted" the territory by his brother, King Charles II), the constable replaced the schout fiscal as the primary law enforcement officer of the colony.

The duties of the New York constable—an unpaid officer elected by a vote of town freeholders to serve for a period of one year—basically were the same as those of any colonial town's constable during that period. Constables were expected to maintain the peace and order of the community; discourage prostitution, gambling, and excessive drinking; keep disturbances to a minimum during church services; watch for vagrants or other questionable strangers; oversee the night watch; administer punishment; and provide at least some sort of police protection during the day (Richardson 1970:7).

The following excerpt from the Duke of York's Laws describes the selection and duties of the early New York constable in greater detail.

* * *

CONSTABLES

That the Constable shall whip or Punish any one to be punished by Order of Authority, where there is not any other Officer appointed to do it, in their own Towns, unless they can get an other person to do it.

That any and every Person tendred to any Constable of this Government, by any other Constable or other Officer belonging to any Jurisdiction within this Government, or by warrant from any Justice shall be presently received and Conveyed forthwith from Constable to Constable till they be brought to the place to which they were sent, or before some Justice of the peace who shall dispose of them as the Justice of the Cause shall require; All Hue & Cryes shall be duly received and diligently pursued to full effect And where no Justice of the Peace is near, Every Constable shall have full power, to make Sign and put forth pursuites or Hue and Cryes after Murtherers Man Slayers Theves Robbers Burglurers and other Capitall Offenders, as also to Apprehend without warrant such as are overtaken with Drink, Swearing, Sabbath breaking, Vagrant persons or night walkers provided they be taken in the manner, either by the Sight of the Constable or by present information from others. As also to make search for all such Persons either on the Sabbath Day or other when there shall be Occasion in all Houses Licensed to sell either Beer or Wine or any other Suspected or disordered place and those to Apprehend and keep in Safe Custody till opportunity Serves to bring them before the Next Justice of the peace to further Examination, Provided that when any Constable is Employed by any Justice for apprehending of any person he shall not do it without a warrant in writing. And if any person shall refuse to Assist any Constable in the Execution of his Office in any of the things aforementioned being by him required thereto, They shall pay for neglect thereof ten Shillings to the use of the Town of which he is Constable To be Levyed by warrant from any Justice before whom such Offender shall be brought And if it appears by good Testimony that any shall wilfully or Contemptuously refuse or neglect to assist any Constable as is before expressed, he shall pay to the use aforesaid forty Shillings And that no man may plead Ignorance for such Neglect or Refusal, Every Constable shall have a Staff of about six foot long, with the Kings armes on it as a badge of his Office which Staff shall be provided at the charge of the Town. And if any Justice of peace Constable or any other, upon urgent Occasion shall refuse to do their best endeavours in raising and presecuting [*sic*] Hue and Cryes by foote and if need by Horse after such as have Committed Capital Crimes: They shall forfeit for every such offence to the use aforesaid forty Shillings The Constable and every two Overseers may take Bayle for any Person Arrested within their precincts if not in Execution or Committed by Special Warrant. . . .

Constables shall be chosen in all Towns upon the first day of April, or Second, yearly, by the plurality of the votes . . . of the free holders in each Town; that is to say one of the four Overseers, in whose places new ones are chosen for the ensuing year, shall be chosen to Officiate as Constable within their Town, Whose name and person shall be presented by the Old Constable and Overseers to the next Sessions ensuing there to be Confirmed by the Justices of the peace by taking the oath appointed for Constables.

Source: The Duke of York's Laws, 1665–75. In *The Colonial Laws of New York from the Year 1664 to the Revolution*, Vol. 1 (Albany: James B. Lyon, State Printer, 1894), 28–30.

DOCUMENT 3: A Bill Concerning the Choice of Constables (1684)

By 1664, English-style constables such as those in New York (see Document 2) were commonplace throughout American colonial towns. However, like the night watch (see Document 1), this system of law enforcement by untrained citizen "draftees" was fraught with problems.

In most cases, constables were elected to serve one-year, unpaid terms. They typically were recruited from among the town's tradesmen and craftsmen, and the job was so time-consuming that their businesses often suffered during their term of service. Moreover, although various fees were paid to the constable for serving warrants and other tasks, monetary penalties often were imposed as well for failing at his assigned duties. Hence, there was little financial incentive to serve (Richardson 1970:7; Rutman 1965:226).

In addition to the wearisome nature of the job, low pay, and interference with the constable's regular occupation, constabulary duties often were unpleasant or dangerous (Bridenbaugh 1938:215–216). For example, it was fairly common for a constable to be assaulted when he tried to make an arrest (Greenberg 1974:158).

Not surprisingly, as early as 1653 there were complaints of numerous men attempting to get out of constable duty in Boston, where the town leaders established a whopping twenty pound fine for refusal to serve (Bridenbaugh 1938:64). In 1684 New York, as the following document shows, the penalty for refusing to serve was five pounds. In many cases, men would pay such fines rather than assume the thankless position.

* * *

[Passed, October 22, 1684.]

Be it Enacted by this Generall Assembly and by the authority of ye same that the Constables in each Respective towne or County shall be Elected att ye same time and according to ye same ways and Methods as have been formerly practiced within this Governm't. That is to say annually on ye third or ffourth day of Aprill by the Majority of voices provided Always that if through the Increase of Inhabitants, enlargements of Bounds or any other ways one Constable is not Capable to officiate the place that then and in such Cases the Inhabitants of the Towne place or County where Such deffect shall happen may make choice of two or more Constables as occasion shall require and if any one being duly elected to serve as Constable shall refuse to serve shall pay ye summe of ffive pounds ffor the use of ye County.

Source: "A Bill Concerning the Choice of Constables," 1684. In *The Colonial Laws of New York from the Year 1664 to the Revolution*, Vol. 1 (Albany: James B. Lyon, State Printer, 1894), 146–147.

DOCUMENT 4: *The Constables Pocket-Book* (Nicholas Boone, 1710)

Despite the numerous problems associated with public participation in law enforcement (see Documents 1 and 3), the constable remained the chief colonial law enforcement officer during the early eighteenth century. In fact, his duties continued to increase—including, in Boston and New York, working on the Sabbath to keep others from working—although his pay and status remained low (Bridenbaugh 1938:215).

As the colonial cities grew, so did their need for constables. However, it also became increasingly difficult to get citizens to perform this public service. More and more people, especially those with successful businesses or careers, preferred to pay the fines (Bridenbaugh 1938: 215; Greenberg 1974:163–164; Regoli and Hewitt 1996:220). As a result, the job often was taken by men of dubious integrity—those who took bribes, assaulted citizens, used the office to advance their personal interests, and committed numerous other crimes. This only served to further lower the status of the position of constable and weaken its authority in the eyes of the colonists (Greenberg 1974:165).

Amid this atmosphere of low public support for the office of constable, Nicholas Boone of Boston, himself a former constable, published *The Constables Pocket-Book*. Written as a dialogue between an old and new constable, it ostensibly was a how-to manual designed to help new constables understand the growing demands of the office. However, it appears from the following passage that the book also may have been intended as a public relations tool to help improve the image of the office and remind citizens of their public duty to serve.

* * *

Old Constable.
Good Morrow Sir, I hear you have an Office this Town-Meeting.
New Constable.
Yes, Sir, and I am afraid a very trouble-some One.
O. C. You must not mind the trouble; but consider the Publick Interest, and that every one ought to Serve his Generation.
N. C. On these thoughts, I have taken the Oath, and hope to do my Duty; and therefore desire you to inform me, How I ought to manage this trust for the Publick good, and my own safety.
O. C. Your Oath lays out your Work chiefly, and therefore we'll begin with that; and so proceed from step to step with the rest.

Constables Oath.

Whereas you A. B. are chosen Constable within the Town of C. for one year now following & until another be Chosen and Sworn in your Place: You do Sware, That you will carefully intend the preservation of the Peace, the discovery and preventing all attempts against the same: That you will duely Execute all Warrants which shall be sent you from Lawful Authority; and faithfully attend all such Directions in the Laws & Orders of Court, as are or shall be committed to your care: That you will faithfully and with what speed you can, Collect and Levy all such Fines, Distresses, Rates, Assessments and Sums of Money, for which you shall have sufficient Warrants according to Law; rendering an Accompt thereof, and paying in the same according to the Direction in your Warrant. And with like faithfulness, speed and diligence, will Serve all Writs, Executions and Distresses in private causes betwixt party & party, and make Returns thereof duely into the same Court where they are Returnable. And in all these things you shall deal seriously and faithfully whilst you shall be in Office, without any sinister respects of favour or displeasure.

So help you God.

Source: Nicholas Boone, *The Constables Pocket-Book* (Boston: Nicholas Boone, 1710), 1–3.

DOCUMENT 5: Benjamin Franklin on the 1737 Philadelphia Night Watch

By 1737, the state of the constabulary and night watch in the bur-geoning—and increasingly crime-ridden—city of Philadelphia was so poor that it made a considerable impression on Benjamin Franklin (1706–1790), who commented on it some fifty years later in his memoirs.

Franklin noted that those who chose not to serve on the night watch were charged six shillings per year, but that the constables did not put this money to use hiring adequate and reputable substitutes. Instead, the constable recruited "ragamuffins" for "a little drink," and pocketed the rest of the money. These substitute watchmen were grossly inadequate at policing the city, often failing to make any rounds at all, and their presence on the watch discouraged "reputable" townsmen from participating, said Franklin.

Although Franklin had suggested to the Philadelphia Junto[3] and other influential local groups that a property-based tax be imposed to raise funds for a proper and efficient night watch, his proposal was not immediately adopted by the town. However, eight years later, in 1745, a provincial law led the city to provide for a "sufficient" watch (Bridenbaugh 1938:377). Hence, Franklin has been credited with initiating a municipal police and fire force in Philadelphia (Schlesinger 1993:89).

* * *

In 1737, Col. Spotswood, late Governor of Virginia, & then Post-master, General, being dissatisfied with the Conduct of his Deputy at Philadelphia, respecting some Negligence in rendering, & Inexactitude of his Accounts, took from him the Commission & offered it to me. I accepted it readily, and found it of great Advantage; for tho' the Salary was small, it facilitated the Correspondence that improv'd my Newspaper, encreas'd the Number demanded, as well as the Advertisements to be inserted, so that it came to afford me a very considerable Income. . . .

I began now to turn my Thoughts a little to public Affairs, beginning however with small Matters. The City Watch was one of the first Things that I conceiv'd to want Regulation. It was managed by the Constables of the respective Wards in Turn. The Constable warn'd a Number of Housekeepers to attend him for the Night. Those who chose never to attend paid him Six Shillings a Year to be excus'd, which was suppos'd to be for hiring Substitutes; but was in reality much more than was necessary for that purpose, and made the Constableship a Place of Profit. And the Constable for a little Drink often got such Ragamuffins about him as a Watch, that reputable Housekeepers did not chuse to mix with. Walking the rounds too was often neglected, and most of the Night spent in Tippling. I thereupon wrote a Paper to be read in Junto, representing these Irregularities, but insisting more particularly on the Inequality of this Six Shilling Tax of the Constables, respecting the Circumstances of those who paid it, since a poor Widow Housekeeper, all whose Property to be guarded by the Watch did not perhaps exceed the Value of Fifty Pounds, paid as much as the wealthiest Merchant who had Thousands of Pounds-worth of Goods in his Stores. On the whole I proposed as a more effectual Watch, the Hiring of proper Men to serve constantly in that Business; and as a more equitable Way of supporting the Charge, the levying a Tax that should be proportion'd to Property. This Idea being approv'd by the Junto, was communicated to the other Clubs, but as arising in each of them. And tho' the Plan was not immediately carried into Execution, yet by preparing the Minds of People for the Change, it paved the Way for the Law obtain'd a few Years after, when the Members of our Clubs were grown into more Influence.

Source: Benjamin Franklin, *Memoirs* (the above excerpt written in Philadelphia in August 1788). This version published as *The Autobiography of Benjamin Franklin* (New York: Heritage Press, 1951), 132–134.

DOCUMENT 6: Southern Slave Patrols as a Precursor to Contemporary Police Forces (1704–circa 1861)

While northern towns such as Boston, New York, and Philadelphia were grappling with law enforcement problems associated with rapid urban growth, the southern colonies were facing a very different set of concerns. As the slave population in these agriculturally oriented communities grew,[4] whites became more and more fearful of slave revolts, which began as early as 1657 (Reichel 1988:55).

Their response was to organize "slave patrols," which were manned by the townspeople and designed both to retrieve runaway slaves and to prevent slave violence and insurrection. First established in South Carolina in 1704, the patrols eventually were commonplace throughout the South prior to the Civil War.

The patrols were given a great deal of authority, which they often abused. Stories of harassment and mistreatment of blacks by the white patrols abound. However, despite their objectionable goals and actions, the slave patrols were important precursors to modern police forces, as both Reichel (see document below) and Walker (1997) have noted.

* * *

The Organization and Operation of Slave Patrols

. . .

In their earliest stages, slave patrols were part of the colonial militias. Royal charters empowered governors to defend colonies and that defense took the form of a militia for coast and frontier defense. . . . All able-bodied males between 16 and 60 were to be enrolled in the militia and had to provide their own weapons and equipment. . . . Although the militias were regionally diverse and constantly changing . . . Anderson's (1984) comments about the Massachusetts Bay Colony militia notes [sic] an important distinction that was reflected in other colonies. At the beginning of the 18th century, Massachusetts' militia was defined not so much as an army but "as an all-purpose military infrastructure" (Anderson, 1984: 27) from which volunteers were drawn for the provincial armies. This concept of the militia as a pool from which persons could be drawn for special duties was the basis for colonial slave patrols. . . .

Despite their link to militia, slave patrols were a separate entity. Each slave state had codes of laws for the regulation of slavery. These slave codes authorized and outlined the duties of the slave patrols. Some towns had their own patrols, but they were more frequent in the rural areas. The presence of constables and a more equal distribution of whites and blacks made the need for the town patrols less immediate. In the rural areas, however, the slaves were more easily able to participate in "dangerous" acts. It is not surprising that the slave patrols came to be viewed as "rural police." . . . South Carolina Governor Bull described the role of the patrols in 1740 by writing:

The interior quiet of the Province is provided for by small Patrols, drawn every two months from each company, who do duty by riding along the roads and among the Negro Houses in small districts in every Parish once a week, or as occasion requires. . . .

Documentation of slave patrols is found for nearly all the Southern colonies and states but South Carolina seems to have been the oldest, most elaborate, and best documented. That is not surprising given the importance of the militia in South Carolina and the presence of large numbers of Blacks. Georgia's developed somewhat later and exemplifies patrols in the late 18th and early 19th centuries. The history and development of slave patrol legislation in South Carolina and Georgia provides a historical review from colonial through antebellum times.

In 1704 the colony of Carolina presented what appears to be the South's first patrol act. The patrol was linked to the militia yet separate from it since patrol duty was an excuse from militia duty. Under this act, militia captains were to select ten men from their companies to form these special patrols. The captain was to

> muster all the men under his command, and with them ride from plantation to plantation, and into any plantation, within the limits or precincts, as the Generall shall think fitt, and take up all slaves which they shall meet without their master's plantation which have not a permit or ticket from their masters, and the same punish. . . .

That initial act seemed particularly concerned with runaway slaves, while an act in 1721 suggests an increased concern with uprisings. The act ordered the patrols to try to "prevent all caballings amongst negroes, by dispersing of them when drumming or playing, and to search all negro houses for arms or other offensive weapons." . . . In addition to that concern the new act also responded to complaints that militia duty was being shirked by the choicest men who were doing patrol duty instead of militia duty. . . . As a result, the separate patrols were merged with the colonial militia and patrol duty was simply rotated among different members of the militia. From 1721 to 1734 there really were no specific slave patrols in South Carolina. The duty of supervising slaves was simply a militia duty.

In 1734 the Provincial Assembly set up a regular patrol once again separate from the militia. . . . "Beat companies" of five men (Captain and four regular militia men) received compensation (captains #50 and privates #25 per year) for patrol duty and exemption from other militia duty. There was one patrol for each of 33 districts in the colony. Patrols obeyed orders from and were appointed by district commissioners and were given elaborate search and seizure powers as well as the right to administer up to twenty lashes. . . .

Since provincial acts usually expired after three years, South Carolina's 1734 Act was revised in 1737 and again in 1740. Under the 1737 revision, the paid recruits were replaced with volunteers who were encouraged to enlist by being excused from militia and other public duty for one year and were allowed to elect their own captain. . . . The number of men on patrol was increased from five to fifteen and they were to make weekly rounds. . . .

The 1740 revision seems to be the first legislation specifically including women plantation owners as answerable for patrol service. . . . The plantation owners (male or female) could, however, procure any white person between 16 and 60 to ride patrol for them. In addition, the 1740 act said patrol duty was not to be required in townships where white inhabitants were in far superior numbers to the Negroes. . . . Such an exemption certainly highlights the role of patrols as being to control what was perceived as a dangerous class.

Source: Philip L. Reichel, "Southern Slave Patrols as a Transitional Police Type," *American Journal of Police* 7, no. 2 (1988): 57–60 (footnotes omitted).

DOCUMENT 7: The Regulators (1767)

Sheriffs (see Document 2) and slave patrols (see Document 6) were not the only forms of law enforcement in the rural southern colonies of the eighteenth century. Vigilantes—citizen groups who took the law into their own hands—originated in the South in 1767 (Regoli and Hewitt 1996:221).

Known as the Regulators, the first such vigilante movement was composed of leading citizens in the crime-ridden back country of South Carolina, where there was little or no formal authority to prevent or punish robberies and other crimes (Hindus 1980:4).

The initial goal of the Regulators was a very reasonable one. The Cherokee War of 1760–1761 had taken a serious economic toll on the back country, in part because many families had been forced to abandon their plantations for the safety of forts. In the wake of this economic devastation, numerous outlaw groups moved into the region and began terrorizing the "respectable" people who had remained there. They robbed houses (often torturing, maiming, or killing the owners and/or raping their wives and daughters in the process), stole horses and slaves, and carried away young girls to their camps. The back countrymen were understandably outraged. In the absence of effective laws, sheriffs, or local courts, which they had long requested from the Charleston government, the leading men of the region banded together informally in 1767 and began a series of counterattacks on the outlaws. Soon after, prompted by retaliatory attacks by the outlaws, the more formal vigilante organization known as the Regulators was formed (Brown 1963:29–39).

By November 1767, the activities of the Regulators had gotten the attention of Charleston's Governor Montagu and the Charleston Assembly, which initiated a circuit court act for the region and also authorized two groups of mounted Rangers—hired from the ranks of the Regulators—to conduct a three-month campaign against the outlaws. Within two months, the Regulator-Rangers had caught and hung sixteen outlaws, brought many others in to await trial, and retrieved thirty-five young girls and more than one hundred stolen horses (Brown 1963: 45–46). All in all, the Regulator-Ranger plan had been a resounding success.

However, in what might be considered one of America's earliest examples of police power gone astray, the Regulators didn't stop there. In 1768, with the outlaw problem under control, many Regulators set their sights on ridding the back country of another problem—the "lower people." Their new "Plan of Regulation" included flogging, ducking, and other corporal punishments for vagrants, idlers, immoral women, and virtually anyone else who didn't measure up to their moral standards and work ethic (Brown 1963:46–51).

By 1769, it had become apparent to many respectable settlers in the back country that the Regulators had gone too far in their campaign against the lower people. They formed another movement—the Moderators—whose strong opposition eventually led to the Regulators' downfall in 1769 (Brown 1963:95). Later that year the Circuit Court Act of 1769 established four circuit court districts in the back country, thus assuaging one of the Regulators' main grievances. Rather ironically, in October 1771, Governor Montagu issued a pardon to seventy-five former Regulators (see document below) that protected them from any actions that might be brought by their victims in the very courts they initially had argued for (Brown 1963:114–115).

* * *

South Carolina George the Third by the Grace of God of Great Britain, France & Ireland, King Defender of the Faith & so forth.

To all & singular our Judges, Justices, Marshalls, Sheriffs, Constables, Bailliffs & others our Peace Officers or loving Subjects within our said province, *Greeting. Whereas* sundry Inhabitants in the Northern parts of our said province, heretofore assembled themselves together under the name of Regulators & committed various Outrages & Acts of Violence in illegally whipping & Imprisoning divers persons under pretence of their being Robbers & Horse-Thieves But for as much as it appeared that sundry well Disposed people, had been unwarily drawn in to join the said Association in some of the said illegal Acts of Violence by them committed. We did by our Proclamation under the Great Seal of our said province bearing Date the sixth Day of August 1768, promise our most Gracious Pardon for the said Outrages & Acts of Violence, Committed by any person or persons on or before the said sixth Day of August 1768, to all such Persons as should thenceforward peaceably Demean themselves & should keep our peace & duly observe the Laws of our said province enacted for the preservation of the same. *And Whereas* very many of the said people who called themselves Regulators did thereupon Desist from the illegal practises aforesaid & peace & Tranquility hath in a manner been restored to the Inhabitants in the back Settlements of our said province. *And Whereas* [names of the seventy-five former Regulators] of our said province planters, have represented unto us that altho' they were present at some of the illegal proceedings, committed on the first Association of the Regulators they have for a long time past duly observed our Peace, & have humbly besought us to grant to them our Pardon for the said Offences. *Now Know Ye* that we being Graciously inclined, have pardoned, Remitted & Released & We do hereby Pardon, Remitt & Release unto the said [names of the seventy-five former Regulators], & to each & every of them all Assaults, Batteries, Tresspasses, Misdemeanors & Crimes whatsoever under the Nature & Degree of a Felony had done, committed & perpetrated by them or any of them on or before the first Day of October Instant, & all Fines, Forfeitures, Americiaments & Imprisonments, or other punishments for the same, & We do hereby further Will & Direct, that no Suit shall henceforward be Instituted or Prosecuted in our Name or at our Instance against all or either of the above named persons for any of the Tresspasses or Misdemeanours aforesaid, of which our Attorney General of our said province & all others whom it may concern, are required to take due Notice & govern themselves accordingly.

Given under the Great Seal of our said
Province *Witness* His Excellency The
Right Honble Lord Chas. Greville Montagu

Source: South Carolina Archives Department, Miscellaneous Records, Volume PP, p. 46–47. In Richard Maxwell Brown, *The South Carolina Regulators* (Cambridge, Mass.: Belknap Press of Harvard University Press, 1963), 159–160.

DOCUMENT 8: The Bill of Rights (1791)

At the same time early American colonists were attempting to develop appropriate and effective means of law enforcement, they also were wrestling with the larger issues of revolution, independence, and the establishment of a new republic.

When the U.S. Constitution was ratified in 1788, its main focus was on preserving the new democracy and protecting against future tyranny by ensuring separation of power among the executive, legislative, and judicial branches of government. However, soon after the Constitution was ratified by the states, its framers realized that by focusing so heavily on these objectives, they had neglected to provide written assurances to protect the rights of individual citizens against possible abuses by the new federal government. This was the main goal of the first ten amendments to the Constitution, also known as the Bill of Rights, adopted December 15, 1791.

Three of these amendments eventually would have significant impact on the way modern police forces operate: the Fourth Amendment (Document 8A), for the limitations it places on police behavior and its protection of individuals' right to privacy; the Fifth Amendment (Document 8B), for its assurance that no person shall be compelled to testify against himself or be detained without due process of law; and the Sixth Amendment (Document 8C), for its promise of the assistance of legal counsel before and during all criminal trials.

* * *

A. THE FOURTH AMENDMENT

The right of the people to be secure in their persons, houses, papers, and effects, against unreasonable searches and seizures, shall not be violated, and no warrants shall issue, but upon probable cause, supported by oath or affirmation, and particularly describing the place to be searched, and the persons or things to be seized.

B. THE FIFTH AMENDMENT

No person shall be held to answer for a capital, or otherwise infamous crime, unless on a presentment or indictment of a Grand Jury, except in cases arising in the land or naval forces, or in the militia, when in actual service in time of war or public danger; nor shall any person be subject for the same offense to be twice put in jeopardy of life or limb; nor shall be compelled in any criminal case to be a witness against himself, nor be deprived of life, liberty, or property, without due process of law; nor shall private property be taken for public use, without just compensation.

C. THE SIXTH AMENDMENT

In all criminal prosecutions, the accused shall enjoy the right to a speedy and public trial, by an impartial jury of the State and district wherein the crime shall have been committed, which district shall have been previously ascertained by law, and to be informed of the nature and cause of the accusation; to be confronted with the witnesses against him; to have compulsory process for obtaining witnesses in his favor, and to have the assistance of counsel for his defense.

Source: United States Constitution.

NOTES

1. In 1658, a paid watch of eight men replaced New York's citizen volunteers, establishing what Bopp and Schultz (1972a) consider "the first police force worthy of the name" (19).

2. *Shire* meaning "county" and *reeve* meaning "judge," or "agent of the king" (Bopp and Schultz 1972a:10; Peak 1997:2).

3. The Philadelphia Junto was a group of noteworthy Philadelphia intellectuals first organized by Benjamin Franklin in 1727 into a club known as the Leather Apron Club, patterned after the Rev. Cotton Mather's Neighborhood Benefit Societies in Boston. The club held regular meetings at taverns to discuss politics, morals, poetry, and philosophy (Bridenbaugh 1938:457–458).

4. Blacks outnumbered whites in South Carolina during most of the eighteenth century, and accounted for about 25–50 percent of the populations of North Carolina, Virginia, and Georgia (Reichel 1992:5).

Part II

Rangers, Marshals, and Municipal Police Forces: The Role of the Police in the Nineteenth Century

During the hundred years after the Revolution began, what had been a relatively homogeneous group of coastal colonies with a population of 4 million grew into a diverse nation of more than 60 million people that spanned a continent. An economy based mostly on agriculture and the export of raw materials had been transformed into a largely unstructured free-for-all dominated by the interests of eastern banking, rail, and industrial monopolies.

Part II follows the emergence and development of policing in the United States during this period of incredible growth and social and economic upheaval. The changing role of police during the nineteenth century reflected attempts by society to maintain order across expanding frontiers and in rapidly growing cities in the face of a tidal wave of immigration and enormous technological change.

FRONTIER POLICING

The expansion westward into the vast frontier brought new challenges, some of which led to new types of policing. Although customs, values, and social roles brought from Europe and east of the Mississippi favored roles for police that were similar to those elsewhere in the nation, the enormous distances and new economic possibilities of the environment also produced an increased need for self-reliance. Railroads and huge livestock industries formed new types of private police forces (Document 13). Private citizens, especially in the least developed places, banded together in times of crisis to form vigilante groups. When disturbances became more widespread, the militia or military were brought in. Some areas, such as Texas, responded to the spatial scope of law enforcement by organizing a territory-wide police force called the Rangers (Document 9) to protect against bandits and Indian raids (Prassel 1972).

As Document 23 shows, with the appearance of U.S. marshals and their deputies in the unorganized territories, more formal law enforcement began to take the place of the often impromptu justice of vigilantes and rangers. Once territorial legislatures were formed, county sheriffs or constables were appointed or, in a few instances, elected. Smaller communities within the territories often found that the county sheriff or constable could fulfill their policing needs. The demand for a strictly local town marshal (Document 24) often did not emerge until towns grew to a thousand or more inhabitants.

Although the deeds of these town lawmen have been romanticized no end by writers and moviemakers, the reality was generally much less exciting. As Prassel described it:

Community lawmen, regarded as a necessary evil, rarely enjoyed public favor. Doing a job few diligently sought, they seldom reflected the heroic romanticism portrayed so frequently in fiction. While the town marshals courted political support, their patrolmen maintained a watchful eye on local activities. Violence occurred, of course, but it usually came in sudden and unexpected form. The empty street, the deadly gunmen, and the structured duel have little foundation in fact. (1972:47)

The actual role of these frontier town marshals was little different from that of their eastern counterparts. Most of their efforts centered around subduing drunks and breaking up fights.

This same role also fell to a very different type of early frontier police officer. Indian police forces (Document 15) were developed in the 1860s and 1870s to handle similar problems on reservations that would, by the end of the century, contain virtually all of the once free Native Americans who had been displaced by the westward advance of U.S. settlers and military forces. In order to free the reservations from military interference, reservation agents like John Clum conclusively demonstrated that Indian police officers could effectively maintain order. By 1890, there were native police forces on fifty-nine different reservations (Hagan 1966: 169).

URBAN POLICING

In 1790 only two U.S. cities had populations exceeding 25,000 (U.S. Bureau of the Census 1975:11, 106). By 1820, due in large part to the influx of a quarter of a million immigrants from northern and central Europe, New York and Philadelphia had more than 100,000 inhabitants, Baltimore 63,000, Boston 43,000, and New Orleans 27,000. By 1860, another three-quarters of a million immigrants had arrived. Although many of them joined the rapid westward expansion, others stayed in the burgeoning port cities. In 1860 the respective populations were: New York 1,080,000; Philadelphia 566,000; Baltimore 212,000; Boston 178,000; New Orleans 169,000. Chicago, which had not even existed in 1820, was a great railroad center by 1860 (Cunliffe 1993: 148).

The already modest ability of traditional night watches and part-time constables to maintain social order and protect lives and property was further strained by rapid growth and increasing cultural diversity. People such as Charles Christian, who in 1812 published an anonymous pamphlet advocating a new role for New York police, began to argue for full-time police systems that would act as deterrents to crime rather than just deal with crime after the fact (Richardson 1970:21). But early advocates like Christian were unable to overcome the long-standing American aversion to anything resembling a standing army—an aversion dating back to the abuses of Cromwell's constabulary in seventeenth-century England and reinforced by the Redcoats' behavior prior to the Revolution.

By the early to mid-1800s, unrestrained growth, frequent mob violence (Lane 1979; Lane and Turner 1978; Weinbaum 1979), and the influx of foreign immigrants into urban areas fueled social disorder and contributed to rising fear among the country's growing middle class. For example, fear of public disorder became so great during this period that every state in New England and the Mid-Atlantic region abolished public executions largely because of concerns that *any* public gathering could lead to a riot (Vila and Morris 1997:33–34). When fears of social disintegration finally became stronger than distrust of a quasi-standing army, America's larger and more disorderly cities began searching for a successful model. Quite naturally, they seized upon the "modern" police model established by the Metropolitan Police Act of 1829, which created the first police force in the world whose primary duty was to *prevent* crime by constant patrolling rather than just apprehending offenders after the fact (Miller 1977:2).

MODERN POLICING ADOPTED BY U.S. CITIES

The London police impressed social reformers in the United States who saw their emphasis on prevention through highly visible, well-coordinated, and pervasive patrols as a way to manage the unwelcome side effects of rampant urban growth. After notable experiments in Philadelphia (1833) and Boston (1837), Americans began to adopt the general structure of the London police, but they were highly selective. In particular, instead of having police report to a national-level cabinet officer, U.S. cities retained control over their police.

In 1845, after several years of political wrangling, New York became the first American city to establish a fully consolidated police force, with 800 paid full-time officers (Document 11). Other cities quickly followed New York's example and established urban police forces. In less than fifteen years, New York–style, full-time consolidated police departments focused on preventive patrol had become standard in all large American cities. Over the next few years the role of urban police gradually evolved from one that included such diverse duties as lamp lighting, election monitoring, and providing overnight lodging and food for the homeless to a clear emphasis on crime control.

PRIVATE POLICING

The nation continued to experience the strains of rapid technological, economic, and demographic change into the late 1800s. Regional, racial, and ethnic divisions that grew out of war and continued immigration were played out violently as Klansmen terrorized blacks and recent immigrants, and thousands of people were lynched each decade by vigilantes (U.S. Bureau of the Census 1975:422). Occupational and class interests also led to violence as strike breakers clashed with unionists. At about the same time that public police agencies were being established to maintain order in the cities, the private police movement also took hold.

Business leaders, concerned over transregional crimes such as thefts from the railroads, as well as the need to control an increasingly restive labor force, relied upon private police such as Pinkerton's Northwest Police Agency (Stead 1977:96). Founded in 1855 by Allan Pinkerton (Document 13) with $10,000 in railroad money, Pinkerton's agency would become a model for private police and detective agencies. In fact, the term "private eye" probably refers to the Pinkerton logo—an open eye. Prior to the Civil War, Pinkerton's was primarily involved in guarding businesses and in cross-jurisdictional detective work which was beyond the authority of America's fledgling police departments with their patchwork jurisdictions. Pinkerton men, as they were known, stepped into this void by tracking desperadoes like Jesse James, Butch Cassidy and the Sundance Kid, and many others across state and municipal boundaries. Often, Pinkerton posses administered "frontier justice" when they caught up with outlaws (Bopp and Schultz 1972a:55–56); other times they worked with local authorities to assist in their capture.

After the Civil War, Pinkerton's became especially well known for its often brutal work against labor unions and strike-breaking in the mines and factories that fueled the nation's burgeoning economy.

POLICE REFORM

The end of the Civil War and the beginning of the industrial revolution were accompanied by even more massive waves of immigration that poured an increasingly diverse group of people from eastern and southern Europe as well as Asia into America's industrializing cities. At the same time, the enormous natural resources of the West fueled the industrial revolution, and capital was amassed at an astounding rate. Americans became intoxicated with their newfound prosperity—prosperity that sometimes fed excess. As S. L. Mayer notes, Americans

did not notice when excess became corruption. Corruption in the last third of the 19th century was of a special order because an entirely new social structure, one of capital and technology, was being developed without the guiding restraints of law. . . . [C]orruption became as acceptable as apple pie. . . . The exuberant young society agreed on one point; a citizen's value could be judged by one standard alone: money. (1993:325)

Reconstruction officials in the South illegally obtained many millions of dollars through fraud and outright theft. Robber barons such as John D. Rockefeller controlled whole legislatures. Scandal after scandal involving high federal and state officials came to light. In the cities, corrupt political organizations openly sold power and position. Machine politicians like New York's Chief of Public Works, William "Boss" Tweed, stole over $200 million in less than six years through kickbacks, fraud, and graft—bringing the city to the verge of bankruptcy. Out west, the depredations of traditional outlaws who robbed stages, banks, and trains at gunpoint were probably more than matched by emerging barons of cattle, mining, land, and railroad who waged a no-holds-barred battle for the young nation's immense resources (see Mayer 1993).

It was against this backdrop of excess and corruption in the cities and on the frontiers that the reform movement emerged as America rediscovered its ideals. American perceptions of the role of police and the limits of police power were influenced to some extent by U.S.

Supreme Court decisions such as *Hopt v. Utah* (Document 16), which established the ground rules under which federal police officers could obtain confessions. However, the development and reform of police during this era came from the efforts of many different types of people. Progressive political leaders such as Theodore Roosevelt triumphed over the domination of police departments by political spoils and instituted merit-based systems of hiring, promotion, and management (Document 22). The Women's Christian Temperance Union and other women's and religious groups fought hard for the establishment of matrons in police departments to look after the needs of arrested women and to protect them from abuse while they were in custody (Document 19). Chiefs of police also began to work together to improve the efficiency and integrity of their departments.

POLICE CHIEFS' ASSOCIATIONS

As early as 1871, when the first national police convention took place (Document 14), law enforcement leaders began to grapple with the need for uniform police regulations, prison and jail reform, and laws to facilitate interagency cooperation. Although initial efforts faltered, they became better organized toward the end of the century as the professionalization movement gained the support of police chiefs across the country.

The first National Chiefs of Police Union meeting took place in 1893 (Document 20) and was attended by fifty-one chiefs from around the country. Most of this meeting dealt with practical matters such as the use of new technologies, civil service rules for police, and the need for a centralized identification bureau. Their first formal resolution was an agreement to assist each other by arresting and detaining criminals wanted for crimes committed in other cities or states (Deakin 1988: 37). The group continued to meet annually, changing its name in 1895 to the National Association of Chiefs of Police of the United States and Canada. In 1902 the group became the International Association of Chiefs of Police (IACP)—a name it still bears. Since that time, it has remained one of the most influential professional law enforcement bodies in the world.

DOCUMENT 9: The Texas Rangers (1823–)

Rapid westward expansion led to new law enforcement challenges in the nineteenth century. Territories were large yet sparsely populated, distances between settlements were vast, and outside threats from bandits and Indians were a problem. As Frank Richard Prassel put it, "The spatial scope of law enforcement demanded expansion with the land" (1972:151).

In the English-speaking land grant settlements in the Mexican territory of Texas, where Indians posed a serious threat, the residents received little or no protection from the Mexican government. Beginning in 1823, they formed small militia groups of their own for protection. These early militia companies, which performed mounted scouting and patrol duties, became known as Rangers (Prassel 1972:151).

Beginning with Texas' successful struggle for independence from Mexico in 1835, and continuing during the period of the Texas Republic from 1836 to 1845, the role of the Rangers was expanded to include guarding the Texas border against Mexicans as well as Indians. After Texas joined the Union in 1845, the Rangers also served as a "mobile striking force" during the Mexican War of 1846–1848 that followed (W. Bailey 1989:614–615; Prassel 1972:151).

During the period between the Mexican War and the Civil War, the role of the Texas Rangers grew to include a variety of policing duties, such as retrieving runaway slaves and fugitives from the law. But their law enforcement activities diminished significantly during the Civil War, when they became part of the Confederate Army (Barker et al. 1994:67).

In 1870, during the period of reconstruction that followed the Civil War, the Rangers were replaced by a new state police force that was both despised and mistrusted by the majority of Texans. However, by 1874, the Democrats were once again in power, a new Texas legislature was in place, the state police had been dismantled, and the Texas Rangers were reinstated (W. Bailey 1989:615; Prassel 1972:153–154).

The oldest state police agency in the country, the Texas Rangers have persisted to this day, although they have undergone several changes. By the early twentieth century, Texas' other state and local police systems had become more formalized and disciplined, and hence the Rangers no longer were a significant means of protection and law enforcement. In 1935, the dwindling force was placed under the Texas Department of Public Safety and its duties limited to activities such as riot control and other special assignments (Barker et al. 1994:68; Prassel 1972:159). However, the role of the Texas Rangers was expanded once again in 1968, when they became the Department of Public Safety's principal investigative unit (Barker et al. 1994:68).

The following "Ranger's Prayer" by Pierre Bernard Hill, a chaplain for the Texas Rangers, provides good insight into the mind-set of nineteenth-century Rangers.

* * *

THE RANGER'S PRAYER

O God, whose end is justice,
Whose strength is all our stay,
Be near and bless my mission
As I go forth today.
Let wisdom guide my actions,
Let courage fill my heart
And help me, Lord, in every hour
To do a Ranger's part.
Protect when danger threatens,
Sustain when trails are rough;
Help me to keep my standard high
And smile at each rebuff.
When night comes down upon me,
I pray thee, Lord, be nigh,
Whether on lonely scout, or camped,
Under the Texas sky.
Keep me, O God, in life
And when my days shall end,
Forgive my sins and take me in,
For Jesus' sake, Amen.
    Pierre Bernard Hill, Chaplain Texas Rangers

Source: In William J. Bopp and Donald O. Schultz, *Principles of American Law Enforcement and Criminal Justice* (Springfield, Ill.: Charles C Thomas, 1972), 52.

DOCUMENT 10: Metropolitan Police Act (London, 1829)

At the same time the first Texas Rangers were riding the western plains, events were taking place on the other side of the Atlantic that eventually would have a significant impact on policing in America (see Document 11). Prompted in part by concerns about London's rapidly increasing crime rate and social upheaval associated with industrialization (Emsley 1991:24; Peak 1997:12), British Home Secretary Sir Robert Peel II (1788–1850) was commissioned by the prime minister in 1822 to establish some sort of a centralized London police force. After seven years of failed attempts due to public and Parliamentary opposition to a professional police force, and several revisions, Peel's "Act for Improving the Police in and near the Metropolis," introduced in April 1829, was passed by Parliament (Peak 1997:12).

The hallmark of Peel's reform was an emphasis on preventing, rather than simply reacting to, crime. It is this focus that earned the London

Metropolitan Police force of 1829 the distinction of being the first "modern" police force (Miller 1977:ix).

In addition to its focus on crime prevention, the new London police force, which replaced the city's night watch and various independent local forces, was a full-time, day and night operation composed of more than 3,000 salaried officers (Miller 1977:2; Regoli and Hewitt 1996:219). Under the command of two commissioners, Colonel Charles Rowan and Richard Mayne, the London "bobbies"—a nickname referring to Sir Robert—patrolled regular beats, wore uniforms, and were distinctively military in terms of structure and discipline (Miller 1977:2). However, although the police force was quasi-military in structure, no military titles other than sergeant were used, and the uniforms were blue, rather than the military's red, in an effort to reinforce their image as a civilian force (Barker et al. 1994:61).

The London Metropolitan Police force was very important from an American perspective because it soon would be used as a model for urban police departments in the United States. In addition to borrowing Peel's structure for police organizations, many U.S. departments also would come to see their primary role as crime prevention. Similarly, the London Metropolitan Police regulations regarding officer demeanor, accountability, and integrity—as well as supervision and management—defined standards that are largely applicable to this day in American policing.

Despite Peel's efforts to create an efficient, civil, and well-disciplined force, the London Metropolitan Police drew early criticism from Londoners, who feared that a stronger police force would impinge on their freedom (Peak 1997:11). The cost, which was considerably higher than that of the old watch system, also was a public concern (Emsley 1991: 25–26; Regoli and Hewitt 1996:219). However, Peel, Rowan, and Mayne's efforts at community relations, including moderating the officers' behavior and ridding the force of many objectionable officers, eventually led to greater public acceptance of the new police force (Peak 1997:12).

Following are excerpts from "An Act for Improving the Police in and near the Metropolis" (Document 10A) and from the *New Police Instructions*, which were reprinted in the *London Times* shortly before the new force went to work on September 29, 1829 (Document 10B).

* * *

A. EXCERPTS FROM "AN ACT FOR IMPROVING THE POLICE IN AND NEAR THE METROPOLIS"

CAP. XLIV.

An Act for improving the Police in and near the
  Metropolis.   [19th *June* 1829.]

Whereas Offences against Property have of late increased in and near the Metropolis; and the local Establishments of Nightly Watch and Nightly Police have been found inadequate to the Prevention and Detection of Crime, by reason of the frequent Unfitness of the Individuals employed, the Insufficiency of their Number, the limited Sphere of their Authority, and their Want of Connection and Co-operation with each other: And whereas it is expedient to substitute a new and more efficient System of Police in lieu of such Establishments of Nightly Watch and Nightly Police, within the Limits herein-after mentioned, and to constitute an Office of Police, which, acting under the immediate Authority of One of His Majesty's Principal Secretaries of State, shall direct and controul the whole of such new System of Police within those Limits: Be it therefore enacted by the King's most Excellent Majesty, by and with the Advice and Consent of the Lords Spiritual and Temporal, and Commons, in this present Parliament assembled, and by the Authority of the same, That it shall be lawful for His Majesty to cause a new Police Office to be established in the City of *Westminster*. . . .

IV. And be it enacted, That the whole of the City and Liberties of *Westminster*, and such of the Parishes, Townships, Precincts, and Places in the Counties of *Middlesex, Surrey*, and *Kent*, as are enumerated in the Schedule to this Act, shall be constituted, for the Purposes of this Act, into One District, to be called "The Metropolitan Police District;" and a sufficient Number of fit and able Men shall from Time to Time, by the Directions of One of His Majesty's Principal Secretaries of State, be appointed as a Police Force for the whole of such District, who shall be sworn in by One of the said Justices to act as Constables for preserving the Peace, and preventing Robberies and other Felonies, and apprehending Offenders against the Peace; and the Men so sworn shall, not only within the said District, but also within the Counties of *Middlesex, Surrey, Hertford, Essex*, and *Kent*, and within all Liberties therein, have all such Powers, Authorities, Privileges, and Advantages, and be liable to all such Duties and Responsibilities, as any Constable duly appointed now has or hereafter may have within his Constablewick by virtue of the Common Law of this Realm, or of any Statutes made or to be made, and shall obey all such lawful Commands as they may from Time to Time receive from any of the said Justices for conducting themselves in the Execution of their Office. . . .

VII. And be it enacted, That it shall be lawful for any Man belonging to the said Police Force, during the Time of his being on Duty, to apprehend all loose, idle, and disorderly Persons whom he shall find disturbing the public Peace, or whom he shall have just Cause to suspect of any evil Designs, and all Persons whom he shall find between Sunset and the Hour of Eight in the Forenoon lying in any Highway, Yard, or other Place, or loitering therein, and not giving a satisfactory Account of themselves, and to deliver any Person so apprehended into the Custody of the Constable appointed under this Act, who shall be in attendance at the nearest Watch-house, in order that such Person may be secured until he can be brought before a Justice of the Peace, to be dealt with according to Law, or may give Bail for his Appearance before a Justice of the Peace, if the Constable shall deem it prudent to take Bail, in the Manner hereinafter mentioned.

VIII. And be it enacted, That if any Person shall assault or resist any Person belonging to the said Police Force in the Execution of his Duty, or shall aid or incite any Person so to assault or resist, every such Offender, being convicted thereof before Two Justices of the Peace, shall for every such Offence forfeit and pay such Sum, not exceeding Five Pounds, as the said Justices shall think meet.

Source: "An Act for Improving the Police in and near the Metropolis." In *Parliamentary Papers*, vol. 2, Bills, N. P., 10° GEORGII IV., Cap. 44 (June 19, 1829), 377–380 (sidenotes omitted).

B. *LONDON TIMES* ARTICLE ON THE NEW POLICE

NEW POLICE INSTRUCTIONS

. . .

It should be understood at the outset, that the object to be attained is "the prevention of crime."

To this great end every effort of the police is to be directed. The security of person and property, the preservation of the public tranquility, and all the other objects of a police establishment, will thus be better effected than by the detection and punishment of the offender after he has succeeded in committing the crime. This should constantly be kept in mind by every member of the police force, as the guide for his own conduct. Officers and police constables should endeavour to distinguish themselves by such vigilance and activity as may render it impossible for any one to commit a crime within that portion of the town under their charge. . . .

SERJEANT

. . .

Each serjeant has under him nine men, and he will be held responsible for their general conduct and good order. He will live much with them, and is expected to make himself thoroughly acquainted with the character of every individual. He will keep in his own hand-writing a journal, according to a prescribed form, of any misconduct or fault they may be guilty of; this book shall be laid before the inspectors and superintendents at stated periods, and will always be consulted before any individual shall receive any reward, or be promoted. The serjeants will therefore feel the importance of entering in this book, fully and fairly, every circumstance which may enable their officers to form a just opinion of the individual's character: in no instance will any neglect or misstatement by the serjeant in such particulars be passed over.

The serjeant for duty will arrive at the division station before the hour fixed by his orders, form his party into ranks, and inspect them, taking care that every man is perfectly sober and correctly dressed. He will read and explain to the men the orders, if any have been given out that day. He will enter in a book the hour the party goes on duty, and the name of each man opposite the number of the beat in his section that such man is to take charge of; he will then report to the inspector, and receive his orders. He marches with his men to the section, and goes round it, and sees every man relieve the man previously on duty. Having done so, he will repair to the spot fixed on for making his first report to the inspector. This report should include any irregularity or disorderly conduct in the men relieved, as well as any other particular. . . .

POLICE CONSTABLE

Every police constable in the force may hope to rise by intelligence and good conduct to the superior stations; it is therefore recommended to each man to endeavour, by studying these instructions, and by reflecting upon the nature of the duty he has to perform, to qualify himself for such promotion. . . .

He will reside in the section, at the house appointed; he will devote the whole of his time and abilities to the service. He is at all times to appear neat in his person, and . . . [be] respectful towards his officers. He shall readily and punctually obey the orders and instructions of the serjeants, inspectors, and superintendents: if they appear to him either unlawful or improper, he may complain to the commissioners, who will pay due attention to him; and any refusal to perform the commands of his superiors, or negligence in doing so, cannot be suffered.

When he has to go on duty, he will take care to be at the appointed place, if not before, precisely at the prescribed hour. He is to fall in with the others of his party; and after inspection by the serjeant, and receiving any orders that may be necessary, he is to be marched by his serjeant to the section. A particular portion of the section is committed to his care; he will have previously received from his serjeant a card with the names of the streets, &c. forming his beat. He will be held responsible for the security of the lives, and safety of all property, of every person within his beat, and for the preservation of the peace and general good order of the whole, during the time he is on duty. . . .

He will be expected to possess a knowledge also of the inhabitants of each house. It must be obvious to him that he will be much assisted in the performance of his duties by making himself acquainted with all such particulars; without knowing them he cannot hope to be a really efficient police-officer, nor expect to rise in the service. He will be able to see every part of his beat, at least once in ten minutes or a quarter of an hour; and this he will be expected to do: so that any person requiring assistance, by remaining in the same spot for that length of time, must certainly meet a constable. . . .

All his duty will be carried on in silence: he is not to call the hour. . . .

On no pretence shall he enter any public house except in the immediate execution of his duty; he is to recollect that now the publican is subject to a severe fine for allowing him to remain in his house. . . .

He must be particularly cautious not to interfere idly or unnecessarily, in order to make a display of his authority; when required to act, he will do so with decision and boldness; on all occasions he may expect to receive the fullest support in the proper exercise of his authority. He must remember that there is no qualification so indispensable to a police-officer as a perfect command of temper, never suffering himself to be moved in the slightest degree by any language or threats that may be used; if he do his duty in a quiet and determined manner, such conduct will probably excite the well-disposed of the by-standers to assist him, if he requires them; but unless in case of urgency, he ought not to interfere without having a force sufficient to prevent any opposition.

Source: London Times, September 25, 1829, 3–4.

DOCUMENT 11: The New York City Police (1845)

In America, as in England, rapid growth and industrialization in urban areas during the nineteenth century brought with it a marked increase in crime that soon highlighted the need for preventive, rather than merely reactive, police systems. Early attempts at more effective policing occurred on a small scale in Philadelphia in 1833 and in Boston in 1838 (Bopp and Schultz 1972a:35–36), but it wasn't until 1845 that America's first unified, prevention-oriented police force was established in New York City.

Patterned after the London Metropolitan Police (see Document 10), established sixteen years earlier, the New York City police force consisted of 800 salaried, full-time officers who patrolled beats both night and day, replacing the city's night watch and the constabulary, as well as dock masters and various inspectors (Astor 1971:19; Miller 1977:x; Peak 1997:13–14). In addition to patrolling the city to help prevent crime, investigating crimes, and arresting lawbreakers, the new police officers also provided a number of other services, including lighting the city's gas lamps at night (Regoli and Hewitt 1996:222).

But while the New York City police force was similar to the London police in many ways, there also were a number of important differences. For instance, unlike its British counterpart, the New York City police force was a highly political entity. Whereas the London police were under the central authority of the Home Secretary, the New York City police answered to politicians in the individual wards they served. Local aldermen selected the officers (with approval from the mayor), which meant that the jobs of the officers in any given district were secure only as long as the alderman who hired them remained in office (Regoli and Hewitt 1996:222).

The New York City police also were more liberal in their use of force than were the English bobbies, and wore no uniforms (Regoli and Hewitt 1996:222; also see document below). Despite the protests of both the public and the officers themselves (see Document 12), this would change in 1853, when uniforms were made mandatory for all New York City officers.

Soon after the New York City department was established, many other urban areas followed suit, including Chicago (1851), New Orleans (1852), Cincinnati (1852), Philadelphia (1854), Boston (1854), St. Louis (1855), Newark (1857), and Baltimore (1857) (Regoli and Hewitt 1996:222).

The following excerpt from a 1970 book by James F. Richardson describes the law that eventually led to the establishment of the new New York City police.

* * *

The law abolished all existing police offices except that of constable; all functions were to be performed by a "Day and Night Police" of not more than eight hundred men. Each ward constituted a patrol district with its own stationhouse. To each ward there was assigned one captain, one first assistant captain, one second assistant captain, and as many policemen as the council should direct. To provide some over-all supervision, the act created the office of chief of police. The chief was to perform the duties of inspector of hacks, omnibuses, cabs, stages, and carts. But his supervisory powers over the police force were very limited. He could not appoint, assign, or remove policemen since these prerogatives were reserved to the mayor and the Common Council. Like the police-men, the chief was appointed for a term of only one year and could be removed before the expiration of his term. The appointment was to be made by the mayor with the approval of the council.

Policemen were to be chosen by the mayor upon the nomination of the alderman, assistant alderman, and the two tax assessors of each ward. The mayor could reject or accept such nominations, and in cases of rejection new names would be submitted in the same manner as the original ones. In such a system the real power of appointment lay with the alderman and assistant alderman of each ward. No provision was made in this act for a uniform, but the policemen were to carry a suitable emblem or device to identify themselves. The emblem subsequently adopted was a star-shaped badge; for this reason the force received the sobriquet "star police."

The act also established maximum salaries. The limit set for the chief of police and the police justices was $1500; for the clerks of the police offices, $800; for the captains of police, $700; for assistant captains, $550; and for policemen, $500. All fees were abolished, and policemen were not allowed to accept any money or other kind of reward without the written permission of the mayor.

Nothing in the act required the mayor and Common Council to adopt it. In his annual message Mayor Harper had dwelt on the need for reform in the city's police and in the administration of criminal justice. The mayor agreed with the Democrats as to the nature of the ills, but he did not subscribe to their proposed cure. All he said about the law of May 7 was that it would soon be submitted to the Common Council. An ordinance for adoption of the law was presented twice in the Board of Aldermen, on June 12 and again on July 30, and in both cases it was defeated. The law was not adopted until the Democrats regained control of the city government in 1845. . . .

The Democrats won the election of 1845, and in his annual message Mayor William F. Havemeyer called for the adoption of the state law. The council bill was signed into law on May 23, 1845, and New York at last achieved a police force akin to London's.

Source: James F. Richardson, *The New York Police: Colonial Times to 1901* (New York: Oxford University Press, 1970), 45–46, 49 (endnotes omitted).

DOCUMENT 12: "The Police Uniform" (1854)

Although police uniforms have been standard issue for patrol officers in the United States for many years now, their initial adoption by America's early police forces was a source of great controversy. In fact, as a result of this controversy, it wasn't until eight years after the New York City Police Department was established in 1845 (see Document 11) that the department's officers wore any official identification other than a star-shaped badge.

The strongest opponents of the police uniform were the officers themselves. They argued that uniforms were demeaning, unmanly, and undemocratic (Peak 1997:14–15). They also contended that losing their anonymity would make their job more dangerous and make it harder for them to catch criminals in the act. (Of course, as Bopp and Schultz [1972a:40–41] pointed out, losing their anonymity also would make it harder for them to shirk their duties.)

The public also opposed the adoption of uniforms for their police, primarily because the idea seemed too militaristic (Bopp and Schultz 1972a:40–41). However, determined to get their officers in uniform, New York's police commissioners finally took action to override opposition from both camps. Beginning in 1853, when many of the officers' four-year terms expired, they made it a policy to rehire only those officers who would agree to wear uniforms. Their plan worked, and despite continued protests (see document below), New York City police became the nation's first uniformed officers (Peak 1997:15).

* * *

THE POLICE UNIFORM.

Indignation Meeting of Policemen in the Park.

A large concourse, numbering from a thousand to fifteen hundred persons, assembled in the Park at 5½ o'clock yesterday afternoon, in accordance with a call issued by order of a previous meeting of the members of the Police.

The objects of the meeting were stated in the following notice, which was posted prominently in the streets and published in the morning papers:

"A meeting of citizens, and all others who feel aggrieved at the ridiculous and oppressive rules, and regulations of the Commissioners of Police and especially that portion of the late order imposing an expensive and fantastical uniform, will be held in the Park."

The meeting was called to order by Mr. BROCK CARROLL who nominated Mr. W. H. STOCKDELL to preside over its deliberations. A Vice-President from each of the different wards was nominated and elected.

The President then proceeded to read the call for the meeting, after which DANIEL B. TAYLOR, Esq., addressed the assemblage.

Mr. TAYLOR objected to the idea that this meeting was one in which only policemen had an interest. He regretted that this meeting had assumed the character of a Police Meeting. It was time that a question of deciding between the merits of the Policemen and the Commissioners of the Police would have to be raised, but to his mind the principles involved in the question were of such a character as to ask the response from every man who claims the name of an American. [Applause.] . . .

Mr. TAYLOR commented upon the decision of the Judges of the Supreme Court, in favor of the Commissioners, in their claims to possess the power of regulating the dress of the Policemen. He conceived that this infraction of the usage of society in the matter of dress, was but the commencement of the establishment in this City of a standing army—a state of facts which Americans could find no sympathy for, they being from their infancy taught to rely upon the spontaneous action of the citizen soldiery—the volunteers—when and where they were needed. The order which the Board of Commissioners had just issued, was the breaking of the ground wherein popular freedom would be buried. He thought that the efficiency lay in the man and not in the coat.

CHARLES S. SPENCER, Esq., was the next speaker. He said that it was the right of any citizen to look into any matter, and to form an opinion on it, and he believed that the members of the Police Department had a right respectfully to protest against any measure which they might consider oppressive to themselves. If this be treason, then, in the language of PATRICK HENRY, let them make the most of it. He was aware of the extent to which despotic power regulated the dress of man—the cut of the hair and the shaving of the beard; but he had yet to learn that in a republican country men were either to be forced to wear badges of nobility or servility.

We were told that the dress did not make the man; but it marked the man, however, and no man bearing the proud title of an American desired to appear in any dress that should make him conspicuous among his fellows. Who entertained any respect for the liveried hackmen who sat in the seats front and rear of the Fifth-avenue *parvenus*.

Mr. SPENCER spoke of the course of the *Tribune* and *Herald* in advocating the use of the proposed uniform. When the Commissioners of the Police could work a change in public opinion upon the subject of wearing liveries, then it would be proper for them, perhaps, to prescribe a dress for the Police to wear. The *Tribune* had said that if the officers did not like the uniform they could resign, and that plenty of men would be ready to fill their places. Were the salary of a policeman only $100, he too could find thousands of men ready to assume the duties. But what could be expected of such men? Of what good would a policeman be who possessed no self-respect?

Source: "The Police Uniform," *New-York Daily Times*, June 30, 1854, 4.

DOCUMENT 13: Allan Pinkerton and Private Policing (1867)

At around the same time America's growing cities were organizing their first modern public police forces, the first private police agencies also were established. One of the first, best known, and largest of these agencies was founded by Allan Pinkerton (1819–1884), a Scottish immigrant who came to the United States in 1842 and opened a barrel-making shop in Dundee, Illinois, the following year. The son of a Glasgow police sergeant, Pinkerton discovered a band of counterfeiters one day while collecting barrel staves on an island, and assisted the local sheriff with their capture. After several similar incidents, he was elected deputy sheriff of his county (Morn 1989:397; Stead 1977:97).

Pinkerton's abolitionist sentiments, which were unpopular in Dundee, led him to move to Chicago in 1850, where he did investigative work for the federal government and for the Cook County sheriff (Deakin 1988:79; Stead 1977:98). In 1855, following a series of train robberies in the region, Pinkerton won a $10,000 contract to establish a private railroad police agency—the North West Police Agency—that would serve six railroads in five states: Illinois, Indiana, Michigan, Ohio, and Wisconsin (Morn 1989:397; Stead 1977:103–104).

By 1858, Pinkerton had expanded his operation to form Pinkerton's Protective Police Patrol—a division of uniformed guards hired out to watch over Chicago banks, offices, stores, and other businesses at night. After the Civil War, he opened additional offices in New York City and Philadelphia (Morn 1989:399; Stead 1977:105–108). Shortly after the expansion of his agency, Pinkerton wrote a manual for his agents in which he outlined what he believed to be the fundamental principles of private law enforcement (see document below).

During the last ten years of his life, Pinkerton turned his attention to writing detective novels—sixteen in all—based on his exploits as a detective. After Pinkerton's death in 1884, his sons William and Robert took over the Pinkerton Detective Agency and became celebrated detectives in their own right. However, toward the end of the century, the agency began to direct its attention more toward the prevention of crime than its detection (Stead 1977:111–112).

* * *

GENERAL PRINCIPLES

This Agency is an individual and private enterprise, and is not in any way connected with, or controlled by, any Municipal Corporation, or

Governmental Authority. It was established for the purpose of the prevention and detection of Crime. The Prevention of Crime will be attended to by the Preventive Police Force, and the sphere of their duties will not extend beyond the City of Chicago. The Detection of Crime will be attended to at the various Branch Agencies which have been established in the several cities of the United States for this purpose, in connection with the Central Office at Chicago.

Only such business will be undertaken as is strictly legitimate and right, and then only, for the purpose of furthering the ends of justice and bringing Criminals to punishment.

The character of the Detective is comparatively new. It is true that, from the earliest ages, there have been officers of some kind for the detection and arrest of Criminals, and the bringing of them to justice; but the manner and style of these operations were entirely different from those of the modern Detective. The existence of the Detective, as an officer should be entirely unknown. All his acts should be surrounded with secrecy, and, in fact, so far from his being known as a Detective, he should be the very last upon whom such a suspicion would be likely to fall. . . .

The profession of the Detective is a high and honorable calling. Few professions excel it. He is an officer of justice, and must himself be pure and above reproach. The public have a right to expect this from their officers, nay, more, they have a right to know that their lives and property are to be guarded by persons, male or female, of whose integrity there can be no question. . . .

It cannot be too strongly impressed upon Detectives that secrecy is the prime condition of success in all their operations. It is the chief strength which the Detective possesses beyond that of an ordinary man. His movements should be quietly conducted; his manner should be unobtrusive; and his address agreeable. He should be able to adapt himself to all persons, in all the various grades of society; although it is not expected that any one class of mind should be able to cope successfully with all classes of Crime; but the Detective should ever study to improve his faculty, to mould himself, as much as possible, to the habits of those with whom he may be brought in contact, whilst engaged in the detection of Crime, bearing in mind that all his movements should be as silent as the "snow flake that falls upon the sod." It frequently becomes necessary for the Detective, when brought in contact with Criminals, to pretend to be a Criminal; in other words, for the time being to assume the garb of Crime, with a view to its detection in another. But when the ends of justice are accomplished, he will return, of course, unblemished by the fiery ordeal through which he has passed, and take his place once more in society. It is, unfortunately necessary to resort to these deceptions, to save society from its enemies; and so long as these enemies exist, so long will this necessity remain operative. The Detective has to act his part, and in order to do so, he has at times, to depart from the strict line of truth, and to resort to deception, so as to carry his assumed character through thoroughly and successfully. Moralists may question whether this be strictly right; but it is a necessity in the detection of Crime, and it is held by the Agency that the ends being for the accomplishment of justice, they justify the means used. . . .

The Detective must, in every instance report everything which is favorable to the suspected party, as well as everything which may be against him. The object of every investigation made by this Agency, is to come at the whole truth, in all the cases that are submitted to it. There must be no endeavoring therefore to overcolor or exaggerate anything against any particular individual, whatever the suspicion may be against him. It is the true function of the Detective to be impartial in all his operations, and to guard himself against prejudice on the one hand, and favor on the other. He is to learn all he can, both for and against the person who may happen to be his quarry for the time being, and report accordingly. He must credit neither good nor ill of any man, upon hearsay. His data should be founded upon knowledge only, and if upon hearsay, the same must be fairly expressed. All suspicions must be verified by facts. No man ought to be made to suffer on suspicion only. Actions alone are amenable to law and justice. These are fundamental axioms of this Agency and must be borne in mind by every Detective who is attached to it.

Source: Allan Pinkerton, *General Principles of Pinkerton's National Police Agency* (Chicago: George H. Fergus, 1867), 5, 6, 8, 11.

DOCUMENT 14: First National Police Convention (1871)

As the nineteenth century progressed, so did the development of the nation's police forces. In 1871, approximately 112 police delegates from twenty-one states and territories and the District of Columbia met in St. Louis, Missouri, for the first National Police Convention ever held in the United States.

Between October 20 and 23, the conventioneers—who hailed from Alabama, Connecticut, Georgia, Indiana, Iowa, Illinois, Kentucky, Kansas, Louisiana, Maryland, Massachusetts, Michigan, Mississippi, Missouri, New Jersey, New York, Nebraska, Ohio, Pennsylvania, Tennessee, Washington, D.C., and Wisconsin—gathered to discuss such issues as crime prevention, prison reform, and promoting uniformity in the management of police agencies.

Following are excerpts from the introductory address delivered at the convention by Charles A. Mantz, chairman of the joint committee, on behalf of the city council of St. Louis.

* * *

Gentlemen, the great majority of you have come from a distance—many of you are from the West, the North, the South and East—and for the first time a large majority of those here present have crossed the "Rubicon," the Mississippi River—the Father of Waters—to attend a Convention, the first of its character or kind ever held in the United States—a Police Convention. . . .

In times past, it has been common for conventions to meet in the interest of capital, trades, professions, religion, politics, emigration, labor, etc.; but never before, in the history of this country, has a convention been held composed of police functionaries or those delegated from States, cities and towns in the United States, to deliberate upon subjects directly connected with, and for the purpose of considering, the police system of the Union; and now, for the first time in our history, you have here assembled for the purpose of taking into consideration such matters as may present themselves calculated to make more perfect the police regulations of the whole land, to the end that the general public may be better served, and small, as well as large communities, may be ultimately benefited by your foresight, wisdom and experience. . . .

As conservators and guardians of the peace and security of the communities in which you and each of you [sic] reside, it will be expected that as intelligent men, having great experience in police matters and business, you will not only make important suggestions for the consideration of legislatures, general assemblies, corporations, municipalities and town trustees, but that you will go further, and, if not at this meeting, you will hereafter, make representation of valuable police regulations, in a national point of view, for the consideration of the Congress of the United States. . . .

At this time, each State, city and town has its own peculiar laws governing the regulation of police matters, and there is no uniformity existing, or international system in force as regards the several States and cities of the Union.

It will be expected of you, that you will take up and act upon various propositions, prominent among which, I may mention, will be a Police Detective system; a Metropolitan Police Force system, which will be under the control of the State as well as the municipality. That you will give attention to prisons, and classify them in such a manner as to separate the young and innocent female child just entering upon a life of shame or crime, from those who have led an abandoned life, and served out terms in State, city and county prisons. That you will see to it that some action be taken as regards the separation of the sexes in prisons, and reformatory institutions, and that they are not brought face to face, and allowed to associate together, where one can educate the other, and learn them [*sic*] how to pick a pocket, enter a house, pick a lock, and all the various and complicated tricks that belong to the murderer, the thief and the burglar; for thus in prison, as well as out, the vicious and bad are made more perfect in rascality, because of the want of proper discipline and more wholesome regulations.

Work houses, calabooses, and houses of refuge or correction, we have no doubt, will receive from you the attention which their importance deserves; for it is in these institutions that criminal acquaintance too often begins. It is in these primary departments where the young and old are thrown together, that they learn each other's history, and the designing and bad corrupt the young and prepare them for a future of infamy and crime; and it has been truly said, that when a youth, caught in petty larceny, is arrested and placed in such places as we have named, among the confirmed criminals—thrust in among them as you would cast a babe into the lion's jaws—the effect is to freeze the germ of manhood, and make callous the youthful heart. The purpose should be to raise up the fallen, and not cast them down—to reclaim, and not destroy.

A recommendation for the passage of laws in the several States of the Union, by and through which the abandoned children in the land—the young evil doer and petty thief—will be watched, cared for, and arrested in his career of crime, and not thrown into work houses, calabooses and jails, among old and expert offenders against the laws, and there compelled to associate with the hardened criminal, and forced to learn from him the "ways that are dark and the tricks that are vain," and, in fact, a criminal education; but placed elsewhere, among the virtuous and the good, where the seeds of badness implanted in their nature may be eradicated by the christian and philanthropist, and the kind and gentle teachers selected to teach them the true and correct principles that should guide them in the pathways of a christian life, teaching them to be frugal, honest, energetic and virtuous.

Your object will be to eradicate every species of villainy and rascality out of States and communities by your labors here, so far as in your power lies, because, in doing so, you protect life and property; therefore, the world has important lessons to learn from your deliberations in this Convention—as practical men you are known, and as such, practical results are expected.

Through the instrumentality of this Convention, great sums of money may be saved to the inhabitants of States, as well as corporations and communities; crime prevented, and the morals of the people benefited and improved. The peace and happiness of the public and society will soon feel the benefit of the work begun by your body, as by and through it you act as one person, because you have resolved, in the future, not to remain isolated and alone, but in all things to act in perfect accord, united and together, for the best interests of all classes and all sections.

As a citizen, we see no good reason why the police system of the entire States composing the Union, cannot be so regulated as to make it most complete—cannot be systematised and managed, and each part made to work with the other, as does the machinery of the General or State governments, and it remains with you, gentlemen of the Convention, to devise some plan by and through which this subject will be brought before the attention of the proper bodies, the Legislatures of the States, and if you cannot succeed at once, you may rest assured you will in time.

Gentlemen, you have a most important duty to perform—a grave responsibility is resting upon you as officers and citizens, and the eyes of the people of this country are directed towards you. May your proceedings be instructive and satisfactory, and the greatest good result from them.

Source: Charles A. Mantz, "Introductory Address," *Official Proceedings of the National Police Convention* (St. Louis: R & T. A. Ennis, 1871). [New York: Arno Press and the New York Times, 1971, 9–11.]

DOCUMENT 15: The Role of the Indian Police in the Western Territories (John P. Clum, 1875)

One of the more unusual and less well-known police institutions in American history was staffed primarily by Native Americans who provided law enforcement services on frontier reservations during the post–Civil War era. Among the earliest instigators of the "Indian Police," as they were called, was John P. Clum, a 23-year-old agent for the Apaches at the San Carlos reservation in southeastern Arizona. Shortly after he arrived at San Carlos in 1874, Clum—who sought to maintain control without resorting to military force—hired four Apaches to serve as police officers for the reservation (Hagan 1966: 31).

Contrary to the expectations of whites in the area who deemed the idea of Apaches policing themselves "preposterous" (Clum 1929:204), within six months Clum and his Apache policemen had things under control on the reservation. Clum eventually increased the size of the police force to eight, then twenty-five, as the Indian population at San Carlos grew (Hagan 1966:31; also see the following document).

Clum's San Carlos Indian Police were so effective that in May 1878 Washington authorized the establishment of Indian police forces throughout the frontier Indian reservations. Twenty-two Indian police forces initially were created—by 1890, there were fifty-nine, for a total of seventy officers and seven hundred privates (Hagan 1966:42–43, 169).

The main duties of the Indian Police included maintaining order on the reservation, protecting agency property, locating and returning lost or stolen property, acting as messengers to the Indian agents, arresting those who were drunk and disorderly, as well as arresting horse thieves, cattle thieves, and whiskey sellers (Hagan 1966:169–170).

Despite the success of the Indian Police "experiment," it had its problems. Compared to cowboys of that era, who earned up to $30 per month (Gillett 1925:14), the Indian officers received low pay—typically $8 per month for officers and $5 per month for privates—and were poorly equipped (Hagan 1966:45, 50). Moreover, many were as reluctant to wear uniforms as the police in New York City and other eastern departments had been during the pre–Civil War era (see Document 12).

Following is an excerpt from a report written by Clum in 1875, in which he described the early successes of the San Carlos Police Force.

* * *

The police force of Indians mentioned in my last report has been continued through the year, and has rendered most efficient service. They have been failthful and vigilant, prompt to quell all disturbances, to arrest criminals, and to give full information regarding all cases that might come under their jurisdiction. So effective have they been in the discharge of their duties that only on special occasions has it been necessary for me or an employe to accompany them when sent to arrest a criminal.

After the arrival of the Rio Verde Indians the number of policemen was increased to eight. On the 31st of July, after the removal of the White Mountain Indians, I increased the number to twenty-five. They were carefully chosen from the various tribes and bands, armed with needle-guns [a new type of rifle that had been issued to the U.S. Army in the 1870s] and fixed ammunition, and placed under the command of Mr. Clay Beauford, who has been guide and scout in this country for several years.

Such is the latest organization of the San Carlos Police Force. The duties of this force are to patrol the Indian camps, to quell disturbances, to arrest offenders, to report any signs of disorder or mutiny, to scour the entire reservation and arrest Indians who are absent from the agency without a pass, and also to arrest whites who trespass contrary to the rules of the reservation. My intention is to mount the police as soon as possible, as a mounted force is far more effective, while the extra expense is but a trifle.

I wish to state further that the police force has entirely superseded the necessity of a military force. I have never yet found it necessary to ask for a single soldier to act as escort, guard, or to do any police duty.

Source: John P. Clum, second annual report to the Commissioner of Indian Affairs, September 1, 1875. In John P. Clum, "The San Carlos Apache Police," *New Mexico Historical Review* 4, no. 3 (July 1929): 204–205.

DOCUMENT 16: *Hopt v. Utah* (1884)

In the western territory of Utah, a murder was committed that eventually led—in a somewhat roundabout way—to the Supreme Court's first articulation on the subject of the inadmissibility of involuntary confessions at federal trials. The case was *Hopt v. People of the Territory of Utah*. Hopt had been convicted of murder in a Utah court and sentenced to death. The judgment was affirmed by the supreme court of the Utah territory, then reversed by the United States Supreme Court, which ordered a new trial. A second trial was held, Hopt again was convicted and sentenced to death, the judgment again was confirmed by the territorial supreme court, and, in 1884, the case again was before the High Court, which again reversed and remanded the decision of the lower court and ordered yet another new trial (110 U.S. 574:575, 583).

The Court's decision to reverse the judgment reached at Hopt's second trial was based on errors made by the Utah court with regard to the jury selection process, admission of certain testimony related to the identification of the victim's body, and the judge's instructions to the jury (101 U.S. 574:575–583). However, the Court also addressed at length the issue of whether Hopt's confession to the murder should have been admissible as evidence during his trial. In doing so, it established the first federal guidelines for what would be considered an involuntary confession. The Court explained that confessions that appear to have been made as the result of "inducements, threats or promises" could not be considered voluntary within the meaning of the law, and therefore should not be admissible in court. While Hopt's confession did not fall into this category—it was deemed by the Court to have been voluntary and therefore admissible (see document below)—the Court's clarification had potential implications for future federal cases involving confessions by defendants, and indirectly provided stricter guidelines for interrogation of suspects by federal law enforcement officers.

* * *

MR. JUSTICE HARLAN delivered the opinion of the court.
   . . .
It appears that the defendant was arrested at the railroad depot in Cheyenne, Wyoming, by the witness Carr, who is a detective, on the charge made in the indictment. The father of the deceased, present at the time, was much excited, and may have made a motion to draw a revolver on the defendant; but of that fact the witness did not speak positively. The witness may have prevented him from drawing a weapon, and thinks he told him to do nothing rash. At the arrest a large crowd gathered around the defendant; Carr hurried him off to jail, sending with him a policeman, while he remained behind, out of the hearing of the policeman and the defendant. In two or three minutes he joined them, and immediately the accused commenced making a confession. What conversation, if any, occurred between the latter and the policeman during the brief period of two or three minutes preceding the confession was not known to the witness. So far as witness knew, the bill of exceptions states, "the confession was voluntary and uninfluenced by hopes of reward or fear of punishment; he held out no inducement, and did not know of any inducement being held out to defendant to confess." This was all the evidence showing or tending to show that the confession was voluntary or uninfluenced by hope of reward or fear of punishment.

While some of the adjudged cases indicate distrust of confessions which are not judicial, it is certain, as observed by Baron Parke, in *Regina* v. *Bald*, . . . that the rule against their admissibility has been sometimes carried too far, and in its application justice and common sense have too frequently been sacrificed at the shrine of mercy. A confession, if freely and voluntarily made, is evidence of the most satisfactory character. Such a confession, said Eyre, C. B., . . . "is deserving of the highest credit, because it is presumed to flow from the strongest sense of guilt, and therefore, it is admitted as proof of the crime to which it refers."

Elementary writers of authority concur in saying that, while from the very nature of such evidence it must be subjected to careful scrutiny and received with great caution, a deliberate, voluntary confession of guilt is among the most effectual proofs in the law, and constitutes the strongest evidence against the party making it that can be given of the facts stated in such confession. . . .

But the presumption upon which weight is given to such evidence, namely, that one who is innocent will not imperil his safety or prejudice his interests by an untrue statement, ceases when the confession appears to have been made either in consequence of inducements of a temporal nature, held out by one in authority, touching the charge preferred, or because of a threat or promise by or in the presence of such person, which, operating upon the fears or hopes of the accused, in reference to the charge, deprives him of that freedom of will or self-control essential to make his confession voluntary within the meaning of the law. Tested by these conditions, there seems to have been no reason to exclude the confession of the accused; for the existence of any such inducements, threats or promises seems to have been negatived by the statement of the circumstances under which it was made.

Source: 110 U.S. 574 (1884), 575, 584–587.

DOCUMENT 17: *Recollections of a New York Chief of Police* (George W. Walling, 1887)

Back in New York, the municipal police force had been in operation for more than four decades at the time George W. Walling published his *Recollections of a New York Chief of Police* in 1887. Walling, who had been with the police department from 1847—just two years after it was formed—until 1885, had served as superintendent of the force from 1874 until his retirement (Richardson 1970:ix).

During an era when romanticized stories about famous crimes, criminals, and heroic police officers were popular with the public, Walling's book offered plenty of the same. However, Walling also offered some insights into the political nature of the police force and its Board of Commissioners (which will be discussed in greater detail in Document 22), and his perception of the role of police, both as it was and as he thought it should be.

Walling also advocated broadening police education, although some of his suggestions sound more like a plan for an officer "charm school" than for the kind of rigorous officer training we associate with police departments today (see document below). Nevertheless, at a time when relations between police and citizens were not always amicable—partly because police officers sometimes stretched the rules to accomplish their goals, and partly because they were expected to enforce unpopular laws that were perceived by the public to be nonsensical, such as anti-gambling statutes and Sunday pub closures (Richardson 1970:viii)—Walling's suggestions for changing the demeanor and appearance of the police appear to be a sincere attempt to improve how the public perceived officers and responded to them. In his view, the role of police officers should not be limited to enforcing the law and preserving public peace—the ideal officer also should be a role model for the community he serves.

* * *

Since I have left active police life I have often thought of the wonderful change that has taken place in the character of the force during the time I was connected with it. Thirty-five years ago but little attention was paid to the *personnel* of applicants for appointment as patrolmen. Now a very close investigation is made of the strength, constitution and general physical well-being of the policemen, and it is unquestionable that great improvement has been the result of the application of the methods of examination now in vogue. But I venture to suggest that there is still very wide room for broadening the field of police education. It is undoubtedly an excellent thing to secure stalwart, hearty and vigorous men; but there are other qualifications which civil service examination does not provide for, but which would most certainly go a long way towards making up the acquirements of an ideal officer. I have sometimes fancied that it might not be wholly impossible to attempt to endow policemen with those elegancies and courtesies of life which make refined social intercourse so pleasant and improving.

Let us imagine an institution in which the guardian of the peace can learn to make a pleasant bow, to walk with grace, to shake hands with dignity, to lift his hat in a courtly way, or to extend his protecting arm to a lady with Chesterfieldian decorum. Such arts are teachable, and could be eloquently lectured upon and illustrated by some great actor, famous for his grace of manner, say Mr. Frank Mayo, for example. Another art which goes far toward making a man popular and effective is the capacity to speak readily and to the point upon matters which come within his ken. In my imaginary School of Deportment I can see Mr. Chauncey M. Depew filling such a "chair," and imparting to his scholars some of the secrets of the fascinating elements which make him so happy a speechmaker; and with what unctuous humor and fine rhetoric could our distinguished senator, Wm. M. Evarts, unfold the mystery of how to crack a pleasant joke.

Another of the amenities of life, which is taught nowhere, is the art of how to wear one's clothes. How often have I seen the effect of a fine new uniform, donned by a well-built policeman, spoiled because the man inside did not know how to wear it; and how much must this detract from the impression sought to be produced by clothing the officer in a uniform? Could he not be taught how to wear it? I maintain that he could, and have but to mention the name of Mr. E. Berry Wall, for every citizen of New York to instantly recognize the proper gentleman to act as instructor of this branch of polite accomplishment.

At first sight, these propositions may seem somewhat fanciful, but if the reader will think a little he will perceive that I am really advocating a most serious matter. Certainly, the practice of the arts which make men agreeable to their fellows is as much to be desired as the practice of the rules which make them formidable. Indeed, more than that. A strong man who is also a polite and affable person is the possessor of enlarged powers for good. I think, if such a curriculum were instituted for policemen, that the beneficial effects which would be obtained would make themselves notable; and that the idea would spread as it ought to, and that before long we should see similar professorships ordained in our public schools. . . .

Imagine a policeman so trained! Why, the transaction of business with him by the average citizen would be both a pleasure and an instruction. A request for the locality of a certain street would be cheerfully answered with a pleasant bow, that would send the citizen on his way refreshed and light of heart. A lady compelled to cross Broadway amid a throng of jostling vehicles, would find herself escorted with a courteous consideration that would land her on the opposite side-walk positively pleased with her perilous trip; and the unfortunate gentleman who should have worshipped too long and too often at the rosy shrine of Bacchus would find himself guided to his home, or when too far "gone," to the nearest police-station, with a dignified and shocked formality that would not only make him feel perfectly safe, but would positively shame him into a better line of conduct, because, for the moment at least, he would be the churl and the officer the gentleman. I do not know whether, in surprising a burglar at his nefarious occupation, a police-officer so schooled could stop to consider how the burglar should be accosted; but I can imagine a policeman brought to such a fine pitch of mental equilibrium that even then he would carefully weigh his words and actions, with a view not only to effect the capture of the burglar, but to preach to him in his person and bearing an effective moral lesson. This, of course, would be an extreme case, but if it could be accomplished, who knows but that the burglar's mind would be so startled and so powerfully affected by the living sermon before him, that it might prove the starting point that would turn his feet into ways of righteousness. What a victory that would be!

There are certain districts in New York, as in all great cities, where life is seen in its crudest and most revolting forms. If the police squads that patrol such districts were living specimens of all that is lovely and courteous in mankind, they would breathe out an atmosphere about them that could not fail to impregnate the minds of the dullest of the denizens of these purlieus; and in due course of time it might come to pass that Mulberry and Baxter streets would begin to rival Rotten Row and the *Bois de Boulogne* in the exchange of courtesies and the practice of politeness; and every philosopher who has ever written bears testimony to the fact that good manners breed good morals. So, not only might the poor creatures named be improved in their style, but ultimately elevated in all their relations with their fellow-men. The development of the Kindergarten system demonstrates that no lessons are so powerful as object lessons; and what more striking and delightful daily instruction can be imagined than the perpetual appearance and reappearance of a corps of policeman so admirably trained as to be positively fascinating.

Source: George W. Walling, *Recollections of a New York Chief of Police* (New York: Caxton Book Concern, 1887). [Montclair, N.J.: Patterson Smith, 1972, 592–595.]

DOCUMENT 18: *Our Police* (George M. Roe, 1890)

At around the same time George W. Walling was waxing poetic about the need for a "School of Deportment" for New York police officers (see Document 17), George M. Roe was extolling the virtues of a physically and mentally fit police force (see Document 18). Toward this end, the Cincinnati police force was one of the first American police departments to establish both a gymnasium and a "School of Instruction" for its officers, in 1887 and 1888, respectively.

The expectations for these two department additions must have been quite high indeed, for as Roe contended in the preface to his book:

[A] model Cincinnati police officer must . . . be a perfect specimen of physical manhood, able to pass a physical examination more exacting than that required of the West Point cadet; as symmetrical as an Apollo, as strong as a Hercules, as enduring as iron. He must have a knowledge of the English language sufficient to make his written reports intelligible, and be well enough versed in criminal and municipal laws to avoid making any mistakes in prosecuting his duties both for the discovery and the prevention of nuisances, of misdemeanors, of crime. (Roe 1890:iii)

Following is an excerpt from Roe's book.

* * *

A few years ago the idea of attaching a fully furnished gymnasium to a police department would have been regarded as chimerical, and even now the number of cities that have made use of the sensible idea can be counted on one's fingers. But it is to the credit of Cincinnati that not only was she among the first to introduce this improvement, but that she has one of the best in the country, and that the police authorities believe in and mean to keep improving it.

At first thought it would not strike the average individual that a gymnasium was of any particular use to a police force that, ordinarily, is on duty from eight to twelve hours each day, largely spent in "walking a beat." But it is of use, nevertheless. The policeman usually has been a hard working man, whose daily labor has kept off all superfluous flesh and hardened all his muscles. When he dons the police uniform his mode of life is changed. He no longer walks briskly for any length of time, he mostly saunters on his beat, or stands quietly at his post on a street corner, where his only exercise comes from an occasional stroll across the street as convoy for a bundle-laden lady among the piratical teams and dashing cable cars. Except for the swinging of his club by his side, his arms get no exercise, save in an infrequent battle with a muscular and recalcitrant law breaker. He may have had the best of wind when he first put on his silver badge, but his official duties are not likely to give him a chance to use it once in three months in chasing a fleeing burglar. All these things have their influence upon his physical welfare, and they begin to make their mark in a year's time, and keep on to his deterioration. It is only a matter of time when the most stalwart gets weak in the arms, asthmatic from accumulated adipose tissue, flabby in the muscles of the body, bilious, and suffers from indigestion, until at last he has a rotundity that in comparison would make Falstaff himself look lank, and the erstwhile Apollo degenerates into plain, wheezy Podger. All this and more can be prevented by a judicious course of "work" in a well-appointed gymnasium, and the policeman's health be preserved, while his physical proportions may remain a joy to those susceptible people who delight in masculinity, surrounded by well-fitting blue flannel and garnished with brass buttons. . . .

The School of Instruction was established in 1888, and is intended to cover some of the deficiencies which would naturally arise were the gaining of police knowledge left to experience only. . . .

The general divisions of the instruction are upon such United States and State laws and city ordinances as pertain to police duties; upon the powers, privileges, duties, discipline and exercises of patrolmen as may be prescribed by the Board of Police Commissioners; upon explanations of the principles, causes, and modes of action under the general orders issued by the mayor and the superintendent of police, and upon the topography of the city, which includes in general the location of all prominent places of interest, such as parks, amusements, buildings, and places of business, and especially in each district its prominent places of interest, even to the location of residences of citizens of any prominence. One additional branch that is not specified by any order of the board, or laid down by any rule, the official instructor has steadily kept in view, and that is the principles that should actuate each officer in the perform-ance of duty, that he must be vigilant, active, and courageous. . . .

With a body well trained in the gymnasium, and by a drillmaster, a mind filled with information imparted by Instructor Warren and gleaned from the manual, the officer is then fitted for a mental and manual ex-amination.

Source: George M. Roe, ed., *Our Police: A History of the Cincinnati Police Force, from the Earliest Period Until the Present Day* (Cincinnati: N.P. 1890). [New York: AMS Press, 1976, 149–162.]

DOCUMENT 19: Police Matrons (1890)

Police work was a decidedly male field throughout the nineteenth century. However, a few women—known as matrons—did participate in law enforcement during this period. The role of the early matrons, beginning in the 1830s, was to oversee the women inmates in local prisons. However, it wasn't until 1878 that matrons first became em-ployed by police departments, where they were in charge of women who had been arrested. Partly as a result of lobbying by women's groups such as the Women's Christian Temperance Union and the General Federation of Women's Clubs, matrons were employed by police departments in thirty-six cities by 1890 (Mishkin 1981:22–25; Reid 1990:233; Schulz 1995:10–13).

Interestingly, New York City, which had employed matrons in its two prisons beginning in 1845, was highly resistant to the notion of employing matrons in its police department. The city rejected the idea when it first was posed by the American Female Reform Society in the 1840s, and did so again in the 1880s, despite the growing number of women who were detained or sheltered by department precincts (Schulz 1995:11, 15; Segrave 1995:7–8).

However, after several years of pressure from the Women's Prison Association and others, including the *New York Times* (see document below), the New York City Police Department finally relented, hir-ing its first police matron in October 1891 (Schulz 1995:16; Segrave 1995:10).

* * *

"Shall we have police matrons?" is the question that is being asked by those who favor advance movements and who see how great is the need for some change in the care that is being given female prisoners. The idea is not a new one, nor a sudden one, but came about gradually, advancing step by step, as new wants suggested themselves, until it spread from a small beginning to its present proportions.

At first the most enthusiastic of women workers thought only of placing a woman for day service at the stations to see that women prisoners were so clothed as to be presentable at court. Now, in many cities, the women as soon as arrested are placed in the hands of other women, who are responsible for them day and night as long as they remain at the police stations.

Portland, Me., was the first city to inaugurate the movement in good earnest. In 1878 a woman physician happened into court and, during a few minutes' stay, saw sights that so aroused her sympathies that she was led to report the matter to the Woman's Christian Temperance Union. Upon application, the union was allowed to place a woman at the stations during the day. Many articles were written for the daily press on the subject and there was, we read, "quite a wave of interest created in various circles."

Providence, R.I., was the next city to follow in Portland's footsteps, and it was here that both day and night service was begun. The idea was widely discussed in all the cities of the United States, and a few at once adopted the plan of thus placing women in the care of women. In every case where it was given a fair trial the result was satisfactory. Now, it is no longer a mere idea, but is a settled and satisfactory institution.

In Chicago there are matrons at five different stations. Philadelphia has also taken up the work. Baltimore has been employing matrons for six years. Manchester, St. Louis, St. Paul, Cleveland, San Francisco, Montreal, Pittsburg [sic], and many other cities have the system fully established. The Massachusetts Legislature some time ago passed a bill providing for police matrons in all cities of over 30,000 inhabitants. This added at once nine cities—Lowell, Fall River, Lawrence, Worcester, Springfield, New Bedford, Cambridge, Lynn, and Boston. . . .

It is not easy to find the right woman, but she can be found. Chief Ebersold of Chicago says: "These women must be of irreproachable reputation, advanced in life, and must have kindly hearts, and keep a close watch upon themselves that they say no word of their business, either in the station or out, speak a kindly word to the girls, and when called into court, sit beside them." Mrs. Barney recommends "a middle-aged woman, scrupulously clean in person and dress, with a face to commend her and manner to compel respect; quiet, calm, observant, with faith in God and hope for humanity; a woman fertile in resources, patient, and sympathetic. She could hardly be this without possessing a generous endowment of good common sense."

The duty of a matron is to receive the prisoners and consign them to cells, giving aid to them if ill, and doing anything that may be necessary in the way of search. When they are to go into court she sees that their clothing is properly arranged, and lends anything that may be needed. In every city the various charitable organizations keep the matrons supplied with such articles as are suggested by womanly thought. Chief Childs of Providence thus describes the duties of matrons in that city:

"All female prisoners are immediately placed under the care of the matron, who has charge of the prisoners' dock, where they await their arraignment or trial before the police or justice courts, and continues her supervision until they are discharged from custody or are taken away to be committed to the State Institutions in Cranston. She also searches all the female prisoners previous to their commitment to the cells, many of whom are charged with larceny and are suspected of having stolen property in their possession."

As to the necessity for having these women, too much cannot be said. Mrs. Charles Russell Lowell, who made a personal examination of six stations in this city, said: "It was evident that the keepers in some of the station houses were doing the best that could be done under existing conditions to keep the women as secluded as possible from the men, but it was also evident that no great degree of privacy, and in many of the houses no privacy at all, could be maintained." In many cases the rows of cells face one another, and the latticed iron doors are the only screens that the occupants of either set of cells have from the other. Many of the cells are so narrow that the screen door reveals about every portion of the inner room. . . .

The presence of the matron in court during the trial of the prisoners is also to be desired. As an instance of this a story is told of a philanthropic lady who went into court to do what she could for a girl arrested for the first time. As a certain case was called, the Judge, who was a personal friend, passed a slip of paper to the lady advising her to retire to the next room.

"May I take the girl with me?"
"No, that is impossible."
"Then I will stay, too."
"We were careful on your account," said the Judge to the lady afterward.
"Didn't you ask all the questions that were necessary?"
"Yes; but if you had not been here, we might have got a little fun out of the case."
"Well! I shall be here every day," replied the lady, "or some one to represent me."

Source: "A Needed Police Reform: The Movement for the Employment of Matrons," New York Times, March 23, 1890, 20.

DOCUMENT 20: William S. Seavey and the National Chiefs of Police Union (1893–1895)

Despite the apparent success of 1871's National Police Convention (see Document 14), a second meeting, which had been scheduled for the following year in Washington, D.C., never materialized as planned (Deakin 1988:35). In fact, it was twenty-two years before the next formal gathering of police chiefs from around the country. The 1893 meeting was instigated by William S. Seavey, chief of police for Omaha, Nebraska, and Robert McLaughrey, superintendent of the Chicago police. In all, fifty-one police chiefs from eighteen states and the District of Columbia attended the first meeting of the National Chiefs of Police Union, which was held in Chicago from May 18 to 20, 1893.

During the meeting, the members of the newly formed organization resolved "to assist each other on all occasions, by arresting and detaining any criminal who may be called for, or any person known to have committed a crime in any other city or state" (in Deakin 1988: 37). This spirit of cooperation, as well as a desire to implement more uniform practices between police agencies nationwide, was a recurring theme throughout the meeting (Bopp and Schultz 1972a:60).

Omaha's Chief Seavey was elected president of the new police organization. A man of interesting and varied background, Seavey had traveled and traded in the South Seas (1881–1887), been the town marshal for Santa Barbara, California (1874–1879), and worked as a clerk aboard a steamboat on the Mississippi River (1866–1873). During the Civil War (1861–1865), he rose through the ranks from private to captain in the 5th Iowa Cavalry. Before that, the enterprising Seavey had left his job as a woodcutter in Wisconsin to take part in the Colorado Gold Rush of 1859 (Deakin 1988:38).

In his opening address at the 1895 meeting of the National Chiefs of Police Union, held May 14–16 in Washington, D.C., Seavey took the opportunity to reflect upon the progress made by the association during its first two years and to discuss the potential for future reforms (see document below).

Unlike its 1871 predecessor, the National Chiefs of Police Union persisted, becoming the country's first professional police association. In 1895, the name of the organization was changed to the National Association of Chiefs of Police of the United States and Canada, and in 1902, the name was changed again to the title it has retained to this day, the International Association of Chiefs of Police (IACP).

* * *

Since our last meeting, which was held in the City of St. Louis a year ago, many changes have been made in the municipal affairs of a number of our cities; but, notwithstanding the alleged "moral wave" which has swept over our country, having for its object the disruption of the police departments in many instances, I believe the interest in our National Chiefs of Police Union is increasing and that the Association will continue to prosper.[1] The number of officials before me today is the best evidence of this fact, and it affords me much pleasure to see this interest and determination displayed by my brother officers for the welfare of our Union.

But two years have elapsed since we organized this Association, and it is extremely gratifying to know that our efforts are universally favored not only by police, city, county, state and government officials generally, but by our legislators and the solid thinking men of this country.

To introduce and accomplish reform; to advance and promote the efficiency of the American Police system, is a grand and noble work which calls for persistent and united effort on the part of our law makers and those having charge and control of our police departments.

This Union, which was organized in Chicago, Ill., May 18, 1893, is, to my mind, a move in the right direction, and the work already performed by the combined efforts of the members of the Association has been productive of much good in the way of the prevention of crime and the apprehension of criminals in the United States during the past two years.

Among the police departments of the larger cities there is a constant telegraphic correspondence, and the effectiveness of one department depends upon the police system of other cities.

To bring these various police departments into more systematic and harmonious action in apprehending criminals is one of the principal objects of this Union.

Telegraphic codes and the Bertillon system of identification will be established, which will enable every department in the Union to work effectively and in harmony with every other department.

Differences in the criminal codes of the various States have most hampered the authorities in apprehending and holding criminals who are wanted at a distance. Through the efforts of our Union a stronger influence may be brought to bear for the removal of obstacles to such arrests. The cities of this country are mutually interested in the detection and punishment of criminals, no matter where the crime may have been committed.

Statistics show that crime is rapidly increasing, and it remains for the police to control and subdue it. In order to bring about a very necessary reform in this matter, the criminal laws in the several States must be more effective and uniform, and the men who have charge of the prosecution of these laws must prosecute in the strongest sense of the term.

The powers that govern, control and discipline the police departments should be composed of men who are honorable and practical, with characters above reproach, who should be non-partisan in their political ideas and have no conscientious scruples about performing their whole duty regardless of political, religious or any other influence, and the law, governing their actions should be as uniform in every city and state as is practical and possible to make it. If all the police of this country were appointed, governed, disciplined, uniformed and drilled the same, America would have a formidable army at a moment's notice for any kind of service.

Nothing is more demoralizing to discipline than the reliance placed by subordinates upon the influence of men, who they have helped into office, to shield them, unless it is the continual scheming of their superiors to secure promotion as a reward for political services rendered.

With united action on the part of the heads of the police departments assisted by the American people who desire to have the police system of this country elevated to a more efficient standard, I believe that crime in the United States will greatly diminish during the next decade.

Source: Excerpts from an address by William S. Seavey, in *Proceedings of the Second Annual Convention of the National Association of Chiefs of Police of the United States and Canada*, Washington, D.C., May 14–16, 1895. [*Proceedings of the Annual Conventions of the International Association of Chiefs of Police: 1893–1905*, Vol. 1. New York: Arno Press and the New York Times, 1971, 8–10.]

DOCUMENT 21: "Improvements in Police Work" (W. J. McKelvey, 1896)

At the third annual convention of the National Association of Chiefs of Police of the United States and Canada, held May 12–14, 1896, W. J. McKelvey, superintendent of the Brooklyn police force in New York,[2] gave an address in which he recounted how various technological advances, such as the advent of the telegraph, telephone, and electricity, had changed police work in recent years. He also noted that sanitary conditions had improved considerably, both in the jail cells and in the lodging rooms where police officers often slept while on call.

The following excerpt from his speech addresses these and other issues, such as the use of patrol wagons and the establishment of official schools of instruction at most police agencies. It also offers some insight into what police work was like in the years before these innovations were available or commonly used by police departments.

* * *

How changed is the work of the policeman in these later days of telegraph, telephone and a thousand and one appliances of that marvelous force, electricity! When I first became a policeman and thirty years is not so long ago, the work was vastly different. Nobody dreamed of telephones and patrol wagons then. Posts were three times as long as they are now in the cities and an officer was forced to lug his tipsy prisoner on a wheelbarrow for miles sometimes to the station. Now under the approved methods the division of labor system holds good. A policeman takes his prisoner to the nearest patrol box, a few blocks at the farthest, presses a button, says a word or two through the telephone and in a jiffy the patrol wagon with two men as a crew is at his service. In Brooklyn we are making the roundsmen keep track of their men through the patrol boxes. It is more sure, it seems to me, than the old system of going the "rounds." While I am in this branch of the topic which has been assigned to me I might say that in every way the police force has kept abreast of the march of progress.

How different are the sanitary conditions of the police stations, for example. Prisons and lodging rooms were located in the cellars, policemen slept in rooms poorly ventilated, the beds so close together as to compel the weary officer to creep over the foot rests. They were forced to sleep in an atmosphere poisoned with the rankest effluvia from the cells and lodging rooms. How changed are the conditions now. We have in Brooklyn about thirty police stations, accommodating a force of nearly nineteen hundred policemen.

Their sleeping rooms are spacious, clean and well ventilated. Most of the houses are new and built on plans approved by the health department, with a cubic air space which guarantees a supply of wholesome air to every man. The prisons are distinct from the main building and the men's quarters are equipped with plunge and shower baths, lavatories and other conveniences of first-class hotels. The municipality does not lose by this generosity to the men. These improvements have caused a positive gain to the city and a decrease of sickness. There is a falling off of sixty per cent in the sick leave now.

I have already spoken about the patrol wagon service, but you will pardon me if I refer to it again, as I do not think we can over estimate its value. Since the advent of the patrol wagon the once not infrequent clubbing by policemen is almost a thing of the past. The policeman is no longer required to pull and haul his prisoner through the public streets, collecting a rabble on the way. The mob in the old days derided and exasperated the officer to such a degree that he frequently lost both temper and judgment and then somebody was clubbed. The wagon is a boon to the prisoner. He is not marched through the street to the court next morning, but is taken as privately as possible to the magistrate.

The up-to-date police force has a school of instruction for the young patrolman with an experienced officer, an inspector, usually, as the class leader. The noviates, (we have a probationary period of six months in Brooklyn before a man can become a full-fledged policeman) are instructed in the laws governing arrests, city ordinances, the rules of the department, military drill and personal deportment. When we turn a young man out he is a full graduate in all these studies and as a rule we have no further trouble with him. He is instructed in a general way that it is his duty to prevent offenses against the law, to prevent calamities as far as possible. The prevention of epidemics, as Bentham teaches, is another of the duties of policemen, as far as lies in his power. But it would be hard to say where the duties of an officer begin and where they end. There is no department of the government more necessary; the preservation of the peace and the safety of personal property are the foundation stones of all successful governments.

How important it is that our police forces should be as near perfection as possible. In my opinion a police department to be effective should have a life tenure and the rank and file should be governed by strict discipline. Civil service can do little toward selecting or defining the requisite qualifications beyond establishing the general intelligence of the applicant. It would be almost impossible to suggest any method that could be applied as a test to prove a man's fitness for police or detective work. Experience is an infallible test after all.

Great care should be exercised in promotions. A man's record should count for more than anything else in his selection for promotion. Political pull should have nothing to do with it. We should never lose sight of the important fact that we are the servants, not the masters of the law-abiding portion of the community. We must insist on our subordinates maintaining in their ordinary intercourse with the public a civil and polite demeanor. Politeness pays and costs nothing. I would say to you, superintendents and chiefs, impress upon your patrolmen the fact that each has a responsibility as great as your own. Too many policemen fail to realize this fact. The people are quick to appreciate good police work. Get on good terms with the public, beneficial legislation will be a logical result.

Source: Excerpts from an address by W. J. McKelvey, in *Proceedings of the Third Annual Convention of the National Association of Chiefs of Police of the United States and Canada*, Atlanta, Ga., May 12–14, 1896. [*Proceedings of the Annual Conventions of the International Association of Chiefs of Police: 1893–1905*, Vol. 1. New York: Arno Press and the New York Times, 1971, 28–29.]

DOCUMENT 22: Theodore Roosevelt and the New York Police (1895–1897)

Despite some early attempts toward improvement—including the establishment of formal training programs in some departments (see Document 18), the formation of a national police association (see Document 20), and the implementation of new technologies such as the telephone—late nineteenth-century police forces were far from what would be considered acceptable by today's standards. In fact, political patronage and corruption were common and widespread throughout many of America's urban police departments (Fogelson 1977:5–11).

One prime example was the New York City Police Department. Under Tammany Hall[3]—which at the time had control of New York City's government—police officers, their supervisors, and many other city employees were beholden to the Tammany leaders for their jobs (Berman 1987:17). Moreover, many police appointments and promotions were dependent upon fees paid to Tammany leaders, and police officers and captains in turn typically recouped those fees by blackmailing local brothel and saloon keepers, gamblers, and others (Astor 1971: 57–64; also see document below).

Prompted in part by the spirit of progressive reform that was prevalent at the time, a special investigative committee chaired by Republican Senator Clarence Lexow was formed in 1894 to examine the nature and extent of corruption in the New York City Police Department[4] (Berman 1987:2–14, 18, 23). The shocking revelations of police corruption made during the committee's hearings led to increased public sentiment against Tammany rule and a subsequent victory for the 1894 anti-Tammany mayoral candidate, William Strong (Berman 1987:32).

One of Strong's first acts as mayor was to instigate a campaign for police reform that included the formation of a new, bipartisan police commission headed by future United States President Theodore Roosevelt (1858–1919). During the two years that Roosevelt served as police commissioner during the height of the progressive reform era, he had a profound effect on police in New York and across the nation. His influential policies and practices and his approach to management and reform, which formed the foundation of modern American policing, are summed up in his first policy statement:

As police commissioner, I shall act solely with a view to the well-being of the city and of the interests of the service, and shall take account only of the efficiency, honesty, and records of the men. Neither in making appointments, nor removals, shall I pay any heed to the political or religious affiliations of anyone. (Berman 1987:43)

At the dawn of the twentieth century, Roosevelt and his contemporaries in the early police reform movement had defined a philosophy and a practical approach to changing law enforcement organizations that would later be known as "police professionalization." This professional model for the role and conduct of police in society would dominate the theory and practice of American policing for the next hundred years (Berman 1987:6–7).

Roosevelt described many of the reforms implemented by the commission in his 1897 book, *American Ideals and Other Essays Social and Political* (see document below).

* * *

In New York, in the fall of 1894, Tammany Hall was overthrown by a coalition composed partly of the regular republicans, partly of anti-Tammany democrats, and partly of independents. Under the latter head must be included a great many men who in national politics habitually act with one or the other of the two great parties, but who feel that in municipal politics good citizens should act independently. The tidal wave, which was running high against the democratic party, was undoubtedly very influential in bringing about the anti-Tammany victory; but the chief factor in producing the result was the wide-spread anger and disgust felt by decent citizens at the corruption which, under the sway of Tammany, had honeycombed every department of the city government, but especially the police force. A few well-meaning people have at times tried to show that this corruption was not really so very great. In reality it would be difficult to overestimate the utter rottenness of many branches of the city administration. There were a few honorable and high-minded Tammany officials, and there were a few bureaus which were administered with more or less efficiency, although dishonestly. But the corruption had become so wide-spread as seriously to impair the work of administration, and to bring us back within measurable distance of the days of Tweed.

The chief centre of corruption was the Police Department. No man not intimately acquainted with both the lower and humbler sides of New

York life—for there is a wide distinction between the two—can realize how far this corruption extended. Except in rare instances, where prominent politicians made demands which could not be refused, both promotions and appointments towards the close of Tammany rule were made almost solely for money, and the prices were discussed with cynical frankness. There was a well-recognized tariff of charges, ranging from two or three hundred dollars for appointment as a patrolman, to twelve or fifteen thousand dollars for promotion to the position of captain. The money was reimbursed to those who paid it by an elaborate system of blackmail. This was chiefly carried on at the expense of gamblers, liquor sellers, and keepers of disorderly houses; but every form of vice and crime contributed more or less, and a great many respectable people who were ignorant or timid were blackmailed under pretence of forbidding or allowing them to violate obscure ordinances and the like. From top to bottom the New York police force was utterly demoralized by the gangrene of such a system, where venality and blackmail went hand in hand with the basest forms of low ward politics, and where the policeman, the ward politician, the liquor seller, and the criminal alternately preyed on one another and helped one another to prey on the general public.

In May, 1895, I was made president of the newly appointed police board, whose duty it was to cut out the chief source of civic corruption in New York by cleansing the police department. The police board consisted of four members. All four of the new men were appointed by Mayor Strong, the reform Mayor, who had taken office in January. . . .

In administering the police force we found, as might be expected, that there was no need of genius, nor indeed of any very unusual qualities. What was needed was exercise of the plain, ordinary virtues, of a rather commonplace type, which all good citizens should be expected to possess. Common sense, common honesty, courage, energy, resolution, readiness to learn, and a desire to be as pleasant with everybody as was compatible with a strict performance of duty—these were the qualities most called for. We soon found that, in spite of the wide-spread corruption which had obtained in the New York police department, the bulk of the men were heartily desirous of being honest. There were some who were incurably dishonest, just as there were some who had remained decent in spite of terrific temptation and pressure; but the great mass came in between. Although not possessing the stamina to war against corruption when the odds seemed well-nigh hopeless, they were nevertheless heartily glad to be decent and to welcome the change to a system under which they were rewarded for doing well, and punished for doing ill. . . .

In re-organizing the force the Board had to make, and did make, more promotions, more appointments, and more dismissals than had ever before been made in the same length of time. We were so hampered by the law that we were not able to dismiss many of the men whom we should have dismissed, but we did turn out 200 men—more than four times as many as had ever been turned out in the same length of time before; all of them being dismissed after formal trial, and after having been given full opportunity to be heard in their own defence. We appointed about 1700 men all told—again more than four times as many as ever before; for we were allowed a large increase of the police force by law. We made 130 promotions; more than had been made in the six preceding years. . . .

Another of our important tasks was seeing that the elections were carried on honestly. Under the old Tammany rule the cheating was gross and flagrant, and the police were often deliberately used to facilitate fraudulent practices at the polls. This came about in part from the very low character of the men put in as election officers. By conducting a written examination of the latter, and supplementing this by a careful inquiry into their character, in which we invited any decent outsiders to assist, we very distinctly raised their calibre. To show how necessary our examinations were, I may mention that before each election held under us we were obliged to reject, for moral or mental shortcomings, over a thousand of the men whom the regular party organizations, exercising their legal rights, proposed as election officers. We then merely had to make the police thoroughly understand that their sole duty was to guarantee an honest election, and that they would be punished with the utmost rigor if they interfered with honest citizens on the one hand, or failed to prevent fraud and violence on the other. The result was that the elections of 1895 and 1896 were by far the most honest and orderly ever held in New York City.

There were a number of other ways in which we sought to reform the police force, less important, and nevertheless very important. We paid particular heed to putting a premium on specially meritorious conduct, by awarding certificates of honorable mention, and medals, where we were unable to promote. We introduced a system of pistol practice by which, for the first time, the policemen were brought to a reasonable standard of efficiency in handling their revolvers. The Bertillion [sic] system for the identification of criminals was introduced. A bicycle squad was organized with remarkable results, this squad speedily becoming a kind of *corps d'elite*, whose individual members distinguished themselves not only by their devotion to duty, but by repeated exhibitions of remarkable daring and skill. . . .

There was a striking increase in the honesty of the force, and there was a like increase in its efficiency. When we took office it is not too much to say that the great majority of the citizens of New York were firmly convinced that no police force could be both honest and efficient.

They felt it to be part of the necessary order of things that a policeman should be corrupt, and they were convinced that the most efficient way of warring against certain forms of crime—notably crimes against person and property—was by enlisting the service of other criminals, and of purveyors of vice generally, giving them immunity in return for their aid. Before we took power the ordinary purveyor of vice was allowed to ply his or her trade unmolested, partly in consideration of paying blackmail to the police, partly in consideration of giving information about any criminal who belonged to the unprotected classes. We at once broke up this whole business of blackmail and protection, and made war upon all criminals alike, instead of getting the assistance of half in warring on the other half. Nevertheless, so great was the improvement in the spirit of the force, that, although deprived of their former vicious allies, they actually did better work than ever before against those criminals who threatened life and property. Relatively to the population, fewer crimes of violence occurred during our administration of the Board than in any previous two years of the city's history in recent times; and the total number of arrests of criminals increased, while the number of cases in which no arrest followed the commission of crime decreased. The detective bureau nearly doubled the number of arrests made compared with the year before we took office; obtaining, moreover, 365 convictions of felons and 215 convictions for misdemeanors, as against 269 and 105 respectively for the previous year. At the same time every attempt at riot or disorder was summarily checked, and all gangs of violent criminals brought into immediate subjection; while on the other hand the immense mass meetings and political parades were handled with such care that not a single case of clubbing of any innocent citizen was reported.

The result of our labors was of value to the city, for we gave the citizens better protection than they had ever before received, and at the same time cut out the corruption which was eating away civic morality. We showed conclusively that it was possible to combine both honesty and efficiency in handling the police. We were attacked with the most bitter animosity by every sensational newspaper and every politician of the baser sort, not because of our shortcomings, but because of what we did that was good. We enforced the laws as they were on the statute books, we broke up blackmail, we kept down the spirit of disorder, and repressed rascality, and we administered the force with an eye single to the welfare of the city. In doing this we encountered, as we had expected, the venomous opposition of all men whose interest it was that corruption should continue, or who were of such dull morality that they were not willing to see honesty triumph at the cost of strife.

Source: Theodore Roosevelt, *American Ideals and Other Essays Social and Political* (New York: G. P. Putnam's Sons, 1897), 160–162, 171–172, 182, 184–188.

DOCUMENT 23: The Role of United States Marshals in the Western Territories (1898)

At the same time more modern, decentralized, uniformed, and better trained local police forces were rapidly developing in American cities east of the Mississippi (see Documents 11, 12, 14, 20, 21, and 22, for example), a very different style of law enforcement was the norm in the expanding western territories and states in the mid-1800s. There, with the exception of Texas (see Document 9) and California, both of which entered statehood with a "heritage of independence and self-rule" (Prassel 1972:220), the federal government provided the main source of law enforcement in the form of United States marshals and their deputies.

The office of U.S. marshal—the first federal law enforcement agency in the country—was established by the federal Judiciary Act of 1789. The main role of the early federal marshals—and one they still fulfill today—was to serve, support, and protect the federal courts and their laws (Regoli and Hewitt 1996:240–241). In 1792, they were given more power by Congress, which proclaimed that "the marshals shall have, in each state, the same powers as sheriffs in executing the laws of the United States" (Ball 1978:7). Hence, in the 1800s, as westward expansion into unorganized—and often federally controlled—territories increased, the U.S. marshals became increasingly responsible for law enforcement on the new frontier (Prassel 1972:221).

As federal officers, the marshals and their deputies were concerned only with crimes against the federal government—such as robbery of the mails and trains. They also became involved when a crime such as murder was committed on federal land, which constituted a large part of the territory at the time. In addition to these duties, they continued to serve the federal courts with regard to various civil matters, such as serving process papers (Peak 1997:21).

As territories became states, local sheriffs and marshals—many of whom had been deputized by federal marshals—typically took over the day-to-day policing duties in the western towns (Calhoun 1989: 150; Peak 1997:21; also see Document 24).

Today, U.S. marshals continue to serve the federal courts (providing security for federal courts, judges, and attorneys, transporting federal prisoners, protecting federal witnesses, etc.) and to perform various law enforcement duties (such as apprehending federal criminals) (Regoli and Hewitt 1996:242).

The following document outlines the duties and responsibilities of U.S. marshals during the late nineteenth century.

* * *

APPOINTMENT, QUALIFICATION, AND DUTIES OF UNITED STATES MARSHALS.

Attention is directed to the following provisions of the Revised Statutes:

SEC. 779. Marshals shall be appointed for a term of four years.

SEC. 1876. There shall be appointed a marshal for each Territory. He shall execute all process issuing from the Territorial courts when exercising their jurisdiction as circuit and district courts of the United States. He shall have the power and perform the duties, and be subject to the regulations and penalties, imposed by law on the marshals for the several judicial districts of the United States. He shall hold his office for four years and until his successor is appointed and qualified, unless sooner removed by the President.

SEC. 787. It shall be the duty of the marshal of each district to attend the district and circuit courts when sitting therein, and to execute, throughout the district, all lawful precepts directed to him, and issued under the authority of the United States, and he shall have power to command all necessary assistance in the execution of his duty.

SEC. 788. The marshals and their deputies shall have, in each State, the same powers, in executing the laws of the United States, as the sheriffs and their deputies in such State may have, by law, in executing the laws thereof. . . .

Attention is invited to the view of this Department that an economical and satisfactory administration of the office of United States marshal depends largely upon the degree of the personal attention which the marshal gives to the duties of his office and upon the honesty and efficiency of the deputies employed by him. It is expected of the marshal that he will personally make such investigation from time to time as will enable him to ascertain whether his field deputies are in fact performing personally all the services for which they are claiming credit, whether all mileage has been actually traveled, and whether the actual expenses for which credit is claimed have been in fact incurred, as indicated by the receipts furnished. The marshal will be held responsible for dishonest or fraudulent practices of his deputies if he does not use the resources at his command to protect the Government against abuses. Examiners of this Department will report upon this matter in their investigations of the manner in which marshals and their deputies perform their official duties.

It is the duty of the marshal, whenever practicable, to aid in serving the process and orders of the courts. He should dismiss at once any deputy who is incompetent, inattentive to his duties, or whom he has reason to believe guilty of any fraud or dishonesty.

Source: U.S Department of Justice, Attorney General's Office, *Instructions to United States Marshals, Attorneys, Clerks, and Commissioners* (Washington, D.C.: U.S. Government Printing Office, 1898), 7–9, 11–12.

DOCUMENT 24: The Nineteenth-Century Town Marshal

At the local level, the chief law enforcement officer on the western frontier was the town marshal, also known as the chief of police in some communities (Calhoun 1989:150). Partly because of their reliance on federal law enforcement (see Document 23), western towns often did not appoint a local marshal until the population had reached one thousand or more (Prassel 1972:44). However, as territories became states, local law enforcement tended to supersede federal law enforcement in most instances (Calhoun 1989:150; Peak 1997:21).

In addition to tracking and/or apprehending outlaws, which actually occurred less frequently than movies and television might lead one to think, duties of the town marshals included maintaining the town jail, collecting taxes, serving civil papers, arresting those who were drunk and disorderly, protecting property, and generally keeping the peace (Peak 1997:22; Prassel 1972:46).

Eventually, many western towns established local police departments, although even today the West still has quite a few local marshals serving as one-person police departments (Prassel 1972:69).

Following is an excerpt from Frank Richard Prassel's 1972 book, *The Western Peace Officer*, in which he gives an excellent overview of the nature and duties of the nineteenth-century western town marshal.

* * *

Earp, Hickok, Masterson—such names are synonymous with the image of the western town marshal. Their legend is one of a tall lone figure, striding down a dusty street in the dim direction of public order and immortality. It is a myth, yet one based on a slim foundation of truth.

The towns of the frontier West did not long remain without some sort of police agency. Many communities found that the county sheriff or constable could supply the necessities of formal law and order. Demand for a strictly local peace officer often did not emerge until the population reached a thousand or more. In many instances settlements developed considerable size before agitation for a community police began.

Village law enforcement among settlers moving across the Mississippi into the West first appeared in Texas. During the 1820s assorted emigrants from the United States had begun colonization of large land grants which later became the seedbed for revolution against Mexico. The Mexican government provided early East Texas with nothing in the form of police. Colonists consequently established their own law enforcement agencies. Within a very few years local *comisarios* of police, such as James B. Patrick in the Gonzales district, began working toward regulation of gambling and other activities. By 1831 the town of San Felipe de Austin established a community patrol to maintain order and warn of approaching danger. Formed at the suggestion of an attorney from Georgia named Robert McAlpin Williamson (locally dubbed "Three-Legged Willie") and placed under the command of Captain Thomas Gay, the force probably comprised the first actually operating local police agency of the English speaking West. Within a short time the guard required the passage of formal rules and regulations by the village governing council. The patrols at San Felipe de Austin, well before the Texas Revolution, did not constitute more than a semiformal organization, but they reflected an established tradition of citizen police and demonstrated both the elemental needs and basic solutions to law enforcement on the frontier.

In later years countless communities throughout the West faced essentially the same conditions as had confronted the early Texans. Subsequently, developing areas normally operated under general but clearly drawn statutory authority for the creation of local law enforcement. Some legislatures, such as that of Kansas, originally provided for the popular election of town constables. More frequently, the term "marshal" was employed, with power of appointment given to the community's mayor and council. Within given formal limits the actual duties of these local peace officers could be prescribed by governing authorities for the village. In later years the title "chief of police" often replaced "constable" or "marshal" to designate law enforcement personnel, but most states still utilize a legislative framework originated in frontier days.

What kinds of men filled these offices? In some villages they came from the ranks of local toughs, on the theory that such persons would most easily gain the fearful respect of the region's criminal element. Occasionally personnel of such dubious qualifications were the only volunteers willing to undertake the work. Unfortunate results, of course, often followed this method of selection. Some local marshals had to flee the community when made to appear cowardly; others resigned after disgraceful public performances caused by drink and gross abuses of offices.

With the passage of time and the growth of population, most villages developed functioning police forces, although the old titles tended to remain. Long before the end of the nineteenth century growing communities in the West established local agencies of considerable sophistication and close interrelationships with existing political structures. By 1866, for example, Chief of Police W. S. Edwards of Virginia City, Nevada, directed a sizable and well-paid force with the advice of a standing committee composed of interested citizens. With the considerable monthly salary of $215 as an attraction, Edwards' appointment depended upon harmonious relations with both local officials and a generally satisfied electorate. The structured agency at his command rarely resorted to firearms. Their primary tasks consisted of arresting those found drunk and disorderly, sleeping on the street, or fighting in public.

The legal authority of town peace officers naturally varied with the provisions of state law. In Kansas they were given, and still possess, the technical power of county sheriffs; in Utah the rights granted are those accorded constables. More typically the legislatures assigned the general authority of community officers in such language as:

The marshal shall be chief of police, and shall at all times have power to make, or order an arrest, with proper process, for any offense against the laws of the State, or of the city, and bring the offender for trial before the proper officer of the city, and to arrest without process, in all cases where any such offense shall be committed, or attempted to be committed in his presence.

In addition, local lawmen have taken on specific duties of attending and serving warrants of corporation courts, quelling riots, and otherwise protecting property and the public peace.

Local marshals encountered a variety of routine tasks in the towns of the frontier West. In some communities they had to prevent bathers from using convenient rivers, or keep the streets clear of obstruction and congestion. In larger towns their duties could be delegated to the lower ranks of town deputies or policemen. Leadville, Colorado, a booming mining camp in 1880, had a sizable but still typical organization:

The members of the police force are elected annually by the city council. The force is governed by the mayor, and its chief executive officer is the city marshal . . . he receives a salary of $180 per month. The rest of the force consists of a captain, with a salary of $125 per month, 2 sergeants and 18 patrolmen, with salaries of $100 per month each. They wear navy-blue uniforms with brass buttons, and each provides his own. They carry clubs and navy revolvers. They serve 8 hours per day each winter and 12 in summer, and patrol about 6 blocks. In 1880 there were 4,320 arrests, the principal causes being intoxication and disturbance of the peace. The mayor may appoint as special policemen without pay any persons of suitable character. . . . The yearly cost of the force is about $30,000.

Community lawmen, regarded as a necessary evil, rarely enjoyed public favor. Doing a job few diligently sought, they seldom reflected the heroic romanticism portrayed so frequently in fiction. While the town marshals courted political support, their patrolmen maintained a watchful eye on local activities. Violence occurred, of course, but it usually came in sudden and unexpected form. The empty street, the deadly gunmen, and the structured duel have little foundation in fact. One study has revealed that in the period from 1870 to 1885 the supposedly roaring trail towns of Abilene, Caldwell, Dodge City, Ellsworth, and Wichita experienced a combined total of 45 homicides, only sixteen of which could be construed as the result of law enforcement. The effective presence of local peace officers could actually reduce violence, and many later very famous marshals never killed anyone in performance of duty.

Source: Frank Richard Prassel, *The Western Peace Officer: A Legacy of Law and Order* (Norman: University of Oklahoma Press, 1972), 44–47 (endnotes omitted). Copyright 1972 by the University of Oklahoma Press, Publishing Division of the University. Reprinted by permission of the University of Oklahoma Press.

NOTES

1. Perhaps this was a reference to reformers' challenges to municipal and police corruption in many jurisdictions.
2. As noted by Donald C. Dilworth, editor of *The Blue and the Brass* (Gaithersburg, Md.: IACP; 1976), Brooklyn did not become a borough of New York City until 1898. Until then, it was a separate city (28).
3. Originally founded as a club called the Society of St. Tammany in 1789, Tammany Hall eventually became the leading Democratic Party organization in New York. By the late nineteenth century, Tammany Hall had become infamous for its political corruption (Berman 1987:16; *Cambridge Encyclopedia* 1990:1184).
4. For several decades to come, the Lexow Committee investigation provided a model for exposing corruption in other urban police departments, including those of Atlanta, Baltimore, Chicago, Los Angeles, Kansas City, Philadelphia, and San Francisco (Fogelson 1977:6).

Part III

Police Reform and Social and Technological Advances in the Early Twentieth Century

PROGRESSIVE GOALS FOR POLICE REFORM ARE DEVELOPED IN A PERIOD OF INTENSE CHANGE

Part III traces the continued development of policing in the United States from 1900 to 1929—a period of intense philosophical, economic, demographic, and technological change. In the span of a single generation, a wave of progressive reforms established women's suffrage and saw the first women elected to high national and state offices. Other electoral reforms of that period that we take for granted today include secret ballots, direct election of U.S. senators and direct presidential primaries, and mechanisms for the recall of elected officials. The sorry lot of industrial workers also began to improve with the first labor protection laws for women and children and the establishment of the first old-age pensions. Work hours for men were reduced to eight hours a day—from twelve to fourteen hours a day, seven days a week (sometimes with a biweekly "stretch-out" where employees worked twenty-four hours straight) (Wade 1993:441–444).

After accomplishing much in the first two decades of the century,

progressive momentum dissipated. America's brief but horrible involvement in World War I also led to disillusionment and a rebounding
of the materialism and hedonism that progressives had struggled
against since the latter part of the eighteenth century. The questionable
outcome of the war also brought on a resurgence of isolationism, racism, and nativism. "Grandfather" laws in the South effectively dis-
enfranchised former slaves and recent immigrants. "Red scares" based
on fears about the growth of communism were used to justify attacks
on organized labor and ethnic minorities like the Irish, Italians, Rus-
sians, and Chinese—and were undoubtedly fueled by some countries'
official practice of sending many jail and asylum inmates to the United
States (Wade 1993:418–419). As the harbingers of depression began
to be felt and unemployment rose, lynchings, brandings, and whippings of blacks and other minorities became more common—often at
the hands of a Ku Klux Klan that was revitalized by economic hardship.

During the first three decades of the new century, the basic structural
changes that began with adoption of "modern" police models based
in part on the London Metropolitan Police crystallized and spread to
most urban police departments in the United States. There they began
to be refined under the influence of the broad-based social and governmental reforms of the progressive movement. By 1929, American
policing had identified its major goals and ideals. The targets toward
which departments across the nation would strive for the rest of the
century had been set—even though progress toward them often was
erratic due to the ebb and flow of broader social trends.

POLICE PROFESSIONALIZATION

The police professionalization movement was driven by two groups
of people: well-educated reformers who usually had no formal connection to any police organization, and reform-minded police chiefs.
As the proportion of the population living in cities continued to grow—
from 40 percent in 1900 to 56 percent in 1929 (U.S. Bureau of the
Census 1975:series A57-A72)—urban police chiefs increasingly came
to dominate the professionalization movement.

Civilian Police Reformers

Three men who never were police officers themselves had a lasting
effect on the development of American law enforcement organizations
in the early twentieth century. Leonhard Fuld (Document 25) and later
Raymond Fosdick (Document 35) compared the organization and administration of U.S. and European police departments. When their
respective results were published in 1909 and 1920, they helped

influence police reforms and research for decades. The trio of eastern civilian progressive police reformers was rounded out by Bruce Smith (Document 42), who conducted more than fifty surveys of U.S. police departments between 1923 and 1950 (Deakin 1988:141–142), authored influential books on the management and administration of state, municipal, and rural police agencies, and was influential in developing the FBI Uniform Crime Reports.

Police Reformers and Innovators

Influential early police executives like Richard Sylvester (Document 27) nurtured the idea of professionalism and advocated novel policing strategies at the beginning of the century. Later leaders like Arthur Woods (Document 32) helped develop a consensus about the need for more well-educated officers and stressed the importance of training for police officers, supervisors, and managers.

Reform wasn't limited to municipal police chiefs. Beginning with his appointment as director of the U.S. Department of Justice's Bureau of Investigation in 1924, J. Edgar Hoover set out to transform what would later become the Federal Bureau of Investigation into a model of professional law enforcement (Regoli and Hewitt 1996:242) and established himself as an advocate for higher educational, training, and professional standards. He also became instrumental in the development of much-needed national fingerprint files, a criminalistics laboratory, and the development of national reporting on crime (Document 43).

Standing head and shoulders above all other American police reformers and innovators of the era—perhaps of all time—was Chief August Vollmer of Berkeley, California. His emphasis on scientific policing, education, centralization of police services, and the highest standards of personal conduct continues to influence how we define the role of police and the standards of behavior to which we hold officers. He also was brought in to reorganize police departments in cities like Los Angeles, San Diego, Minneapolis, Detroit, Kansas City, Dallas, Portland, and Chicago. A leader in administrative and organizational reforms, Vollmer also pioneered the use of many new technologies.

Continuing Problems with Corruption

Despite the continuing efforts of police reformers, corruption remained a problem. In fact, one of the worst disasters for police reform was one of the progressive movement's own reforms—national prohibition of alcohol. With the passage of the Eighteenth Amendment in 1919 and the Volstead Act which implemented it in 1920, the very real social problems associated with alcohol use and abuse were magnified rather than diminished. Wealthy organized crime syndicates emerged, fueled by the enormous profits associated with producing, smuggling, and retailing alcohol. The extensive corruption of politicians, police, and other public officials that accompanied Prohibition seriously undermined public respect for the law and government in general. By the time Prohibition was repealed in 1933, more than 300,000 people had been convicted of violating federal prohibition laws (Wade 1993:444), which also would affect the development of constitutional law restraining police behavior.

Legal Constraints on Police Behavior

This era also marked the beginning of the Supreme Court's efforts to constrain the behavior of police officers by ruling that evidence obtained in violation of the Bill of Rights was inadmissible in court. Although initially they applied only to federal law enforcement officers, these rulings, including the Supreme Court's decision in *Weeks v. United States* (Document 31), laid the foundation for the extensive legal restrictions on police search and seizure that still are being refined today.

At the same time, *Carroll et al. v. United States* (Document 38) illustrates the difficulty of striking a balance between the Fourth Amendment's guarantee that "the right of the people to be secure in their persons, houses, papers, and effects, against unreasonable searches and seizures, shall not be violated" (Document 8) and the practical necessity for intrusive investigative techniques generated by social reforms like Prohibition. As is the case in contemporary drug law enforcement, the enforcement of Prohibition often required that officers intrude into people's personal lives without any complaint having been made. This was very different from the investigation of crimes like robbery, rape, and theft, which had complaining victims.

EVOLVING STRATEGIES AND TECHNOLOGY

Technological change also presented police with new opportunities and challenges as airplanes, radio and telephone communication, and new scientific techniques became more widely available. But perhaps no innovation affected the capabilities and responsibilities of the police as greatly as the rapid proliferation of the automobile.

As early as 1908, police departments in at least nine major cities were using automobiles to replace slower, less reliable, and more expensive horse-drawn wagons (Document 26). A decade later, nearly all medium-to-large departments were using them (Regoli and Hewitt 1996:226).

Another important innovation of the era was the widespread development of firearms training. Although American police were much more heavily armed than their English counterparts, there was almost no systematic firearms training for recruits, and continuing training to maintain officers' skills was even more rare. The National Rifle Association (NRA) stepped into this gap in 1920 (Document 37) and began adapting training programs based on traditional army cavalry pistol training for the police (see Morrison and Vila 1998).

Technological change also presented the police with some serious challenges. As officers moved from the intimacy of foot beats to the isolation of the radio car, casual day-to-day contact with the average citizen diminished substantially. Worse still, when officers did come in contact with the "noncriminal" general public, it now often was while issuing a traffic citation. With increased involvement by police in traffic enforcement, many people who previously regarded police officers as their protectors came to see them as adversaries.

The mixed blessing of widespread automobile ownership also translated into more accidents. Motor vehicle death rates rose over 250 percent from 1913 to 1929 (U.S. Bureau of the Census 1975:series Q209). Motor vehicle theft rates increased dramatically as well. And automobiles provided criminals with added mobility which made many types of crime more difficult to detect and solve.

GENDER, RACE, AND THE POLICE

Learning to Deal with Women

Widespread social changes during the early twentieth century pushed police to adopt new policies toward women. Such changes also brought about important developments in the role of police in society because the first female police officers' duties placed more emphasis on protecting minors and women, crime prevention, and community problem solving than on making arrests. At the start of the twentieth century women generally were limited to jobs as matrons in police departments (see Document 19) and there were no regularly appointed female police officers. By 1925, however, 145 U.S. police departments had hired policewomen. In addition to clerical duties, working with juvenile and female victims and prisoners, and handling missing person cases, the duties of these "municipal mothers" (Myers 1995) also included preventing lewd and immoral acts in public places, helping families in crisis, and sheltering youths from violent or morally offensive movies (Document 28). Although policewomen earned substantially less than their male counterparts (Bopp and Schultz 1972a:82), their duties often were more complex and their moral authority in the communities they served often was substantially stronger than that of the average cop on the beat.

Race Relations and the Difficult Role of Black Police Officers

From 1900 to 1929 many blacks were drawn to large urban areas from the rural South by industrial jobs that promised them a substantially improved quality of life. Moving north provided little respite from racial prejudice, although the prevalence of lynchings and overt systematic violence against African Americans probably was lower than in the South during the early twentieth century. Pervasive racial strain and violence culminated in more than twenty major race riots in 1919 (Deakin 1988:110), including the Chicago riot that summer (Document 36). Foreshadowing a pattern that remains common today, the six-day-long riot was fueled by strained relations between the black community and the police over discriminatory practices and was ignited by police officers exercising poor judgment.

Prior to World War II, African American police officers were very rare in urban areas. Often allowed to police only blacks, African American officers typically were discriminated against officially in terms of which sleeping, eating, and restroom facilities they could use. They also had very limited hiring or promotional opportunities and tended to suffer substantial day-to-day discrimination at the hands of their peers (Document 30).

DEFINING THE ROLE AND DUTIES OF POLICE

Aside from reform issues dealing with how police officers should perform their duties and what personal attributes they should exhibit, another key issue was *what* police officers should do. In contrast to widespread calls for honest, diligent, well-educated, and well-trained officers, there was far less consensus about whether the attention of those officers should be focused primarily on enforcing the law (i.e., "thief catching") or whether their role should be cast more broadly as "peace officers." At one extreme police were cast in the role of anti-crime warriors. Perhaps reflecting World War I militarism, this era appears to be the first in which the term "War on Crime" was used (see Documents 39 and 40). At the other extreme, police officers were seen as front-line social workers whose role was to maintain safe and orderly communities while helping individuals and families in crisis. As was discussed previously, the latter role was one in which early policewomen often were cast (Document 28) and one advocated by the International Association of Policewomen (Palmiotto 1997:231).

This debate had important practical consequences. Police forces were expensive: per capita expenditures for policing increased 140 percent from 1900 to 1929, and policing claimed a significant share of many municipal budgets (Document 41). Limiting the role of the police to law enforcement would focus the attention of this expensive public resource on problems that required the special expertise and legal authority of a police officer. Only police could effectively arrest criminals, break up fights, and quell riots. Moreover, restricting their role in this manner would tend to maintain broad support from law abiding citizens.

But expanding the role of police to many other activities also was attractive. For one thing, crimes are relatively rare events; police officers who did nothing but directly enforce the law would have less to do. Like all good bureaucratic entrepreneurs, many chiefs recognized that more duties meant more personnel, and that larger organizations wielded more power. Despite the complications and problems associated with taking on duties such as traffic enforcement (Document 29), dog catching, and social work, many reformers favored an expanded role for the police (e.g., Document 33). In addition to political and bureaucratic issues associated with defining the role of police more or less broadly, there also were problems with personnel—what one expected of an officer had a great deal to do with the kind of people required for the job.

THE REALITY OF WORKING-CLASS PATROLMEN

In contrast to the idealized images of patrol officers around which reform chiefs built their ideals was a reality that remains to this day: police work is a blue-collar occupation (Bayley 1994:66–75). The ideal of highly trained and well-rounded college men who approached their jobs with gentlemanly demeanor and knightly virtue was a far cry from the grossly underpaid, poorly trained, and undereducated men who policed the streets. Their social peers were laborers who built and maintained the cities and the cars that began to crowd their streets, not the lawyers, accountants, bankers, and merchants who sat in offices (Bopp and Schultz 1972a:73–76). It would take another forty years before college-educated police officers became common. And even then, officers who were college graduates tended to move quickly into supervisory or management positions rather than stay on the streets.

Disastrous early experiences associated with police unionization present perhaps the most vivid examples of disparities among lofty rhetorical ideals, the reality of police working conditions, and society's treatment of officers (Document 34). The efforts of officers in many cities to organize in order to improve work hours, pay, and working conditions that were declining rapidly relative to their unionized peers in industry came to a sudden halt after Boston fired all of the officers who went on strike—nearly 75 percent of the force—and easily replaced them with new workers.

DOCUMENT 25: *Police Administration* (Leonhard Felix Fuld, 1909)

One of the most important police reformers of the early twentieth century was a young man with no experience as a police officer or administrator. His name was Leonhard Felix Fuld. Fuld (1883–1965), the son of a New York City merchant, was an exceptional scholar who earned five degrees in just seven years—including two law degrees—at New York's Columbia University (W. Bailey 1989:246). During his last two years at Columbia (1908–1909), Fuld conducted extensive research on police departments in Europe and the United States for his doctoral dissertation, "Police Administration: A Critical Study of Police Organizations in the United States and Abroad." His dissertation was published as a book by G. P. Putnam's Sons in 1909, when Fuld was twenty-six years old.

The book, which Fuld himself believed was "the first attempt to present a logical exposition of the principles of police administration" (Fuld 1909: xviii), was extremely well received, despite the fact that Fuld had no previous experience with the police (W. Bailey 1989: 246). In his book, Fuld was one of the first police reformers—along with August Vollmer, then police chief for Berkeley, California (see Document 33)—to argue for higher education for police officers (W. Bailey 1989: 657; Chapman 1971: xii; Peak 1997: 24; also see document below).

Fuld also discussed the police function and duties, including the importance of police patrol as a preventive crime control measure; the appointment and examination of police officers; detective work; police discipline; the maintenance of police records; police control of prostitution, gambling, and alcohol; the importance and duties of police matrons (see Document 19); and many other relevant topics.

Despite the influence of his book, Fuld did not stay involved in police issues throughout his life. He helped plan the New York Police Academy shortly after his book was published, and then went on to earn millions in real estate and the stock market. Much later, in 1963, Fuld's attention returned to the police when he established an officer training fund for the New Jersey State Police Academy (Chapman 1971: ix; W. Bailey 1989:247).

* * *

In considering the qualifications required of candidates for appointment as police patrolmen, we noticed with what scrupulous care the examiners inquire into the candidate's physical efficiency, and we also learned that the inquiry into the candidate's intellectual fitness is generally confined to a short examination in the common branches. In the professional training received by the policemen during their probationary period, we noticed again that the training is principally in the duties of their position, and that the intellectual training is confined to instruction in the rules and regulations of the department by the obsolete method of catechetical instruction. It is certainly true that the police officer must possess physical powers rather than intellectual powers, that he must act rather than think, but a moment's reflection will convince anyone that he must think as well as act.

It is this element of individual discretion which distinguishes the police officer from the soldier. The soldier is merely a part of a great military machine; it is his duty to obey the orders of his superior without individual reflection. The policeman, on the other hand, does not always nor even generally act under the immediate supervision of his superior officer and, accordingly, he must himself determine by the exercise of a sound discretion whether he shall act or not, and if he decides to act, what he shall do and how he shall do it. To fit him for the performance of this important function the ideal police officer ought to receive a professional training similar in some respects to that now required of applicants for the position of probation officer,—a good secondary education followed by a special course of study in sociology and the special problems of police duty. It is probably impracticable to demand of policemen such an education at the present time as a condition precedent to appointment, but, bearing this ideal in mind, we can improve the present unsatisfactory intellectual ability of the police officer in two respects,—by supplying to the police officers during their probationary period suitable instruction by competent teachers in place of the old-fashioned catechetical instruction, and by offering inducements to men of good general education, high-school graduates and college-bred men, to enter the higher ranks of the uniformed force and make the police business their lifework.

Source: Leonhard Felix Fuld, *Police Administration* (New York: G. P. Putnam's Sons, 1909). [Montclair, N.J.: Patterson Smith, 1971, 152–153.]

DOCUMENT 26: "The Automobile as a Police Department Adjunct" (J. H. Haager, 1909)

The technological advances of the late nineteenth and early twentieth centuries, including telephone and radio (see Documents 21 and 40) and the automobile (see document below), had a profound impact on policing. Louisville, Kentucky, was among the first police departments to use the automobile in police work. Under the direction of Police Chief J. H. Haager, the department purchased three vehicles to replace its horse-drawn patrol wagons in October 1908 (Haager 1909: 66).

In a presentation made at the sixteenth annual meeting of the International Association of Chiefs of Police, Chief Haager, who also was a member of the IACP executive committee and of the board of governors of the National Bureau of Identification, discussed the advantages of the automobile compared to the horse-drawn wagon.

Haager explained that the automobile was more economical than the wagon, both in terms of shortened police response time and maintenance costs. He also noted such assets as the automobile's usefulness in manhunts and its endurance.

In concluding his speech, Haager predicted that the automobile soon would be in use in police departments nationwide. His prediction was accurate. At the time, automobile patrol wagons already were being used by several departments, including Atlantic City, Baltimore, Hartford, Los Angeles, Minneapolis, Omaha, Richmond, and Toronto (International Association of Chiefs of Police 1909: 71). By the late 1920s, nearly all medium-to-large police departments nationwide utilized the automobile for patrol service (Regoli and Hewitt 1996: 226). However, as Regoli and Hewitt (1996: 226) pointed out, while the patrol car revolutionized police work in many ways, it also had its disadvantages, such as alienating police officers from their public.

* * *

I am proud to say that the police department of Louisville is in such a line of progress that we feel ourselves beyond the utility of the horse, and can now boast of three power-driven vehicles. . . .

The prime advantage of the automobile over this horse-drawn vehicle is its economy. Consider the economy of time in a suburban run of twelve miles from the city as compared with the time consumed by a horse-drawn vehicle over the same distance, and you will find a difference of several hours. Can you tell me where time is more truly money than in this great department of public service? I think each of us can readily recall numerous instances where, if we had been just a few minutes earlier in getting to the scene of trouble, we might have saved later on endless hours of work in our efforts to locate and apprehend fugitives.

With the now common use of telephones, there are many instances where police stations are called up at all hours of the night by female members of households who may hear noises or see suspicious persons lurking about their places. Since almost every home is now provided with a telephone, the quick response of the automobile has resulted in much good and general satisfaction to our people. On several occasions we were able to reach residences and surround the house before the burglars came out with their loot, whereas, if response had been made to these calls in the old-fashioned way, I am quite sure the birds would have flown long before the wagon reached the scene.

The quick response of the automobile is a most welcome sight to a patrolman on many occasions when he has one or more unruly persons in custody. Frequently, during busy times, especially on Saturday night, when the horse-drawn vehicle was used, officers were compelled to stand with prisoners until the wagon had made runs in other parts of the district. This naturally causes a crowd to congregate, and with their customary jeers and taunts from the small boy and the friends of the prisoner, the officer's position, especially in negro districts, becomes a defenseless if not a dangerous one. During these periods of delay a peaceable thoroughfare can be transformed into a scene of rowdyism and disorder.

Our experience has been that we can make four long runs with the automobile in the time that it formerly took us to answer one long run with the horse-drawn vehicle. . . .

I recall several cases where we used the machine to great advantage. Only recently, we had a case where a party attempted to shuffle off this mortal coil via the poison route. Within ten minutes from the time we received the call, we had the patient landed in the portals of the city hospital, where, by prompt medical attendance his life was saved.

During the last street-car strike . . . , I was called over the telephone by a citizen who informed me that a large crowd of riotous strikers and sympathizers were passing through the alley in the rear of his home, armed with missiles, and from their actions he inferred that they intended to attack a street car, two blocks away. We instantly manned a machine with six officers and reached the point of attack, a mile from headquarters, in three minutes, just as the band of strikers were coming out of the alley, however, not before the approaching car, containing women and children, received a fusilade of pistol shots, boulders, etc. Our sudden and quiet descent upon the mob spread consternation into their ranks, and they were instantly dispersed, and we succeeded in arresting forty-five of the rioters within two hours.

On one occasion, while fighting a fire, one of our firemen was severely cut by falling glass, and was in great danger of bleeding to death. The medical authorities at the city hospital made the statement that had we been one or two minutes later in our arrival, the unfortunate man's life would have been despaired of.

From the standpoint of economy, the automobile has an advantage over the horse-drawn vehicle. Our patrol wagons, equipped with horses, harness, etc., cost us in the neighborhood of $1,800 each. Our automobiles cost us in the neighborhood of $1,900 each. The average life of the automobile, when properly cared for, is just as great as that of the ordinary patrol wagon, and the automobile has the advantage, as, when it has outlived its usefulness in the police department, it may be disposed of for a considerable sum, while the worn-out patrol wagon is of practically no value. . . .

When the first automobile was put into commission some of our citizens seemed to view it as a display of extravagance, but the splendid results we obtained in the new departure have completely convinced the most skeptical, and now we hear but words of praise for the automobile.

The machine has also been of incalculable service to the detective bureau in man hunts, and we have been able to run down many criminals owing to our ability to get over ground quickly. The detective bureau has also used the machine to great advantage in taking prisoners to various places for the purpose of identification.

The horse as a means of locomotion is restricted in strength, speed and endurance, but the automobile never tires, and in my opinion it will only be a short time when it will be universally adopted for patrol service in all of the police departments of the country.

Source: J. H. Haager, "The Automobile as a Police Department Adjunct," in *International Association of Chiefs of Police: Sixteenth Annual Session*, Buffalo, N.Y., June 15–18, 1909. [*Proceedings of the Annual Conventions of the International Association of Chiefs of Police: 1906–1912*, Vol. 2. New York: Arno Press and the New York Times, 1971, 66–71.]

DOCUMENT 27: "A History of the 'Sweat Box' and 'Third Degree' " (Richard Sylvester, 1910)

Another prominent police reformer of the early twentieth century was Richard Sylvester. Like several other well-known reform advocates of his era, such as William S. Seavey (Document 20), Theodore Roosevelt (Document 22), and Leonhard Felix Fuld (Document 25), Sylvester's background and interests were diverse. Sylvester had studied law, then worked as a journalist, a disbursement officer for the Ute Indian Commission, and chief clerk for the Washington, D.C., police department. He wrote a book on the history of the Washington, D.C., police in 1894, and was appointed superintendent of that police department in 1898, a position he held until 1915 (Deakin 1988:38–39; Palmiotto 1997:17).

Sylvester also served as president of the International Association of Chiefs of Police from 1901 until 1915. In this role, he became an early instigator of the notion of police professionalism. Under his leadership, the annual IACP conventions focused on a number of topical issues relevant to police work and crime prevention (Deakin 1988:39; Fogelson 1977:154; Palmiotto 1997:17).

One of Sylvester's best known IACP presentations during his tenure as president was "A History of the 'Sweat Box' and 'Third Degree' " (see document below). At Sylvester's urging, the IACP unanimously voted in favor of a resolution condemning any such maltreatment of prisoners in order to get them to confess to their crimes (Deakin 1988: 40, 85; Sylvester 1910: 58).

* * *

While there was a cessation of visitations of the criminal classes to our shores during the War of the Revolution, the War of the Rebellion, eighty years later, at a time when our population had grown to tremendous proportions, and our commercialism extended from ocean to ocean, the disruption demanded extraordinary military and civil police activity. The marauder, the bank robber and highwayman, thieves and criminals of every kind, took advantage of the exciting times to engage in their nefarious undertakings. At the close of the conflict, during the period of reconstruction, soldiers and the police were required to meet unusual conditions in the cities.

Many of those arrested, criminals and suspects, were subjected to many kinds of inquisition and torture prior to court trials, in order that convicting confessions, implicating themselves or others in the commission of violations, might be had. It was clearly following upon these exciting times that the practical "sweat box" was described.

As pictured, it was a cell adjoining which in close proximity was a high iron stove of drum formation. The subject indisposed to disclose information which might be securely locked within his bosom, without ceremony or formality, it is given, would be confined within the cell, a scorching fire would be encouraged in the monster stove adjoining, into which vegetable matter, old bones, pieces of rubber shoes and kindred trophies would be thrown, all to make a terrible heat, offensive as it was hot, to at last become so torturous and terrible as to cause the sickened and perspiring object of punishment to reveal the innermost secrets he possessed as the compensation for release from the "sweat box." This is the origin of the torrid appelation [sic] which has been so much discussed within the past few and preceding years.

The existence of any such character of contrivance in these enlightened days would be followed by raid and suppression. On the other hand, the criminal and those who would use the criminal vernacular, apply the effervescent term to the office, or room adjacent, at a Detective Head-quarters, where consultation may be had or questions be asked in secrecy of prisoners under investigation.

In this progressive age when the heads of police departments, mainly at individual expense, gather in convention annually and advocate the establishment of Houses of Detention; in other words, separate respect-able looking edifices for the placing therein of women and juvenile offenders rather than in station houses, when these men endorse the probation system, when they study the infirmities and defects of crimi-nals of record in order that the Courts may be enlightened in these re-spects before penalties are imposed, when these members argue for kind treatment of the child and the establishment of Juvenile Courts, when these Chiefs submit intelligent written discussions as to the humane treatment of prisoners, it should be argument sufficient to condemn any assertion that "little drops of water" or superheated moisture weep through the pores of a prisoner's skin through torture in a "sweat box"—in criminal parlance.

It is to be regretted that there are exceptions to such rules; but the members of the International Police Association, who number quite two hundred chiefs, have subscribed to the principles of humanity. There are officials who do not practice what they preach, some who are imposed upon by ignorant subordinates, but the well disposed superiors will far outclass the others of his calling.

We have heard of the other vulgarity, "Third Degree." . . .

In the pursuit of their investigations there is no law to prevent the officers of the law questioning any person who, in their opinion, may be able to give information which may enable them to discover the perpe-trator of a crime. It becomes the bounden duty of the police to locate the violator. There is no justification for personal violence, inhuman or unfair conduct, in order to extort confessions. The officer who understands his position will offer admissions obtained from prisoners in no other man-ner than that which is sanctioned by the law. If a confession, preceded by customary caution, obtains [sic] through remorse or a desire to make reparation for a crime, is advanced by a prisoner, it surely should not be regarded as unfair.

No well-informed and schooled police officer would undertake to make himself liable before the Court for disreputable practices. . . .

Some years ago a rough usage was resorted to in some cities, in order to secure confessions, but such procedure does not maintain at large nowadays. There are those who come in contact with the authorities who are always ready to condemn on slight provocation. Those who are waiting to even up for some fancied wrong, or for some contact with the police they may have had through their own wrong-doing, and who are ever ready to condemn the police.

On the other hand the principles of the police, as announced and discussed in their own circle, are to the end that the closest co-operation and friendly feeling should exist between them and the good citizen. If the latter would applaud the creditable deeds of the police and criticize their shortcomings, it would be just, and lead to a better condition for all concerned.

Source: Richard Sylvester, "A History of the 'Sweat Box' and 'Third Degree,' " in *International Association of Chiefs of Police: Seventeenth Annual Session*, Birmingham, Ala., May 10–13, 1910. [*Proceedings of the Annual Conventions of the International Association of Chiefs of Police: 1906–1912*, Vol. 2. New York: Arno Press and the New York Times, 1971, 55–57.]

DOCUMENT 28: Alice Stebbins Wells (1910)

Among the many police reforms that took place during the early twentieth century was the hiring of the first official female police officer, Alice Stebbins Wells, in 1910. Previously, most women's participation in law enforcement had been limited to serving as matrons in jails (see Document 19). One woman, Marie Owens, had been hired as a "patrolman" with the Chicago Police Department in 1893 after her police officer husband's death—a job she held for thirty years. Another woman, Lola Baldwin, had been hired by the Portland Police Department in 1905 to provide protection and assistance for young women and children at the Lewis and Clark Centennial Exposition (Bopp and Schultz 1972a:81; Palmiotto 1997:229; Regoli and Hewitt 1996:359; Reid 1990:233; Segrave 1995:11–12). However, Baldwin, who later received a permanent job with the Portland Police Department, was considered an "operative" rather than a police officer (Palmiotto 1997:229; Segrave 1995:12).

Wells, who reported for duty with the Los Angeles Police Department on September 13, 1910, had lobbied hard for the job. Her efforts included a petition urging the admission of women to the police force that was signed by one hundred notable Los Angeles residents and organizations (Bopp and Schultz 1972a:81; Peak 1997:94; Segrave 1995:13).

Wells, who was given a badge but no uniform or baton, was responsible for patrolling such places as "penny arcades, moving picture shows, skating rinks, dance halls, and other places of public amusement, including the parks on Sunday" (see Document 28B) to discover "places and people with immoral tendencies" (see Document 28A). She also gave aid to lost children, assisted juvenile and female crime victims and lawbreakers, and counseled families with problem children (Palmiotto 1997:232; also see Document 28B, below).

Following the example of the Los Angeles Police Department, the departments of several other cities soon hired policewomen of their own. By 1915, when the National Association of Policewomen was formed and Wells named its first president, police departments in twenty-five cities employed women police. By 1925, 145 police departments nationwide had hired female police officers (Bopp and Schultz 1972a:81; Palmiotto 1997:231; Regoli and Hewitt 1996: 359).

* * *

A. *LOS ANGELES TIMES* ARTICLE ANNOUNCING WELLS' APPOINTMENT

The first woman policeman, if such an anomaly is possible, in Los Angeles, will be Mrs. Alice Stebbins Wells, and she will report this morning to Chief Galloway for duty. The appointment was made by the Police Commission last night, after only two and one-half months' preparation, which is unusually rapid for a Los Angeles governmental department.

Mrs. Wells receives a probationary emergency appointment which will be subject later to civil service examination. The first suggestion of such a position from the Friday Morning Club and the W.C.T.U. to the Police Commission, were [sic] accompanied by her application and indorsements.

Mrs. Wells has had experience in settlement and semi-official police work in the East, and it is her purpose here to make inspections of the dance halls, rinks and other places where young people congregate, in an effort to perform preventive service against immorality. She is not to wear a uniform or carry a baton, but is to discover places and people with immoral tendencies, and bring to her aid the operation of agencies of reclamation.

Source: "First Woman 'Policeman,'" *Los Angeles Times*, September 13, 1910, Part II, 9.

B. *GOOD HOUSEKEEPING* MAGAZINE ARTICLE ABOUT WELLS

Alice Stebbins Wells has received her commission as a regular police officer of the city of Los Angeles, Cal., and has been presented by the chief of police with a policeman's star. This in accord with a new ordinance permitting the appointment of women as police officers. In handing her the badge, the chief said he was sorry to offer a woman so plain an insignia of office; that when he had a squad of Amazons he would ask the police commission to design a star edged with lace ruffles.

A star with lace ruffles is exactly what Mrs. Wells does not want. She wears no uniform, carries no weapon, and as often as possible keeps her star in her handbag. Measuring not much over five feet, she has no idea of using physical force in the discharge of her duties, which are no less varied than those of her brother officers, and often identical with them. She goes about her work quietly and unostentatiously, with the hope of applying preventive rather than punitive measures, and eagerly taking advantage of the opportunity offered by her position for the study of crime, and particularly that phase of crime commonly known as the social evil. . . .

Mrs. Wells was for some years a religious student and worker in the East. Later in California she became interested in the scientific study of crime. Each experience illuminated the other, and she came to feel that the proper handling of crime should be regarded as one of the greatest fields of applied Christianity. In order to get at the very root of the question, she decided to become a policewoman. As she puts it:

"The police department represents the strategic point at which virtue can meet vice, strength can meet weakness, and guide them into preventive and redemptive channels."

Continuing to discuss her motives in adopting this as her life work, Mrs. Wells says:

"The thinking world is more and more recognizing the causes of crime as a vital part of the problem of crime. Since many of these causes arise from improper home conditions, their correction necessarily depends in a large measure upon the intelligent co-operation of women. As all the world knows, the perfect home training of every child would largely eliminate the need of police work. But we must take the situation as we find it, many degrees below the ideal.

"Multitudes of young girls are walking up and down the streets of every city whose minds are so void of any real purpose in life that their controlling motive, apparently, is to dress and attract attention.

"In many instances their mothers are respectable, hard-working women who need the help of these idle, incapable, pleasure-seeking daughters. But, untrained themselves, they did not know how to implant early a loving co-operation and interest in the family duties, which constitute one of the very best safeguards any girl can have.

"Again, in many homes, deferential treatment toward all womankind is not insisted upon. A girl accustomed to easy familiarity within the home is not quickly affronted by undue freedom from the chance acquaintance.

"Then there is the exceedingly difficult task of finding the happy medium between unquestioning servile obedience and the over-ruling of a child's growing personality and will. As all who deal with the erring know, a multitude of young people know no law but that of their own imperious wills. These things, together with wrong ideals, bad blood, poorly nourished bodies, and industrial strife, produce a large part of the tide endlessly sweeping into the precincts of the police.

"Under modern conditions, much of the remedy must be applied directly or indirectly by women. Insistence upon a single standard of morality, the elevation of domestic service to a plane equal to other respected occupations, wider teaching of industrial arts and science, and other plain, vital truths in our public schools, will do much toward stemming the tide.

"One or more women in the police department of every city can learn much concerning the need of changes in worn-out and ineffective laws, and the practical handling of wrongdoers, which other women can embody in their manifold labors for the city's good. This is more important than may be obvious. The police department is the organized, empowered body, and all other upbuilding social agencies should work in harmony with it. For lack of this, much well-intended, laborious effort goes wide of the mark.

"There is no doubt in my mind that with time the appointment of women police officers will work out much good along these fundamental lines, but in the meantime the innovation is proving its own justification day by day in the greater freedom and confidence with which girls and women appeal to the department for advice and protection, in the handling of special cases where a woman's sympathy may be more effective than a man's power, and in the care given to young girls or women brought to the police station for the first time, and who might otherwise come under the degrading influence of confinement with old offenders." . . .

Although Mrs. Wells has been in office but a few months, the demands on her time are so numerous that already she feels the need of an assistant, and there could be no better justification of her appointment. Yet always she insists:

"All one woman can do is but little—to find the needs and point the way. Where she leaves off many women may begin and do much toward the betterment of social conditions."

Source: Bertha H. Smith, "The Policewoman," *Good Housekeeping* 52 (February 1911): 296–298.

DOCUMENT 29: "Police Regulation of Motor Vehicles" (C. E. Sebastian, 1911)

During the early 1900s, the police were not the only ones making use of the automobile (see Document 26). The American public also was becoming increasingly mobile, as is evident by the increase in car registrations between 1900 and 1930—from 8,000 to almost 27 million (U.S. Bureau of the Census 1975:series Q148, 150, 152).

This increase in vehicular traffic created new challenges for police departments, whose duties typically had included traffic control since the days of horse-drawn vehicles. In Los Angeles, where temperate weather and tourism contributed to what was then considered heavy motor traffic, it soon became apparent to the police chief, Charles E. Sebastian, that better and more uniform traffic regulations were needed.

Sebastian, who had joined the Los Angeles Police Department in 1900 and became its chief in January 1911 (G. Woods 1993:37), advocated uniform speed laws, rules of the road, and automobile registration practices. He also stressed that drunken driving should be prohibited, and that intoxicated drivers who hit pedestrians or other vehicles should be charged with a felony. Moreover, he argued that all drivers should be required to pass a driver's test before being allowed to operate a vehicle (at the time, California had no such requirement).

However, not all police reformers of the early 1900s believed, as Sebastian apparently did, that it was the duty and responsibility of the police to either help establish or enforce uniform traffic laws. A few, including August Vollmer (see Document 33), thought that traffic regulation should be the responsibility of some other municipal department, leaving the police to devote their time and resources to preventing and detecting crime (Fogelson 1977:60).

Another concern was that traffic enforcement by the police might harm relations between them and the general public, as more and more typically law-abiding citizens began to be cited for traffic and parking violations (Peak 1997:179).

* * *

I do not believe there is a more serious, beneficial-to-all problem before the police officials today than that of providing for nation-wide laws aimed to control and regulate the automobile traffic. No person can safely get away with the statement that the horse-drawn vehicle is not a thing of the past. It has not quite passed to the status of the relegated spinning-wheel and the old-fashioned well-sweep, but it is rapidly traveling in the direction taken by those and other antiquated articles of domesticity.

Those who have had police and hospital experience with automobile ambulance and patrol wagon service dare not dispute the statement that these power-propelled vehicles have by their speed and promptness in answering "Hurry" calls greatly reduced the mortality reports. That is one of the arguments advanced for their permanency, stability and advance over the old-fashioned methods of removing the ill and injured in horse-drawn wagons or ambulances.

Those of you who have traveled up and down or across the land are more or less informed in the fact that the laws and ordinances regulating the rate of speed to be traveled by motor-propelled vehicles—the automobile and motorcycle—and the drivers and riders thereof, vary to a confusing degree. . . .

The problem I want to present to you, gentlemen, is the strong and ever present necessity of agitating in your own states and cities the demand of the motorists and police for uniform laws. . . .

In thirty-eight states in which I have cognizance of the rate of speed at which an automobile may travel, the maximum ranges from eight to thirty miles an hour. This includes speed rates of eight, ten, twelve, fifteen, eighteen, twenty, twenty-four, twenty-five and thirty miles an hour. Sixteen states have a maximum speed law of twenty-five miles; three place the maximum at thirty miles; two at twenty-four miles; fifteen at twenty miles; one at eighteen and one at fifteen. In the majority of the larger cities the maximum speed limit is fifteen miles or under; in only two states is a speed rate of twenty miles permitted in the cities. . . .

The question of regulating traffic is being considered in many states and cities and also in states and municipalities that possess traffic laws which require revision up or down as the problem may demand. . . .

As to the general provisions of the State laws, I believe they should be uniform concerning regulations of movements of vehicles along highways and city streets. After a careful study of the laws of several states, I believe the maximum speed in congested districts where traffic is heavy, as within the shopping district, should be TWELVE MILES PER HOUR and have this district determined and described by the city lawmaking body. Outside of this district and inside the city limits, a maximum speed of TWENTY MILES PER HOUR would not be objectionable. Outside incorporated cities and towns, a maximum of TWENTY-FIVE MILES PER HOUR would not operate as a hardship on any rational motorist. Speed on crossings within the congested district should not be more than EIGHT MILES PER HOUR and outside the congested district no more than FIFTEEN MILES at any railroad crossing or where the view of the driver is obscured from cross streets or roads. Where local authorities designate a restricted district, they should be required to place signs in all principal streets leading into said district for the purpose of notifying the drivers to slow down to the legal speed limit of TWELVE MILES.

Source: C. E. Sebastian, "Police Regulation of Motor Vehicles," in *International Association of Chiefs of Police: Proceedings of the 19th Annual Convention*, Toronto, Canada, June 9–12, 1912. [*Proceedings of the Annual Conventions of the International Association of Chiefs of Police: 1906–1912*, Vol. 2. New York: Arno Press and the New York Times, 1971, 117–124.]

DOCUMENT 30: "Troubles of a Black Policeman" (1912)

Women weren't the only ones who had a slow and difficult entry into the field of law enforcement (see Documents 19 and 28). Prior to World War II, police departments were composed primarily of white males—for example, by 1900, only about 3 percent of all urban police officers were African American (Peak 1997:100; Regoli and Hewitt 1996:362–363).

The few minority officers who were hired typically were discriminated against in a number of ways. According to James S. Griffin, "race riots followed the efforts of African American officers to 'police' members of the white community, and such officers were relegated to African American communities and often not allowed to wear uniforms for fear of offending members of the white community" (quoted in Peak 1997:101).

By 1912, some things had changed. Samuel J. Battle, the only black police officer in New York City at the time, was not limited to patrolling African American communities, nor did he appear to be prohibited from wearing a uniform or arresting whites. However, blatant discrimination persisted. For example, despite the fact that they all spoke highly of him as a person and of his performance as a police officer, none of the white officers would speak to Battle at the station house (see document below).

* * *

Judging by the experiences of Samuel J. Battle, the only negro policeman in the State of New York, we must take note with *The Sun* that the lot of even the best of his race is a hard one. For Battle, *The Sun* reports, is probably one of the most conscientious, right-minded black men in the United States. He is painstaking in his duties, he is willing—even eager—to take upon himself the work of others, and in all ways, we are told, is the right kind of a man for New York's renovated police department. But Battle has his troubles. For altho—any man of the precinct will tell you "Battle's a thorough gentleman," yet in the station-house nobody talks to him, and on patrol the few who venture to say, "Hello, Battle," speak from a corner of the mouth, and are sure no other policeman is in sight. For the "silence" that began when Battle entered the precinct last June is as deep as ever to-day, not because Battle is a negro—altho that was the reason at first—but because every white policeman is afraid of what would be said to and about him if he made any attempt to bring the "silence" to an end. Six months ago the men thought that Battle could be hazed into resigning, or at least into asking for a transfer. Now they know he isn't that sort and he has made himself so respected that most of them would be sorry to see him depart, but he remains in Coventry because none of his white mates has the courage to suggest to the others that he has earned release.

Battle's own story, as told to a *Sun* reporter, is interesting. Says he:

I was born in Newbern, S.C., twenty-nine years ago, and had a grammar-school education. When I came North I went to West Glastonbury, Conn., and found myself the only colored man in town. A boarding-house took me in without question, and I went to the boss of a cotton-mill for a job. He said: "I don't know about this, Battle. We need men, but we've never employed a negro." "Well," I said to the boss, "if you've never had a colored man you don't know whether there'll be any trouble or not. Take me on and see." He did, and there wasn't a speck of trouble.

Eight years ago I became one of those red-capped porters at the Grand Central Station. I stayed there until last June, and never had a complaint against me. I got to be assistant-chief of the porters, married, and was content, until one day it struck me that assistant-chief was all I could ever hope to be and there wouldn't be any pension when I got to be an old man. So I said to myself, "I'm going to be a policeman." I took the examination and stood 199th among 638 men. When my name got to the top of the eligible list I was passed over twice because the surgeon said I had a "murmuring heart," altho I am positive my heart never murmured in its whole life. Then Mr. Waldo became commissioner, the civil-service law was enforced, and here I am.

Battle informed the reporter that he hadn't a single complaint to make of his treatment by the other policemen. "And as for the captains and lieutenants"—they had simply gone out of their way to be kind to him. But the "silence" still exists. Said a member of the force recently:

I haven't heard of anybody having a word with him except on police business since he got on probation, and that's more than six months. I never talk to him myself except when we meet at the end of our beats with no other police ears in the vicinity. I ain't got the nerve.

But if you won't repeat it at the house I'll tell you that we regard Battle as a gentleman. He has never said anything uncivil, and he does more than his share of the work. For instance, one day there was a mess of a grocery-cart and an automobile on Central Park West. There were three prisoners, and all I could tend to under the circumstances was two. Along comes Battle on his way to the house. Says he: "Want me to take one of them in?" Breakin' my rule about not speakin' to him, I says: "I certainly would be obliged." So he takes the prisoner to the house as cheerful as you please; and if you know how the ordinary policeman hates to do anybody else's work you know what that means.

But as for sayin' "howdydo" to Battle in the station-house—not me.

If any New-Yorker cares to make an examination for himself, Battle, we are informed, is stationed in the Park district, and patrols Central Park West from the Circle to Sixty-seventh Street. He says, however, that he is willing to go to the negro quarter, if asked to, or anywhere else. His one complaint is that under the regulations he cannot be examined for promotion until five years are up—and by that time, says *The Sun*, "Oh, well, some of the men may speak to him, and then perhaps their conversation will prove to be neither as agreeable, nor as interesting, as their silence."

Source: "Troubles of a Black Policeman," *Literary Digest* 44, no. 4 (January 27, 1912): 177–179.

DOCUMENT 31: *Weeks v. United States* (1914)

In 1914, the United States Supreme Court issued a ruling that would have a profound impact on the admissibility in federal trials of evidence seized by police. The case was *Weeks v. United States*. The petitioner in the case, Freemont Weeks, had been convicted of illegal use of the mails. His conviction was based in large part on papers taken from his home following his arrest by police officers who had no search warrant. The police officers handed these papers over to the U.S. marshal, who subsequently searched Weeks' house himself and found and took more evidence, again without a warrant.

Although Weeks and his attorney petitioned the court before the trial for the return of the illegally seized documents, their request was denied. The papers were used against Weeks in court, despite his attorney's objections, and Weeks was convicted.

The Supreme Court overturned Weeks' conviction, explaining:

If letters and private documents can thus be seized and held and used in evidence against a citizen accused of an offense, the protection of the Fourth Amendment declaring his right to be secure against such searches and seizures is of no value, and, so far as those thus placed are concerned, might as well be stricken from the Constitution. (232 U.S. 383:393)

The Court's ruling established what is known as the "exclusionary rule" disallowing the use of illegally obtained evidence in a criminal trial. However, the new rule applied only to federal trials—the High Court had yet to establish such guidelines with regard to state trials.

* * *

MR. JUSTICE DAY delivered the opinion of the court....

The case in the aspect in which we are dealing with it involves the right of the court in a criminal prosecution to retain for the purposes of evidence the letters and correspondence of the accused, seized in his house in his absence and without his authority, by a United States Marshal holding no warrant for his arrest and none for the search of his premises. The accused, without awaiting his trial, made timely application to the court for an order for the return of these letters, as well as other property. This application was denied, the letters retained and put in evidence, after a further application at the beginning of the trial, both applications asserting the rights of the accused under the Fourth and Fifth Amendments to the Constitution. If letters and private documents can thus be seized and held and used in evidence against a citizen accused of an offense, the protection of the Fourth Amendment declaring his right to be secure against such searches and seizures is of no value, and, so far as those thus placed are concerned, might as well be stricken from the Constitution. The efforts of the courts and their officials to bring the guilty to punishment, praiseworthy as they are, are not to be aided by the sacrifice of those great principles established by years of endeavor and suffering which have resulted in their embodiment in the fundamental law of the land. The United States Marshal could only have invaded the house of the accused when armed with a warrant issued as required by the Constitution, upon sworn information and describing with reasonable particularity the thing for which the search was to be made. Instead, he acted without sanction of law, doubtless prompted by the desire to bring further proof to the aid of the Government, and under color of his office undertook to make a seizure of private papers in direct violation of the constitutional prohibition against such action. Under such circumstances, without sworn information and particular description, not even an order of court would have justified such procedure, much less was it within the authority of the United States Marshal to thus invade the house and privacy of the accused. In *Adams* v. *New York*, 192 U.S. 585, this court said that the Fourth Amendment was intended to secure the citizen in person and property against unlawful invasion of the sanctity of his home by officers of the law acting under legislative or judicial sanction. This protection is equally extended to the action of the Government and officers of the law acting under it. . . . To sanction such proceedings would be to affirm by judicial decision a manifest neglect if not an open defiance of the prohibitions of the Constitution, intended for the protection of the people against such unauthorized action.

Source: 232 U.S. 383 (1914), 386–394.

DOCUMENT 32: *Policeman and Public* (Arthur Woods, 1919)

In addition to a growing awareness of the benefits associated with higher education for police officers (see Document 25, for example), police reformers of the early twentieth century also stressed the need for better basic training, not only for patrolmen but for their commanding officers as well. For example, in his book *Policeman and Public*, Arthur Woods (1870–1942), who served as police commissioner for New York City from 1914 to 1918, stated that "a properly equipped and administered school is perhaps the most indispensable single feature of the police force of a large city" (A. Woods 1919:156).

Woods believed that specialized training was just as important for police sergeants, lieutenants, and other higher ranking officers as for new recruits and regular patrol officers, yet at the time, he said, there were no training programs designed to help prepare a patrolman for new leadership duties associated with promotion to a higher rank (A. Woods 1919:148–149).

Moreover, Woods emphasized the need for better firearms training for all police officers, noting that in some instances "officers are taken on the force and turned out on the street to go about their duty armed with loaded revolvers, and yet with no training in the care or use of the weapon" (A. Woods 1919: 159).

These and other concerns raised by Woods would remain the subject of continued debate throughout the twentieth century (e.g., Documents 37, 42, 44, 48, 74).

* * *

In American cities there is no special course of training for officers of higher grades. They have all been patrolmen, have all risen from the ranks, and they are given no special preparation for the duty of the higher rank. All they know of it is what they have observed from below. . . .

To higher officers on police forces this is a handicap which is little understood. When we think of the methods taken by armies to train officers, with the four-year course at West Point, and now in war time with Officers' Training Camps, we cannot help wondering why it is that people are content to trust their safety to the care of police commanding officers who have had no training other than that given to patrolmen. . . .

What can be done in American police forces to improve the quality of leadership among the higher officers? . . . [A] good deal can be accomplished by training; and fairness to the officers, as well as the interest of the city, demands that policemen promoted to higher duty be given instruction to fit them to meet the added responsibility.

This can be done by police Training Schools, and a properly equipped and administered school is perhaps the most indispensable single feature of the police force of a large city.

Such a school has two main functions: to train raw recruits so as to fit them for service as patrolmen, and to train officers.

Recruits cannot be turned out trained as they should be, mentally and physically, in less than three months, and at least twice as much time as this could well be devoted to them. For they must be taught the laws, and the ways to enforce them. They must also be given a most rigorous course of physical training, and be taught how to fight, to defend themselves, to handle prisoners who resist so as to subdue them without battering them with clubs. . . .

Besides mental and physical training, recruits must develop morale, and learn their obligations, their powers, and the limitations of their powers. For a well-taught and well-trained policeman may be only a menace on the street if he has not also learned self-restraint and *noblesse oblige*. . . .

No policeman should be promoted without being given such instruction and training as is necessary to fit him to do the work of his new higher rank. Regular courses can be given in the training school to prepare candidates for promotion to each of the successive higher grades, and no one should be permitted to enter a new grade until he has qualified in the school and shown that he can reasonably be expected to perform his duties capably.

This is one part of the assistance a police training school can give to higher officers. The other is to provide continual freshening-up courses, so that every sergeant, lieutenant, etc., can put in a fortnight a year in further training to keep him up to date and prevent him from falling into perfunctory ruts.

One of the most important things these officers should be taught is a rudimentary proficiency in military drill, so that when they are called on to handle groups of men they shall be able to do so with confidence, and with a fair chance of being able to get the group where they want it to be, and in the formation that will best meet the needs of the situation. . . .

It is vital to successful work, and an obligation to the men, that they be given the most careful kind of training in self-defense. Policemen must be armed, trained, and kept in training. It will be found in some places that officers are taken on the force and turned out on the street to go about their duty armed with loaded revolvers, and yet with no training in the care or use of the weapon. This was the situation in New York only a few years ago. The result of it was that if an officer took a shot at anyone on the street, about the only safe individual within the range of his gun was the criminal he was shooting at. The policeman is entitled to a thorough course of training in revolver shooting, starting with methods of sighting the revolver, and of squeezing the trigger, and not ending until he is proficient at snap-shooting without sighting. It is only fair also that before being sent out on the street to perform duty, he should be put into first-class physical condition, should be taught to box and to wrestle, should have mastered a few simple jiu jitsu tricks which will enable him to handle a fighting prisoner without clubbing or mauling him. And then the policeman should be encouraged to keep himself fit. The courage of the men will be made more sturdy and instinctive if they have confidence in their own powers, in their marksmanship, their ability to use their hands and bodies, and if they keep themselves in sound physical condition, hard and supple.

It is really a grave question whether policemen should be allowed to carry revolvers at all unless they qualify periodically, showing that they still know how to handle the weapon and can shoot straight enough not to be a menace in the street. It is a fairly dangerous thing to arm an officer with as destructive a weapon as a six-shooter and give him a certain amount of authority to use it, when he is completely incompetent to use it properly, and cannot even hit near the bull's-eye of a stationary target in a quiet pistol range, to say nothing of a moving, escaping felon in a crowded, excited street. It is a question further as to whether a police administration is not responsible, at least morally, for any harm that may be done with a revolver by an officer who has not been properly trained to handle and fire it. Unless he is trained and has passed satisfactory tests the administration knows, and should probably be held responsible for acting on the knowledge, that he is an unsafe man to be allowed to use a revolver.

It is certainly unwise to give police power to anyone who has not been thoroughly trained and tested, and found to be qualified to exercise it wisely, with restraint, yet strongly when the occasion calls for force. It is unfair to the public as well as to the individual officer. For the public can hardly help suffering repeatedly at the hands of ignorant officers who do not know clearly what their duties are and what are the limitations of their duties, who have not been made to realize their responsibility, and been taught how to act so as to measure up to the important demands made upon them. The policeman is entitled to thorough, able training which does not stop the moment he goes on the street but continues during his police life. If he acts harshly or cruelly or ignorantly, it is no one's fault except that of the public and the police administration, unless everything that could reasonably be done to fit him to perform his job well was done for him before the shield was pinned on his breast and he was called to his post for duty.

Source: Arthur Woods, *Policeman and Public* (New Haven, Conn.: Yale University Press, 1919). [New York: Arno Press and the New York Times, 1971, 148–161.]

DOCUMENT 33: "The Policeman as a Social Worker" (August Vollmer, 1919)

The best known and most respected police reformer of the early twentieth century—perhaps of all time—was August Vollmer (1876–1955). Vollmer, who repeatedly has been called the "father of modern professional policing in the United States" (MacNamara 1989:657; Stead 1977:178), was born in New Orleans, the son of German immigrants. His father, a grocer, died when he was eight, and his mother took young Vollmer and his sisters back to Germany. The family returned to New Orleans a few years later, then moved to the San Francisco Bay area in 1888 and to Berkeley, California, in 1891. In Berkeley, young Vollmer ran a coal and feed store with a friend before serving as an Army Artillery man in the Philippines during the Spanish-American War. He returned to Berkeley as a decorated war hero in 1899, worked as a mailman there for five years, and then was elected town marshal in 1905 (Deakin 1988:90; MacNamara 1989:657; Peak 1997:23; Stead 1977:180–181).

The 29-year-old Vollmer soon earned a reputation as a police innovator and reformer. He immediately began asking the Berkeley Board of Trustees for more personnel and equipment, and although he met with some opposition at first, most of his requests gradually were granted (A. Parker 1972:8–9). For example, by 1907 Vollmer had expanded the Berkeley department from four deputies to twenty-six deputies and one special officer, and still was asking the board for more deputies (Deakin 1988:90; A. Parker 1972:12; Peak 1997:24). In 1906, he established one of the first modern police signal systems and a centralized police records system, among other innovations (Deakin 1988: 91; Stead 1977:181).

One of the first reformers to advocate higher education for police officers (also see Document 25), Vollmer also initiated a formal training school for his deputies—the first to educate officers in scientific methods of crime detection—in 1908 (Deakin 1988:95; MacNamara 1989: 657; Peak 1997:24).[1]

After Berkeley underwent municipal restructuring in 1909, Vollmer's title changed from town marshal to chief of police—a position he held until his retirement in 1932. During that time, he was responsible for numerous additional innovations, including putting his entire police force on bicycles by 1911, establishing motorcycle patrols beginning in 1912 and automobile patrols beginning in 1913, and utilizing the first police radio car in 1921 (Deakin 1988:91; A. Parker 1972:24; Peak 1997:25). He also was the first to put the lie detector to use in a police laboratory (1921), established innovative classification systems for fingerprints and handwriting samples (1922), reorganized numerous police departments across the country, served as president of the International Association of Chiefs of Police (1922), and supervised the preparation of the *Report on Police* for the Wickersham Commission— the first national study of law enforcement in the United States—in 1931 (see Document 44) (Deakin 1988:89; MacNamara 1989:657; Stead 1977:182–183).

Although he held no college degree, Vollmer became the first professor of police administration in the United States, first teaching at the University of Chicago, where he helped establish a course of study in criminology, and then at the University of California, Berkeley, where he taught from 1931 until 1937 (Deakin 1988:96; Peak 1997:27). He also was the author or co-author of a number of books, including *Crime and the State Police* (with A. E. Parker, 1935), *The Police and Modern Society* (1936), *Crime, Crooks and Cops* (with A. E. Parker, 1937), and *The Criminal* (1949).

Apparently driven to suicide by declining health and failing eyesight, Vollmer ended his life with a bullet to the right temple on November 4, 1955, at the age of 79 (MacNamara 1989:657; Stead 1977:178).

Although Vollmer's advocacy and implementation of police education generally are considered to be the most valuable and noteworthy of his many contributions to police reform, he also is known for his lifelong emphasis on professional integrity, and for his innovative views on the police officer's role in crime prevention (Deakin 1988:94–95; Stead 1977:179–180, 188). With regard to the latter, in particular, Vollmer was well ahead of his time, and, indeed, might still be considered an innovator in ours (see document below).

* * *

Crime prevention, that all-important police function, is compelling the attention of some of the world's greatest thinkers, and though the appreciation of criminology as a science is still in its infancy, and the surface has been merely scratched, sufficient light has been thrown on the subject to prove that old methods of dealing with crime must be changed, and newer ones adopted. The time to begin is past but the time to keep going what has been started is now.

Ordinarily, the policeman feels that his duty is well done when the offender is promptly apprehended and placed behind the bars. His failure to note that the prisoner may be the sole support of a large family, who, left to shift for themselves, must steal or starve, is only one of numerous mistakes that our peace guardians are making, in their efforts to serve the public faithfully.

Big, healthy, honest, and kind, ready to die without hesitancy when duty calls them, their usefulness is impaired by reason of their ignorance of the many causes of delinquency. Even though the experienced policeman knows that poverty, unemployment, defective home conditions, bad companions, sickness, alcohol, gambling and prostitution are crime factors, he does not feel that it is any part of his duty to assist in the correction or elimination of these great contributors to criminality.

Co-operation with social service agencies is out of the question; they can do nothing to help him, nor has he the time nor the inclination to assist them. Policemen do aid the injured, give the needy lodger a cot to sleep on, search for missing persons, and render other services not necessarily police duties, but here ends their activities as humanitarians.

However, the pendulum is beginning to swing the other way, and the policeman is beginning to realize his power as a social worker, and the future is frought [sic] with wonderful possibilities, if all will realize their potential worth.

The policeman is learning that dependency, criminality, and industrial unrest have a common origin, and that upon him rest far more important and far greater obligations than the mere apprehending and prosecuting of lawbreakers. He is fast learning that dealing with criminals after the evil habits have been formed is a hopeless task as far as the eradication, or even lessening of crime is concerned.

If he would serve his community by reducing crime he must go up the stream a little further and dam it up at its source, and not wait until it is a rushing torrent, uncontrollable and resistless. Moreover, if he would succeed in his efforts he must utilize to the fullest extent every helpful agency in the community, such as schools, churches, recreation and juvenile departments, public welfare and employment bureaus, clinics, dispensaries, hospitals and fraternal and labor organizations. Cooperation is also necessary with character forming organizations, such as Boy Scouts, Campfire Girls, well organized boys' clubs, community social centers and auxiliary and junior police forces. . . .

You will ask what can the policeman do, and how shall he proceed to get the best results. My answer is,—fight for everything which helps to decrease crime and dependency, and in this connection a few suggestions are offered for social service work in the community and state. And let me add that these are merely a few suggestions. There are many, many possibilities.

In many cities the schools are unable to accommodate all of the school children. This results in many of them being on the streets, with the attendant evils. The policeman can do his share to correct this condition by stating the facts to the voters whenever an opportunity is afforded.

It is also true that no city in this country gives sufficient thought to the physical welfare of the children. Supervised recreation grounds are few in number, and we know from experience that much of our juvenile problem may be traced to misdirected energy. Here again, the policeman in his rounds, and in contact with people generally, can be useful by calling attention to the community's need for sufficient play ground space for children to give expression to their play tendencies. . . .

Public welfare bureaus, like the clinics and dispensaries, actually have to fight for existence in this civilized country. Their efforts are often viewed with suspicion, due to the lack of knowledge of social service work. Often the public does not understand that the rehabilitation of the family by scientific social service is more beneficial than sporadic donations of money, food, fuel, clothing and shelter. The public welfare bureau performs excellent crime preventive work, and should have the support of every police official. Where is there a police department that has not dealt with the man or woman who in desperation has stolen to keep the family from starving, and further, that has not dealt with the product of the other family which starved rather than steal?

Considering at this time only the unemployed, and not the unemployable (the latter being institutional problems), the police should not only advocate the establishment of municipal, state and federal employment bureaus, but in addition thereto, should cooperate with such bureaus to the fullest extent in finding positions for the deserving and capable. Friendly relations must be established with labor unions as their assistance is occasionally required in these cases.

Furthering the cause of laws to provide funds for orphans, industrial compensation for the injured, prevention of child labor, eight hour labor laws, probation laws, prohibition, veneral [sic] disease control and other legislative acts having for their purpose the prevention of feeblemind-edness, insanity, criminality, prostitution, dependency, and the protec-tion of the family, is the bounden duty of every member of the police force. . . .

We have discussed briefly what can be done by the policeman in the city and state. Let us next consider the neighborhood, or in language more familiar to the police, the beat. No single individual in the com-munity has more opportunities to do good, solid, constructive social service than the intelligent, sympathetic and trained policeman. His in-timate knowledge of the character of the people residing on his beat makes it possible for him to acquaint immigrants living therein with the laws of this country, protect them from petty political and business graft-ers, as well as from other unscrupulous persons, and help them to be-come decent, law-abiding citizens.

By close co-operation with schools and public welfare agencies, he will soon learn who the potential delinquents and dependents are, and can do much to assist in preventing them from becoming social failures. Boy gangs may be transformed into juvenile police and taught to be friendly helpers, or they may be helped to join boy scouts or similar boys' or-ganizations, and through these agencies become helpful members of the community.

Wayward girls may be saved from taking the final plunge into a life of evil, and many homes saved from disgrace and sadness, by the kindly counsel of the policeman. Sick and poor may be directed to the estab-lished places for their relief. These cases should be carefully followed up and nothing left undone which would be of assistance in their rehabili-tation. . . .

Regardless of the policeman's efforts to contribute to social and eco-nomic betterment in the manner described above, we cannot close our eyes to the fact that crime will always be with us. Much can be done to further reduce the evil, providing we raise the educational and intellec-tual standard of our police departments, elevate the position of the po-liceman to that of a profession, eliminate politics entirely from the force, and secure the people's confidence, sympathy, respect and co-operation.

Policemen should jealously guard the reputation of their profession, and establish a code of ethics. Any and every member of the force who violates the provisions of the code should be vigorously prosecuted and expelled from the ranks. Policemens' [sic] lives must be dominated by the highest ideals if they hope to establish themselves in the affections of the people, and win for the profession such an exalted plane that positions on the force will be sought for by the nation's best manhood. Let us speed the day when the appointment as a policeman shall be considered the greatest honor that the municipality may bestow upon one of its citizens.

Source: August Vollmer, "The Policeman as a Social Worker," in *International Association of Chiefs of Police: Proceedings 26th Convention*, New Orleans, La., April 14–16, 1919. [*Proceedings of the Annual Conventions of the International Association of Chiefs of Police: 1913–1920*, Vol. 3. New York: Arno Press and the New York Times, 1971, 32–38.]

DOCUMENT 34: The Boston Police Strike (1919)

Police labor disputes and the issue of unionization received considerable attention in the years following World War I. Inflation was high—with the cost of living rising 25 percent between 1900 and 1915 alone. Moreover, while the wages of many factory workers and others had kept up with inflation, largely as a result of unionization, police salaries had remained static (Deakin 1988:112). In Boston, for example, police officers had not received a raise since 1898 (Deakin 1988: 113).

Dissatisfied both with low wages and with working conditions, a Boston police officers' group called the Boston Social Club sought and was granted a union charter by the American Federation of Labor in August 1919.[2] However, the city's new police commissioner, Edwin U. Curtis, promptly issued an order—known as Rule 35—forbidding membership in the union (Deakin 1988:113). Most officers ignored the order, and Curtis subsequently pressed charges against nineteen of their newly elected union leaders (Bopp and Schultz 1972a :74–75; Deakin 1988:113).

The officers responded in turn by going on strike on September 9, 1919. Nearly three-quarters of the Boston police force—1,117 of 1,544 officers—participated in the strike, which lasted for three days (Fogelson 1977:194). Fueled by sensationalistic media accounts of crime and violence in the city as a result of the strike,[3] as well as official denunciations of the strike by President Woodrow Wilson and Governor Calvin Coolidge of Massachusetts (see Documents 34A, 34B, and 34C, below), public sentiment turned against the striking police officers. All of the striking police officers were fired and replaced, and the union was destroyed.

Although there were some attempts to organize police unions in the years that followed (see Document 51, for example), the experience of the Boston police left the movement largely defunct until the late 1950s (Peak 1997:134; Pfuhl 1989:598).

* * *

A. GOVERNOR COOLIDGE'S RESPONSE TO THE STRIKE (1)

In the opinion of Gov Coolidge, expressed in an interview today with the State House reporters, the members of the Boston Policemen's Union are not strikers, but are guilty of desertion of duty. There can be no arbitration, the Governor says, of the question whether they should be permitted to join the A.F. of L., because such action is expressly forbidden by the rules of the Police Department, which are "the law of the Commonwealth." The Governor says there can be "no arbitration of Government and law." The Governor could not think of any circumstances, he said, under which the striking police officers could be reinstated. . . .

"There is No Strike On"

The next query put to the Governor was: "Will you negotiate with the strikers to see if a basis can be arrived at for their return?"

To this the Governor replied, "The present situation should not be called a strike. There is no strike on. These men are public officials, not employes. It is improperly referred to as a strike."

"What do you call their act of leaving their positions?"

"Desertion of duty," replied the Governor.

Source: "Governor Opposes Reinstatement," *Boston Globe*, September 12, 1919, 1, 5.

B. PRESIDENT WILSON'S RESPONSE TO THE STRIKE

HELENA, Mont, Sept 12—In his speech here last night President Wilson referred to the Boston police strike, saying:

"I want to say this, that a strike of the policemen of a great city, leaving that city at the mercy of an army of thugs, is a crime against civilization.

"In my judgment the obligation of a policeman is as sacred and direct as the obligation of a soldier. He is a public servant, not a private employe, and the whole honor of the community is in his hands. He has no right to prefer any private advantage to the public safety."

Source: M. E. Hennessy, "Police Strike Denounced by Wilson," *Boston Globe*, September 12, 1919, 1.

C. GOVERNOR COOLIDGE'S RESPONSE TO THE STRIKE (2)
GOV COOLIDGE'S REPLY TO SAMUEL GOMPERS

Gov Coolidge yesterday sent the following telegram in reply to the one received by him from Samuel Gompers, printed in the Sunday Globe:

Boston, Mass, Sept 14, 1919.

Mr Samuel Gompers,
    President American Federation of Labor,
        New York City.

Replying to your telegram: I have already refused to remove the Police Commissioner of Boston. I did not appoint him. He can assume no position which the courts would uphold except what the people have by the authority of their law vested in him. He speaks only with their voice.

The right of the police of Boston to affiliate has always been questioned, never granted, is now prohibited. The suggestion of President Wilson to Washington does not apply to Boston. There the police have remained on duty. Here the Policemen's Union left their duty, an action which President Wilson characterized as a crime against civilization.

Your assertion that the commissioner was wrong cannot justify the wrong of leaving the city unguarded. . . . There is no right to strike against the public safety by anybody, anywhere, any time. . . .

Calvin Coolidge,
Governor of Massachusetts.

Source: "Gov Coolidge's Reply to Samuel Gompers," *Boston Globe*, September 15, 1919, 1.

DOCUMENT 35: *American Police Systems* (Raymond B. Fosdick, 1920)

One of the harshest critics of American police during the reform era of the early twentieth century was Raymond Blaine Fosdick (1883–1972). Fosdick was born in Buffalo, New York, and educated at Princeton and New York Law School. After receiving his law degree in 1908, he went to work for Mayor George B. McClellan of New York City, first as assistant corporate counsel and later as commissioner of accounts.

In 1913, Fosdick was recruited by the Rockefeller Bureau of Social Hygiene—a Progressive era "think tank"—to study police organizations in Europe. His glowing account of police administration, training, and practices in European cities, titled *European Police Systems*, was published in 1915. The Rockefeller Bureau of Social Hygiene subsequently asked Fosdick to conduct a similar study in the United States.

Between 1915 and 1917, Fosdick visited the police departments of seventy-two American cities (W. Bailey 1989:239). The results of this study were published in his 1920 book, *American Police Systems*. However, in stark contrast to the high praise he had given to the European police, Fosdick had little good to say about their American counterparts. He cited numerous problems, including political influence, recruitment standards, and training (Deakin 1988:29).

While Fosdick's book was no doubt unpopular with the American police departments it denigrated, it received considerable public attention and also became a definitive source for students of police administration for many years (Deakin 1988:29). Moreover, Fosdick's criticisms and the public concern they focused on American police departments increased those departments' motivation to improve police training and to implement other reforms as well (W. Bailey 1989: 240; Bopp and Schultz 1972a:84).

* * *

To an American who has intimately studied the operation of European police systems, nothing can be more discouraging than a similar survey of the police of the United States. As he travels from east to west across the continent he is oppressed with the contrasts that meet him on every side. He remembers the conscious pride of European cities in their police, and the atmosphere of public confidence in which they carry on their work. He recalls the unbroken record of rectitude which many of their forces maintain and their endeavor to create, with the aid of expert leadership, a maturing profession. He remembers the infinite pains with which the police administrators are trained and chosen, and the care with which the forces are shielded from political influence. . . .

In America, on the other hand, the student of police travels from one political squabble to another, too often from one scandal to another. He finds a shifting leadership of mediocre calibre—varied now and then by flashes of real ability which are snuffed out when the political wheel turns. There is little conception of policing as a profession or a science to be matured and developed. It is a *job*, held, perhaps, by the grace of some mysterious political influence, and conducted in an atmosphere sordid and unhealthy. It is a treadmill, worked without imagination or aim, and with little incentive except the desire to keep out of trouble. Instead of confidence and trust, the attitude of the public toward the police is far more often than not one of cynicism and suspicion, expressing itself, occasionally, in violent attacks which are as unjust as they are ineffective. In the interim between these spasms of publicity the average police force sinks in its rut, while crime and violence flourish.

This is not a happy picture, and the contrast between the situation on the two sides of the Atlantic is frankly disillusioning. It is only when we approach the facts from another angle that any ray of encouragement can be seen. A basis of comparison, perhaps fairer than the juxtaposition of European police and our own, is the contrast between what our system is today and what it was ten, twenty and forty years ago. Assuming that our present measurement by European standards is below our hopes, what has our own growth been?

It is this perspective which furnishes a substantial basis for encouragement. London's police department had thirty-five years of established tradition and achievement behind it when the draft riots broke out in New York in 1863. And what was New York's police force then? It was an undisciplined, half-uniformed mob, armed with clubs. Between that day and this a revolution has been wrought in our police administration. In the early seventies the police of San Francisco were little more than a sheriff's posse, and the hue and cry was the method of apprehending criminals. San Francisco's police force today, with all its imperfections, represents a new era in public service. As late as the eighties our police everywhere were regarded by the citizens with a resignation bordering on complacence, as the private armies of the political parties in power. Today the open and avowed connection of the police with politics arouses widespread though often futile protest. It was in 1895 that the Lexow Commission in New York unearthed scandals in the police department of a kind and to a degree that would be almost inconceivable today. Such flagrant conditions, in open defiance of public right and decency, may exist here and there even now, but unlike 1895, they represent the exception and not the rule. . . .

There is hardly a police department in the United States where similar evidences of improvement cannot be found. Only a blind man could fail to see that with all our shuffling incompetence in municipal affairs—and it is ominous enough—the cumulative effort of forty years for a decent standard of local government in the United States is bearing fruit, not so evident as yet, perhaps in constructive results—although even here it has registered substantial gains—as in the general toning up of our political life, and in a public opinion far more sensitive to betrayal and abuse, and increasingly intolerant of laxity and ineptitude. From the influence of these silent but potent forces in American life our police departments have not escaped. Measured against the background of the past they show a real advance.

But the advance has been discouragingly irregular—a step forward, a slip back, with a net achievement slight and inadequate. Improvement is not permanent; we do not hold our gains. The constructive efforts of a progressive administration are likely to be wiped out by a reactionary successor, and carefully laid plans whose installation and development bear promise of good results are abandoned over night. Every police department is a graveyard of projects and improvements which, had they been developed to maturity, would have reconstituted the police work of the city. They have died because the particular administration sponsoring them has met the fate of all municipal administrations, and the succeeding regime, to justify its existence, has had to discredit the work and aims of its predecessor. In this mean play of politics, this recurring advance and reaction, our gains are often illusory.

We have, indeed, little to be proud of. It cannot be denied that our achievement in respect to policing is sordid and unworthy. Contrasted with other countries in this regard we stand ashamed. With all allowances for the peculiar conditions which make our task so difficult, we have made a poor job of it. Our progress has fallen far behind our needs. Successful in the organization of business and commerce, pre-eminent in many lines of activity, we must confess failure in the elemental responsibility laid on all peoples who call themselves civilized, of preserving order in their communities. Surely in the new era upon which we are entering, with its challenge to forms of government and political faiths, the vision of America will not be blind to the grave importance of the problem and the resourcefulness of America will not be baffled in attempting the solution.

Source: Raymond B. Fosdick, *American Police Systems* (New York: Century Co., 1920), 379–383.

DOCUMENT 36: Race Relations and the Police in Chicago (1922)

Police reform efforts of the early twentieth century addressed not only administration, recruitment, and training issues (for example, see Documents 25 and 32), but racial discrimination as well. Between 1900 and 1920, racial tensions had been steadily increasing in America's cities—resulting in more than twenty riots in 1919 alone (Deakin 1988:110).

Perhaps the most notorious of these riots occurred in Chicago, where twenty-three blacks and fifteen whites were killed, 537 people were injured, and hundreds more were left homeless during a riot that took place between July 27 and August 2, 1919 (Chicago Commission on Race Relations 1922:xv). The riot began after a dispute between whites and blacks at a beach used primarily by whites. The whites tried to drive away a group of blacks, and a fight broke out that resulted in stone-throwing between the two groups.

Meanwhile, a 17-year-old black youth who had been swimming offshore before the altercation began drowned. Several black witnesses on shore claimed he had been hit by a stone thrown by a white man,[4] but a white police officer who had intervened in the fight supposedly refused to arrest the accused man. To make matters worse, the officer not only failed to arrest the white man the blacks had accused of murder, but subsequently arrested a black man involved in the fight based on a complaint of a white man. The combination of these events, along with a long-standing mistrust of the police by Chicago's black citizens, instigated the riot that continued for six days (Chicago Commission on Race Relations 1922:4–5).

In the aftermath of the riot, the Chicago Commission on Race Relations was formed to investigate the causes of the riot and the events that had occurred, and to seek solutions to the problem. The commission—which was composed of eighty-one leading citizens, both black and white—included in its report an examination of the role of the police in the riot, the problems they encountered in attempting to control the riot, examples of discrimination by police officers against black citizens before and during the riot, and a general discussion of strained relations between blacks and the police in Chicago (Chicago Commission on Race Relations 1922:33–40). Following is an excerpt from this portion of the report.

* * *

Police.—There has been much criticism of the manner in which the riot was handled by the authorities, but it may be pointed out that the riot was not quelled until at least four groups of peace guardians had taken part in handling it. The two most important groups were the police and the militia; the others were composed of deputy sheriffs and Negro ex-soldiers.

Testimony before the coroner's jury and in hearings before this Commission throws considerable light on the actions of the Police Department as a whole during the riot, its methods in meeting the unusual situation, and on the conduct of individual policemen. First-hand information and opinion was obtained from Chief of Police Garrity and State's Attorney Hoyne.

The police had two severe handicaps at the outset of the rioting. The first, as declared by Chief Garrity, was lack of sufficient numbers adequately to cope with the situation. The coroner's jury found that "the police force should be enlarged. It is too small to cope with the needs of Chicago." The grand jury added: "The police force is also inadequate in numbers, and at least one thousand (1,000) officers should be added to the existing force." This number approximates the need urged by Chief Garrity, who, when asked before the Commission as to the sufficiency of his force, answered: "No. I haven't sufficient force. I haven't got a sufficient force now to properly police the city of Chicago by one-third." Militia officers and other police officials held the same general opinion.

The second handicap, distrust of white policemen by all Negroes, while implied and not admitted by Chief Garrity, was frankly explained by State's Attorney Hoyne. He said before the Commission: "There is no doubt that a great many police officers were grossly unfair in making arrests. They shut their eyes to offenses committed by white men while they were very vigorous in getting all the colored men they could get."

Leaders among the Negroes clearly indicate that discrimination in arrest was a principal cause of widespread and long-standing distrust. Whether justified or not, this feeling was actual and bitter. This distrust had grown seriously during the six months preceding the riot because no arrests were made in bombing cases. State's Attorney Hoyne said before the commission: "I don't know of a single case where the police have apprehended any man who has blown up a house."

Charles S. Duke, a well-educated and fair-minded Negro, gave his reaction to the bombings when he said that he did not "believe a Negro would have been allowed to go unpunished five minutes." Mrs. Clarke, Negro, said her house was bombed three times, once while a plainclothes policeman was inside waiting for bombers, but no arrests were made. One suspect was put under surveillance but was not held.

The trial of the three Negro policemen before the Merit Committee of the Police Department because they refused to use the "Jim Crow" sleeping quarters in a police station doubtless added to race feeling, particularly in view of the publicity it received in the "Black Belt."

Negro distrust of the police increased among the Negroes during the period of the riot. With each clash a new cause for suspicion seemed to spring up. The most striking instance occurred on the first afternoon when Policeman Callahan refused to arrest the white man whom the Negro crowd accused of causing the drowning of Williams, the Negro boy. This refusal has been called the beginning of the riot because it led to mob violence of grave consequences. However that may have been, the fact remains that this refusal was heralded broadcast by the Negroes as the kind of action they might expect from the police. . . .

A report on 229 Negroes and whites accused of various criminal activities disclosed the fact that 154 were Negroes and seventy-five were whites. The state's attorney reported eighty-one indictments against Negroes and forty-seven against whites after all riot cases were cleared up. These figures show that twice as many Negroes appeared as defendants and twice as many were indicted as whites.

At first glance these figures indicate greater riot activity on the part of Negroes, and therefore one would expect to find twice as many whites injured as Negroes. But out of a total of 520 injured persons whose race was definitely reported, 342 were Negroes and 178 whites. The fact that twice as many Negroes appeared as defendants and twice as many were injured as whites suggests the conclusion that whites were not apprehended as readily as Negroes.

Source: Chicago Commission on Race Relations, *The Negro in Chicago* (Chicago: University of Chicago Press, 1922), 33–35.

DOCUMENT 37: "Adding Policemen to the List of Those Who Know How to Shoot" (1923)

In addition to increased racial tensions (see Document 36), the period following World War I also was marked by increased crime—including violent crime, such as armed bank robbery (Johnson 1981: 125–127). Media accounts of such crimes, though often sensationalized, helped focus public attention on the need for more and better firearms training for police officers. At the same time, the National Rifle Association (NRA) assumed a leading role both in promoting and assisting police marksmanship training (G. Morrison 1995:336–358). Until this time, police firearms training typically was sporadic and inefficient.

Part of the reason for this problem was that although police officers had been carrying firearms for fifty years or more, it often had been without official sanction. For example, in 1857 New York, police officers officially were armed only with billy clubs. However, as a result of increased violence and attacks on police officers that year, they also were equipped with.32 caliber revolvers, although the police commissioners "never officially authorized the weapons and in fact denied they purchased them for the men's use" (Miller 1977:52). As Gregory Morrison explained, "This leaves little doubt about why training suffered from neglect: One obviously cannot conduct firearms training for police officers who officially do not possess them" (1995:196).

As various departments gradually began to officially equip officers with firearms, such as Boston in 1884 and New York in 1895 (Deakin 1988:13), some firearms training programs were begun. For example, the first revolver training program for police officers—the School of Pistol Practice—appears to have been instigated by Theodore Roosevelt, then head of the New York City police commission (see Document 22), as a result of "firearms-related accidents" and "failure by officers to shoot properly at critical moments" (G. Morrison 1995:219–224).

However, it wasn't until the 1920s that police firearms training began in earnest, with the assistance of the NRA. Local NRA clubs provided many police departments' officers with access to local firing ranges, which most police departments did not have at the time, and also provided opportunities to test their skills at national marksmanship matches held at Camp Perry in Ohio (G. Morrison 1995:336–348). The following document appeared in the September 1, 1923, issue of *The American Rifleman.*

* * *

The ignorance of the average police officer in the proper handling of his weapons have been topics [*sic*] of before breakfast and after dinner conversation among American shooters and American criminals for years. A distinct trend has finally set toward the proper training of officers of the law in the one arm on which they can in final emergency depend for enforcement of the law. The surface has, as yet, been barely scratched, but the results beginning to show are most encouraging.

For a number of years the police in Toledo, Philadelphia, and Detroit have been prominent figures on the Pistol Range at Perry. Last year a police high power rifle club was organized in New Orleans with a membership of over two hundred of the cities [*sic*] blue-coats. This spring thirty-six officers in Hartford, Conn., affiliated with the N.R.A. as individual members. Just a few months ago the entire Boston police force affiliated in the form of twenty precinct rifle clubs. Now comes word that the police force in Toledo have constructed a Municipal Rifle and Pistol Range which will be used primarily for their own instruction, and the instruction and practice of civilian rifle clubs, and secondarily for the training of any American in Toledo who is interested enough in the enforcement of the law and the preservation of the United States to want to learn to shoot. Toledo has set an example which may profitably be followed by the Department of Public Safety in every state in the Union, and it would appear that the atmosphere at Perry, which has turned many a luke-warm rifleman into a bug, has similarly inoculated the guardians of the law at Toledo.

Finally, we have evidence of a definite step forward in police marksmanship in the announcement that the New Jersey State Police will hold an inter-state police match at Sea Girt, New Jersey, immediately following the Sea Girt matches. The entire New Jersey State Police force affilited [*sic*] with the N.R.A. last year, and has shown unmistakable signs that it is their intention to take advantage of the service which the N.R.A. is able to render. This match, putting the matter of police practice squarely up to the state police organizations in Connecticut, New York, Pennsylvania, and Maryland will, without doubt, go far toward boosting the entire idea of police marksmanship, and Colonel Schwarzkopf, Superintendent of Police, and his able assistant, Major Kimberling, deserve a foremost place in the ranks of men who realize that training in police marksmanship is fully as important to the nation as the training of the National Guard.

Source: "Adding Policemen to the List of Those Who Know How to Shoot," *American Rifleman* 71, no. 7 (September 1, 1923): 14.

DOCUMENT 38: *Carroll et al. v. United States* (1925)

The illegal production and sale of bootleg liquor, or "moonshine," during Prohibition (1920–1933)[5] prompted several challenges to search and seizure laws during the 1920s. One such challenge led to an important Supreme Court ruling with regard to police search and seizure activities.

The case, *Carroll et al. v. United States,* involved the arrest and conviction of a known bootlegger, George Carroll, and his associates, based on evidence—sixty-eight bottles of whiskey and gin—seized by three federal prohibition officers and one state officer during a warrantless search of Carroll's automobile.

The defendants claimed that the warrantless search and seizure by the officers violated their Fourth Amendment rights, and therefore that the seized liquor used as evidence in their trial should have been deemed inadmissible (267 U.S. 132, 134).

The Supreme Court disagreed, ruling that the search and seizure had been justified, despite the fact that no warrant had been issued. Writing the opinion of the Court, Chief Justice Taft explained that the search of an automobile or other moving vehicle, such as a water vessel or mobile home, differs from that of a home in that it may be moved quickly, and therefore evidence may be lost to police forever unless they are able to act immediately upon suspicion of a crime. Therefore, if sufficient probable cause of illegal activity exists, the police may conduct a search of a vehicle without a warrant. This ruling has become known as the "Carroll Doctrine" (Peak 1997:279–280; Regoli and Hewitt 1996:303).

* * *

A. OPINION OF THE COURT

MR. CHIEF JUSTICE TAFT, after stating the case as above, delivered the opinion of the Court.

. . .

. . . [T]he guaranty of freedom from unreasonable searches and seizures by the Fourth Amendment has been construed, practically since the beginning of the Government, as recognizing a necessary difference between a search of a store, dwelling house or other structure in respect of which a proper official warrant readily may be obtained, and a search of a ship, motor boat, wagon or automobile, for contraband goods, where it is not practicable to secure a warrant because the vehicle can be quickly moved out of the locality or jurisdiction in which the warrant must be sought.

Having thus established that contraband goods concealed and illegally transported in an automobile or other vehicle may be searched for without a warrant, we come now to consider under what circumstances such search may be made. It would be intolerable and unreasonable if a prohibition agent were authorized to stop every automobile on the chance of finding liquor and thus subject all persons lawfully using the highways to the inconvenience and indignity of such a search. Travellers may be so stopped in crossing an international boundary because of national self protection reasonably requiring one entering the country to identify himself as entitled to come in, and his belongings as effects which may be lawfully brought in. But those lawfully within the country, entitled to use the public highways, have a right to free passage without interruption or search unless there is known to a competent official authorized to search, probable cause for believing that their vehicles are carrying contraband or illegal merchandise. . . .

. . . [I]f an officer seizes an automobile or the liquor in it without a warrant and the facts as subsequently developed do not justify a judgment of condemnation and forfeiture, the officer may escape costs or a suit for damages by showing that he had reasonable or probable cause for the seizure. . . . The measure of legality of such a seizure is, therefore, that the seizing officer shall have reasonable or probable cause for believing that the automobile which he stops and seizes has contraband liquor therein which is being illegally transported. . . .

Such a rule fulfills the guaranty of the Fourth Amendment. In cases where the securing of a warrant is reasonably practicable, it must be used, and when properly supported by affidavit and issued after judicial approval protects the seizing officer against a suit for damages. In cases where seizure is impossible except without a warrant, the seizing officer acts unlawfully and at his peril unless he can show the court probable cause.

B. DISSENTING OPINION

The separate opinion of MR. JUSTICE MCREYNOLDS concurred in by MR. JUSTICE SUTHERLAND.

1. The damnable character of the "bootlegger's" business should not close our eyes to the mischief which will surely follow any attempt to destroy it by unwarranted methods. "To press forward to a great principle by breaking through every other great principle that stands in the way of its establishment; . . . in short, to procure an eminent good by

means that are unlawful, is as little consonant to private morality as to public justice." Sir William Scott, *The Louis*, 2 Dodson 210, 257.

While quietly driving an ordinary automobile along a much frequented public road, plaintiffs in error were arrested by Federal officers without a warrant and upon mere suspicion—ill founded, as I think. The officers then searched the machine and discovered carefully secreted whisky, which was seized and thereafter used as evidence against plaintiffs in error when on trial for transporting intoxicating liquor contrary to the Volstead Act. . . . They maintain that both arrest and seizure were unlawful and that use of the liquor as evidence violated their constitutional rights. . . .

3.

. . .

While the Fourth Amendment denounces only unreasonable seizures, unreasonableness often depends upon the means adopted. Here the seizure followed an unlawful arrest, and therefore became itself unlawful—as plainly unlawful as the seizure within the home so vigorously denounced in *Weeks* v. *United States.* . . .

5. When Congress has intended that seizures or arrests might be made upon suspicion it has been careful to say so. The history and terms of the Volstead Act are not consistent with the suggestion that it was the purpose of Congress to grant the power here claimed for enforcement officers. The facts known when the arrest occurred were wholly insufficient to engender reasonable belief that plaintiffs in error were committing a misdemeanor, and the legality of the arrest cannot be supported by facts ascertained through the search which followed.

Source: 267 U.S. 132 (1925), 143–175.

DOCUMENT 39: J. Edgar Hoover (1925)

In 1924, a young man by the name of John Edgar Hoover (1895–1972) was appointed director of the Department of Justice's Bureau of Investigation, which in 1935 would be renamed the Federal Bureau of Investigation (FBI). Hoover, then just twenty-nine, previously had worked as a law clerk for the Department of Justice (1917–1919), special assistant to the U.S. Attorney General (1919–1921), and assistant director of the Bureau of Investigation (1921–1924). When he took over as director of the bureau, it was in sorry shape, tainted by the Teapot Dome scandal[6] and other corrupt dealings of the former Harding administration (Murphy 1977:263, 265). Hoover immediately went to work to revamp and professionalize the bureau. Toward this end, he fired many of its agents and established new hiring criteria, which included educational and physical fitness requirements, and also implemented a more extensive training program for new agents (W. Bailey 1989:268; Murphy 1977:265; Peak 1997:34–45; Regoli and Hewitt 1996:242).

During his forty-eight years as director of the FBI, during which time he served under eight presidents (Murphy 1977:262), Hoover was responsible for establishing a large national fingerprint file, a criminalistics laboratory, and a national police training academy (see Document 48), and for coordinating the development of a uniform crime reporting system, among other accomplishments (Peak 1997:35; Regoli and Hewitt 1996:242).

These other accomplishments include the establishment of an Identification Division within the Bureau of Investigation during his first year as director of the bureau (Peak 1997:36). Speaking at the thirty-second annual convention of the IACP (see document below), Hoover reported on the progress of the new division.

* * *

I am glad of the opportunity to meet my old friends and to gain new ones, among the ranks of the members of the Association to whom we owe so much, to whose contributions of material and unwavering, unselfish, devoted support in the dark and trying days of the first year of our existence, is due our present condition of substantial accomplishment, the beginning of something of actual and potential worth, of an organization that we truly trust will grow into a service-unit, unique in the history of crime prevention and detection, of invaluable and vital import and necessity to the Chiefs of Police of not only this, the greatest and best of the sub-divisions of humanity, but all the countries of the world.

Basically, the existence of our Bureau's Identification Division is due to a recognition on the part of the members of this Association that any real development and progress in crime detection and punishment must, if the modern criminal and latter-day crime is [sic] to be successfully combated, be founded upon the rock of universal co-operation. This is not a strange or novel discovery or doctrine. The entire history of humankind is simply the record of the development of the idea of universal co-operation.

I may safely assume, I fancy, that none may realize the value and necessity of co-operation, of mutual assistance and help, better and more fully than those who are engaged in the never-ending pursuit of the criminal. . . .

In these days we are compelled to recognize the universalism of crime and to all practical intents and purposes the omnipresence of the criminal. In times past (and not so far distant past) crime or the criminal was a more or less local issue. Our local or neighborhood criminal was known, his haunts could be watched, his associates shadowed, the method and nature of the crime often bore within itself the recognizable identity of the criminal. He could often be captured on the scene of the crime, the fastest means of locomotion being either human or equine. Then, too, his means of travel, which were limited, could be traced with comparative ease. Should he escape to some other community, the danger of his capture was still imminent. Every stranger was a marked man, every newcomer aroused suspicion. When there did not yet exist the great urban centers of population of today, the opportunities and possibilities of securing almost untraceable hiding-places were proportionately fewer. The world of today offers almost endless means and channels of escape for the wary fugitive. The modern motor-car, steam, electricity, all are at his service. The airplane is, or soon will be. His lairs and hiding-places have multiplied almost infinitely. The means by which he may conceal his tracks have increased many-fold. A crime may be committed in a great city of the east and the criminal travel undetected to some other great city in the west, there to take a place and rank among the seemingly respectable and solid citizens of the commonwealth, to become a power in the realm of finance and commerce, notwithstanding his real character, that of a potential wolf in the sheepfold of unsuspecting innocence. These developments therefore, the mighty, irresistible current of world-wide, cosmic forces, have created the necessity and impetus for the inception and growth of an organization which will serve to centralize and crystallize the efforts of those who would meet the exigencies of our changing times by a pooling of all of the wisdom and power of the guardians of civilization, the protectors of Society.

Such was the genesis of the Division of Identification of the Bureau of Investigation of the United States Department of Justice. To you gentlemen of the International Association of Chiefs of Police is due the credit and honor of an early and timely recognition of the urgent necessity for the establishment of a vast, central storehouse of information, a library of criminal records, a collection of identification data. Here would be suitably recorded for all time the results of the trained, toilsome and devoted efforts of each and every one of you, finger-print records of criminals, great and small, the changeless fingertip-signatures of the violators of the laws and the foes of the institutions upon which rest all that we possess of good and all that we hold that is fair. . . .

. . . We have now on hand 914,848 finger-print records. We have in our files 1,051,347 alphabetical index cards. We know, of course, the necessity for card-indexing each and every alias of a criminal. We have one "gentleman of easy virtue" recorded under 144 aliases. We have a conservatively estimated number of Bertillon photographs and records on hand aggregating 225,000. We no longer dread the coming of a new day with its accumulation of inquiries and unclassified prints. We are fully abreast with our current inquiries and work. I might mention that our daily receipt of finger-print records approximates the substantial figure of 500.

Source: Excerpts from an address by J. Edgar Hoover, in *International Association of Chiefs of Police: Proceedings 32nd Convention*, Indianapolis, Ind., July 13–16, 1925. [*Proceedings of the Annual Conventions of the International Association of Chiefs of Police: 1921–1925*, Vol. 4. New York: Arno Press and the New York Times, 1971, 48–51.]

DOCUMENT 40: "Radio in Police Work" (William P. Rutledge, 1929)

By the 1920s, radio broadcasting of news and entertainment programs had become routinely available to the American public. However, while the first two-way radio car was put into service by August Vollmer's Berkeley Police Department in 1921 (see Document 33), it wasn't until the 1930s that the radio became a common feature in patrol vehicles (Regoli and Hewitt 1996:226–227).

Part of the reason for the relatively slow adoption of radio by the police undoubtedly was inherent in the need to streamline and improve the technology itself. For example, as William P. Rutledge, commissioner of the Detroit Police Department noted, although his department had been experimenting with radio cars since 1921, as had Vollmer's department, it wasn't until the spring of 1928 that their radio system first began to "function satisfactorily." However, another problem cited by Rutledge was the reluctance of the Federal Radio Commission to recognize the utility and importance of radio to police work. For example, his police department initially was not given its own wavelength, and therefore all of its broadcasts were made over public airwaves. Moreover, the department was forced to include entertainment in its broadcasts, therefore, "[i]f we wished to broadcast an alarm of a murder or a holdup, we must first play a tune on a fiddle" (Rutledge 1929:69).

Despite these initial obstacles, by the late 1920s radio use by police departments was on the rise. And as radio use increased, the Detroit police, and other departments that soon followed their example, reported significantly improved police response time to crime and to requests for help. Radios also made it easier for police administrators to supervise their officers in the field (Regoli and Hewitt 1996:226–227; Rutledge 1929:69–70).

* * *

The possibilities of radio as a most effective weapon in our never-ending war against crime have been discussed by police officials for ten years or more. Not until recently has a sustained success been achieved.

Detroit was among the early pioneers in police radio development. It was the first police department in the country to have a municipally owned station, operated by licensed police operators and devoted exclusively to police work.

Ten years ago when radio was in its infancy, I realized its potential value as a new and powerful weapon. When the subject of installing our own broadcasting equipment was first discussed, there was openly expressed skepticism. But I was convinced that we could find a successful and practical method of applying this new police weapon, not only as a means of instant communication between police departments of cities and states, as was suggested by Commissioner Higgins at the St. Louis Convention in 1920, but to accomplish something that has proven to be of far greater importance—radio communication between the heads of our Department and the personnel in traveling police automobiles.

It was in the early part of 1921 that we placed our first car, equipped with a receiving set, on the streets of Detroit. In 1922 I arranged for a statewide broadcast of the license numbers of stolen cars and sent letters to every sheriff and police chief in the State of Michigan, urging them to adopt radio as a most effective instrument against crime.

Our station was operated intermittently and with varying success. We had to overcome the obstacles that beset the path of pioneers in any line of endeavor. The skeptics continued to belittle our efforts. The Government radio authorities seemed reluctant to accept our opinion as to the importance of giving some preference to police radio stations. They failed to show any keen interest in our experiment. We were forced to broadcast important police information on a wave length that made our messages public. The radio authorities stipulated that an entertainment feature must be included. If we wished to broadcast an alarm of a murder or a holdup, we must first play a tune on a fiddle. We refused to continue under such ridiculous and discouraging restrictions. We closed the station for a short time. When we resumed operations, it was under an amateur license that eliminated all entertainment features.

The first receiving sets that we made and installed in police cars, easily picked up the messages from our own station, but being of a selective type, they could also be tuned in on commercial stations. When we found one of our crews listening in on outside musical programs, which comprise about ninety per cent of radio broadcasting, we rebuilt the sets. Since then the sets are locked in cabinets and it is impossible to tune out our station.

In spite of numerous setbacks and discouragements, we persisted in our efforts. Seven years of hard unrelenting toil, was at last rewarded. In the spring of 1928 our radio began to function satisfactorily. Since then we have accomplished so great a number of important arrests that the press throughout the world has carried the details of the impressive manner in which radio is being used to combat crime in Detroit.

Letters began to arrive from police officials throughout the United States and abroad, requesting information as to our equipment, cost of operation, etc. Police departments from all over the world sent representatives to Detroit to inspect our radio equipment. Even the far-famed Scotland Yard requested information. Invariably the visiting officials conducted a thorough investigation, during which they witnessed demonstrations that proved without doubt the efficiency and practicability of police radio communication.

Snaring criminals in a radio network, woven by broadcasting to radio equipped pursuit cars, has become a matter of seconds. Seconds are precious to the lawbreaker. They spell the difference between escape and capture. The wider the margin of time, the better his chances to escape apprehension. By the use of radio we are catching the criminal red-handed. We are eliminating the introduction of circumstantial evidence in trials by indisputable proof of guilt. Economically, we are cutting down the cost of law enforcement by catching the crook with the goods on, instead of getting him after a long chase. We have quickened and lengthened the arm of the law. We have synchronized the arrest with the depredation. Instead of trailing behind in the criminal's dust, we are as near abreast of him as it is humanely [sic] possible to be.

Murderers have been caught at the scene of the crime before they had a chance to dispose of their weapons. Burglars have been captured while still piling up their loot in homes. Bewildered auto thieves have gasped as the police cruiser roared alongside of them a few moments after they had stolen a car. Speeding hit-run drivers have been captured and returned to the spot where they had run down and left their hopeless victim a few seconds before. Thugs have been captured while in the act of robbing their victims. Racketeers and bad check passers have been caught. Bank stickup men have been in handcuffs within sixty seconds of the time they fled from the bank.

Six hundred important arrests in an average time of eighty seconds per arrest,—the most astounding record ever entered in police annals. . . .

It is not so many years ago that there were no means of communication between a policeman walking his beat, from the time he left his station, until he returned hours later. In the interval he was completely away from control of his superior officers. The introduction of the street telephone patrol box was hailed as an epoch-making improvement. Later the flash system was regarded as the last word in quick communication between the men on the beat and his [sic] station. The efficiency of such means pales into insignificance when compared to the new crime-fighting agency which science has given us in radio. And yet, we know that radio is only in its infancy. Before long, every officer on the beat will be equipped with a small radio receiver. Every man and every car patrolling our streets night or day will be directed by radio orders. The value of police service to our citizens will be increased a hundredfold.

However, before much further progress can be made, we must have understanding and cooperation in our own departments. We must also receive full cooperation and consideration from those who control the future destinies of police radio—the Federal Radio Commission at Washington.

When the staggering, almost unbelievable sum of four billion dollars each year is the cost of crime in this country, and a further six billion dollars is expended yearly in law enforcement, we believe we are justified in asking the Federal Radio Commission to give first consideration to police radio wave-band requests. It would seem to us that the Radio Commission does not fully realize the importance of radio in law enforcement. What is needed now is a wave band of from 105 to 109 meters for police work; first, because it will assure privacy for police information, and, secondly, this frequency or wave band is the most efficient for service of this kind as it can be handled with less power with better results.

The importance of enlisting every possible means of law enforcement in combatting crime cannot be exaggerated. President Hoover has stated that he believes that the enforcement and obedience to the laws of the United States, both Federal and State, is the dominant issue before the American people. He reminded us that nine thousand human beings are lawlessly killed in the United States each year; that little more than half as many arrests follow; that murders can apparently be committed with impunity and that burglaries and robberies are common. He expressed the opinion that one of the immediate problems before us is the reorganization of our police systems in such a manner as to eliminate its weaknesses.

What is the most effective means we can employ to stem the tide of lawlessness? What weapon is the most formidable with which to battle the unseen army of criminals which constitutes the vicious minority—an army which acts as one man because it is bound together by a common desire to make a living by defying the law and preying upon society?

I am convinced that in police radio we have found the weapon. The psychological effect of quick capture acts as a powerful deterrent to crime. The actual effect is being recorded daily on the log of our police radio in Detroit. We are catching and convicting more stickup men, robbers and other vicious criminals, than ever before. Prosecutions have increased fifty-four per cent. All of which is discouraging the criminally inclined parasite, who will soon find it best to adopt honest employment as his means of livelihood.

Source: William P. Rutledge, "Radio in Police Work," in *International Association of Chiefs of Police: Proceedings Thirty-Sixth Convention*, Atlanta, Ga., June 3–6, 1929. [*Proceedings of the Annual Conventions of the International Association of Chiefs of Police: 1926–1930*, Vol. 5. New York: Arno Press and the New York Times, 1971, 68–71.]

DOCUMENT 41: "Our Inefficient Police" (Howard McLellan, 1929)

Throughout the 1920s, American police departments continued to expand significantly—both in terms of personnel and operating costs. Yet despite these increases, and the use of new technologies such as the automobile (Document 26), telephone, teletype, telephotography, and radio (Document 40), crime rates remained relatively high, leading at least one critic to question the efficiency of American police departments.

In his article, "Our Inefficient Police," which appeared in the February issue of the *North American Review*, Howard McLellan noted that the annual per capita costs of urban policing almost doubled from 1916 to 1926, rising from $2.10 to $4.09.[7]

McLellan also noted that in New York, 3,522 new officers were added to the force in 1926 and 1927, increasing the department's operating costs by about $6 million. Yet by the end of 1927, New York's crime rate had decreased by just 4 percent since 1926. In McLellan's view, such a low rate of return called for increased scrutiny of the police and their operations (McLellan 1929:222, 225–226).

* * *

On New Year's Day, 1928, the Department of Commerce, regarding the occasion as appropriate for retrospection and new resolutions, put out a bulletin showing that the cost of policing American cities is ascending the same steep road travelled by the costs of being respectably born, correctly married, adequately doctored and decently buried. Statisticians in the Department of Commerce laid emphasis upon the revelation that police departments in 250 American cities in 1926 cost almost double what they had cost in 1916.

In 1926 the cost of operating and maintaining police departments in 250 cities, representing 35 per cent. of the country's total population, was $171,167,243, exclusive of pensions, interest on city bonds and charges for equipment and buildings. Expenditures for police represented 10.4 per cent. of the entire cost of the city government, while the *per capita* cost was $4.09. In 1916 the cost of policing 213 cities in the same population class was $67,647,508 and the *per capita* cost $2.10; an increase of $103,520,000 or almost threefold in ten years.

Weighing these figures, one's mind may run presumptively to the conclusion that a police machine that has doubled in cost in a decade must be twice as efficient. Bigness reflected in tremendous costs is impressive. It staggers the citizen and it should stagger the crook. And to be sure there are more policemen on the streets, who dress better, smile oftener and excite the taxpayers' admiration. In a detached way the citizen feels safe, but unfortunately in spite of the increasing cost and size of American police machines the crook, too, shares that sense of security and reflects it in demonstrable ways. Are there not more gunmen and bandits at work, operating oftener and for bigger returns, and organized on a basis hitherto unknown in history? . . .

In 1927 the New York department had a personnel of 17,672 policemen, or about three policemen to 1,000 inhabitants. The cost of operating it in that year was $45,018,725, which was $3,714,147 more than was spent upon the same task in 1926. Salaries of patrolmen range from $1,769 to $2,500 annually. In 1917, when war called forth one grand protective movement and all, including youngsters, were enlisted in protective organizations of one kind or another, the New York force consisted of 10,916 men, and the cost of the department was $18,200,000, or approximately only 40 per cent. of the cost in 1927.

The $3,714,147 increase in 1927 over the previous year went for salaries of 1,722 new men added to the force. In 1926 1,800 men were added to the force, making a total increase in personnel of 3,522 police, added at a cost of $6,000,000. At the end of 1927 the crime rate in New York city, according to police statistics, was four per cent. lower than the previous year.

If a business man had employed 3,522 new salesmen in his private business, thereby adding $6,000,000 to his payroll, and discovered only a four per cent. increase in sales, very likely he would not call in efficiency experts but would, instead, get rid of the entire new increment.

Source: Howard McLellan, "Our Inefficient Police," *North American Review* 227, no. 2 (February 1929): 219–228.

DOCUMENT 42: "Municipal Police Administration" (Bruce Smith, 1929)

While critics such as Howard McLellan (Document 41) focused on police efficiency as measured by the impact—or lack thereof—of increased police personnel and expenditures on crime rates, police reformer Bruce Smith (1892–1955) looked at the larger picture in his assessment entitled "Municipal Police Administration."

Smith, a highly respected police consultant who ultimately surveyed approximately fifty police departments in eighteen states (W. Bailey 1989:582) and also was instrumental in developing the Uniform Crime Reports adopted by the FBI (see Document 43), acknowledged the need for improvement in police administration, recruitment and training, and other areas. However, he also recognized that the growing and changing role of the police, legislative vagaries, media sensationalism, and public misperceptions (see document below) all helped make the police officer's job more difficult. In his own words, "The achievements of American police forces under these adverse circumstances are truly amazing" (Bruce Smith 1929:2).

Like many police reformers of the early twentieth century, such as Leonhard Felix Fuld (Document 25) and Raymond Fosdick (Document 35), Smith never worked as a police officer. Instead, he got his start working with the police as assistant to Charles Beard, director of the New York Bureau of Municipal Research (later named the Institute of Public Administration). Smith remained with the institute for many years, serving as a manager from 1921 to 1928, as acting director from 1941 to 1946 and again from 1950 to 1952, and then as director in 1954 until his death the following year. During that time, he not only conducted numerous police surveys, but also served on a number of commissions dealing with the administration of justice and related topics, and was a key participant in the International Association of Chiefs of Police (W. Bailey 1989:582–583; Reppetto 1977:195–197).

Unlike many police reformers, Smith was well liked and respected by most police administrators and street cops, even though many of his proposed reforms and recommendations for individual departments never were adopted (W. Bailey 1989:582–583). Perhaps this was because many of his criticisms and suggestions for improvement were offered with an understanding of the difficulties faced by both police administrators and officers, and in the spirit of working together toward a solution. In the following excerpt from the introduction to his article,

Smith focused on the changing role of the police and on the environment in which they operated.

* * *

The role of police in modern society steadily tends to become more difficult. Viewing the rudimentary police organizations of a little more than a century ago, one is filled with wonder that their work was not more defective than it actually proved to be. There seems to be only one satisfactory explanation. The police of that day were almost exclusively "thief-takers." In other words they were ranged against a fairly definite group of offenders who plied their criminal trades entirely outside of the law. The urgent need for protection made the ordinary citizen a natural ally of the police even when the latter did not enjoy any large degree of public confidence.

GENERAL CONSIDERATIONS

It is not so today. The police no longer confine their attention to groups and individuals who are essentially outlaws. The police function has come to involve intimate regulation of the day-to-day life of nearly every person with whom the police officer comes into contact. Inevitably there has followed an ill-defined yet none the less positive reaction against police restrictions. In the last analysis, this unfavorable result has been due more to the increasing complexities of daily life than to any failure of the police to adjust themselves to the new conditions.

There have, of course, been such failures of adjustment, although they would appear to have been a result rather than a cause. For it must be remembered that police are creatures of legislative enactments, and that their control has sometimes been dictated by some of the wildest vagaries of the legislative imagination. This definition and restriction of powers has at times been carried so far, and the police have found themselves confined within such narrow limits in both administration and criminal investigation, that they have made furtive, and occasionally open efforts to circumvent the laws under which they operate. Laws and ordinances which were unpopular have been ignored, and others which were persistently violated have only occasionally been enforced. For the most part, such departures from the legislative intent have been dictated by practical, rather than corrupt, considerations. In either case, however, they have had a most unfortunate effect upon both police and public. The standard of performance which the penal law should provide has been taken away, the police have drifted with the tides of expediency, and the public, viewing all this, has drawn its own conclusions.

The press, as the mouthpiece of the public, through which the latter hopes and expects to find its views coherently expressed, has scarcely done its part. The most enlightened editorial policies, through which might be secured able discussion of police problems, have often been offset by a news policy designed to appeal to the unschooled and the ignorant. But even editorial policies have frequently been at fault in condemning the police when they were right, and praising them when they were wrong. So there have been few influences at work for the instruction of the public in the realities and the objective standards of police duty.

Nor have we been able to profit greatly from foreign experience, because of the greater simplicity of the police problem there. We can turn with a considerable degree of confidence to European practices concerning police organization and technique, but we can discover little there which has a direct bearing upon our problems of "law enforcement" and the relations of police, press and public. Legislative self-restraint across the seas has succeeded in avoiding most of the pitfalls into which we have blindly stumbled.

The plight in which American police forces recurrently find themselves has a serious effect upon police administration. Being denounced both when they act vigorously and when they adopt a more complaisant attitude, consistent performance is thrown to the winds, each day's work is done without relation to any larger program, and the police force, from top to bottom, becomes chiefly engaged in propitiating those who possess the greatest power to do them injury.

The achievements of American police forces under these adverse circumstances are truly amazing. Foreign observers who perceive the essential unsoundness of much of our legislative provision and police organization are impressed with the quality of work performed by individual police officers. These last represent both the strength and the weakness of our system of crime repression, because while they are responsible for occasional brilliant results, their numbers are relatively so few and their influence upon the entire police organism so slight that they can never be counted as important factors in the effort to improve police service.

Such improvement is now, as in the past, largely dependent upon influences which lie outside the rank and file. Until the statutory basis of police forces is radically revised, the police administrator and the policeman alike will be hedged about and confined in their efforts. Until that revision is accomplished, the work of improving the details of police administration and police duty will necessarily rest upon insecure foundations.

Source: Bruce Smith, "Municipal Police Administration," *The Annals of the American Academy of Political and Social Science* 146 (November 1929): 1–2.

NOTES

1. By 1917, the police school had expanded to become a three-year program that covered subjects ranging from chemistry, biology, anthropology, and toxicology to criminal psychology, theoretical and applied criminology, police administration, methods, and procedures (Peak 1997:24).

2. Washington, D.C., and about thirty other cities also were issued union charters during this period (Fogelson 1977:193–194).

3. In all, eight or nine people were killed and twenty-one to twenty-three were seriously injured and there was about $300,000 in property damage during the three-day period (Deakin 1988:113; Peak 1997:134; Pfuhl 1989:598). While not discounting these losses, they seem minor compared to race riots in other cities during this period (Deakin 1988:113). Indeed, they were relatively and unexpectedly low when compared with the media's reports of mass anarchy and violence.

4. However, the coroner's report later showed no signs of stone bruising on the drowned boy. Instead, it was concluded that he had most likely drowned because he had become tired but was afraid to return to shore because of the stone-throwing that was going on there (Chicago Commission on Race Relations 1922:4).

5. Prohibition was an attempt to forbid alcohol consumption in the United States that was authorized by the Eighteenth Amendment to the U.S. Constitution (1919) and the Volstead Act (1920) and ended with the repeal of the Eighteenth Amendment in 1933.

6. A government scandal that involved the leasing of land for oil exploration in California and Teapot Dome, Wyoming (*Cambridge Encyclopedia* 1990:1190).

7. What McLellan neglected to say was that rampant inflation had diminished the value of the dollar by 38 percent during the same period—a 1916 dollar could buy only 62 cents worth of goods in 1926 (U.S. Bureau of the Census 1975:series E135 and E185). This meant that actual per capita costs had increased by only 21 percent, not 95 percent, as McLellan claimed.

Part IV

A Growing Emphasis on Police Training, Professionalism, Efficiency, and Ethics, 1930–1959

In the twenty years following 1930 the United States survived a desperate economic depression and World War II, and entered the Korean War. By the early 1950s, however, a period of unprecedented prosperity and population growth had begun. Economic incentives and new technology also encouraged fundamental changes in the size and structure of American families and the way they lived their lives. Urbanization continued to increase throughout the period; during the three decades from 1930 to 1959, the proportion of the population living in towns larger than 2,500 grew from 56 percent to 70 percent. Prosperity and post–World War II demobilization of young males led to a boom in births which would overwhelm social institutions for decades (Easterlin 1987). The proportion of women in the labor force rose from 25 percent in 1930 to 42 percent in 1959. Nearly two-thirds of those women were married. Technology, too, had a major influence on family life as television began to invade quiet family evenings. Against this backdrop of rapid demographic, economic, and social change the role of police in American society also underwent substantial change.

MAPPING A PATH TO PROFESSIONALISM

In 1930, the state of police was dismal. Despite the aspirations of progressive reformers and the pronouncements of practitioners, two dozen crime commissions at the local, state, and national levels had found American police organizations sorely deficient. For example, the 1931 National Commission on Law Observance and Enforcement (popularly called the Wickersham Commission) found that police departments generally were inept, inefficient, and poorly run. Corruption and political manipulation were rampant—as was the use of physical and psychological torture to coerce confessions from suspects. Training was almost nonexistent.

According to the Wickersham Commission, police reform faced formidable challenges. In addition to bureaucratic and institutional inertia, policing had been seriously tainted by the corruption and cynicism fostered by illicit money from Prohibition's powerful underground economy. Although the "noble experiment" of alcohol prohibition was ended in 1933 with the repeal of the Eighteenth Amendment, the damage to policing would take years to repair.

Fortunately, the Wickersham Commission report did more than condemn the police. The chapter on police written under the direction of August Vollmer (see Document 44B) provided a detailed set of guidelines that would serve as a map for police reform efforts and technological improvements. Over the next two generations, it would guide the professionalization movement, and in time the commission's ten specific recommendations would be adopted by most U.S. law enforcement organizations.

DEVELOPING PROFESSIONAL AND EFFICIENT ORGANIZATIONS

Performance Benchmarks

In addition to the generally low esteem in which police in the 1930s were held by the public, media dramatization of the activities of bootleggers, organized crime syndicates, and bank robbers in that decade added to perceptions of their ineptness. This put police in the unenviable position of trying to refute public perceptions of a national crime wave without the support of comprehensive and credible crime statistics. Under the leadership of the International Association of Chiefs of Police and the FBI, a long-awaited national system for counting serious crime finally was instituted. Jurisdictions across the United States gradually began to make annual reports about serious violent and property crime to the FBI in 1930. These Uniform Crime Reports (Document 43) provided an important benchmark against which crime trends and police performance could be evaluated. They also were an important milestone in the development of links among the nation's thousands of independent law enforcement agencies.

Cross-Jurisdictional Cooperation

The gross decentralization of police in the United States also continued to hamper their ability to coordinate crime control efforts and limited their efficiency. Americans faced a quandary that is a classic example of the tension between the need to maintain order in society and the need to preserve individual rights and liberties. On the one hand, it obviously was inefficient to have so many independent law enforcement agencies attempting to control crime and apprehend increasingly mobile criminals. On the other, calls for a strong national police agency (for example, Vollmer 1936) ran counter to Americans' traditional distrust of government—especially national government.

Instead of moving toward a national police agency, as had most of the United States' European contemporaries, a concerted effort was made by the U.S. Department of Justice to nurture strong informal links between agencies. The mechanism for accomplishing this was a national training school for police which was opened by the FBI in 1935 (Document 48). The National Police Academy provided sorely needed training for promising police officers from around the country. At the same time, the camaraderie inspired by the intensive training program provided each class of attendees with a network of personal contacts upon whom they could call for help. To this day, the informal network of National Academy graduates, as they now are known, is one of the most useful cross-jurisdictional law enforcement tools in the United States.

Models for Professional Police Organizations

Throughout the Depression and war years, many departments made progress toward the standards set by Vollmer and his colleagues in the Wickersham Commission's report (Document 44). The day-to-day operations of progressive departments gradually became less affected by political machinations; better qualified police chiefs were selected—often from the ranks of National Academy graduates—and better records systems were developed. The selection, training, salary, and benefits of patrolmen also improved, as did the tools available to them. Radios and motorized vehicles became the norm, and investigative tools continued to improve.

The improvements made between 1930 and 1950 were solidified when O. W. Wilson, a protégé of Vollmer's and the most influential reform police chief in the country, published *Police Administration* (Document 52). The textbook clearly defined a "professional model" for police organizations. The key concepts of Wilson's approach were administrative efficiency fostered by a semi-military hierarchy. Other essential elements were police integrity, education, and training. The textbook, which also dealt with a variety of technical, administrative, and management topics, became required reading for any police officer who aspired to promotion.

Police Administration and another book, *Municipal Police Administration, Third Edition*, edited by Wilson for the International City Managers Association, provided a durable core around which police reforms could crystallize. Within a relatively brief period, Wilson's philosophy spread to departments across the country. A notable example was the Los Angeles Police Department, which was taken over by Wilson protégé William H. Parker (Document 53) in 1950 after a corruption scandal. Following the principles developed by Vollmer and Wilson, over the next sixteen years Parker developed the department into one of the most widely recognized professional police agencies in the world.

Selecting and Training the Right People

Like Vollmer, Wilson, and other reform chiefs of the 1950s, Parker placed great emphasis on the importance of selecting the right people and subjecting them to rigorous training. This emphasis on training continued throughout an officer's career with daily roll-call training sessions and periodic in-service training.

In addition to the FBI National Police Academy (Document 48), another important source of training for the nation's scattered police forces emerged at the state level. Following Vollmer's recommendations in the Wickersham report (Document 44), all but one state established a state police force—often directed and supervised by distinguished local veterans of World War I—to provide protective and investigative services outside the cities. Many state police forces also were responsible for traffic enforcement on highways as well as for assisting smaller police departments with complex investigations. The rigorous recruit training programs developed by state police agencies motivated municipal departments to establish their own training programs and provided models for them to follow. It was not unusual for outstanding local officers to attend state police academies (Bopp and Schultz 1972a:111).

Giving more officers the skills needed to investigate crimes, take reports, and make arrests was a major step forward. But it was much more difficult to provide officers with ethical guidelines for negotiating the treacherous moral dilemmas and corrosive work environment of everyday policing.

CONSTRAINING POLICE BEHAVIOR

Police Ethics

The Wickersham Commission's 347-page chapter on lawlessness in law enforcement and Ernest J. Hopkins' 1931 book *Our Lawless Police: A Study of the Unlawful Enforcement of the Law* (Document 45) underscored the prevalence of police practices that were contrary to fundamental American principles. The candid memoirs of a retired New York police captain (Document 46) also confirmed the common police use of physical and psychological coercion, illegal beatings, and perjury by the police to obtain convictions.

In addition to recommendations for closer supervision and administrative oversight to constrain illegal police behavior, during this era police executives and reformers began to grapple with tough ethical issues regarding the moral construction of police work. The FBI's 1937 "Pledge for Law Enforcement Officers" (Document 49) casts police in the role of model citizens who are principled and dispassionate warriors against crime and defenders of the Constitution. In somewhat less dramatic language, the IACP's 1957 "Law Enforcement Code of Ethics" (Document 54) provides similar direction, emphasizing honesty, integrity, courage, and respect for "the Constitutional rights of all men to liberty, equality and justice."

Constitutional Constraints

The Supreme Court also played an important role in defining limits for police behavior during this period. In the 1936 case of *Brown et al. v. Mississippi* (Document 47), the High Court made it clear that confessions obtained from suspected criminals by torture were inadmissible as evidence. Perhaps more important, the Court's ruling in *Brown* applied the prohibition against physically coerced confessions at the *state* level.

The Court extended this line of reasoning in 1940 to exclude confessions obtained by psychological coercion with regard to a weeklong interrogation in *Chambers et al. v. Florida* (Document 50). In the 1944 case of *Ashcraft et al. v. Tennessee*, the Court went even further, ruling that an alleged confession made by the petitioner was inadmissible in court because the questioning procedure used by the police—

in this case a 36-hour interrogation session—was inherently coercive, and therefore a violation of the petitioner's constitutional rights.

DOCUMENT 43: Uniform Crime Reporting (1930)

As early as 1871, police chiefs nationwide had recognized the need for a standardized system for collecting and reporting criminal statistics from law enforcement agencies nationwide.[1] Such a system would provide the police with vital, long-term information about the nature and magnitude of crime, including increases or decreases, and trends in the types of crimes being committed. However, due to various difficulties and some failed attempts, it was not until 1930 that a uniform crime reporting system was finally put into action (Deakin 1988:138–139; Vaughn 1989b:635).

Public perceptions of a massive crime wave during the 1920s, often fueled by media sensationalism (but not supported by adequate statistics), helped motivate the International Association of Chiefs of Police to take action during the late 1920s (Deakin 1988:140). Determined to discover the *true* extent of the nation's crime problem by developing a method for accurately and uniformly compiling crime statistics, the IACP formed a Committee on Uniform Crime Statistics, chaired by Detroit Police Commissioner William P. Rutledge (see Document 40), at its 1927 meeting. With funding from the Laura Spelman Rockefeller Fund, the committee hired prominent police consultant Bruce Smith (see Document 42) and his staff from New York's National Institute of Public Administration to direct the planning and creation of the system, assisted by an advisory board of noted criminologists and others. The proposed Uniform Crime Reporting (UCR) system was completed by June 1929 and adopted by the members of the IACP at their annual meeting that year (Deakin 1988:142; Vaughn 1989b:635). A 464-page manual, *Uniform Crime Reporting,* written by Smith and his staff and the IACP committee, was sent to police administrators nationwide.

Smith and the IACP then took their plan to Congress, which subsequently passed legislation in 1930 to enable the Department of Justice's Bureau of Identification to operate and manage the UCR. The bureau took over the operation of the system on September 1, 1930 (Deakin 1988:143; Repetto 1977:197). UCR results still are produced each year by the FBI under the title *Crime in the United States.*

Though a monumental achievement at the time of its creation, and still in use to this day, the UCR has been criticized over the years for a number of reasons, including its inability to estimate the number of unreported crimes (Vaughn 1989b:637) and the fact that UCR reporting rules count only the most serious crime associated with a given incident (for example, an incident in which a man breaks into a home, rapes the occupant, then kills her counts only as a murder; the burglary and rape are not reported by UCR).

* * *

The Meaning of National Crime Statistics

[I]t should be stated that the present task has not been undertaken from any desire merely to add to the growing list of statistical year books. The aim throughout has been to confine the police returns to those matters which are essential to the police executive, the legislator, the sociologist, and the public generally. Lack of such essential data has made scientific police management extremely difficult. As stated by our chairman, Commissioner Rutledge, in presenting the resolution which led to the appointment of this Committee, "We are in the absurd position of endeavoring to diagnose and cure a social disease with little knowledge of its causes, its nature, and its prevalence."

For the general public, also, such compilations will have a substantial value. The ever-increasing attention devoted by the daily and periodical press to crime topics has resulted in an ill-defined yet wide-spread feeling of uncertainty in a belief that one is not secure in his life and his goods, that the police have failed in their task of protection, and that all forms of crime are steadily mounting.

In the absence of data on the subject, irresponsible parties have often manufactured so-called "crime waves" out of whole cloth, to the discredit of police departments and the confusion of the public concerning effective measures for reducing the volume of crime. It is true that during recent years there appears to have been an unusual increase in certain types of offenses, such as hold-up and auto theft, the magnitude of which could not be recognized until the agencies of criminal justice had been overwhelmed by the task of combating them. Those in close touch with the situation have recognized what was going on. Their practical experience has convinced them that in certain cases substantial additions to the man power of police forces, or extensive administrative reforms, were necessary. Often, however, the lack of authentic and comparable records of the extent and incidence of crime has made it impossible to demonstrate what substantial changes should be adopted for improvement in the administration of criminal justice.

It is towards this general goal that the efforts of the Committee on Uniform Crime Records have been directed. Its work has been initiated by police authorities and conducted under police auspices. In consequence, there is large promise of constructive achievement, because of all the public and private agencies concerned with the administration of justice, the police alone are in a position to report extensively upon the volume of criminal acts, and the great mass of offenders. Moreover, the police have the greatest stake in the game. They have the most to lose from a continuance of our present ignorance of actual conditions, and the most to gain from its correction. Under these favoring circumstances, this report is submitted in the confident belief that a sound basis for criminal statistics in the United States is about to be laid. With the continuing support of police authorities, that purpose cannot fail of realization.

Source: Committee on Uniform Crime Records, International Association of Chiefs of Police, *Uniform Crime Reporting: A Complete Manual for Police*, second edition (New York: J. J. Little and Ives, 1930), 16–18 (footnotes omitted).

DOCUMENT 44: *Report on Police* (Wickersham Commission, 1931)

Public perceptions of a growing crime problem catapulted the issue of crime control into the national spotlight during the 1920s and early 1930s. President Calvin Coolidge acknowledged the seriousness of the problem in 1925, when he formed the first National Crime Commission. In 1929, President Herbert Hoover took Coolidge's strategy a step further by replacing the original commission with a National Commission on Law Observance and Enforcement (Deakin 1988:114).

Known as the Wickersham Commission in honor of its chairman, former United States Attorney General George Woodward Wickersham, the new commission was charged primarily with examining law enforcement concerns related to Prohibition. However, in doing so, the commission conducted the first national study of crime and the American criminal justice system (Deakin 1988:115; Peak 1997:28–29). In 1931, the commission released fourteen reports on such topics as the enforcement of Prohibition, criminal statistics, prosecution, deportation laws, child offenders, federal courts, criminal procedures, penal institutions, immigrant crime, crime costs, and the causes of crime. Of these, Report No. 14, *Report on Police*, is especially pertinent to this documentary history on the role of police in the United States.

The *Report on Police*, prepared under the direction of August Vollmer (also see Document 33), then professor of police administration at the University of Chicago, by two of his research assistants, David G. Monroe and Earle W. Garrett, analyzed problems inherent in many police departments, paying particular attention to police executives, the selection and training of police personnel, communications and equipment, records, and crime prevention. The report concluded with ten recommendations for improving police professionalism (W. Bailey 1989: 679; Deakin 1988: 115–117; Peak 1997:29; also see document below).

Although many of the findings and recommendations from the fourteen Wickersham Commission reports were not adopted (W. Bailey 1989:680), the ten recommendations made by Garrett, Monroe, and Vollmer eventually were voluntarily implemented by most police departments nationwide. The FBI also adopted many of the report's recommendations for professionalization of the police (Deakin 1988:116).

Following is a summary of the report and its findings written by the Wickersham Commission (Document 44A) and the ten recommendations suggested in the report (Document 44B).

* * *

A. SUMMARY OF THE *REPORT ON POLICE* WRITTEN BY THE WICKERSHAM COMMISSION

POLICE

The general failure of the police to detect and arrest criminals guilty of the many murders, spectacular bank, pay-roll, and other hold-ups, and sensational robberies with guns, frequently resulting in the death of the robbed victim, has caused a loss of public confidence in the police of our country. . . .

1. The chief evil, in our opinion, lies in the insecure, short term of service of the chief or executive head of the police force and in his being subject while in office to the control by politicians in the discharge of his duties. A questionnaire was sent out under the authority of this commission to the officials of 745 cities, to ascertain the length of service of the head of the police force in each city, and replies received from 575 cities, ranging in population from 10,000 to those over 500,000, showed that the average term of service in any of the classifications is considerably less than five years. . . .

It goes without saying that corporate business of any magnitude conducted on such short terms of service by its executive officials and responsible subordinates would have restless, worried and inefficient employees and the corporation would soon find itself bankrupt. . . .

2. The second outstanding evil of such poor police administration is the lack of competent, efficient, and honest patrolmen and subordinate officers. The latter are with rare exceptions selected or promoted from the rank and file of the patrolmen, possibly by reason of seniority, but

more likely by direction of politicians whose private interests are to be subserved. Even where there are civil service examinations, the hand of the politician is all too plainly visible in such promotions. . . .

3. The third great defect of our police administration is the lack of efficient communication systems . . . and . . . equipment. . . .

4. The well-known and oft proven alliance between criminals and corrupt politicians which controls, in part, at least, where it does not wholly do so, the police force of our large cities, might well be taken as a primary cause of police inefficiency, since it rules the head and every subordinate, and lays a paralyzing hand upon determined action against such major criminals. . . .

5. But the inefficiency of our police in failing to detect, arrest, and prosecute the gang criminals can not all be laid to insufficient equipment, incompetency, and corrupt politics.

The excessively rapid growth of our cities in the past half century, together with the incoming of so many millions of immigrants, ignorant of our language, laws and customs, and necessarily adhering in their racial segregations in large cities, to the language and customs of their native lands, has immensely increased the difficulties of the police in detecting crime among the foreign born in such localities and arresting the criminal. The inborn suspicion by the foreigner of all police officers and their unwillingness to expose a criminal of their race has made much more difficult, if not impossible, in our country than in cities abroad, the arrest and prosecution of a criminal and especially any notorious one of such race. . . .

In view of the diversity of non-English speaking nationals resident in our large cities, it seems to us important to suggest that more police officers should be on each force who are of such races and familiar with their language, habits, customs, and cultural background. . . .

6. There are too many duties cast upon each officer and patrolman. This is the outcome of the transition from rural or small-town policing to city communities.

As the urban population increased, no diversification was made in the duties of officers or patrolmen. Numbers were added to the force as the exigencies of the time required without changing the duty of the officer to watch for breaches of all laws and ordinances. This system is virtually in existence in all police forces. It was and is too much a burden upon the capacity of the individual officer and his superiors.

Source: National Commission on Law Observance and Enforcement, *Report on Police* (Washington, D.C.: U.S. Government Printing Office, 1931). [New York: Arno Press and the New York Times, 1971, 1–8.]

B. CONCLUSIONS REACHED BY GARRETT, MONROE, AND VOLLMER IN THEIR *REPORT ON POLICE*

1. The corrupting influence of politics should be removed from the police organization.

2. The head of the department should be selected at large for competence, a leader, preferably a man of considerable police experience, and removable from office only after preferment of charges and a public hearing.

3. Patrolmen should be able to rate a "B" on the Alpha test, be able-bodied and of good character, weigh 150 pounds, measure 5 feet 9 inches tall, and be between 21 and 31 years of age. These requirements may be disregarded by the chief for good and sufficient reasons.

4. Salaries should permit decent living standards, housing should be adequate, eight hours of work, one day off weekly, annual vacation, fair sick leave with pay, just accident and death benefits when in performance of duty, reasonable pension provisions on an actuarial basis.

5. Adequate training for recruits, officers, and those already on the roll is imperative.

6. The communication system should provide for call boxes, telephones, recall system, and . . . teletype and radio.

7. Records should be complete, adequate, but as simple as possible. They should be used to secure administrative control of investigations and of department units in the interest of efficiency.

8. A crime-prevention unit should be established if circumstances warrant this action and qualified women police should be engaged to handle juvenile delinquents' and women's cases.

9. State police forces should be established in States where rural protection of this character is required.

10. State bureaus of criminal investigation and information should be established in every State.

Source: National Commission on Law Observance and Enforcement, *Report on Police* (Washington, D.C.: U.S. Government Printing Office, 1931). [New York: Arno Press and the New York Times, 1971, 140.]

DOCUMENT 45: *Our Lawless Police* (Ernest Jerome Hopkins, 1931)

Although the Wickersham Commission's *Report on Police* (see Document 44) had the greater long-term influence on American police departments, the commission's Report No. 11, *Report on Lawlessness in Law Enforcement*, generated greater public attention and concern (Deakin 1988:115–117; Peak 1997:29).

This 347-page report focused on police misconduct, particularly the continued use of the "third degree"—including the infliction of physical and mental suffering—in the questioning of suspects. Although this method of obtaining confessions had been condemned by a resolution passed at the 1910 meeting of the International Association of Chiefs of Police in Birmingham, Alabama (see Document 27), the study found that it still was practiced in many police departments nationwide. In addition to outlining the problems associated with third degree interrogation and other unlawful practices, the report also offered eleven recommendations for change.

In his popular 1931 book, *Our Lawless Police: A Study of the Unlawful Enforcement of the Law*, Ernest Jerome Hopkins expanded on the findings of the report. Following is an excerpt from Hopkins' book.

* * *

That "Americans are a lawless people" has become the tritest of sayings. We have, in fact, not one kind of lawlessness only, but three: the lawlessness of the criminal, the lawlessness of the average man, and the lawlessness among law-enforcing authorities, particularly the municipal police. . . .

The lawlessness within law enforcement, by its results, might reasonably be considered the most fundamentally subversive of all forms of law-breaking. It attacks the very basis of government. Law-breaking by the police, not of the character of graft, but of the forceful, positive sort, strongly characterizes our national struggle against crime. . . . For the police are obviously our main reliance in the entire trouble of crime that has come upon the nation. The public hires guardians for one purpose: to establish, in daily practice, our accepted system of government, justice and order. They are not hired to warp or to undermine that system, or to establish in its stead some plan of vigilantism, of direct action, which they, from their point of view, may think superior. . . .

. . . No nation whose paid agents were lawless, and trampled upon public and individual rights, ever had anything but a disorderly people and a serious problem of smoldering rebellion and crime. That is true of nations whose governments have made no such humanitarian guarantees as ours. We are not immune from the law of cause and effect in social matters; besides, we have made those guarantees. Citizens must suffer the effects of whatever hatred and antagonism against our public institutions may be bred by the departures of our police from constitutional justice and law. . . .

In no previous period of our national life has a general popular antagonism toward public authority, and distrust of it, been more prevalent throughout the United States. . . . Police graft, paralyzing certain laws, has played a very large part in creating the distrust; but the more positive antagonism has been engendered by the high-handedness and over-riding abuses of authority occurring when police were doing, not forgetting, their work. Street brutality by policemen, loose kidnaping or false arrest, unlawful imprisonment and "incommunicado" imprisonment in police jails, the use of unfair pressure to get evidence and confessions, the perjury indulged in by policemen to gain convictions—these practices have greatly operated to turn the average man against his police and to deprive them of his support in turn. Outrageous incidents are published, and the citizen wonders: "What if I were next?"

This antagonism, thoroughly fatal to successful law enforcement, is discernible today in every class of society, from the more prominent citizens to the foreign-language groups in congested districts. And perhaps no condition has more to do with the failure of police to cope with the emergency of crime than this removal of general public support behind law enforcement. Business men will not confide to the police the names of the racketeers who prey upon them. Witnesses to gangster-shootings turn the other way and tell the police they have seen nothing. Much crime goes unreported because the victims have the intuitive feeling that the police do not represent the law but have become an irresponsible and unpredictable force.

So the police themselves are abnormally helpless; and, in turn, they resort to more and more violent methods—to the direct punishment of arrested persons against whom they cannot produce proper evidence in court, to the eliciting of confessions by third-degree pressure because in that way the suspect, at least, will talk. So lawlessness begets more lawlessness, and the situation shows a vicious circle. Meanwhile, the public suffers from crimes of reprisal, though it has established the rules of justice, laid down the lines of official restraint, and—while it may violate certain sumptuary and business laws itself—fundamentally wants the great standards of American justice, of Americanism, to be maintained. . . .

Attorney-General William D. Mitchell has said: "Nothing has a greater tendency to create lawlessness than lawless methods of law enforcement." The Wickersham Commission put the case severely when it declared: "The fight against lawless men, if waged by forbidden means, is degraded almost to the level of a struggle between two law-breaking gangs." Police have their reply; it consists in the well-worn phrase: "By criticizing the police you are encouraging the criminal." But the answer to that is competent. Only law discourages the criminal. Lawlessness imitates, infuriates, and sanctions him. Our national need is for stronger police; brutality and violence are not strength.

Source: Ernest Jerome Hopkins, *Our Lawless Police: A Study of the Unlawful Enforcement of the Law* (New York: Viking, 1931), 3–13.

DOCUMENT 46: *A Cop Remembers* (Cornelius W. Willemse, 1933)

At a time when police departments were under fire for corruption and lawlessness (Document 45), and reform efforts focused on professionalism (Document 44), Police Captain Cornelius W. Willemse published a book of memoirs from his many years with the New York Police Department that showed another side to the police.

While Willemse made no bones about the fact that police officers generally gave cop-fighters and wife-beaters "some of their own medicine" and often accepted "a few bucks" from grateful citizens whom they helped while on duty, he also painted a picture of police officers as caring and charitable types who nursed lost children and gave their own money away to citizens in need. Moreover, he claimed that "in all my experience I never saw a harmless drunk struck or anyone beaten up who was not looking for trouble" (see document below).

In the following excerpt from his book, Willemse describes a typical scene from the back room of a station house during the "old days" of the New York Police Department. While Willemse's account may be somewhat idealized, it provides an interesting contrast to some of the harsh criticisms of the police that were common at the time.

* * *

ON POST AND ON RESERVE

The back room of the Station House is the experience exchange for the man on post. Every phase of life handled by the Police Department forms a part of the "shop talk" that goes on between the men on reserve or off duty for a few hours. What tales those rooms could tell, and what secrets lie buried within those walls! Sometimes a few words injudiciously carried from those conversations might scatter the good reputation of a life time, but there is rarely a leak from the back room.

To the casual visitor today, the back room would present a quiet, homelike resting place for the men coming from or going on patrol, but in the old days, when one quarter of the entire force was held on reserve and lived in dormitories and back rooms, it was a different story.

Let me picture the back room of the old 17th Precinct on West Twentieth Street. A dingy room about twenty-five by forty feet. On one side of the entrance there was a rack for night sticks and batons. About forty wooden chairs, two large sinks, the only available places for washing off the grime of the streets, a big round table, a pot-bellied stove, a blackboard on which were posted general and special orders and alarms, and here and there pictures of persons wanted. Hooks along the sides of the room held the coats, belts and helmets of the men.

Along with the Station House dog and cat, for every back room has its pets, there were usually lost children. A little girl, asleep on the bench beside the Station House cat, had been there for several hours. A paper bag had dropped from her little fist after she and the Station House pooch had cleaned it up to the last crumb of the cakes it had contained, showing that some cop had done his best to make her comfortable before she nodded off, too tired to wonder any more at her strange surroundings.

Over in the corner a little boy played with the checkers, building and rebuilding imaginary castles. The grizzled old doorman had quizzed the little fellow trying to find out his name and address, for children usually know the nearest fire house, the place where brother goes to school, or perhaps the name of the candy man at the corner or the priest of the neighborhood, but this time he had found out nothing about the child except that his name was Timmy.

It's surprising how far from home these adventurous toddlers can go before they realize they're completely lost and are picked up by somebody. Very often it's the cop on post who finds them and it's lucky for the child if he falls into the cop's hands. Frequently he can identify the youngster from having seen him on the post or, if not, he's a trustworthy guardian and can be depended upon to take good care of the runaway at the Station House until its parents come for it. You'll find him in the back room with the child fast asleep in his arms, doing his best to shush some bird who is making a noise. There he sits, the big lummox, afraid to move for fear of waking the kid—a fine nurse he is, too, with a big black pipe or a wad of chewing tobacco in his face, a gun in his back pocket and a set of wristlets (steel chains or wrist breakers for use on reluctant prisoners) hanging from his belt. . . .

Another glimpse shows a yelling drunk being brought in. When he arrives in the back room, hell breaks loose. The children, if there are any, begin to cry, the dog barks and if the drunk is profane he's hustled out to the cell block with a few kicks or slaps, not enough to hurt him, but just to let him understand he's in the Station House.

When a real bad man is brought in things are different. Wise lieutenants generally send a superior officer down the cell block with this type of prisoner, for, after all the Lieutenant or Sergeant is held responsible for these charges. Cop-fighters and wife-beaters generally get some of their own medicine. But in all my experience I never saw a harmless drunk struck or anyone beaten up who was not looking for trouble. The ones the cop hates most are those bums with political influence who get away with everything in court.

Haven't you ever picked up the paper and read about some criminal who is brought in for committing a dastardly crime and wanted to take a wallop at him yourself? Well, that same feeling exists in the back room. Most of the cops are family men and when a man is arrested for assaulting a child, for instance, you've got to be very careful that nothing serious happens while he's in the hands of the police. Human feelings are the same in and out of the Station House. They're a rough crowd, but they demand fair play, and that type of criminal can't expect to be handled with much sympathy.

Cops, as a class, are exceptionally charitable. They're not the saving kind. They depend on their pensions to take care of them in their old age, so as they meet deserving cases while on duty, they do their best to help. They pick up an extra dollar, now and then, to be sure, but they usually spend it as fast as they get it. Easy come, easy go. I was no exception to this rule. I'm not trying to pose as a saint or a reformer, or one who was shocked by anything I saw. If I found an open door on post, or picked up a man for safe keeping while helplessly drunk, or if I brought a drunk home, found a lost child or warned a man of a violation before taking action, and they felt like slipping me a few bucks, I took it and my conscience didn't bother me then nor does it now. Of course there are cops who have never taken a dollar, at least I've heard about them, but I never saw one. However, if they exist, I give them credit for being so good or for being on bum posts.

Source: Cornelius W. Willemse, *A Cop Remembers* (New York: E. P. Dutton, 1933), 101–105.

DOCUMENT 47: *Brown et al. v. Mississippi* (1936)

Fifty-two years after the U.S. Supreme Court established the first guidelines with regard to the inadmissibility of involuntary confessions at federal trials (see *Hopt v. Utah*, Document 16), the Court made a ruling establishing the inadmissibility of involuntarily obtained confessions at *state* trials.

The case, *Brown et al. v. Mississippi*, involved three African Americans—Ed Brown, Yank Ellington, and Henry Shields—who were accused of murdering Raymond Stewart, a white man. The three men were convicted and sentenced to death in the absence of any evidence against them except confessions by them that had been extorted via whippings and other tortures by the deputy sheriff investigating the case. At trial, Brown, Ellington, and Shields testified that their confessions were false, and had only been made after they had been physically coerced by the deputy and others.

Ellington, for example, had been hanged from a tree with a rope by a mob of white men (with participation from the deputy), then tied to the tree and whipped, at which time he had repeatedly protested his innocence. A couple of days later the same deputy arrested Ellington at his home, and on his way to the jail he stopped and whipped Ellington, "declaring that he would continue the whipping until he [Ellington] confessed" (297 U.S. 278: 281–282). It was then that Ellington finally agreed to confess to any statement the deputy dictated.

Upon being arrested and taken to jail, Brown and Shields also were whipped with leather straps by the same deputy, another officer, a jailer, and several other white men until they confessed, and "as the whippings progressed and were repeated, they changed or adjusted their confession in all particulars of detail so as to conform to the demands of their torturers" (297 U.S. 278: 282).

At their trial, the defendants described the physical abuses they had undergone, and the deputy and others who had participated in these acts did not deny them. Yet despite this undisputed evidence, the three defendants were convicted and sentenced to death.

The Supreme Court overturned the convictions on the grounds that the defendants' "confessions" were void under the due process clause of the Fourteenth Amendment (see document below).

* * *

Mr. Chief Justice Hughes delivered the opinion of the Court. . . .
1. . . .
The State is free to regulate the procedure of its courts in accordance with its own conceptions of policy, unless in so doing it "offends some principle of justice so rooted in the traditions and conscience of our people as to be ranked as fundamental.". . . The State may abolish trial by jury. It may dispense with indictment by a grand jury and substitute complaint or information. . . . But the freedom of the State in establishing its policy is the freedom of constitutional government and is limited by the requirement of due process of law. Because a State may dispense with a jury trial, it does not follow that it may substitute trial by ordeal. The rack and torture chamber may not be substituted for the witness stand. The State may not permit an accused to be hurried to conviction under mob domination—where the whole proceeding is but a mask—without supplying corrective process. . . . The State may not deny to the accused the aid of counsel. . . . Nor may a State, through the action of its

officers, contrive a conviction through the pretense of a trial which in truth is "but used as a means of depriving a defendant of liberty through a deliberate deception of court and jury by the presentation of testimony known to be perjured.".... And the trial equally is a mere pretense where the state authorities have contrived a conviction resting solely upon confessions obtained by violence. The due process clause requires "that state action, whether through one agency or another, shall be consistent with the fundamental principles of liberty and justice which lie at the base of all our civil and political institutions.".... It would be difficult to conceive of methods more revolting to the sense of justice than those taken to procure the confessions of these petitioners, and the use of the confessions thus obtained as the basis for conviction and sentence was a clear denial of due process.

2. . . .

In the instant case, the trial court was fully advised by the undisputed evidence of the way in which the confessions had been procured. The trial court knew that there was no other evidence upon which conviction and sentence could be based. Yet it proceeded to permit conviction and to pronounce sentence. The conviction and sentence were void for want of the essential elements of due process, and the proceeding thus vitiated could be challenged in any appropriate manner. . . . It was challenged before the Supreme Court of the State by the express invocation of the Fourteenth Amendment. That court entertained the challenge, considered the federal question thus presented, but declined to enforce petitioners' constitutional right. The court thus denied a federal right fully established and specially set up and claimed and the judgment must be
Reversed.

Source: 297 U.S. 278 (1936), 279–287.

DOCUMENT 48: FBI National Police Academy (J. Edgar Hoover, 1937)

One of the most notable improvements in law enforcement that occurred during the 1930s was in the area of police training. It was then that the recommendations for increased police training made by numerous Progressive era police reformers, including Leonhard Felix Fuld (Document 25), Arthur Woods (Document 32), August Vollmer (Document 33), Raymond B. Fosdick (Document 35), and Bruce Smith (Document 42), first began to be implemented on a wide scale.

For example, the many new state police forces being created during the 1930s, beginning with New York, typically established their own training academies. The success and prevalence of these state training schools in turn helped encourage local police departments to establish training programs of their own (Bopp and Schultz 1972a:111).

However, perhaps the most noteworthy police training program of the decade was the National Police Academy, established by the Federal Bureau of Investigation in 1935 to provide extensive instruction to exceptional officers from municipal, county, and state law enforcement agencies nationwide (Bopp and Schultz 1972a:102; Fogelson 1977: 144). The FBI academy was the brainchild of U.S. Attorney General Homer S. Cummings, who suggested such an educational center during his Conference on Crime in 1934. Cummings' idea was implemented by J. Edgar Hoover, who, with strong backing from the International Association of Chiefs of Police, opened the national police training school in Washington, D.C., the following year (Deakin 1988:165–166).

Following is an excerpt from Hoover's address at the IACP 1937 annual meeting in Baltimore, Maryland, in which he discussed a number of issues, including the "mounting success" of the new National Police Academy.

* * *

I am extremely happy over the constantly mounting success of the FBI National Police Academy. For this, we of the FBI owe to all of you a deep debt of gratitude for the primary interest which caused you to send your picked men as students and for the spirit of cooperation which has followed their graduation.

You have made this idea and this institution possible. Had you of the International Association of Chiefs of Police not given the National Police Academy your wholehearted cooperation; had you not picked intelligent, fine men to become the members of this student body; had you not followed their progress with the greatest of interest and of friendly helpfulness; had you not upon their return had the foresight and the vision by which to profit from what they learned, the FBI National Police Academy would indeed have been a failure. But today it stands as a constantly growing success, not only of the Federal Bureau of Investigation but for law-enforcement bodies everywhere.

We are only the agency; we possess certain knowledge, certain technical equipment, certain methods of training which you have been good enough to say were foreminded in the field of criminal apprehension. We have been more than happy to act as instructors to your selected men and to give them everything we possess. We have been over-joyed to learn the results and to watch the constantly mounting number of graduates who have received promotion, a number of whom I am more than happy to welcome here as newly installed chiefs of police. Through this police academy, I look forward to the day when there shall be no longer the sickening petty jealousies between the Federal, the state, and the local officer which too often arise to impede the successful consummation of a case. Through education, we shall advance. If we can learn from you and you can learn from us, if together we can advance toward a goal of integrity, of intelligence, of perseverance, of efficiency, then indeed shall we command the respect of everyone and possess the enthusiastic support of every good citizen in our battle against many foes.

Source: John Edgar Hoover, *Present-Day Police Problems*, address before the Convention of the International Association of Chiefs of Police, Baltimore, Md., Oct. 4, 1937 (Washington, D.C.: U.S. Department of Justice, Federal Bureau of Investigation, 1937), 9–10.

DOCUMENT 49: "FBI Pledge for Law Enforcement Officers" (1937)

In December 1937, the growing idea of police professionalism took another step forward with the announcement of the "FBI Pledge for Law Enforcement Officers." The pledge was written by Hugh H. Clegg, a former professor and FBI Director J. Edgar Hoover's assistant director for training, and published in the *FBI Law Enforcement Bulletin*. The pledge was intended not only for FBI agents, but for law enforcement officers nationwide. It was reprinted frequently in the *Bulletin* between 1937 and 1944 (Kleinig with Zhang 1993:43).

* * *

Humbly recognizing the responsibilities entrusted to me, I do vow that I shall always consider the high calling of law enforcement to be an honorable profession, the duties of which are recognized by me as both an art and a science. I recognize fully my responsibilities to defend the right, to protect the weak, to aid the distressed, and to uphold the law in public duty and in private living. I accept the obligation in connection with my assignments to report facts and to testify without bias or display of emotion, and to consider the information coming to my knowledge by virtue of my position as a sacred trust, to be used solely for official purposes. To the responsibilities entrusted to me of seeking to prevent crime, of finding the facts of law violations and of apprehending fugitives and criminals, I shall give my loyal and faithful attention and shall always be equally alert in striving to acquit the innocent and to convict the guilty. In the performance of my duties and assignments, I shall not engage in unlawful and unethical practices but shall perform the functions of my office without fear, without favor, and without prejudice. At no time shall I disclose to an unauthorized person any fact, testimony, or information in any pending matter coming to my official knowledge which may be calculated to prejudice the minds of existing or prospective judicial bodies either to favor or to disfavor any person or issue. While occupying the status of a law enforcement officer or at any other time subsequent thereto, I shall not seek to benefit personally because of my knowledge of any confidential matter which has come to my attention. I am aware of the serious responsibilities of my office and in the performance of my duties I shall, as a minister, seek to supply comfort, advice and aid to those who may be in need of such benefits; as a soldier, I shall wage vigorous warfare against the enemies of my country, of its laws and of its principles; and as a physician, I shall seek to eliminate the criminal parasite which preys upon our social order and to strengthen the lawful processes of our body politic. I shall strive to be both a teacher and a pupil in the art and science of law enforcement. As a lawyer, I shall acquire due knowledge of the laws of my domain and seek to preserve and maintain the majesty and dignity of the law; as a scientist, it will be my endeavor to learn all pertinent truth about accusations and complaints which come to my lawful knowledge; as an artist, I shall seek to use my skill for the purpose of making each assignment a masterpiece; as a neighbor, I shall bear an attitude of true friendship and courteous respect to all citizens; and as an officer, I shall always be loyal to my duty, my organization, and my country. I will support and defend the Constitution of the United States against all enemies, foreign and domestic; I will bear true faith and allegiance to the same, and will constantly strive to cooperate with and promote cooperation between all regularly constituted law enforcement agencies and officers in the performance of duties of mutual interest and obligation.

Source: "The FBI Pledge for Law Enforcement Officers," *FBI Law Enforcement Bulletin* 6 no. 12 (December 1937): 2. Reprinted in John Kleinig with Yurong Zhang, *Professional Law Enforcement Codes: A Documentary Collection* (Westport, Conn.: Greenwood Press, 1993), 43–44.

DOCUMENT 50: *Chambers et al. v. Florida* (1940)

In 1940, four years after the U.S. Supreme Court ruled on the inadmissibility of involuntary confessions at state trials (see *Brown et al. v. Mississippi*, Document 47), it further defined what it considered to be coerced or involuntarily obtained confessions in the case of *Chambers et al. v. Florida.*

As in *Brown*, the case involved several African American men who had been convicted and sentenced to death for the murder of a white man. Also as in *Brown*, their convictions were based solely on their confessions.

In this case, however, it was not necessarily physical coercion,[2] but several days of continued questioning "without friends, advisers or counselors" (309 U.S. 227:238) that eventually led the four defendants to "confess."

The Supreme Court reversed the convictions, explaining that the use of such coerced confessions by the state court was a violation of the defendants' Fourteenth Amendment right to due process (309 U.S. 227: 227–228).

* * *

Mr. Justice Black delivered the opinion of the Court. . . .

Third. . . . [A]s assurance against ancient evils, our country, in order to preserve "the blessings of liberty," wrote into its basic law the requirement, among others, that the forfeiture of the lives, liberties or property of people accused of crime can only follow if procedural safeguards of due process have been obeyed.

The determination to preserve an accused's right to procedural due process sprang in large part from knowledge of the historical truth that the rights and liberties of people accused of crime could not be safely entrusted to secret inquisitorial processes. The testimony of centuries, in governments of varying kinds over populations of different races and beliefs, stood as proof that physical and mental torture and coercion had brought about the tragically unjust sacrifices of some who were the noblest and most useful of their generations. The rack, the thumbscrew, the wheel, solitary confinement, protracted questioning and cross questioning, and other ingenious forms of entrapment of the helpless or unpopular had left their wake of mutilated bodies and shattered minds along the way to the cross, the guillotine, the stake and the hangman's noose. And they who have suffered most from secret and dictatorial proceedings have almost always been the poor, the ignorant, the numerically weak, the friendless, and the powerless.

This requirement—of conforming to fundamental standards of procedure in criminal trials—was made operative against the States by the Fourteenth Amendment. Where one of several accused had limped into the trial court as a result of admitted physical mistreatment inflicted to obtain confessions upon which a jury had returned a verdict of guilty of murder, this Court recently declared, *Brown* v. *Mississippi*, that "It would be difficult to conceive of methods more revolting to the sense of justice than those taken to procure the confessions of these petitioners, and the use of the confessions thus obtained as the basis for conviction and sentence was clear denial of due process."

Here, the record develops a sharp conflict upon the issue of physical violence and mistreatment, but shows, without conflict, the dragnet methods of arrest on suspicion without warrant, and the protracted questioning and cross questioning of these ignorant young colored tenant farmers by state officers and other white citizens, in a fourth floor jail room, where as prisoners they were without friends, advisers or counselors, and under circumstances calculated to break the strongest nerves and the stoutest resistance. Just as our decision in *Brown* v. *Mississippi* was based upon the fact that the confessions were the result of compulsion, so in the present case, the admitted practices were such as to justify the statement that "The undisputed facts showed that compulsion was applied."

For five days petitioners were subjected to interrogations culminating in Saturday's (May 20th) all night examination. Over a period of five days they steadily refused to confess and disclaimed any guilt. The very circumstances surrounding their confinement and their questioning without any formal charges having been brought, were such as to fill petitioners with terror and frightful misgivings. Some were practical strangers in the community; three were arrested in a one-room farm tenant house which was their home; the haunting fear of mob violence was around them in an atmosphere charged with excitement and public indignation. From virtually the moment of their arrest until their eventual confessions, they never knew just when any one would be called back to the fourth floor room, and there, surrounded by his accusers and others, interrogated by men who held their very lives—so far as these ignorant petitioners could know—in the balance. The rejection of petitioner Woodward's first "confession," given in the early hours of Sunday morning, because it was found wanting, demonstrates the relentless tenacity which "broke" petitioners' will and rendered them helpless to resist their accusers further. To permit human lives to be forfeited upon confessions thus obtained would make of the constitutional requirement of due process of law a meaningless symbol.

We are not impressed by the argument that law enforcement methods such as those under review are necessary to uphold our laws. The Constitution proscribes such lawless means irrespective of the end. And this argument flouts the basic principle that all people must stand on an equality before the bar of justice in every American court. Today, as in ages past, we are not without tragic proof that the exalted power of some governments to punish manufactured crime dictatorially is the handmaid of tyranny. Under our constitutional system, courts stand against any winds that blow as havens of refuge for those who might otherwise suffer because they are helpless, weak, outnumbered, or because they are nonconforming victims of prejudice and public excitement. Due process of law, preserved for all by our Constitution, commands that no such practice as that disclosed by this record shall send any accused to his death. No higher duty, no more solemn responsibility, rests upon this Court, than that of translating into living law and maintaining this constitutional shield deliberately planned and inscribed for the benefit of every human being subject to our Constitution—of whatever race, creed or persuasion.

Source: 309 U.S. 227 (1940), 227–241 (footnotes omitted).

DOCUMENT 51: *Police Unions and Other Police Organizations* (1944)

During the 1940s, there was another short-lived effort to unionize America's police forces, similar in some respects to the failed attempt at unionization that occurred between 1917 and 1920 (see Document 34). Like the earlier police union movement, which was prompted in part by high inflation combined with static police salaries following World War I, the police union activity of the 1940s also was precipitated by wartime inflation (Fogelson 1977:195).

This second campaign to organize the police was led by the American Federation of State, County, and Municipal Employees (an American Federation of Labor affiliate) and the State, County and Municipal Workers of America (a Congress of Industrial Organizations affiliate), which issued union charters to dozens of local union branches nationwide (Fogelson 1977:195; Peak 1997:134).

In response to this revived effort to unionize the police, the International Association of Chiefs of Police published a bulletin, *Police Unions and Other Police Organizations*, that made clear its position against unionization. In his foreword to the bulletin, IACP Executive Secretary Edward J. Kelly stated that police unions were "contrary to the basic nature of police duties" and "powerless to engage in collective bargaining or benefit from the closed shop, check-off system, or strike privileges," and that "state and municipal governments are vested with constitutional authority to adopt a policy prohibiting public employees from affiliating with such organizations" (International Association of Chiefs of Police 1944:ii).

The bulletin, which included a review of the Boston union precedent, an overview of the contemporary union movement based primarily on a questionnaire distributed to 198 cities (168 responded) as well as state police agencies (30 of which responded), and a discussion of bans on police unions, among other topics, concluded by arguing that there was little or no advantage to be gained by police officers through union membership (see document below).

In addition to this condemnation of the police union movement by the IACP, the fledgling police unions in Los Angeles, St. Louis, Detroit, Chicago, and other cities were banned by local police authorities, and those officers who refused to cooperate were fired. The courts subsequently upheld the bans, using a military analogy to explain why police, like soldiers, were prohibited from organizing, and by 1945 most of the police unions again were defunct (Fogelson 1977:196; Peak 1997:134).

* * *

WHAT COULD POLICE UNIONS ACCOMPLISH?

Labor unions have accomplished a great deal for employees in private industry, and their legal existence has been recognized by courts of the nation. They afford a medium of collective bargaining to large groups of employees to promote their common interest. The constitutions of the recognized trade and labor unions dwell upon the objectives of securing redress of grievances and of promoting agreements with employers relating to pay and conditions of work. Their tool for furthering such objectives is the walkout or strike. There are few who question either the legality or propriety of *private* employees affiliating with a union for these expressed objectives.

On the other hand, there are many who question the legality and propriety of *public* employees seeking personal advantages through channels normally open to private employees, for they occupy a special position in government and in the eyes of the public—the taxpayer, their employer. . . .

There are many legal citations and legal precedents which bear out the distinctive nature of the obligations and duties of a policeman which supersede the normal personal prerogatives of private employees. Many of these are quoted in full elsewhere in these pages.

Let us examine closely the application of the union principle to police forces. Union benefits to private employees are usually termed collective bargaining in matters pertaining to wage and working conditions, the closed shop, the check-off system, and the strike to enforce these benefits.

1. Collective Bargaining. This benefit is denied to police employees, since courts of the nation have declared that a municipality, county or

state is without power to enter into collective bargaining agreements with its employees. Appropriations for police salaries are fixed by statute or through certain statutory provisions. The legislative body of the state, county or municipality cannot bargain away or delegate its statutory powers and responsibilities.

2. THE CLOSED SHOP. The closed shop benefit is denied to police employees. Statutes, charters, civil service rules and regulations stemming from statutory provisions, departmental rules, or other instruments define the procedure under which police employees are selected and appointed. In public employment there can be no discrimination of citizen against citizen, of union member against non-union member, where other eligibility requirements are met. This has been declared by courts of the nation.

3. THE CHECK-OFF SYSTEM. The check-off system provides that the employer shall deduct at stated intervals the union membership fees of a union member. This cannot apply to police union members, since state or local governments cannot be used as an agency for the collection of private debts.

4. THE STRIKE. Police union members cannot hope to exercise the right of strike to enforce demands. In almost every instance where there has been agitation for a labor union, or where such union has been organized, the constitution contains a no-strike clause. The American Federation of Labor in March, 1943, at [a] meeting of the General Executive Board of the American Federation of State, County and Municipal Employees, directed that a no-strike provision be included in all charters issued to affiliated local unions which comprise police officers. Public opinion is so overwhelmingly against strikes by police officers that to exercise this weapon of private employees would bring immediate disaster to the group. It was demonstrated in Jackson, Mississippi, when 36 officers were dismissed for failing to withdraw from a police union. It was demonstrated in Boston in 1919.

Therefore, if the original tenets and expressed objectives of a recognized trade or labor union are to be adhered to, there is very little advantage, if any, offered to police officers by union membership. Police employees, along with other public employees, are now contributing generously to charitable and welfare causes in addition to deductions for retirement benefits, and perhaps the only privilege afforded them by union membership would be that of adding union dues to their already sizeable contribution list.

Source: International Association of Chiefs of Police, *Police Unions and Other Police Organizations* (Washington, D.C.: IACP, 1944). [New York: Arno Press and the New York Times, 1971, 28–30.]

DOCUMENT 52: *Police Administration* (O. W. Wilson, 1950)*

Orlando Winfield Wilson (1900–1972), like his mentor, August Vollmer (see Document 33), was perhaps the most influential police administrator and educator of his day. One of Vollmer's new breed of "college cops," Wilson was a student at the University of California, Berkeley, when he became a patrol officer with the Berkeley police department, which Vollmer then headed, in 1921. Wilson stayed on the Berkeley police force until shortly after he received his bachelor's degree, with an emphasis in criminology, in 1924. With Vollmer's assistance and encouragement, he then went on to become chief of the Fullerton, California, police department in 1925. However, his ideas proved to be too progressive for the small community, and Wilson was asked to resign after less than a year (W. Bailey 1989:682; Bopp 1977: 6; Deakin 1988:213).

Wilson worked as an investigator for Pacific Finance Corporation for two years before Vollmer persuaded him to return to law enforcement, this time as chief of police in Wichita, Kansas, a position he held from 1928 to 1939 (W. Bailey 1989:682; Bopp 1977:6–7), during which time he made a name for himself as an honest, innovative, and dedicated leader (Bopp and Schultz 1972a:104–105).

In 1939, Wilson accepted a position as a tenured professor in the UC Berkeley School of Criminology. With the exception of military service during World War II, Wilson remained at UC Berkeley until 1960, and served as dean of the School of Criminology during his last ten years on the faculty. Upon his retirement from the university, Wilson was appointed superintendent of the Chicago police force, which was badly in need of reform. He served in this role until his sixty-seventh birthday (Barker et al. 1994:64–65; Bopp 1977:3).

While Wilson's reorganization of the Chicago department was perhaps the accomplishment that earned him the most public attention, his 1950 textbook, *Police Administration*, might be considered his most lasting legacy to the field of law enforcement. This book, and subsequent editions in 1963 and 1972, has been called the "bible" for U.S. police chiefs (Barker et al. 1994:64; Walker 1998:172), a "classic" (Bopp and Schultz 1972a:132), and "the most widely circulated police administration textbook in history" (Bopp 1977:7). The book outlined what has been called the "professional model" of police organization, in which administrative efficiency and a military hierarchy were key, and police integrity, education, and training also were considered essential elements (Barker et al. 1994:194; Deakin 1988:216). In addition to these basic tenets, the book covered such specific topics as police patrol, crime investigation, traffic administration, vice control, the prevention of criminality, juvenile offenders, police record-keeping, police equipment, the design and location of police stations, public relations, planning, and leadership (O. Wilson 1950:ix–x).

In the following excerpt from the first chapter of Wilson's book, he describes the role of police as he saw it, and also discusses some of the problems and challenges faced by the police at that time.

* * *

The Police Function. The protection of life and property against criminal attack and the preservation of the peace have always been the primary purpose of police departments. Police protection must also be provided against the harmful acts, both willful and inadvertent, of the noncriminal as well as the criminal class. In addition, police departments are charged with the enforcement of a wide variety of state and local laws, ordinances, and regulations dealing with all sorts of subjects. Many of these are designed to safeguard the morals of the community, and through their enforcement the police department becomes the principal agency of society for protection against immoral conduct. For every ill or abuse the typical American response is "There ought to be a law against that," with the result that the statute books and city ordinances are filled with prohibitions against conduct which many persons regard as innocent. The American faith in the efficacy of laws, and failure to recognize the difficulties of enforcement, have made more arduous the task of police departments.

Police Duties. In order to accomplish their purpose, the police must control people and their environment in such a manner as to obtain compliance with criminal laws and other regulations. Failing in this objective, they must apprehend offenders so that they may be subjected to treatment intended to diminish the likelihood of future violations by them and by others. Police duties may be classified according to their more immediate objectives as (1) the prevention of the development of criminal and antisocial tendencies in individuals; (2) the repression of the criminal activities of those so inclined; (3) the arrest of criminals, the recovery of stolen property, and the preparation of cases for presentation in court; and (4) the regulation of people in their noncriminal activities (as, for example, the regulation of traffic) and the performance of a variety of nonregulatory services.

Police Problems of Today. New threats to the peace, comfort, security, and welfare of citizens make police tasks today different from those of a hundred years ago, although this fundamental purpose remains unchanged. New inventions and social changes have caused new problems, and the solutions of many of them have required new procedures. It is asserted that crime has been stimulated by immigration and migration, with their problems of assimilation; by blighted slum areas resulting from rapid urban population increases, concentrations, and movements; by the misuse of the press and radio; by alliances between criminals and ostensibly law-abiding citizens, some of them officeholders and political figures in the community; and by the inevitable backwash of war. The adaptation of new inventions to criminal use has imposed additional burdens on the police. The use of the automobile by criminals, its influence in reducing the effectiveness of the home in social and family control, and its more direct influence on delinquency also have affected the crime rate. Traffic accidents and congestion now demand a large part of police attention, and transient populations resulting from rapid and easy transportation have increased the growing list of police problems.

Broadened Social Concept. A broader social concept on the part of the police has resulted in a more positive philosophy of service. . . . The old police philosophy of "throw 'em in jail" has changed to a new philosophy of keeping people out of jail. Police service has broadened to include certain aspects of social service for which the police are particularly well suited; some cases have more than ordinary social-welfare significance, notably those involving the mentally defective, the very young, the very old, and family relationships. Police service today extends beyond mere routine investigation and disposition of complaints; it also has as its objective the welfare of the individual and of society. If society is to be effectively safeguarded against crime, the police must actively seek out and destroy delinquency-inducing influences in the community and assist in providing suitable treatment for the maladjusted.

Source: O. W. Wilson, *Police Administration* (New York: McGraw-Hill, 1950), 2–4 (footnotes omitted).

DOCUMENT 53: Los Angeles Police Chief William H. Parker (1954)

Another noted police reformer of the post–World War II era was William Henry Parker (1902–1966). Parker joined the Los Angeles Police Department (LAPD) in 1927 and worked his way up through the ranks while also pursuing an education (he received his LL.B. from the

Los Angeles College of Law in 1930) and furthering his police training through a number of specialized courses (Bopp and Schultz 1972a: 127–128; O. Wilson 1957:x).

In 1950, in the wake of a corruption scandal, Parker was appointed chief of the LAPD, a position he held until his death in 1966 (Deakin 1988:226–227; Palmiotto 1997:22). He immediately began implementing long-needed reforms within the department, particularly with regard to raising recruitment standards. According to Bopp and Schultz (1972a:128), "six months after his appointment, the Los Angeles Police Department probably had the most stringent selection procedures in the country." In addition to enforcing higher recruitment standards, Parker, like August Vollmer (Document 33) and O. W. Wilson (Document 52), stressed the importance of education and training for police officers. He also promoted the concepts of police discipline, efficiency, and overall professionalism via a militaristic, "war on crime" style (Deakin 1988:228–229; Walker 1998:174).

Parker also was highly skilled at public relations.[3] For example, he and his department served as consultants to the popular television show *Dragnet*[4] which promoted an extremely positive, professional image of the LAPD to the public (W. Bailey 1989:382; Walker 1998: 174).

Although the LAPD and its "California professionalism" served as an example that was followed by many other police departments across the country, the department was not without its problems. For example, Parker's focus on the "war on crime" often prevented him from paying adequate attention to other important concerns such as race relations— a mistake the LAPD continued to make well into the 1990s (W. Bailey 1989:382; Walker 1998:174; also see Documents 59, 87, and 88).

The following document is an excerpt from Parker's 1954 article, "The Police Challenge in Our Great Cities," which was reprinted in a book edited by Parker's strong supporter, O. W. Wilson, titled *Parker on Police*.

* * *

It would be difficult to devise a combination of factors more conducive to crime and disorder than is found in the typical great city of the United States. Rarely does history record so many people of varied beliefs and modes of conduct grouped together in so competitive and complex a social structure. The confusing variety of religious and political creeds, national origins, and diverse cultures is matched only by the extremes of ideals, emotions, and conduct found in the individual. Although proud of their independence, these people live so interdependently that food, shelter, and even their very movement on the streets require delicately balanced co-operation. Although sharing a tradition of individual liberty, their activities are regulated by the greatest and most complicated concentration of laws to be found anywhere.

Charged with maintaining this precarious order by enforcing this confusion of laws is the city police department. Although this would prove a difficult task under ideal conditions, it is aggravated by unusual factors. The police function is rarely considered by the members of the electorate to be a vital element of their life together. Further, its past operation is one of alternating inefficiency, corruption, and brutality. As a result, the individual police officer operates with a remarkable lack of public support, co-operation, or trust. Although this past is a legacy from corrupt political machines erected and supported by the people themselves, the policeman has become a public symbol upon which the wrath for such conditions is vented.

It must also be conceded that the police themselves have failed. Instead of analyzing the causes for lack of support and working toward their eventual removal, police have all too often withdrawn into a shell of "minorityism." There has been a near-fatal inability to recognize police dependence on public opinion, and the result has been great tugging at bootstraps without appreciable elevation.

Increased Interest Manifest

This is the "police problem" that has characterized every major American city in the past and complicates the administration of most police departments today. Yet there are indications that at least some factors are changing. The last few years have seen a great upsurge of attention to this aspect of government and, even more heartening, a growing appreciation of the vital part it plays in the affairs of men. If this rising tide of interest can be sustained, the professional police services our country so critically needs may, within our lifetime, be planned and their foundations laid.

It is inevitable that the police of our great cities will be thrust into leadership in this reformation. The reason is not that size alone attracts superior personnel or confers any monopoly on creative thinking. Rather, it is because the weaknesses of our system are more apparent there. Urban life concentrates and multiplies law enforcement problems. Police inefficiencies which may go nearly unnoticed in the relatively stable pattern of rural life are cast into prominence and grave import by the fast-paced social and economic turmoil of the larger cities. Million-dollar budgets, strangling traffic congestion, and lucrative markets for organized crime make for spectacular police failures. It is here that the public outcry is heard first and loudest, and it is here that sheer necessity puts law enforcement to its crucial test.

The Basis for Improvement

Despite the most aggressive and enlightened leadership, law enforcement cannot rise above the level set by the electorate. *A condition prece-*

dent to the establishment of efficient, professional law enforcement in a community is a desire and a demand on the part of the residents for that type of service.

In this respect, law enforcement does not differ greatly from private industry. The one factor which predetermines the success of any business is the market. Unless the ultimate recipient of a product or service is convinced that he requires it, the most skillful organization and techniques are wasted.

A second lesson the police administrator can draw from industry is that markets are created. They seldom spring full-blown from the unshaped desires of the people. The vital elements of civilized life, including our most sacred institutions, at one time or another have been laboriously *sold* to the people. In this respect, it is heartening that unreceptiveness is not one of the faults of Americans. They respond quickly to new ideas, and peculiarly relish being proved wrong. Despite opinion to the contrary, they respond to large ideas as well as to the small and trivial. They buy comic books, but they also make best sellers of works on art, philosophy, and religion. This is of tremendous importance to the police administrator, because the ideas and ideals he must sell are not trivial ones.

The police administrator's first step toward professionalism must be to introduce to the public a fact which is elemental to every society. This fact is, *the police function is a basic component of man's government by man which has determined the character and permanence of every social structure since human beings first sought collective security.* In the face of the extremes of conduct possible in human affairs, we manage to exist only because we set up and enforce certain limits of conduct. These rules or laws are promulgated, not because men agree on attitudes or conduct, but because they do *not* agree. Thus law, an artificial standard, is necessary to mark the limits of activity beyond which society is injured. Law, standing alone, is a fiction. It achieves reality only when it is observed. The character of every society lies in its method of establishing observance, and its permanence lies in its success in securing it.

Source: William H. Parker, "The Police Challenge in Our Great Cities," *The Annals of the American Academy of Political and Social Science* (January 1954). Reprinted in O. W. Wilson, ed., *Parker on Police* (Springfield, Ill.: Charles C Thomas, 1957), 187–189.

DOCUMENT 54: "Law Enforcement Code of Ethics" (IACP, 1957)

In 1957, the International Association of Chiefs of Police adopted a "Law Enforcement Code of Ethics" that has endured to this day, in a slightly modified form (see Document 86), as the standard for ethical police conduct.

In a somewhat roundabout way, O. W. Wilson (see Document 52) is considered the "father" of the code, which is largely based on the "Square Deal Code" he developed in 1928 as chief of police in Wichita, Kansas (Bopp 1977:42–43; Kleinig with Zhang 1993:91).

During the 1950s, as dean of the School of Criminology at the University of California, Berkeley, and as a member of the Peace Officers' Research Association of California (PORAC), Wilson participated in a PORAC subcommittee that drafted a local code of ethics for the California Peace Officers' Association (CPOA). This code, which is noticeably similar to Wilson's 1928 Wichita code, was adopted by both the CPOA and PORAC in 1955. The National Conference of Police Associations adopted the code in 1956, and the following year it became the national standard when it was ratified by the IACP, which added a set of eleven "Canons of Police Ethics" to accompany the code (Kleinig with Zhang 1993:91).

* * *

AS A LAW ENFORCEMENT OFFICER . . .
my fundamental duty is to serve mankind; to safeguard lives and property; to protect the innocent against deception, the weak against oppression or intimidation, and the peaceful against violence or disorder; and to respect the Constitutional rights of all men to liberty, equality and justice.

I WILL . . .
keep my private life unsullied as an example to all; maintain courageous calm in the face of danger, scorn, or ridicule; develop self-restraint; and be constantly mindful of the welfare of others. Honest in thought and deed in both my personal and official life, I will be exemplary in obeying the laws of the land and the regulations of my department. Whatever I see or hear of a confidential nature or that is confided to me in my official capacity will be kept ever secret unless revelation is necessary in the performance of my duty.

I WILL . . .

never act officiously or permit personal feelings, prejudices, animosities or friendships to influence my decisions. With no compromise for crime and with relentless prosecution of criminals, I will enforce the law courteously and appropriately without fear or favor, malice or ill will, never employing unnecessary force or violence and never accepting gratuities.

I WILL RECOGNIZE . . .

the badge of my office as a symbol of public faith, and I accept it as a public trust to be held so long as I am true to the ethics of the law enforcement service. I will constantly strive to achieve these objectives and ideals, dedicating myself before God to my chosen profession . . . Law Enforcement.

Source: International Association of Chiefs of Police, "Law Enforcement Code of Ethics and Canons of Police Ethics," *The Police Chief* 24, no. 12 (December 1957): 4–6. Reprinted in John Kleinig with Yurong Zhang, *Professional Law Enforcement Codes: A Documentary Collection* (Westport, Conn.: Greenwood Press, 1993), 92.

NOTES

1. At the first National Police Convention, held October 20–23, 1871, in St. Louis, Missouri (see Document 14), some 112 police delegates from twenty-one states and territories and the District of Columbia adopted a resolution in which it was stated that one of the purposes of the National Police Association was "to procure and digest statistics for the use of police departments" (*Official Proceedings of the National Police Convention*: R. & T. A. Ennis. 1871 [New York: Arno Press and the New York Times, 1971]).

2. Unlike *Brown et al. v. Mississippi*, there was conflicting testimony in this case as to whether the defendants had been threatened or physically mistreated during the course of their interrogation (309 U.S. 227:231).

3. For this reason, along with his "ruthlessly authoritarian administrative style," Parker often has been called the "J. Edgar Hoover of municipal policing" (Deakin 1988:228).

4. *Dragnet* first began as a radio series in 1949 and then became a television series in 1952 (W. Bailey 1989:382).

Part V

Social Change and Conflicting Expectations of the Police Role, 1960–1978

CONFLICT BETWEEN IMAGE, EXPECTATIONS, AND REALITY

There was substantial conflict over the role of police in American society during the 1960s and 1970s. Part of this reflected broader social conflict over the just and equal distribution of opportunities and legal protections to all people. Other sources of conflict included disparities between the symbolic role of the police, everyday social expectations about police services and behavior, and the reality of the working-class cop on the beat.

As society's most visible representatives, police officers during this period often were caught between powerful social forces. In public demonstrations, civil rights and political activists counted on being able to provoke an excessive response from the police—or at least being able to create the appearance of one (Document 57)—in order to gain sympathy for their causes. Political leaders and legislators depended upon the police to enforce controversial laws and maintain public order in the face of protests against unpopular and often ill-considered policies. And all the while the Supreme Court produced increasingly restrictive interpretations of constitutional constraints on police behavior. In a time of deep-seated social and political unrest over civil rights, equal rights, the Vietnam War, and which drugs and lifestyles were to be legal, idealized images of the police promoted during the 1950s were pummeled by the fierce political reality of an increasingly diverse and contentious society.

The documents presented in Part V show police work as an exaggerated battleground where many social issues were contested. Symbolically, police officers were portrayed as agents of oppression when they clashed with protesters and demonstrators. At the same time, however, police departments were dealing with the practical realities of increasing racial integration (Documents 57, 59, and 63) and expanding the role of women (Document 56). The actions of police ignited riots in many major American cities during this period (Documents 59 and 63). Yet in many instances it was not the officers themselves who were at fault but rather broad social and economic problems.

On the other hand, public confidence in the police continued to be eroded by officer misconduct. While, with some notable exceptions (Document 69), economic and political corruption was on the wane, it became increasingly obvious that other types of misconduct still were rampant. Police use of excessive force was pervasive, especially against racial and ethnic minorities and the poor (for example, see Document 66). The disrespectful manner in which many officers dealt with minorities and the poor also contributed to tensions and encouraged many of the people most in need of protection by the police to view cops as the enemy.

Despite 1950s reforms in the administration of police organizations (Documents 52, 53, and 54), more adept media relations (Document 53), and substantial progress against corruption, it became increasingly obvious during the 1960s and 1970s that the manner in which police carried out their role in society left much to be desired. Many reforms during this era were driven by government programs that grew out of a series of commissions established in the wake of riots and civil disturbances. Academic researchers also played an important role in helping to identify what the police were capable of doing—and what their role should be—in an increasingly mobile, diverse, and unequal democratic society. Pressure for reform also came from an activist Supreme Court that handed down a series of decisions that set more elaborate constitutional boundaries for police behavior.

NEW FORCES FOR REFORM

Review Commissions and Government Programs

Local, state, and national commissions established to determine the causes of riots in Los Angeles, Detroit, Washington, D.C., New York, Chicago, Atlanta, Miami, and many other American cities during the 1960s drew attention to serious problems with the way police handled relations with minority communities and allegations of police brutality and disrespect (Documents 59, 61, and 63). Recommendations from these committees led most major law enforcement agencies to establish community relations programs that attempted to strengthen ties with minority communities and improve police services in them. They also resulted in more careful review and handling of citizen complaints against officers. Another important change was a concerted push to increase the hiring of minority officers in order to correct the enormous differences between the racial and ethnic makeup of most police departments and those of the communities they served.

The passage in 1968 of the Omnibus Crime Control and Safe Streets Act (Document 64) was another outgrowth of the findings of review commissions and widespread public concern over civil unrest. Unlike previous attempts to legislate improvements in policing, the act provided funds to support plans, projects, and programs aimed at improving law enforcement, reducing crime, and strengthening ties between police and the communities they served. The act also funded research and provided financial assistance that helped thousands of law enforcement officers earn college degrees, at last providing the means for achieving a key goal of progressive reformers like August Vollmer.

The act was expensive and often was criticized, eventually losing most of its funding in 1982. But the act provided a nucleus of college-trained police officers whose ranks include most current-day police managers and executives. It also provided the impetus for criminal justice research that developed steadily and just now is beginning to mature.

Scholarly Reconceptualization of Policing

Scholarly inquiry regarding the police ranged from the esoteric to the applied. Philosophical analyses examined the need for change in the authority and role of police officers (Document 67) as well as the central role that the potential for use of force plays in defining what constitutes police work (Document 68). Psychiatric analyses focused on the ways that frustration arising from conflicting demands associated with the police role could affect officers (Rubin 1972:23–25). Other investigations assessed the extent and prevalence of police abuse of power (Document 66) and the quality of police education (Document 74). In response to challenges raised by his students, one college professor even became a police officer and reported on the surprising differences between policing in theory and policing in reality (Document 71).

Some of the most influential research examined varieties of police behavior (Document 65) and the effectiveness of traditional police tactics. A test of the actual capacity of the police to control crime through preventive patrol—a mainstay of administrative reformers—found that capacity to be very limited (Document 70). Scholarly research, however, probably had less impact upon the everyday actions of police officers during that period than did judicial decisions.

Constitutional Constraints

While scholars worked at the core of the problem of what role police should play in American society, the judiciary was busy defining constitutional boundaries for everyday police behavior. Beginning with the *Mapp* decision (Document 55), which extended the exclusionary rule (Document 31) to the states, the U.S. Supreme Court restricted the conditions under which police could interrogate suspects and the manner in which those interrogations could proceed. It also placed a positive burden on police to advise suspected criminals of their constitutional rights (Document 60).

Search and seizure decisions affirmed the right of police to collect important physical evidence (*Schmerber v. California* 1966) and to perform cursory "pat-down" searches for weapons (*Terry v. Ohio* 1968, Document 62). But, for the most part, the High Court's decisions in this domain restricted the scope of legal searches and when evidence legally could be seized (e.g., *Katz v. U.S.* 1967; *Bumper v. North Carolina* 1968; *Harris v. U.S.* 1968; and *Chimel v. California* 1969). The clear message from these decisions was that police at all levels have an affirmative responsibility to uphold the Constitution, even if doing so makes it more difficult to arrest criminals and assist with their successful prosecution.

DOCUMENT 55: *Mapp v. Ohio* (1961)

In the 1914 case *Weeks v. United States* (see Document 31), the United States Supreme Court established the "exclusionary rule" disallowing the use of illegally obtained evidence in criminal trials. However, the rule applied only to federal trials—no such guidelines had been established for state trials (Peak 1997:268; Regoli and Hewitt 1996:292).

Although some states established exclusionary rules of their own during the years that followed, it was not until 1961 that the Supreme Court made a definitive ruling in which it extended the federal exclusionary rule to the states.

Mapp v. Ohio involved a blatant case of unlawful entry and search and seizure by the police, and a minor crime by the defendant, Dollree Mapp, who was convicted of having "certain lewd and lascivious books, pictures, and photographs" in her possession, which at the time was a violation of Ohio law (367 U.S. 643:643).

The illegal search resulting in Mapp's conviction took place on May 23, 1957. Acting on a tip that Mapp was harboring a fugitive and also hiding illegal gambling paraphernalia, three Cleveland police officers went to her home and demanded entrance. On advice from her lawyer, Mapp refused to admit them without a search warrant. The officers left, but came back three hours later with more officers and forced their way into the house. When Mapp's attorney arrived at the scene, the police refused to allow him to enter the house or speak to Mapp.

When Mapp demanded to see the officers' search warrant, they flashed a piece of paper they claimed was a warrant. Mapp attempted to confiscate the "warrant," but the officers wrested it away from her and proceeded to search her home from top to bottom. They found no fugitive and no gambling paraphernalia, only the obscene materials for which she was arrested (367 U.S. 643:645).

At Mapp's trial, the prosecution was unable to produce any evidence that the officers had ever had a search warrant. In fact, the Ohio court admitted, "There is, in the record, considerable doubt as to whether there ever was any warrant for the search of defendant's home" (in 367 U.S. 643:645). Despite this obvious breach, Mapp was convicted, and the Ohio Supreme Court upheld her conviction on appeal. However, the U.S. Supreme Court reversed the lower court's decision, recognizing that the Fourteenth Amendment made the Fourth Amendment's guarantee of the right to privacy applicable to the states (367 U.S. 643: 660).

* * *

A. OPINION OF THE COURT

Mr. Justice Clark delivered the opinion of the Court. . . .

V.

. . . There is no war between the Constitution and common sense. Presently, a federal prosecutor may make no use of evidence illegally seized, but a State's attorney across the street may, although he supposedly is operating under the enforceable prohibitions of the same Amendment. Thus the State, by admitting evidence unlawfully seized, serves to encourage disobedience to the Federal Constitution which it is bound to uphold. Moreover, as was said in *Elkins*, "[t]he very essence of a healthy federalism depends upon the avoidance of needless conflict between state and federal courts." . . .

Federal-state cooperation in the solution of crime under constitutional standards will be promoted, if only by recognition of their now mutual obligation to respect the same fundamental criteria in their approaches. . . .

. . . Having once recognized that the right to privacy embodied in the Fourth Amendment is enforceable against the States, and that the right to be secure against rude invasions of privacy by state officers is, therefore, constitutional in origin, we can no longer permit that right to remain an empty promise. Because it is enforceable in the same manner and to like effect as other basic rights secured by the Due Process Clause, we can no longer permit it to be revocable at the whim of any police officer who, in the name of law enforcement itself, chooses to suspend its enjoyment. Our decision, founded on reason and truth, gives to the individual no more than that which the Constitution guarantees him, to the police officer no less than that to which honest law enforcement is entitled, and to the courts, that judicial integrity so necessary in the true administration of justice.

B. DISSENTING OPINION

MR. JUSTICE HARLAN, whom MR. JUSTICE FRANKFURTER and MR. JUSTICE WHITTAKER join, dissenting. . . .

II. . . .

I would not impose upon the States this federal exclusionary remedy. . . .

The preservation of a proper balance between state and federal responsibility in the administration of criminal justice demands patience on the part of those who might like to see things move faster among the States in this respect. Problems of criminal law enforcement vary widely from State to State. One State, in considering the totality of its legal picture, may conclude that the need for embracing the *Weeks* rule is pressing because other remedies are unavailable or inadequate to secure compliance with the substantive Constitutional principle involved. Another, though equally solicitous of Constitutional rights, may choose to pursue one purpose at a time, allowing all evidence relevant to guilt to be brought into a criminal trial, and dealing with Constitutional infractions by other means. Still another may consider the exclusionary rule too rough-and-ready a remedy, in that it reaches only unconstitutional intrusions which eventuate in criminal prosecution of the victims. Further, a State after experimenting with the *Weeks* rule for a time may, because of unsatisfactory experience with it, decide to revert to a non-exclusionary rule. And so on. . . . For us the question remains, as it has always been, one of state power, not one of passing judgment on the wisdom of one state course or another. In my view this Court should continue to forbear from fettering the States with an adamant rule which may embarrass them in coping with their own peculiar problems in criminal law enforcement. . . .

I regret that I find so unwise in principle and so inexpedient in policy a decision motivated by the high purpose of increasing respect for Constitutional rights. But in the last analysis I think this Court can increase respect for the Constitution only if it rigidly respects the limitations which the Constitution places upon it, and respects as well the principles inherent in its own processes. In the present case I think we exceed both, and that our voice becomes only a voice of power, not of reason.

Source: 367 U.S. 643 (1961), 643–686.

DOCUMENT 56: *Policewoman's Manual* (Lois Lundell Higgins, 1961)

In 1961, more than fifty years after Alice Stebbins Wells had been hired as the first official female police officer (see Document 28), the role of policewomen still remained, as it had been in Wells' day, largely different from that of their male counterparts.

The prevailing attitude of and toward policewomen at the time is reflected in a statement made by Lois Lundell Higgins, then director of the Crime Prevention Bureau of Illinois and president of the International Association of Women Police (IAWP), in the introduction to her 1961 *Policewoman's Manual*:

If policewomen are here to stay, which seems today to be an established fact, not only in the United States but all over the world, it is not because they have tried to compete against men in work that always has been and will always be predominately [sic] a man's job. It is because they have brought to their work talents that are generally considered peculiarly feminine—an unusually highly developed interest in human relationships—and have accentuated, rather than subordinated, their femininity. (xiii)

Indeed, as Schulz (1995:119) notes, not only Higgins but a majority of IAWP members advocated professional, yet separate, gender-based roles for policewomen. They believed that women were best suited to working with female offenders and juveniles, and until 1972 supported the creation of separate women's bureaus that focused on crime prevention and the protection of women and children (Higgins 1961:xiv; Schulz 1995:119; Segrave 1995:93).

However, while the IAWP continued to promote the idea of separate roles for policewomen until the 1970s, the equal rights and women's rights movements of the 1960s led many policewomen, particularly those in the younger age groups, to seek police roles and promotions on a par with male police officers. They would not be successful until the 1970s (Lord 1989:493; Schulz 1995:127; also see Document 79).

Following is an excerpt from *Policewoman's Manual* in which Higgins describes the policewoman's role, circa 1961, with regard to arresting suspects.

* * *

The apprehension of male suspects or offenders will usually be carried out by male officers, if the arrest is to be made by virtue of a warrant. In such cases, the policewoman will at most *cooperate* with her fellow officers, usually in the role of a decoy or under-cover agent.

Occasionally the patrolwoman may encounter a crime in progress, and, even if the offender is a male, she is obliged by her position to take action in defense of the community. In these instances it is advisable to summon a male officer to aid in the arrest. If none is at hand, the policewoman must rely upon her training in the use of weapons and in the art of self-defense. The employment of judo has been found to be a particularly effective means of subduing male offenders who are inclined to resist arrest.

Besides her superior training the policewoman has another advantage in dealing with men—the element of surprise. A male offender is usually totally unprepared for the intervention of a woman and can frequently be caught off guard and subdued with little difficulty.

Fortunately, however, this type of work is the exception to the rule. The policewoman's powers of arrest should generally be used sparingly, and in many if not most situations her efforts will be directed towards avoiding the making of arrest, towards keeping cases out of court. Furthermore, where an arrest is necessary, she is usually handling members of her own sex.

Male officers frequently experience grave difficulty in the arrest and detention of female prisoners. It is a common adage that a policeman "would rather handle ten men than one woman." Policewomen, on the other hand, are entirely unaffected and unmoved by the usual feminine ruses, such as the use of tears, pleas and sex appeal. Moreover, when a policewoman carries out an arrest, the possibility that the arresting officer may be accused of improper conduct with the prisoner is successfully obviated.

Source: Lois Lundell Higgins, *Policewoman's Manual* (Springfield, Ill.: Charles C Thomas, 1961), 49–51.

DOCUMENT 57: *The Police Role in Racial Conflicts* (Juby E. Towler, 1964)

The civil rights movement that began in the 1950s and intensified during the 1960s created new and often unique challenges for police officers nationwide.

Mass demonstrations and protests were staged in cities across the country, as African Americans sought to enforce constitutional guarantees of racial equality. While most of the protests were nonviolent acts of civil disobedience, demonstrators often sought publicity via arrest and other forms of police response. For example, according to Bopp and Schultz, "Stokely Carmichael, an early leader of the Student Non-Violent Coordinating Committee (SNCC), stated that a demonstration which did not provoke a police response was unsuccessful" (1972a:142).

Such actions often put police officers in a difficult position. On the one hand, they were sworn to uphold the law and arrest those who broke it. On the other, they often were reluctant to escalate the situation via the use of force, or to be perceived as hostile or abusive toward the protesters. As Bopp and Schultz noted, when demonstrations elicited an "extreme" police response, "the entire law enforcement community suffered" (1972a:142).

To help police officers better understand what their role, duties, and obligations should be in handling civil rights demonstrations, Juby E. Towler, captain and commanding officer of the detective bureau for the Danville, Virginia, police department, published *The Police Role in Racial Conflicts* in 1964. The book included descriptions of typical demonstrations so that officers would have a better idea of what to expect, as well as suggestions for appropriate police actions and responses.

* * *

The police role in racial conflicts could involve many situations. This treatment of the subject is more specifically defined as handling civil rights demonstrations relative to law enforcement. It must be assumed that local governments and community citizens desire that law and order prevail. If existing laws are to be compromised as a policy because of fear, or in order to avoid undesirable conflict, then this treatment of the problems of law enforcement will be useless. It is designed to help the administration of law enforcement plan and act to maintain peace and good order in a community torn with racial strife. The police officer must keep a cool head indeed to cope with the legal problems that such tasks thrust upon him. This treatment is predicated upon the assumption that if he is forewarned his task should be easier. . . .

Racial aggressions that stem from civil rights demonstrations are usually well organized. There is usually no real physical danger to the police from the Negro demonstrator. This situation changes, of course, if the races become embroiled in combat. The efficiency of the police effort can do much to prevent racial battles. The community that has confidence in its police department will leave it alone to handle the problem. By a show of adequate police manpower at the points of activity, the public will be inspired to merely be onlookers. Whenever the police department shirks its unbiased responsibility, or when it shows inadequate capability the community then is in for real trouble.

The demonstrators are arrogant in the face of any ordinance or law that restrains them. They break laws with the obscession [sic] that if they think the law is unfair to them, it should not apply to them. An interesting development probably would occur if this obscession was enlarged to the felony crimes. The civil disobedience, however, controls itself with non-violence. This gives the police more opportunity to be alert in protecting the rights of everybody. His own safety is not really in danger unless he brings it on himself by bad decisions or inefficiency. The officer has no cause to be angry because a person violates the law. He has a sworn duty to arrest the violator, but he has no right to inflict punishment. In fact, if he arrests a person, he has the added responsibility of giving that person specific protection. His responsibility to that person after the arrest is greater than to the general public, because then he has taken many of that person's freedoms away from him. Regardless of how arrogant the demonstrator appears against the law, he apparently has no intention of doing physical battle with the police officer. . . .

The racial demonstrators on the move in the streets are actually seeking to go to jail. If they are ignored, they only get worse. To arrest them when and where they break the law is the only honorable thing to do. Unless the community desires to establish two standards of law enforcement the police have no other choice.

Source: Juby E. Towler, *The Police Role in Racial Conflicts* (Springfield, Ill.: Charles C Thomas, 1964), 4–8.

DOCUMENT 58: Police Unionization (1965)

Although two early attempts to unionize the police were firmly defeated (see Documents 34 and 51), a third movement that began in the mid-1950s and gained momentum in the 1960s eventually met with success, due in large part to the changing social and political climate (Peak 1997:135; Walker 1998:199).

Like the two previous organization efforts, the unionization campaign of the 1960s was motivated in large part by economic grievances. However, other concerns, including public criticisms of the police, accusations of discrimination, and the Supreme Court's growing emphasis on the due process rights of criminal defendants (for example, see Documents 55 and 60), also played a role in the rank and file's push for union representation (Deakin 1988:111; Walker 1998:199).

As in years past, the International Association of Chiefs of Police and others attempted to quash this union movement, but the majority of elected officials eventually realized that it might not be in their best political interests to do so (Barker et al. 1994:296; Fogelson 1977:206–207; Peak 1997:135). The courts already had established that other municipal employees, such as firemen, sanitation engineers, and teachers had the right to join unions, and Americans were beginning to support the right of policemen to join unions (see document below). Hence, by the 1970s, police unions had been established nationwide at the local, state, and national level. Today, almost three-quarters of all police officers are represented by unions (Barker et al. 1994:296).

* * *

Unionization of Policemen

Question: "Should policemen be permitted to join unions, or not?"

. . .

	YES	NO	NO OPINION
	%	%	%
NATIONAL	50	38	12
SEX			
Men	46	46	8
Women	54	31	15

Source: Gallup Political Index, American Institute of Public Opinion (October 1965), 17. Reprinted by permission of The Gallup Organization.

DOCUMENT 59: Governor's Commission on the Los Angeles Riots (1965)

In the summer of 1965—just one year after the Urban League named Los Angeles the best U.S. city for blacks to live in—racial tensions there ignited a massive riot that eventually spanned more than forty-six square miles and lasted for six days.

The incident that set off the riot was the drunken driving arrest of a black driver, Marquette Frye, by a white California Highway Patrol (CHP) officer in a predominantly black neighborhood near Watts. During the incident Frye's brother, who also was in the car, went to the Fryes' nearby home to get their mother. He returned with her as a second CHP officer and a tow truck arrived at the scene. Assisted by his brother and mother, Marquette resisted arrest in front of a large crowd of onlookers. Eventually, all three Fryes were arrested, along with two of the onlookers—one of whom had spat on one of the officers and another who reportedly had attempted to incite the crowd to violence (Governor's Commission 1965:10–12).

Exaggerated and inaccurate accounts of the incident and the officers' treatment of the arrestees spread quickly, and the rioting began soon after. Over the next six days, 34 people were killed, 1,032 were wounded, and 3,952 were arrested, and property losses exceeded $40 million. It eventually took more than 13,000 peace officers, including Los Angeles police and sheriff's deputies, California National Guardsmen, and U.S. Army soldiers, to get the rioting under control (Governor's Commission 1965:1, 23; Walker 1998:196; G. Woods 1993: 236–239).

In the aftermath of the riot, the Los Angeles Police Department and its chief, William H. Parker (see Document 53), who long had been criticized for his inattention to race relations (W. Bailey 1989:382; Walker 1998:174), came under fire from the black community and liberal whites for their handling of the situation. They demanded that Parker resign[1] and that a civilian review board be created to look into allegations of police brutality in Los Angeles. On the other hand, many people, especially conservative whites, thought Parker's department had responded admirably (G. Woods 1993:237–238).

To help resolve some of these issues, the Governor's Commission on the Los Angeles Riots, chaired by John A. McCone, investigated a number of allegations against the LAPD and also examined the role the

LAPD had played in controlling the riots, their relations with the black community in general, and ways to improve those relations.

The McCone Commission, as it was known, reported that most blacks disliked and distrusted Chief Parker and saw Los Angeles police officers as "the enemy" (Governor's Commission 1965:28). Many also made claims of police brutality and/or disrespect. To help remedy the problem, the commission made several recommendations, including a larger role in police-community relations for the Board of Police Commissioners, improved citizen complaint procedures, expanded community relations programs, and the hiring of more African American and Mexican American police officers.

* * *

The Problem—Deep and Serious

The conduct of law enforcement agencies, most particularly the Los Angeles Police Department, has been subject to severe criticism by many Negroes who have appeared before the Commission as witnesses. The bitter criticism we have heard evidences a deep and long-standing schism between a substantial portion of the Negro community and the Police Department. "Police brutality" has been the recurring charge. One witness after another has recounted instances in which, in their opinion, the police have used excessive force or have been disrespectful and abusive in their language or manner.

On the other hand, the police have explained to us the extent to which the conduct of some Negroes when apprehended has required the use of force in making arrests. Example after example has been recited of arrestees, both men and women, becoming violent, struggling to resist arrest, and thus requiring removal by physical force. Other actions, each provocative to the police and each requiring more than normal action by the police in order to make an arrest or to perform other duties, have been described to us. . . .

The reasons for the feeling that law enforcement officers are the enemy of the Negro are manifold and it is well to reflect on them before they are accepted. An examination of seven riots in northern cities of the United States in 1964 reveals that each one was started over a police incident, just as the Los Angeles riot started with the arrest of Marquette Frye. In each of the 1964 riots, "police brutality" was an issue, as it was here, and, indeed, as it has been in riots and insurrections elsewhere in the world. The fact that this charge is repeatedly made must not go unnoticed, for there is a real danger that persistent criticism will reduce and perhaps destroy the effectiveness of law enforcement.

Our society is held together by respect for law. A group of officers who represent a tiny fraction of one percent of the population is the thin thread that enforces observance of law by those few who would do otherwise. If police authority is destroyed, if their effectiveness is impaired, and if their determination to use the authority vested in them to preserve a law abiding community is frustrated, all of society will suffer because groups would feel free to disobey the law and inevitably their number would increase. Chaos might easily result. So, while we must examine carefully the claim of police brutality and must see that justice is done to all groups within our society, we must, at the same time, be sure that law enforcement agencies, upon which so much depends, are not rendered impotent. . . .

Complaint Procedures—A New Approach to an Old Problem

A strained relationship such as we have observed as existing between the police and the Negro community can be relieved only if the citizen knows that he will be fairly and properly treated, that his complaints of police misconduct will be heard and investigated, and that, if justified, disciplinary action will be taken against the offending officer. . . .

Under the existing procedure, the impression is widespread that complaints by civilians go unnoticed, that police officers are free to conduct themselves as they will, and that the manner in which they handle the public is of little concern to the higher authorities. This impression is not consistent with fact. Departmental policies set high standards of conduct for police officers in their contacts with citizens, and these standards are conscientiously enforced. In 1964, 412 complaints of police misconduct were received from citizens. Forty-two complaints alleging police misconduct in contacts with citizens were sustained. Despite these facts, the impression that citizen complaints are ignored continues because of deficiencies in the existing procedure. Thus, the clamor is raised from many sources for an independent civilian review board. . . .

To insure independent investigation of complaints, we recommend that an "Inspector General" should be established in the Police Department, under the authority of the Chief of Police but outside the chain of command. Properly staffed with sworn officers and civilian personnel, the Inspector General would perform the functions of the present Internal Affairs Division and would be responsible for making investigations and recommendations on all citizen complaints, whether filed with the Board or the Department. An adequate hearing process for the complainant should be made available at some point in the procedure, and he should be informed of the action taken on his complaint. . . .

Community-Police Relations—A Responsibility for Crime Prevention

. . .

We commend the Board of Police Commissioners and the Chief of

Police for the community relations activities which the Department has undertaken in 1965. These have included the appointment of a Coordinator of Community Relations Activity and a Community-Police Relations Advisory Committee, and an increase in the staff of the community relations unit. Visitation programs to elementary schools and command level seminars on community relations have also been useful steps. But, we believe, a greater effort is indicated.

We propose more intensive in-service human relations training programs for officer personnel; youth programs such as the Deputy Auxiliary Police program; periodic open forums and workshops in which the police and residents of the minority communities will engage in discussions of law enforcement; and frequent contact between the police and the students in junior and senior high schools.

Such programs are a basic responsibility of the Police Department. They serve to prevent crime, and, in the opinion of this Commission, crime prevention is a responsibility of the Police Department, equal in importance to law enforcement. . . .

More Negroes and Mexican-Americans Must Enter Careers in Law Enforcement

Finally, the Commission expresses its concern over the relatively few sworn officer personnel in the Police Department and the Sheriff's Department who are Negroes or Mexican-Americans. Only four percent of the sworn personnel of the Police Department and six percent of the Sheriff's Department are Negroes and an even smaller percentage are Mexican-American. Both of these departments recruit their personnel through the civil service agencies and selections are made on a basis of qualifications without regard for race, religion, or national origin. Despite efforts by the civil service agencies, the law enforcement departments, and some elected officials to encourage Negroes and Mexican-Americans to enter the law enforcement field, the results have been unsatisfactory.

We believe it essential that the number of sworn officers of each minority group should be increased substantially. To bring this about, more active recruitment by the Police and Sheriff's Departments and the civil service must be undertaken. Furthermore, educational and private institutions and organizations, and political leaders as well, should encourage members of the minority groups to enter careers in law enforcement. Finally, budget support for extensive efforts in recruitment, which should perhaps include pre-employment preparatory training, should be provided by both the City Council and the Board of Supervisors.

Source: Governor's Commission on the Los Angeles Riots, *Violence in the City—An End or a Beginning?* (Sacramento: California State Government, 1965), 27–37 (footnotes omitted).

DOCUMENT 60: *Miranda v. Arizona* (1966)

In the landmark case of *Miranda v. Arizona*, the U.S. Supreme Court ruled that once a criminal suspect has been taken into police custody, he may not be interrogated unless he has been informed of his Fifth Amendment right against self-incrimination (Document 8B), his right to remain silent, and his Sixth Amendment right to an attorney (Document 8C). This case is especially important because it cast the police in the role of defending the Constitution.

The petitioner in the case was Ernesto Miranda, a 23-year-old with little education, a long history of trouble with the police, and an undesirable discharge from the U.S. Army. On March 13, 1963, Miranda was arrested and taken into police custody, where a witness identified him as the man who had kidnapped and raped her (Peak 1997:284).

By their own admission, the two police officers who subsequently interrogated Miranda did not tell him that he had a right to have an attorney present. Within two hours, Miranda had confessed. His confession included a statement in which he declared that the confession was made voluntarily, "with full knowledge of my legal rights, understanding any statement I make may be used against me" (384 U.S. 436: 492).

The confession was used in court, over the objections of Miranda's lawyer, and Miranda was given two concurrent sentences of twenty to thirty years in prison for kidnapping and rape. The Supreme Court reversed the judgment,[2] explaining:

From the testimony of the officers and by the admission of respondent, it is clear that Miranda was not in any way apprised of his right to consult with an attorney and to have one present during the interrogation, nor was his right not to be compelled to incriminate himself effectively protected in any other manner. Without these warnings the statements were inadmissible. (384 U.S 436:492)

In a 5–4 decision that included the reversals of three other cases involving similar circumstances, the Court elaborated on these points at length (see document below). Excerpts from its decision formed the foundation for the "Miranda Warning," which is read to all suspects being taken into police custody.

While this warning is well known to most people today, perhaps mostly from television and movies, the Court's ruling in *Miranda* was highly controversial at the time. On the one hand, police officers feared it would hamper their efforts to investigate crimes and gain convictions, and many conservatives agreed. On the other hand, many liberals felt it was an important measure for enforcing citizens' constitutional rights and curbing police pressure (Dowling 1989:608; Regoli and Hewitt 1996:291).

Miranda did serve to increase suspects' awareness of their constitutional rights. However, in most cases "Police officers found it easy to go through the motions of *Miranda* and still get suspects to confess" (Walker 1998:182).

* * *

A. OPINION OF THE COURT

MR. CHIEF JUSTICE WARREN delivered the opinion of the Court. . . .

. . . [W]e hold that when an individual is taken into custody or otherwise deprived of his freedom by the authorities in any significant way and is subjected to questioning, the privilege against self-incrimination is jeopardized. Procedural safeguards must be employed to protect the privilege, and unless other fully effective means are adopted to notify the person of his right of silence and to assure that the exercise of the right will be scrupulously honored, the following measures are required. He must be warned prior to any questioning that he has the right to remain silent, that anything he says can be used against him in a court of law, that he has the right to the presence of an attorney, and that if he cannot afford an attorney one will be appointed for him prior to any questioning if he so desires. Opportunity to exercise these rights must be afforded to him throughout the interrogation. After such warnings have been given, and such opportunity afforded him, the individual may knowingly and intelligently waive these rights and agree to answer questions or make a statement. But unless and until such warnings and waiver are demonstrated by the prosecution at trial, no evidence obtained as a result of interrogation can be used against him.

B. DISSENTING OPINION

MR. JUSTICE HARLAN, whom MR. JUSTICE STEWART AND MR. JUSTICE WHITE join, dissenting. . . .

I. INTRODUCTION.

At the outset, it is well to note exactly what is required by the Court's new constitutional code of rules for confessions. The foremost requirement, upon which later admissibility of a confession depends, is that a fourfold warning be given to a person in custody before he is questioned, namely, that he has a right to remain silent, that anything he says may be used against him, that he has a right to have present an attorney during the questioning, and that if indigent he has a right to a lawyer without charge. To forgo these rights, some affirmative statement of rejection is seemingly required, and threats, tricks, or cajolings to obtain this waiver are forbidden. If before or during questioning the suspect seeks to invoke his right to remain silent, interrogation must be forgone or cease; a request for counsel brings about the same result until a lawyer is procured. Finally, there are a miscellany of minor directives, for example, the burden of proof of waiver is on the State, admissions and exculpatory statements are treated just like confessions, withdrawal of a waiver is always permitted, and so forth.

While the fine points of this scheme are far less clear than the Court admits, the tenor is quite apparent. The new rules are not designed to guard against police brutality or other unmistakably banned forms of coercion. Those who use third-degree tactics and deny them in court are equally able and destined to lie as skillfully about warnings and waivers. Rather, the thrust of the new rules is to negate all pressures, to reinforce the nervous or ignorant suspect, and ultimately to discourage any confession at all. The aim in short is toward "voluntariness" in a utopian sense, or to view it from a different angle, voluntariness with a vengeance.

Source: 384 U.S. 436 (1966), 439, 478–479, 504–505 (footnotes omitted).

DOCUMENT 61: U.S. Task Force Report on the Police (1967)

The social and political upheaval of the 1960s—including civil rights demonstrations and Vietnam War protests, widespread rioting in many urban areas, assassinations, Supreme Court decisions that put new restrictions on police while increasing the rights of criminal suspects, and rising crime rates—led to a renewed interest in the role of police in American society.

For example, in 1965 President Lyndon Johnson established the President's Commission on Law Enforcement and Administration of Justice, much of which focused on the police. Shortly after the commission released its 1967 general report, *The Challenge of Crime in a Free Society*, it issued a separate task force report on the police.

Rather than either attacking or applauding some 40,000 police agencies and 420,000 police employees working nationwide at the time, *Task Force Report: The Police* took a more measured approach to the contemporary problems facing the police and the communities they served. As Bopp and Schultz put it, "The approach [of the report] was conservative, the language was guarded, and criticism was tempered by reason" (1972a:150).

The report addressed and elaborated on many of the issues and recommendations made by the commission's general report. Particular attention was paid to the issue of community relations, which were especially strained in minority communities at the time. The following document is an excerpt from this section of the report, in which the panel discussed at length the importance of strengthening police-community relations, the impact of poor community relations on police departments, the need for increased and improved community relations units within departments, the need to recruit more minority police officers, and the need to provide adequate citizen complaint procedures and reduce police misconduct through improved internal disciplinary policies.

* * *

THE SCOPE OF THE PROBLEM

THE IMPORTANCE OF POLICE-COMMUNITY RELATIONS

The need for strengthening police relationships with the communities they serve is critical today in the Nation's large cities and in many small cities and towns as well. The Negro, Puerto Rican, Mexican-American, and other minority groups are taking action to acquire rights and services which have been historically denied them. As the most visible representative of the society from which these groups are demanding fair treatment and equal opportunity, law enforcement agencies are faced with unprecedented situations on the street which require that they develop policies and practices governing their actions when dealing with minority groups and other citizens.

Even if fairer treatment of minority groups were the sole consideration, police departments would have an obligation to attempt to achieve and maintain good police-community relations. In fact, however, much more is at stake. Police-community relationships have a direct bearing on the character of life in our cities, and on the community's ability to maintain stability and to solve its problems. At the same time, the police department's capacity to deal with crime depends to a large extent upon its relationship with the citizenry. Indeed, no lasting improvement in law enforcement is likely in this country unless police-community relations are substantially improved. . . .

POLICE-COMMUNITY RELATIONS UNITS

Although the Commission's surveys clearly indicate that most police departments are keenly aware of serious community relations problems, they have been slow to institute programs to confront them. A 1964 survey conducted by the International Association of Chiefs of Police and the United States Conference of Mayors found that only 46 of 165 cities either with populations over 100,000, or with more than 30,000 population and 5 percent non-white population, had extensive community relations programs; of these only 37 had a community-relations unit within the department. Only 6 out of 145 cities with between 30,000 and 100,000 population and less than 5 percent nonwhite residents, had a formal community relations program of any kind.

In the last few years there has been some progress. In several major departments community relations units recently have been established. The need for such a unit or its expansion has often been recognized after a major disorder, as in Watts, or after an inflammatory racial incident, as in Seattle. . . . [Nevertheless], most of the smaller departments still have no unit or program; and in many large cities, community relations are handled without any central organization because of lack of sufficient funds, personnel, initiative, or other reasons.

The belief is prevalent in many departments that it is enough if "every policeman is a community relations officer" and if the chief's "door is always open" to citizen complaints, suggestions, and problems. . . .

Although, ideally, every man on the force should indeed be a community relations officer, he also has a full-time job of patrol or investigation. What is in effect every officer's business can end up being no one's business. Even if, as in some departments, community relations officers are appointed in each precinct, this is not a total solution. Without a central unit to plan overall programs, conduct training, represent the force with citywide citizen groups, and supervise precinct-community relations efforts, the job will either not get done or will lack the expertise, coordination, and leadership which are needed. . . .

MINORITY GROUP PERSONNEL

Attraction and Selection

   . . .

In order to gain the general confidence and acceptance of a community, personnel within a police department should be representative of the community as a whole. But the need for competent minority group officers is more than a symbolic one. The frequent contact of white officers with officers from minority groups on an equal basis can help to reduce stereotyping and prejudice of white officers. Minority officers can provide to a department an understanding of minority groups, their languages, and subcultures, that it often does not have today. This obviously has great practical benefits to successful policing. In some cities, for example, the lack of knowledge of Spanish has led to conflicts between the police and Spanish-speaking people. Personal knowledge of minority groups and slum neighborhoods can lead to information not otherwise available, to earlier anticipation of trouble, and to increased solution of crime. . . .

POLICE FIELD PRACTICES

A community's attitude toward the police is influenced most by the action of individual officers on the street. While community relations units, neighborhood advisory committees, and fair procedures for processing citizen complaints are essential for reducing existing friction between the police and the community, these programs will have little enduring effect if persons are not treated justly in their contacts with police officers. This is particularly true of persons in slums or minority group neighborhoods who, because of more frequent contact with the police, are more aware of police practices.

Although many allegations of police misconduct or discriminatory treatment are unwarranted, Commission surveys reveal that police practices exist which cannot be justified. For example, the Commission found that abusive treatment of minority groups and the poor continues to occur. Many established police policies—such as the use of arrests for investigative purposes—alienate the community and have no legal basis. Departments may utilize procedures, such as the use of dogs to control crowds, without balancing the potential harm to police-community relations. And some valuable law enforcement techniques, like field interrogation, are frequently abused to the detriment of community relations. Too few departments give necessary guidance to assist their personnel in resolving potentially explosive social and criminal problems. . . .

ENSURING FAIRNESS

INTERNAL PROCEDURES

. . .

Without question, the best means for ensuring that personnel are complying with departmental policies and general notions of fairness is through effective internal police procedures. Internal discipline can be swifter and, because imposed by the officers' own superiors, more effective. If properly carried out, internal discipline can assure the public that the department's policies concerning community relations are fully meant and enforced. This is particularly true when the department's own investigation discovers misconduct without any citizen complaint.

Strong discipline shows the public that misconduct is merely the action of individual officers—the few who violate the rules in any organization—and not action which is customarily tolerated in the department. Consequently, high priority should be given to improving internal police procedures so that they can satisfy as much of the public as possible concerning their fairness and effectiveness.

Source: President's Commission on Law Enforcement and Administration of Justice, *Task Force Report: The Police* (Washington, D.C.: U.S. Government Printing Office, 1967), 144–145, 150–151, 167, 178, 193–194 (footnotes omitted).

DOCUMENT 62: *Terry v. Ohio* (1968)

During a decade in which the Supreme Court was noted for rulings that often focused on the constitutional rights of criminal suspects—and consequently placed greater restrictions on police behavior (for example, see Documents 55 and 60)—the 1968 case of *Terry v. Ohio* stands out because it expanded, rather than limited, the power of the police.

The petitioner in the case, John Terry, had been convicted along with another man, Richard Chilton, of carrying a concealed weapon. The weapon had been discovered by a Cleveland police detective, Martin McFadden, who had noticed the two men acting suspiciously—walking back and forth in front of the same store window many times, looking inside repeatedly, and conferring with each other and a third man periodically. McFadden, convinced that the men were "casing" the store for a robbery, approached the three men, told them he was a police officer, and asked them for their names. The men "mumbled something" in response, and McFadden subsequently grabbed Terry, turned him around, and patted him down. Feeling a pistol in the left breast pocket of Terry's overcoat, he ordered the three men inside the store, where he removed Terry's overcoat and retrieved the gun. A pat down search of the other two men revealed a revolver in Chilton's overcoat as well. The third man had no gun. Terry and Chilton were arrested, charged, and convicted of carrying concealed weapons (392 U.S. 1: 5–8).

On appeal to the U.S. Supreme Court, Terry[3] claimed that the "stop and frisk" search by Officer McFadden had violated his Fourth Amendment right against unreasonable searches and seizures, and therefore that the revolver should not have been admissible as evidence against him in court.

The Court disagreed, ruling that if a police officer has reasonable suspicion that a person may be armed and dangerous, or about to commit a criminal act, the officer may stop the person and make reasonable inquiries of that person. If those inquiries do not dispel the officer's reasonable fear for his own safety or that of others, the officer may conduct a limited search of the person's outer clothing for weapons, regardless of whether he has probable cause for arrest, without violating that person's Fourth Amendment rights (see document below).

The Court's ruling established for the first time the legal right of the police to stop, question, and frisk a person who is behaving suspiciously, as long as the police officer has reasonable grounds for perceiving the person's behavior as suspicious (Regoli and Hewitt 1996: 300). As Peak pointed out, "This case instantly became, and remains, a major tool for the police" (1997:278).

* * *

A. OPINION OF THE COURT

Mr. Chief Justice Warren delivered the opinion of the Court.

This case presents serious questions concerning the role of the Fourth Amendment in the confrontation on the street between the citizen and the policeman investigating suspicious circumstances. . . .

I.

. . .

. . . Unquestionably petitioner was entitled to the protection of the Fourth Amendment as he walked down the street in Cleveland. . . . The question is whether in all the circumstances of this on-the-street encounter, his right to personal security was violated by an unreasonable search and seizure. . . .

III.

If this case involved police conduct subject to the Warrant Clause of the Fourth Amendment, we would have to ascertain whether "probable cause" existed to justify the search and seizure which took place. However, that is not the case. We do not retreat from our holdings that the police must, whenever practicable, obtain advance judicial approval of searches and seizures through the warrant procedure, . . . or that in most instances failure to comply with the warrant requirement can only be excused by exigent circumstances. . . . But we deal here with an entire rubric of police conduct—necessarily swift action predicated upon the on-the-spot observations of the officer on the beat—which historically has not been, and as a practical matter could not be, subjected to the warrant procedure. Instead, the conduct involved in this case must be tested by the Fourth Amendment's general proscription against unreasonable searches and seizures. . . .

V.

We conclude that the revolver seized from Terry was properly admitted in evidence against him. At the time he seized petitioner and searched him for weapons, Officer McFadden had reasonable grounds to believe that petitioner was armed and dangerous, and it was necessary for the protection of himself and others to take swift measures to discover the true facts and neutralize the threat of harm if it materialized. The policeman carefully restricted his search to what was appropriate to the discovery of the particular items which he sought. Each case of this sort will, of course, have to be decided on its own facts. We merely hold today that where a police officer observes unusual conduct which leads him reasonably to conclude in light of his experience that criminal activity may be afoot and that the persons with whom he is dealing may be armed and presently dangerous, where in the course of investigating this behavior he identifies himself as a policeman and makes reasonable inquiries, and where nothing in the initial stages of the encounter serves to dispel his reasonable fear for his own or others' safety, he is entitled for the protection of himself and others in the area to conduct a carefully limited search of the outer clothing of such persons in an attempt to discover weapons which might be used to assault him. Such a search is a reasonable search under the Fourth Amendment, and any weapons seized may properly be introduced in evidence against the person from whom they were taken.

B. DISSENTING OPINION

MR. JUSTICE DOUGLAS, dissenting.

I agree that petitioner was "seized" within the meaning of the Fourth Amendment. I also agree that frisking petitioner and his companions for guns was a "search." But it is a mystery how that "search" and that "seizure" can be constitutional by Fourth Amendment standards, unless there was "probable cause" to believe that (1) a crime had been committed or (2) a crime was in the process of being committed or (3) a crime was about to be committed.

The opinion of the Court disclaims the existence of "probable cause." If loitering were in issue and that was the offense charged, there would be "probable cause" shown. But the crime here is carrying concealed weapons; and there is no basis for concluding that the officer had "probable cause" for believing that that crime was being committed. Had a warrant been sought, a magistrate would, therefore, have been unauthorized to issue one, for he can act only if there is a showing of "probable cause." We hold today that the police have greater authority to make a "seizure" and conduct a "search" than a judge has to authorize such action. We have said precisely the opposite over and over again. . . .

To give the police greater power than a magistrate is to take a long step down the totalitarian path. Perhaps such a step is desirable to cope with modern forms of lawlessness. But if it is taken, it should be the deliberate choice of the people through a constitutional amendment. Until the Fourth Amendment, which is closely allied with the Fifth, is rewritten, the person and the effects of the individual are beyond the reach of all government agencies until there are reasonable grounds to believe (probable cause) that a criminal venture has been launched or is about to be launched.

There have been powerful hydraulic pressures throughout our history that bear heavily on the Court to water down constitutional guarantees and give the police the upper hand. That hydraulic pressure has probably never been greater than it is today.

Yet if the individual is no longer to be sovereign, if the police can pick him up whenever they do not like the cut of his jib, if they can "seize" and "search" him in their discretion, we enter a new regime. The decision to enter it should be made only after a full debate by the people of this country.

Source: 392 U.S. 1 (1968), 4–39 (footnotes omitted).

DOCUMENT 63: *The Kerner Report* (1968)

By 1967, race riots had become an annual summer phenomenon in America's urban ghettos. The first wave of riots occurred in New York City, Rochester, Philadelphia, and Jersey City in the summer of 1964. The notorious Watts riot of 1965 (see Document 59) was followed by rioting in Atlanta, Chicago, Cleveland, Dayton, Omaha, San Francisco, and some thirty-eight other cities in the summer of 1966. And in July 1967, riots in Newark and Detroit left many people dead and millions of dollars worth of property destroyed in both cities (Walker 1998:196).

On July 27, 1967, President Lyndon B. Johnson appointed a National Advisory Commission on Civil Disorders to answer the following questions: "What happened?" "Why did it happen?" and "What can be done to prevent it from happening again?" (National Advisory Commission on Civil Disorders 1968:1).

The commission, typically called the Kerner Commission after its chairman, Governor Otto Kerner of Illinois, initially held a series of formal hearings in which they listened to testimony from 130 witnesses, including Dr. Martin Luther King, Jr., and FBI Director J. Edgar Hoover (see Documents 39 and 48). The commission members then broke into small teams and visited eight of the cities where riots had occurred. In addition, commission staff members and consultants conducted approximately twelve hundred interviews, opinion surveys, and other research in twenty-three cities across the country. Finally, the Kerner Commission members convened for forty-four days between December 1967 and February 1968 to analyze their findings and write their report (Harris 1988:x).

The main conclusion reached by the commission in its report, disseminated in 1968, was that "[o]ur nation is moving toward two societies, one black, one white—separate and unequal." In other words, the problem was racism, discrimination, and inequality in American society (National Advisory Commission on Civil Disorders 1968:1).

The Kerner Commission made a number of recommendations for change at the local, state, and national level. Moreover, citing "deep hostility between police and ghetto communities as a primary cause of the disorders surveyed by the Commission" (see document below), the commission made a number of suggestions for change within police departments and with regard to police patrol practices in ghetto communities. Many of these recommendations, such as increased recruitment and training of minority police officers, mirrored the recommendations already made by the President's Commission on Law Enforcement and Administration of Justice's task force report on the police (see Document 61).

The following excerpt from the Kerner Commission report discusses the general underlying tensions between the police and the black community, and outlines five specific problem areas addressed at length later in the report.

* * *

We have cited deep hostility between police and ghetto communities as a primary cause of the disorders surveyed by the Commission. In Newark, Detroit, Watts, and Harlem—in practically every city that has experienced racial disruption since the summer of 1964—abrasive relationships between police and Negroes and other minority groups have been a major source of grievance, tension and, ultimately, disorder.

In a fundamental sense, however, it is wrong to define the problem solely as hostility to police. In many ways, the policeman only symbolizes much deeper problems.

The policeman in the ghetto is a symbol not only of law, but of the entire system of law enforcement and criminal justice.

As such, he becomes the tangible target for grievances against shortcomings throughout that system: Against assembly-line justice in teeming lower courts; against wide disparities in sentences; against antiquated correctional facilities; against the basic inequities imposed by the system on the poor—to whom, for example, the option of bail means only jail.

The policeman in the ghetto is a symbol of increasingly bitter social debate over law enforcement.

One side, disturbed and perplexed by sharp rises in crime and urban violence, exerts extreme pressure on police for tougher law enforcement. Another group, inflamed against police as agents of repression, tends toward defiance of what it regards as order maintained at the expense of justice.

The policeman in the ghetto is the most visible symbol, finally, of a society from which many ghetto Negroes are increasingly alienated.

At the same time, police responsibilities in the ghetto are even greater than elsewhere in the community since the other institutions of social control have so little authority: The schools, because so many are segregated, old and inferior; religion, which has become irrelevant to those who have lost faith as they lost hope; career aspirations, which for many young Negroes are totally lacking; the family, because its bonds are so often snapped. It is the policeman who must deal with the consequences of this institutional vacuum and is then resented for the presence and the measures this effort demands.

Alone, the policeman in the ghetto cannot solve these problems. His role is already one of the most difficult in our society. He must deal daily with a range of problems and people that test his patience, ingenuity, character, and courage in ways that few of us are ever tested. Without positive leadership, goals, operational guidance, and public support, the individual policeman can only feel victimized. Nor are these problems the responsibility only of police administrators; they are deep enough to tax the courage, intelligence and leadership of mayors, city officials, and community leaders. As Dr. Kenneth B. Clark told the Commission:

This society knows . . . that if human beings are confined in ghetto compounds of our cities and are subjected to criminally inferior education, pervasive economic and job discrimination, committed to houses unfit for human habitation, subjected to unspeakable conditions of municipal services, such as sanitation, that such human beings are not likely to be responsive to appeals to be lawful, to be respectful, to be concerned with property of others.

And yet, precisely because the policeman in the ghetto is a symbol— precisely because he symbolizes so much—it is of critical importance that the police and society take every possible step to allay grievances that flow from a sense of injustice and increased tension and turmoil.

In this work, the police bear a major responsibility for making needed changes. In the first instance, they have the prime responsibility for safeguarding the minimum goal of any civilized society: Security of life and property. To do so, they are given society's maximum power: Discretion in the use of force. Second, it is axiomatic that effective law enforcement requires the support of the community. Such support will not be present when a substantial segment of the community feels threatened by the police and regards the police as an occupying force.

At the same time, public officials also have a clear duty to help the police make any necessary changes to minimize so far as possible the risk of further disorders.

We see five basic problem areas:

- The need for change in police operations in the ghetto, to ensure proper conduct by individual officers and to eliminate abrasive practices.
- The need for more adequate police protection of ghetto residents, to eliminate the present high sense of insecurity to person and property.
- The need for effective mechanisms for resolving citizen grievances against the police.
- The need for policy guidelines to assist police in areas where police conduct can create tension.
- The need to develop community support for law enforcement.

Source: National Advisory Commission on Civil Disorders, *Report of the National Advisory Commission on Civil Disorders* (Washington, D.C.: U.S. Government Printing Office, 1968), 157–158.

DOCUMENT 64: The Omnibus Crime Control and Safe Streets Act of 1968

In 1968, Congress passed the Omnibus Crime Control and Safe Streets Act. Once called "the most comprehensive piece of crime legislation in the nation's history" (Bopp and Schultz 1972a:153), the act was prompted in part by public fears about increasing crime and civil disorder, as well as the findings of two recent presidential commissions (see Documents 61 and 63) that pointed out numerous deficiencies in law enforcement systems and practices.

Title I of the act established the Law Enforcement Assistance Administration (LEAA) within the U.S. Department of Justice. The LEAA provided federal grants to the states to support the development of comprehensive state and local law enforcement plans. It also funded projects and programs outlined under these plans that were aimed at improving and expanding law enforcement capabilities and facilities, reducing crime, recruiting and training officers, educating the public about crime prevention and cooperation with law enforcement, developing specialty units within police departments, and other areas.

Title I of the act also established, under the authority of the LEAA, the National Institute of Law Enforcement and Criminal Justice, which promoted law enforcement research and the development of new ways to prevent and reduce crime, and the Law Enforcement Education Program (LEEP), which provided financial assistance to law enforcement officers who chose to further their formal education, and also to college students planning to enter the field of law enforcement.

The goals of the LEAA were lofty and its expenditures large, and the agency often was criticized during its fourteen years in operation for its "disappointing" research program (Walker 1998:205), lack of central priorities (Deakin 1988:275), and numerous other reasons. Federal funding was withdrawn by Congress in 1982, after nearly $8 billion had been spent through the LEAA, with little apparent impact on America's crime problem (Schmalleger 1995:153).

Despite its shortcomings, however, the LEAA instigated a number of important programs which today remain a part of the U.S. Justice Department, including the National Institute of Justice, the National Institute of Corrections, the Bureau of Justice Statistics, and the National Institute for Juvenile Justice and Delinquency Prevention (Vaughn 1989a:309). Moreover, the LEAA's contribution to police higher education through LEEP was an important step toward improving police administration and services (Barker et al. 1994:304). As Deakin pointed out, "LEEP, and its parent LEAA, lasted little more than a decade, but provided a nucleus of college-educated officers, many of whom have advanced today to leadership positions in their police agencies, and a tremendous number of officers with associate degrees or at least some exposure to college" (1988:274).

* * *

TITLE I—LAW ENFORCEMENT ASSISTANCE
DECLARATIONS AND PURPOSE

Congress finds that the high incidence of crime in the United States threatens the peace, security, and general welfare of the Nation and its citizens. To prevent crime and to insure the greater safety of the people, law enforcement efforts must be better coordinated, intensified, and made more effective at all levels of government.

Congress finds further that crime is essentially a local problem that must be dealt with by State and local governments if it is to be controlled effectively.

It is therefore the declared policy of the Congress to assist State and local governments in strengthening and improving law enforcement at every level by national assistance. It is the purpose of this title to (1) encourage States and units of general local government to prepare and adopt comprehensive plans based upon their evaluation of State and local problems of law enforcement; (2) authorize grants to States and units of local government in order to improve and strengthen law enforcement; and (3) encourage research and development directed toward the improvement of law enforcement and the development of new methods for the prevention and reduction of crime and the detection and apprehension of criminals.

PART A—LAW ENFORCEMENT ASSISTANCE ADMINISTRATION

SEC. 101. (a) There is hereby established within the Department of Justice, under the general authority of the Attorney General, a Law Enforcement Assistance Administration (hereafter referred to in this title as "Administration"). . . .

PART B—PLANNING GRANTS

SEC. 201. It is the purpose of this part to encourage States and units of general local government to prepare and adopt comprehensive law enforcement plans based on their evaluation of State and local problems of law enforcement.

SEC. 202. The Administration shall make grants to the States for the establishment and operation of State law enforcement planning agencies (hereinafter referred to in this title as "State planning agencies") for the preparation, development, and revision of the State plans required under section 303 of this title. Any State may make application to the Administration for such grants within six months of the date of enactment of this Act. . . .

PART C—GRANTS FOR LAW ENFORCEMENT PURPOSES

SEC. 301. (a) It is the purpose of this part to encourage States and units of general local government to carry out programs and projects to improve and strengthen law enforcement.

(b) The Administration is authorized to make grants to States having comprehensive State plans approved by it under this part, for—

(1) Public protection, including the development, demonstration, evaluation, implementation, and purchase of methods, devices, facilities, and equipment designed to improve and strengthen law enforcement and reduce crime in public and private places.

(2) The recruiting of law enforcement personnel and the training of personnel in law enforcement.

(3) Public education relating to crime prevention and encouraging respect for law and order, including education programs in schools and programs to improve public understanding of and cooperation with law enforcement agencies.

(4) Construction of buildings or other physical facilities which would fulfill or implement the purposes of this section.

(5) The organization, education, and training of special law enforcement units to

combat organized crime, including the establishment and development of State organized crime prevention councils, the recruiting and training of special investigative and prosecuting personnel, and the development of systems for collecting, storing, and disseminating information relating to the control of organized crime.

(6) The organization, education, and training of regular law enforcement officers, special law enforcement units, and law enforcement reserve units for the prevention, detection, and control of riots and other violent civil disorders, including the acquisition of riot control equipment.

(7) The recruiting, organization, training and education of community service officers to serve with and assist local and State law enforcement agencies in the discharge of their duties through such activities as recruiting; improvement of police-community relations and grievance resolution mechanisms; community patrol activities; encouragement of neighborhood participation in crime prevention and public safety efforts; and other activities designed to improve police capabilities, public safety and the objectives of this section: *Provided,* That in no case shall a grant be made under this subcategory without the approval of the local government or local law enforcement agency. . . .

PART D—TRAINING, EDUCATION, RESEARCH, DEMONSTRATION, AND SPECIAL GRANTS

SEC. 401. It is the purpose of this part to provide for and encourage training, education, research, and development for the purpose of improving law enforcement and developing new methods for the prevention and reduction of crime, and the detection and apprehension of criminals.

SEC. 402. (a) There is established within the Department of Justice a National Institute of Law Enforcement and Criminal Justice (hereafter referred to in this part as "Institute"). The Institute shall be under the general authority of the Administration. It shall be the purpose of the Institute to encourage research and development to improve and strengthen law enforcement. . . .

SEC. 406. (a) Pursuant to the provisions of subsections (b) and (c) of this section, the Administration is authorized, after appropriate consultation with the Commissioner of Education, to carry out programs of academic educational assistance to improve and strengthen law enforcement.

(b) The Administration is authorized to enter into contracts to make, and make, payments to institutions of higher education for loans, not exceeding $1,800 per academic year to any person, to persons enrolled on a full-time basis in undergraduate or graduate programs approved by the Administration and leading to degrees or certificates in areas directly related to law enforcement or preparing for employment in law enforcement, with special consideration to police or correctional personnel of States or units of general local government on academic leave to earn such degrees or certificates. Loans to persons assisted under this subsection shall be made on such terms and conditions as the Administration and the institution offering such programs may determine, except that the total amount of any such loan, plus interest, shall be canceled for service as a full-time officer or employee of a law enforcement agency at the rate of 25 per centum of the total amount of such loans plus interest for each complete year of such service or its equivalent of such service, as determined under regulations of the Administration.

(c) The Administration is authorized to enter into contracts to make, and make, payments to institutions of higher education for tuition and fees, not exceeding $200 per academic quarter or $300 per semester for any person, for officers of any publicly funded law enforcement agency enrolled on a full-time or part-time basis in courses included in an undergraduate or graduate program which is approved by the Administration and which leads to a degree or certificate in an area related to law enforcement or an area suitable for persons employed in law enforcement. Assistance under this subsection may be granted only on behalf of an applicant who enters into an agreement to remain in the service of the law enforcement agency employing such applicant for a period of two years following completion of any course for which payments are provided under this subsection, and in the event such service is not completed, to repay the full amount of such payments on such terms and in such manner as the Administration may prescribe.

Source: Public Law 90–351, "Omnibus Crime Control and Safe Streets Act of 1968," in *United States Statutes at Large* (Washington, D.C.: U.S. Government Printing Office, 1969), 197–200, 203–205 (sidenotes omitted).

DOCUMENT 65: *Varieties of Police Behavior* (James Q. Wilson, 1968)

In 1968 James Q. Wilson,[4] then professor of government at Harvard University, reported the findings of his in-depth study of police behavior in eight communities in New York, Illinois, and California. It was the first study to explore the very different styles of policing that were implemented in different kinds of communities (Palmiotto 1997:162).

Wilson identified three different styles of policing—the "watchman" style, the "legalistic" style, and the "service" style (see document below). These styles later were described by Roberg and Kuykendall (1990:41–48) as "neighbor," "soldier," and "teacher," respectively (also see Peak 1997:60). As Peak (1997:60–61) pointed out, the style of policing that a community adopts typically is dependent on three variables: the nature and preferences of the community, the police chief, and the law enforcement officers.

* * *

Five   The Watchman Style

In some communities, the police in dealing with situations that do not involve "serious" crime act as if order maintenance rather than law enforcement were their principal function. What is the defining characteristic of the patrolman's role thus becomes the style or strategy of the department as a whole because it is reinforced by the attitudes and policies of the police administrator. I shall call this the "watchman" style, employing here for analytical purposes a term that was once—in the early nineteenth century—descriptive generally of the mission of the American municipal police.

In every city, of course, all patrolmen display a watchman style, that is, a concern for the order maintenance aspect of their function, some of the time, but in a few places this style becomes the operating code of the department. To the extent the administrator can influence the discretion of his men, he does so by allowing them to ignore many common minor violations, especially traffic and juvenile offenses, to tolerate, though gradually less so, a certain amount of vice and gambling, to use the law more as a means of maintaining order than of regulating conduct, and to judge the requirements of order differently depending on the character of the group in which the infraction occurs. Juveniles are "expected" to misbehave, and thus infractions among this group—unless they are serious or committed by a "wise guy"—are best ignored or treated informally. Negroes are thought to want, and to deserve, less law enforcement because to the police their conduct suggests a low level of public and private morality, an unwillingness to cooperate with the police or offer information, and widespread criminality. Serious crimes, of course, should be dealt with seriously; further, when Negroes offend whites, who, in the eyes of the police, have a different standard of public order, then an arrest must be made. Motorists, unless a departmental administrator wants to "make a record" by giving a few men the job of writing tickets, will often be left alone if their driving does not endanger or annoy others and if they do not resist or insult police authority. Vice and gambling are crimes only because the law says they are; they become problems only when the currently accepted standards of public order are violated (how accurately the political process measures those standards is another question). Private disputes—assaults among friends or family—are treated informally or ignored, unless the circumstances (a serious infraction, a violent person, a flouting of police authority) require an arrest. And disputes that are a normal business risk, such as getting a bad check, should be handled by civil procedures if possible. With exceptions to be noted, the watchman style is displayed in Albany, Amsterdam, and Newburgh. . . .

Six   The Legalistic Style

In some departments, the police administrator uses such control as he has over the patrolmen's behavior to induce them to handle commonplace situations as if they were matters of law enforcement rather than order maintenance. He realizes, of course, that the officer cannot always act as if his duty were merely to compare observed behavior with a legal standard and make an arrest if that standard has been violated—the law itself, especially that governing misdemeanor arrests, does not always permit the application of its sanctions. But whenever he acts on his own initiative or to the extent he can influence the outcome of disorderly situations in which he acts on the initiative of the citizen, the patrolman is expected to take a law enforcement view of his role. Such a police style will be called "legalistic," and it can be found in varying degrees in Oakland and Highland Park and to a growing extent in Syracuse.

A legalistic department will issue traffic tickets at a high rate, detain and arrest a high proportion of juvenile offenders, act vigorously against illicit enterprises, and make a large number of misdemeanor arrests even when, as with petty larceny, the public order has not been breached. The police will act, on the whole, as if there were a single standard of community conduct—that which the law prescribes—rather than different standards for juveniles, Negroes, drunks, and the like. Indeed, because such persons are more likely than certain others to commit crimes, the law will fall heavily on them and be experienced as "harassment." . . .

The concept "legalistic" does not necessarily imply that the police regard all laws as equally important or that they love the law for its own sake. In all the cities here discussed, officers distinguish between major and minor crimes, feel that private disputes are usually less important than public disorders, and are willing to overlook some offenses and accept some excuses. . . .

The legalistic style does mean that, on the whole, the department will produce many arrests and citations, especially with respect to those matters in which the police and not the public invoke the law; even when the police are called by the public to intervene, they are likely to intervene formally, by making an arrest or urging the signing of a complaint, rather than informally, as through conciliation or by delaying an arrest in hopes that the situation will take care of itself. . . .

Seven   The Service Style

In some communities, the police take seriously all requests for either law enforcement or order maintenance (unlike police with a watchman style) but are less likely to respond by making an arrest or otherwise imposing formal sanctions (unlike police with a legalistic style). The police intervene frequently but not formally. This style is often found in homogeneous, middle-class communities in which there is a high level of apparent agreement among citizens on the need for and definition of public order but in which there is no administrative demand for a legalistic style. In these places, the police see their chief responsibility as protecting a common definition of public order against the minor and occasional threats posed by unruly teenagers and "outsiders" (tramps, derelicts, visiting college boys). Though there will be family quarrels, they will be few in number, private in nature, and constrained by general understandings requiring seemly conduct. The middle-class character of such communities makes the suppression of illegal enterprises both easy (they are more visible) and necessary (public opinion will not tolerate them) and reduces the rate of serious crime committed by residents; thus, the police will be freer to concentrate on managing traffic, regulating juveniles, and providing services.

Such a police policy will be called the "service" style, and it can be found especially in Brighton and Nassau County. In such communities, which are not deeply divided along class or racial lines, the police can act as if their task were to estimate the "market" for police services and to produce a "product" that meets the demand. For patrolmen especially, the pace of police work is more leisurely (there are fewer radio messages per tour of duty than in a community with a substantial lower class) and the community is normally peaceful, thus apparent threats to order are more easily detected. Furthermore, the citizenry expects its police officers to display the same qualities as its department store salesmen, local merchants, and public officials—courtesy, a neat appearance, and a deferential manner. Serious matters—burglaries, robberies, assaults—are of course taken seriously and thus "suspicious" persons are carefully watched or questioned. But with regard to minor infractions of the law, arrests are avoided when possible (the rates at which traffic tickets are issued and juveniles referred to Family Court will be much lower than in legalistic departments) but there will be frequent use of informal, nonarrest sanctions (warnings issued to motorists, juveniles taken to headquarters or visited in their homes for lectures).

Source: James Q. Wilson, *Varieties of Police Behavior* (Cambridge, Mass.: Harvard University Press, 1968), 140–142, 172–173, 200–201 (footnotes omitted).

DOCUMENT 66: *Police Power* (Paul Chevigny, 1969)

In 1966, Harvard-educated lawyer Paul Chevigny, whose legal experience ranged from working at a Wall Street law firm to running a neighborhood law office in Harlem, embarked on a two-year study of police abuses in New York City for the New York Civil Liberties Union. The goal of the study was to collect and investigate complaints of police abuse, particularly police brutality, in order to better understand the problem and seek potential solutions (Chevigny 1969:xi–xiii).

Between March 1, 1966, and July 31, 1967, Chevigny received 441 complaints of police abuse, 123 of which he investigated further based on the presence of corroborating evidence, and 71 of which were ultimately authenticated (i.e., the complaint was corroborated by at least one independent witness and the defendant was not convicted on a charge that might explain the alleged police abuse, such as resisting arrest). With some overlap between categories, these 71 complaints included assault by an officer (10), assault by an officer combined with false arrest (18), false arrest alone (17), the search of a home (11), an outdoor search (7), a "frame" by the police (3), misuse of a firearm by an officer (7), not being allowed to speak to an attorney (1), a racial slur made by an officer (1), detention without charge (3), and discrimination (3). Forty percent of the complainants in the 71 authenticated cases were black or Puerto Rican (Chevigny 1969:285–286).

Chevigny presented these findings, along with anecdotal accounts of many of the authenticated complaints, in his 1969 book, *Police Power*. In the following excerpt from the concluding chapter of the book, Chevigny discusses the problem of police abuse of power within the greater context of the police role in society as it then was perceived by police officers—and by the public.

* * *

Police abuses are a set of consistent responses in similar situations, and not very surprising responses at that. The policeman identifies with the office with which he is vested, and considers a threat to that office the most serious of threats to good order. It is misleading to say that his views are unlawful or unethical. They may participate in a different ethic, and perhaps even in a somewhat different law from the criminal law of the modern, liberal state, but unquestionably there are ethics and law at work here. It is a "good guys versus bad guys" ethic, free of the strictures of procedure: the person who is "wise to a cop" has no respect for authority and deserves to be punished. Deviants are undesirable, and the police should ride herd on them to keep them from intruding on the rest of society. A criminal ought to be caught and put in jail the quickest way that one can get him there.

Is this really such an unfamiliar canon of ethics? Doesn't it rather ring of the opinion reflected in most of our newspaper editorials and shared by thousands of citizens? We should realize that the appeals courts ask an extraordinary act of will from the policeman. They ask him to be concerned solely with "enforcing law," not with simply catching wrong-doers. It is an abstract distinction that most of us treat with the same suspicion as does the policeman, and the policeman continues to ignore it partly because we encourage him to do so. . . .

. . . Our criminal law is becoming increasingly rational in the formal sense, as economic and political relations become more abstract, while the police continue to adhere to a kind of substantive rationality. Formal rationality is increasing partly because the rough rules of the police are simply inadequate to the social changes taking place in our society, and to the ideal of equal justice. The conflict in which the police are placed—between their own code and the formal code—is the conflict of modern city administration, and indeed, of the people who live in the cities. The question which the citizens of New York, and of every city which pretends to a liberal administration, must ask themselves is whether they would rather have the police follow their old-fashioned rules, or whether they really want the police to adhere to the formally rational (and substantively different) rules of due process of law. It is clear that there is something in most of us that does not want the police to change; the landslide vote against a civilian review board demonstrated that, if nothing else. We want efficiency, quick work, order above all, though we claim to want due process and equal justice as well. Without basic changes to eliminate the obvious injustices in our society, we cannot expect to have all these, but if all else fails, we think we would like to preserve at least the appearance of order ("peace and quiet"). It is for the police to play the tough, no-nonsense half of this conflict. The enlightened feel a little guilty about their own impulse to coerce respect by force, and it is easier for them to turn the police into a whipping boy than to admit to such instincts themselves. The police do all the "wrong" things—club people who are outcasts or defiant of authority—but the unfortunate truth is that much public disapproval of their actions is sheer hypocrisy. Many, perhaps most, citizens feel that it is desirable for a policeman to coerce adherence to his code by punching a "wise kid" or ransacking an apartment without a warrant. They hide from themselves the fact that every act which coerces obedience from a man by unlawful means is by definition an act of oppression. . . .

For legislators and judges the police are a godsend, because all the acts of oppression that must be performed in this society to keep it running smoothly are pushed upon the police. The police get the blame, and the officials stay free of the stigma of approving their highhanded acts. The police have become the repository of all the illiberal impulses in this liberal society; they are under heavy fire because most of us no longer admit so readily to our illiberal impulses as we once did.

The welter of statutes intended to control morality by penalizing the possession of some contraband, or the act of vagrancy or loitering, pointedly reveals the hypocrisy in the administration of our laws. The legislature passes such statutes, knowing quite well that their enforcement encourages a host of police abuses, including unlawful searches, dragnet arrests, and systematic harassment. The links between these abuses and morals legislation is no accident; the impulse in each is the same. It is the drive to legislate the lives of others and to force them to adhere to an accepted mode of life; that impulse cannot be enforced without abusing the rights of citizens.

Viewed in this light, the distortions of fact by policemen, which we have pronounced at once the most dangerous and the most pervasive of abuses, do not seem quite so shocking or unnatural. Lying is a bridge between the substantively rational rules of the police and the formally rational ones of the criminal law, by which the first are made to appear to conform to the second.

The actions of the police probably embody a natural tendency of any group of bureaucrats, working out in the field where their decisions have low visibility, to avoid the effect of restrictive regulations that conflict with existing practices. A book similar to this could perhaps be written about welfare workers or even public school administrators. The effects of the conflict between rule and practice are more dramatic in the case of the police than of other bureaucrats because the victims of their practices wind up in jail, and more prolonged and exaggerated because of the traditional solidarity and secrecy of the police. Like many other minor bureaucrats before them, however, the police continue to adhere to their old customs because they know that their superiors and much of the rest of society approves. They have no motive to change. . . .

The saddest aspect of police abuses is that they defeat their avowed purposes. The rationalization for street abuses is that they create or at least maintain respect for authority. Punishment for the wise guy is supposed to "teach him a lesson," but the system of police abuses creates only contempt for authority. A man, and especially the already defiant black man in this country, does not feel respect when he is clubbed, when he is charged with a crime, and when he loses his only job because he has been convicted. Words cannot convey the despair, the hatred, induced by a system which injures a man and then brands him as a criminal. It is not enough to say that the behavior of all the administrators involved—the officer, his superiors, the prosecutor, the judge—is understandable The system within which the police work is evil, for the simplest of reasons: because it injures people and destroys their respect for the legal process. It is not for nothing that ghetto people have chosen police abuses as the symbol of oppression; it is because they actually *are* acts of oppression.

This brings us back to the importance of police abuses and the urgency of the problem they present. They are hardly the only acts of oppression in our cities, but they are the easiest to recognize. The anger they instill is part of the fuel for the violent uprisings in our cities during the past five years. As an indispensable condition for ending those uprisings, the police must change their allegiance from a private code to a publicly recognized rule of law, and it is only when society itself demands this change that it will take place.

Source: Paul Chevigny, *Police Power: Police Abuses in New York City* (New York: Vintage Books, 1969), 278–283.

DOCUMENT 67: "The Role of the Police in Modern Society" (T. A. Fleek and T. J. Newnam, 1969)

As the turbulent 1960s came to a close, it seemed apparent to some researchers that it was time to redefine the role of police in American society. In the March–April 1969 issue of the journal *Police*, Colonel T. A. Fleek, then Director of Security Police for the Pacific Air Forces, and Lt. Colonel T. J. Newnam, then Executive, Directorate of Security Police for the United States Air Force headquarters, argued that amid an atmosphere of social discord, increasing crime and violence, and civil disorder, traditional societal views of the role and mission of police were no longer adequate for maintaining social control. Their article is excerpted below.

* * *

Whatever else future historians may say of the mid 1960's, it is likely that they will recognize these years as the period when the problems of police operations in a modern society finally became matters of direct interest to practically all segments of that society.

... [I]n this present period of social unrest, when crime, lawlessness, civil disorder and violence have intruded into all our daily affairs and have threatened our personal well-being, the role of the police, as protectors of the public welfare and as the primary means of exercising social control, has become justifiably a matter of widespread social concern.

This resulting spotlight on police activities has highlighted a distinct and glaring need for clarification of the police mission itself. It seems all too plain that our traditional ideas of what a policeman should be, what he should do, and how a police department should be organized, manned and operated, will not serve to meet the demands and problems of social control inherent in the development of our twentieth century society.

At the same time, it has also become obvious that not all our complex problems of social control are going to be alleviated merely by improving the capability to police ourselves. Rising crime rates, riots, racial unrest and disturbances, all point to the existence of deeper, more basic issues inherent in the growth and evolution of an extremely complex, urban-centered, highly technological society.

The policing activity must necessarily be only one aspect of social control; a problem which, in a highly-organized society, should inevitably directly affect and concern every member of that society. The public must not only understand complicated control and regulatory problems, but also have an understanding of and participation in the formulation of the police role and mission. . . .

Source: T. A. Fleek and T. J. Newnam, "The Role of the Police in Modern Society," *Police*, March–April 1969, 21–27. Reprinted in Harry W. More, Jr., ed., *Critical Issues in Law Enforcement* (Cincinnati: W. H. Anderson, 1972), 7–8.

DOCUMENT 68: "The Capacity to Use Force as the Core of the Police Role" (Egon Bittner, 1970)

In 1970, Brandeis University professor Egon Bittner proposed the concept that the central, unifying theme underlying the police role was not law enforcement or crime control, but rather the capacity to use force. In his monograph *The Functions of the Police in Modern Society*, published by the National Institute of Mental Health as part of its series on current issues and directions in crime and delinquency, Bittner argued that "the role of the police is to address all sorts of human problems when and insofar as their solutions do or may possibly require the use of force at the point of their occurrence" (1970:44).

Bittner acknowledged that it was likely that very few routine police encounters with the public involved the direct use of force. However, he pointed out, "What matters is that police procedure is defined by the feature that it may not be opposed in its course, and that force can be used if it is opposed" (1970:41).

Following is an excerpt from Bittner's monograph.

* * *

After reviewing briefly what the public appears to expect of the police, the range of activities police actually engage in, and the theme that unifies all these activities, it was suggested that *the role of the police is best understood as a mechanism for the distribution of non-negotiably coercive force employed in accordance with the dictates of an intuitive grasp of situational exigencies.*

It is, of course, not surprising that a society committed to the establishment of peace by pacific means and to the abolishment of all forms of violence from the fabric of its social relations, at least as a matter of official morality and policy, would establish a corps of specially deputized officials endowed with the exclusive monopoly of using force contingently where limitations of foresight fail to provide alternatives. That is, given the melancholy appreciation of the fact that the total abolition of force is not attainable, the closest approximation to the ideal is to limit it as a special and exclusive trust. If it is the case, however, that the mandate of the police is organized around their capacity and authority to use force, that is, if this is what the institution's existence makes available to society, then the evaluation of that institution's performance must focus on it. While it is quite true that policemen will have to be judged on other dimensions of competence, too—for example, the exercise of force against criminal suspects requires some knowledge about crime and criminal law—their methods as society's agents of coercion will have to be considered central to the overall judgment.

The proposed definition of the police role entails a difficult moral problem. How can we arrive at a favorable or even accepting judgment about an activity which is, in its very conception, opposed to the ethos of the polity that authorizes it? Is it not well nigh inevitable that this mandate be concealed in circumlocution? While solving puzzles of moral philosophy is beyond the scope of this analysis, we will have to address this question in a somewhat more mundane formulation: namely, on what terms can a society dedicated to peace institutionalize the exercise of force?

It appears that in our society two answers to this question are acceptable. One defines the targets of legitimate force as enemies and the coercive advance against them as warfare. Those who wage this war are expected to be possessed by the military virtues of valor, obedience, and *esprit de corps.* The enterprise as a whole is justified as a sacrificial and glorious mission in which the warrior's duty is "not to reason why." The other answer involves an altogether different imagery. The targets of force are conceived as practical objectives and their attainment a matter of practical expediency. The process involves prudence, economy, and considered judgment, from case to case. The enterprise as a whole is conceived as a public trust, the exercise of which is vested in individual practitioners who are personally responsible for their decisions and actions.

Reflection suggests that the two patterns are profoundly incompatible. Remarkably, however, our police departments have not been deterred from attempting the reconciliation of the irreconcilable. Thus, our policemen are exposed to the demand of a conflicting nature in that their actions are supposed to reflect both military prowess and professional acumen.

Source: Egon Bittner, *The Functions of the Police in Modern Society* (Chevy Chase, Md.: National Institute of Mental Health, Center for Studies of Crime and Delinquency, 1970), 46–47.

DOCUMENT 69: *The Knapp Commission Report on Police Corruption* (1972)

The New York City Police Department, infamous during the late nineteenth century for widespread corruption under Tammany rule (see Document 22), was rocked by an even greater police corruption scandal during the early 1970s. Long before the scandal became public, New York City police officer Frank Serpico[5] made allegations of corruption within the department that were largely ignored by police officials and politicians. Unable to get results within the system, Serpico finally went to the press with his story (Maas 1973:11). On April 25, 1970, following a six-month investigation prompted by Serpico's allegations, the *New York Times* printed a lengthy exposé of New York City police corruption (Burnham 1970). In response to the *Times* article, Mayor John V. Lindsay of New York City appointed an interdepartmental committee to review these charges. The committee in turn recommended that an independent citizens' commission be established to determine the nature and extent of police corruption, evaluate the department's procedures for handling reports of corruption, and recommend ways to improve these procedures (Commission to Investigate Allegations of Police Corruption 1973:1).

Called the Knapp Commission after its chairman, United States District Judge Whitman Knapp, the commission took two and one-half years to complete its investigation, during which time Serpico and numerous others testified before the commission in a series of widely publicized and televised hearings. The findings of the commission—a summary was released on August 3, 1972, and the complete report was issued on December 26, 1972—were shocking. According to the report, more than 50 percent of the city's 29,600 police officers had participated in some form of corrupt activity (Inciardi 1993:277).

The commission report divided these corrupt cops into two categories—"grass eaters," who did not seek bribes and payoffs but took them when they were offered, and "meat eaters," who actively and aggressively engaged in corrupt practices, such as collecting regular payments from illegal gambling establishments or narcotics violators. Although the commission concluded that most corrupt police officers were of the more minor "grass eater" variety, this finding did not detract from the disheartening fact that many of New York's "finest" were corrupt.

By the time the Knapp Commission report was released in late 1972, many reforms already were under way within the department. Police Commissioner Howard R. Leary, who resigned in 1970 in the wake of the *New York Times* article, had been replaced by Patrick V. Murphy (see Document 73), who immediately set out to reform the department and eliminate corruption. Murphy's efforts, combined with the work of the commission, led Mayor Lindsay to assert, "There is good reason to believe that the problems faced by Patrolman Serpico six years ago would not recur today" (Commission to Investitate Allegations of Police Corruption 1973).

* * *

SUMMARY

The Extent of Police Corruption

We found corruption to be widespread. It took various forms depending upon the activity involved, appearing at its most sophisticated among plainclothesmen assigned to enforcing gambling laws. In the five plainclothes divisions where our investigations were concentrated we found a strikingly standardized pattern of corruption. Plainclothesmen, participating in what is known in police parlance as a "pad," collected regular bi-weekly or monthly payments amounting to as much as $3,500 from each of the gambling establishments in the area under their jurisdiction, and divided the take in equal shares. The monthly share per man (called the "nut") ranged from $300 and $400 in midtown Manhattan to $1,500 in Harlem. When supervisors were involved they received a share and a half. A newly assigned plainclothesman was not entitled to his share for about two months, while he was checked out for reliability, but the earnings lost by the delay were made up to him in the form of two months' severance pay when he left the division.

Evidence before us led us to the conclusion that the same pattern existed in the remaining divisions which we did not investigate in depth. This conclusion was confirmed by events occurring before and after the period of our investigation. Prior to the Commission's existence, exposures by former plainclothesman Frank Serpico had led to indictments or departmental charges against nineteen plainclothesmen in a Bronx division for involvement in a pad where the nut was $800. After our public hearings had been completed, an investigation conducted by the Kings County District Attorney and the Department's Internal Affairs Division—which investigation neither the Commission nor its staff had even known about—resulted in indictments and charges against thirty-seven Brooklyn plainclothesmen who had participated in a pad with a nut of $1,200. The manner of operation of the pad involved in each of these situations was in every detail identical to that described at the Commission hearings, and in each almost every plainclothesman in the division, including supervisory lieutenants, was implicated.

Corruption in narcotics enforcement lacked the organization of the gambling pads, but individual payments—known as "scores"—were commonly received and could be staggering in amount. Our investigation, a concurrent probe by the State Investigation Commission and prosecutions by Federal and local authorities all revealed a pattern whereby corrupt officers customarily collected scores in substantial amounts from narcotics violators. These scores were either kept by the individual officer or shared with a partner and, perhaps, a superior officer. They ranged from minor shakedowns to payments of many thousands of dollars, the largest narcotics payoff uncovered in our investigation having been $80,000. According to information developed by the S.I.C. and in recent Federal investigations, the size of this score was by no means unique.

Corruption among detectives assigned to general investigative duties also took the form of shakedowns of individual targets of opportunity. Although these scores were not in the huge amounts found in narcotics, they not infrequently came to several thousand dollars.

Uniformed patrolmen assigned to street duties were not found to receive money on nearly so grand or organized a scale, but the large number of small payments they received present an equally serious if less dramatic problem. Uniformed patrolmen, particularly those assigned to radio patrol cars, participated in gambling pads more modest in size than those received by plainclothes units and received regular payments from construction sites, bars, grocery stores and other business establishments. These payments were usually made on a regular basis to sector car patrolmen and on a haphazard basis to others. While individual payments to uniformed men were small, mostly under $20, they were often so numerous as to add substantially to a patrolman's income. Other less regular payments to uniformed patrolmen included those made by after-hours bars, bottle clubs, tow trucks, motorists, cab drivers, parking lots, prostitutes and defendants wanting to fix their cases in court. Another practice found to be widespread was the payment of gratuities by policemen to other policemen to expedite normal police procedures or to gain favorable assignments.

Sergeants and lieutenants who were so inclined participated in the same kind of corruption as the men they supervised. In addition, some sergeants had their own pads from which patrolmen were excluded.

Although the Commission was unable to develop hard evidence establishing that officers above the rank of lieutenant received payoffs, considerable circumstantial evidence and some testimony so indicated. Most often when a superior officer is corrupt, he uses a patrolman as his "bagman" who collects for him and keeps a percentage of the take. Because the bagman may keep the money for himself, although he claims to be collecting for his superior, it is extremely difficult to determine with any accuracy when the superior actually is involved.

Of course, not all policemen are corrupt. If we are to exclude such petty infractions as free meals, an appreciable number do not engage in any corrupt activities. Yet, with extremely rare exceptions, even those who themselves engage in no corrupt activities are involved in corruption in the sense that they take no steps to prevent what they know or suspect to be going on about them.

It must be made clear that—in a little over a year with a staff having as few as two and never more than twelve field investigators—we did not examine every precinct in the Department. Our conclusion that corruption is widespread throughout the Department is based on the fact that information supplied to us by hundreds of sources within and without the Department was consistently borne out by specific observations made in areas we were able to investigate in detail.

Source: Commission to Investigate Allegations of Police Corruption, *The Knapp Commission Report on Police Corruption* (New York: George Braziller, 1973), 1–3.

DOCUMENT 70: *The Kansas City Preventive Patrol Experiment* (George L. Kelling et al., 1974)

From the earliest days of policing, routine patrol was considered an important part of the police role. The widely held but unsubstantiated belief was that a highly visible police presence deterred potential criminals and helped allay public fears about crime.

However, *The Kansas City Preventive Patrol Experiment,* a controversial study published in 1974, poked more than a few holes in that theory. The one-year experiment, conducted from October 1972 through September 1973, found that decreasing or increasing the level of police patrol in a given area had no significant impact on the level of crime, police response time, people's fear of crime, or their attitudes toward police service in that area.

The study was led by George L. Kelling and funded by the Washington, D.C.–based Police Foundation, an independent nonprofit organization established by the Ford Foundation in 1970 to support "innovation and improvement in policing" (Kelling et al. 1974:ii). According to Patrick V. Murphy, former New York City Police Commissioner (see Document 73), who then was president of the Police Foundation, "The experiment was unique in that never before had there been such an attempt to determine through such extensive scientific evaluation the value of visible police patrol" (Kelling et al. 1974: iii).

Kelling and his team's real-life testbed for the study consisted of fifteen Kansas City police beats. These beats were divided into three different groups—termed "reactive," "proactive," and "control"—of five beats each. The reactive group received no preventive patrol—police officers entered these five beats only when citizens called for service. The five beats in the proactive group received increased patrol—about two to three times the normal level. No changes in the level of patrol were made in the control group (Kelling et al. 1974:3). Throughout the year-long experiment, the researchers monitored the crime rate and police response times within each beat, and interviewed citizens about their fear of crime, satisfaction with police services, and other issues.

The results of their study—which suggested that police officers' "noncommitted" time might be put to other, possibly more productive, uses than patrol without a negative impact on public safety—are excerpted below.

* * *

The experiment found that the three experimental patrol conditions appeared not to affect crime, service delivery and citizen feelings of security in ways the public and the police often assume they do. For example,

- as revealed in the victimization surveys, the experimental conditions had no significant effect on residence and non-residence burglaries, auto thefts, larcenies involving auto accessories, robberies, or vandalism—crimes traditionally considered to be deterrable through preventive patrol;

- in terms of rates of reporting crime to the police, few differences and no consistent patterns of differences occurred across experimental conditions;

- in terms of departmental reported crime, only one set of differences across experimental conditions was found and this one was judged likely to have been a random occurrence.

- few significant differences and no consistent pattern of differences occurred across experimental conditions in terms of citizen attitudes toward police services;

- citizen fear of crime, overall, was not affected by experimental conditions;

- there were few differences and no consistent pattern of differences across experimental conditions in the number and types of anti-crime protective measures used by citizens;

- in general, the attitudes of businessmen toward crime and police services were not affected by experimental conditions;

- experimental conditions did not appear to affect significantly citizen satisfaction with the police as a result of their encounters with police officers;

- experimental conditions had no significant effect on either police response time or citizen satisfaction with police response time;

- although few measures were used to assess the impact of experimental conditions on traffic accidents and injuries, no significant differences were apparent;

- about 60 percent of a police officer's time is typically noncommitted (available for calls); of this time, police officers spent approximately as much time on non-police related activities as they did on police-related mobile patrol; and

- in general, police officers are given neither a uniform definition of preventive patrol nor any objective methods for gauging its effectiveness; while officers tend to be ambivalent in their estimates of preventive patrol's effectiveness in deterring crime, many attach great importance to preventive patrol as a police function.

Some of these findings pose a direct challenge to traditionally held beliefs. Some point only to an acute need for further research. But many point to what those in the police field have long suspected—an extensive disparity between what we want the police to do, what we often believe they do, and what they can and should do. . . .

. . . The findings of this experiment do not establish that the police are not important to the solution of crime or that police presence in some situations may not be helpful in reducing crime. Nor do they automatically justify reductions in the level of policing. They do not suggest that because the majority of a police officer's time is typically spent on non-crime related matters, the amount of time spent on crime is of any lesser importance.

Nor do the findings imply that the provision of public services and maintenance of order should overshadow police work on crime. While one of the three patrol conditions used in this experiment reduced police visibility in certain areas, the condition did not withdraw police availability from these areas. The findings in this regard should therefore not be interpreted to suggest that total police withdrawal from an area is an answer to crime. The reduction in routine police patrol was but one of three patrol conditions examined, and the implications must be treated with care.

It could be argued that because of its large geographical area and relatively low population density, Kansas City is not representative of the more populous urban areas of the United States. However, many of the critical problems and situations facing Kansas City are common to other large cities. For example, in terms of rates of aggravated assault, Kansas City ranks close to Detroit and San Francisco. The rate of murder and manslaughter per 100,000 persons in Kansas City is similar to that of Los Angeles, Denver and Cincinnati. And in terms of burglary, Kansas City is comparable to Boston and Birmingham. Furthermore, the experimental area itself was diverse socio-economically, and had a population density much higher than Kansas City's average, making the experimental area far more representative and comparative than Kansas City as a whole might be. In these respects, the conclusions and implications of this study can be widely applied.

Source: George L. Kelling, Tony Pate, Duane Dieckman, and Charles E. Brown, *The Kansas City Preventive Patrol Experiment: A Summary Report*. Washington, D.C.: Police Foundation, 1974, 3–5. Reprinted with permission of the Police Foundation.

DOCUMENT 71: "A Professor's 'Street Lessons' " (George L. Kirkham, 1974)

At a time when many academics, including Florida State University criminology professor George L. Kirkham, were highly critical of the police, Kirkham decided to put his criticisms to the test by becoming a police officer himself. In doing so, Kirkham expected to establish "once and for all the accuracy of what I and other criminologists had been saying about the police for so long" (Kirkham 1974:15).

With permission from Sheriff Dale Carson and Undersheriff D. K. Brown of Jacksonville, Florida, Kirkham—then a 31-year-old professor, husband, and father—went through four months of training at a certified police academy in the Tallahassee area, and then worked six months as a Jacksonville patrolman.

However, rather than confirming his criticisms of the police, the experience gave Kirkham a new perspective on the police and a new respect for the police role. Said Kirkham:

Those few steps have given me a profoundly new understanding and appreciation of our police, and have left me with the humbling realization that possession of a Ph.D. does not give a man a corner on knowledge, or place him in the lofty position where he cannot take lessons from those less educated than himself. (Kirkham 1974:22)

Following is an excerpt from Kirkham's article about his experiences, "A Professor's 'Street Lessons,' " which appeared in the March 1974 issue of the *FBI Law Enforcement Bulletin,* and by 1988 was that journal's most widely reprinted article of all time (Deakin 1988:191).

* * *

As policemen have come under increasing criticism by various individuals and groups in our society in recent years, I cannot help but wonder how many times they have clenched their teeth and wished they could expose their critics to only a few of the harsh realities which their job involves.

Persons such as myself, members of the academic community, have traditionally been quick to find fault with the police. From isolated incidents reported in the various news media, we have fashioned for ourselves a stereotyped image of the police officer which conveniently conforms to our notions of what he is. We see the brutal cop, the racist cop, the grafting cop, the discourteous cop. What we do not see, however, is the image of thousands of dedicated men and women struggling against almost impossible odds to preserve our society and everything in it which we cherish.

For some years, first as a student and later as a professor of criminology, I found myself troubled by the fact that most of us who write books and articles on the police have never been policemen ourselves. I began to be bothered increasingly by many of my students who were former policemen. Time and again, they would respond to my frequently critical lectures on the police with the argument that I could not possibly understand what a police officer has to endure in modern society until I had been one myself. Under the weight of this frustration, and my personal conviction that knowledge has an applied as well as a theoretical dimension, I decided to take up this challenge: I would become a policeman myself as a means of establishing once and for all the accuracy of what I and other criminologists had been saying about the police for so long. . . .

The School of Hard Knocks

. . .

I had always personally been of the opinion that police officers greatly exaggerate the amount of verbal disrespect and physical abuse to which they are subjected in the line of duty. During my first few hours as a street officer, I lived blissfully in a magic bubble which was soon to burst. As a college professor, I had grown accustomed to being treated with uniform respect and deference by those I encountered. I somehow naively assumed this same quality of respect would carry over into my new role as a policeman. I was, after all, a representative of the law, identifiable to all by the badge and uniform I wore as someone dedicated to the protection of society. Surely that fact would entitle me to a measure of respect and cooperation—or so I thought. I quickly found that my badge and uniform, rather than serving to shield me from such things as disrespect and violence, only acted as a magnet which drew me toward many individuals who hated what I represented.

I had discounted on my first evening the warning of a veteran sergeant who, after hearing that I was about to begin work as a patrolman, shook his head and cautioned, "You'd better watch yourself out there, Professor! It gets pretty rough sometimes!" I was soon to find out what he meant.

Several hours into my first evening on the streets, my partner and I were dispatched to a bar in the downtown area to handle a disturbance complaint. Inside, we encountered a large and boisterous drunk who was arguing with the bartender and loudly refusing to leave. As someone with considerable experience as a correctional counselor and mental health worker, I hastened to take charge of the situation. "Excuse me, Sir," I smiled pleasantly at the drunk, "but I wonder if I could ask you to step outside and talk with me for just a minute?" The man stared at me through bloodshot eyes in disbelief for a second, raising one hand to scratch the stubble of several days growth of beard. Then suddenly, without warning, it happened. He swung at me, luckily missing my face and striking me on the right shoulder. I couldn't believe it. What on earth had I done to provoke such a reaction? Before I could recover from my startled condition, he swung again—this time tearing my whistle chain from a shoulder epaulet. After a brief struggle, we had the still shouting, cursing man locked in the back of our cruiser. I stood there, breathing heavily with my hair in my eyes as I surveyed the damage to my new uniform and looked in bewilderment at my partner, who only smiled and clapped me affectionately on the back. . . .

A Different Perspective

The same kinds of daily stresses which affected my fellow officers soon began to take their toll on me. I became sick and tired of being reviled and attacked by criminals who could usually find a most sympathetic audience in judges and jurors eager to understand their side of things and provide them with "another chance." I grew tired of living under the ax of the news media and community pressure groups, eager to seize upon the slightest mistake made by myself or a fellow police officer.

As a criminology professor, I had always enjoyed the luxury of having great amounts of time in which to make difficult decisions. As a police officer, however, I found myself forced to make the most critical choices in a time frame of seconds, rather than days: to shoot or not to shoot, to arrest or not to arrest, to give chase or let go—always with the nagging certainty that others, those with great amounts of time in which to analyze and think, stood ready to judge and condemn me for whatever action I might take or fail to take. I found myself not only forced to live a life consisting of seconds and adrenalin, but also forced to deal with human problems which were infinitely more difficult than anything I had ever confronted in a correctional or mental health setting. Family fights, mental illness, potentially explosive crowd situations, dangerous individuals—I found myself progressively awed by the complexity of tasks faced by men whose work I once thought was fairly simple and straightforward. . . .

A Complex Challenge

As someone who had always regarded policemen as a "paranoid" lot, I discovered in the daily round of violence which became part of my life that chronic suspiciousness is something that a good cop cultivates in the interest of going home to his family each evening. Like so many other officers, my daily exposure to street crime soon had me carrying an off-duty weapon virtually everywhere I went. I began to become watchful of who and what was around me, as things began to acquire a new meaning: an open door, someone loitering on a dark corner, a rear license plate covered with dirt. My personality began to change slowly according to my family, friends, and colleagues as my career as a policeman progressed. Once quick to drop critical barbs about policemen to intellectual friends, I now became extremely sensitive about such remarks—and several times became engaged in heated arguments over them.

As a police officer myself, I found that society demands too much of its policemen: not only are they expected to enforce the law, but to be curbside psychiatrists, marriage counselors, social workers, and even ministers, and doctors. I found that a good street officer combines in his daily work splinters of each of these complex professions and many more. Certainly it is unreasonable for us to ask so much of the men in blue; yet we must, for there is simply no one else to whom we can turn for help in the kind of crises and problems policemen deal with. No one else wants to counsel a family with problems at 3 a.m. on Sunday; no one else wants to enter a darkened building after a burglary; no one else wants to confront a robber or madman with a gun. No one else wants to stare poverty, mental illness, and human tragedy in the face day after day, to pick up the pieces of shattered lives.

As a policeman myself, I have often asked myself the questions: "Why does a man become a cop?" "What makes him stay with it?" Surely it's not the disrespect, the legal restrictions which make the job increasingly rough, the long hours and low pay, or the risk of being killed or injured trying to protect people who often don't seem to care.

The only answer to this question I have been able to arrive at is one based on my own limited experience as a policeman. Night after night, I came home and took off the badge and blue uniform with a sense of satisfaction and contribution to society that I have never known in any other job. Somehow that feeling seemed to make everything—the disrespect, the danger, the boredom—worthwhile.

Source: George L. Kirkham, "A Professor's 'Street Lessons,'" *FBI Law Enforcement Bulletin* 43, no. 3 (March 1974): 15, 17, 20–22.

DOCUMENT 72: "Law Enforcement and Affirmative Action" (Samuel L. Williams, 1975)

The 1972 Equal Employment Opportunity Act and subsequent employment discrimination lawsuits led to the establishment of affirmative action hiring programs within many police departments (Walker 1998: 236). By 1975, federal court orders in Boston, New Jersey, Philadelphia, San Francisco, Toledo and other cities also had established mandatory minority hiring and promotion quotas within police departments (Williams 1975:72).

The intention of such programs was to remedy the wrongs of past discrimination. However, critics of affirmative action and hiring quotas argued that they actually went against the 1964 Civil Rights Act in that they linked hiring decisions to race (Regoli and Hewitt 1996:366). Others, such as Samuel L. Williams, president of the Los Angeles Board of Commissioners and himself an African American, saw court-ordered racial quotas as "an unfortunate way for a police department to meet the challenge of equal opportunity" (Williams 1975:72).

Williams believed that affirmative action should come from within police departments, through a serious commitment by police administrators to meet the challenge of equal opportunity, rather than being imposed by court order from outside the organization. Such a commitment, he said, would accomplish the goals of affirmative action without giving rise to racial hostilities within the department that can result from the imposition of hiring quotas (Williams 1975:72–73).

All criticisms aside, the Equal Employment Opportunity Act of 1972, affirmative action programs, and hiring quotas all contributed to the creation of new opportunities for minorities and women in law enforcement, and significantly changed the demographic composition of those who fill the police role in the United States. For example, only 5 percent of all police officers in Detroit were African American back in 1968, and by 1992 that figure had increased to 53 percent. In Miami, 47 percent of police officers were Hispanic and 22 percent were African American as of 1992 (Walker 1998:236).

* * *

Court-ordered quotas . . . to achieve racial balance are powerful medicines. These quotas, however benign, are nothing short of legal dynamite placed at the doors of closed institutions—institutions closed to minorities through either the will or the incompetence of those charged with their administration and their future.

Doubtless racial quotas are effective in springing open the doors of police departments which meet this description. Doubtless after their imposition, recruit classes contain more black faces and brown faces than before. But, when all is said and done, a court-ordered racial quota has got to be not so much an ill conceived as an unfortunate way for a police department to meet the challenge of equal opportunity.

First of all, as a personal matter, I just don't like quotas. As a black man, I have met more than a few of them in my life—as Roy Wilkins used to say, "zero quotas." As a member of a minority group, I may have recently and reluctantly come to accept "justice by percentile" but I have never and still do not really trust it. It used to be called "tokenism."

But even more importantly—and here I speak from the standpoint of a president of a board of police commissioners—I think numerical quotas are unfortunate because their imposition must represent a confession of serious failure on the part of the institution involved.

In the police context, this failure can have serious consequences. The entrance of minorities into a department under a judge-fashioned statistical umbrella can only lead to an organization that will be divided for the foreseeable future. I am talking here about one and two generations at the least, twenty to fifty years. I am talking of departments torn by factions and laced with angry mutterings. I am talking of police departments which are deprived of that crucial cooperation among brother officers so critically essential to effective service.

It is considerations like these which make so apparent the basic fallacy in the thinking of the police administrators who "go it slow" in response to the challenge of equal opportunity—those who prefer to wait for a court-ordered quota which is increasingly certain to be at the end of the tunnel. Surely, along with the responsibility, the unpopularity of the decision in many quarters is shifted from the police administrator to the judge. But there is the fallacy. Judges move on to hear and decide other cases. Police administrators, on the other hand, remain to confront the consequences for their departments—consequences which stem from their failure to act in a timely and resolute manner, that is, before those failures become the necessary occasions for court intervention.

I do not mean to suggest that the other alternative approaches to equal opportunity do not contain risks for the innovative police administrator. They undoubtedly do. My point rather is that the risks involved are largely personal ones assumed chiefly by the individual administrator rather than by his organization. And further, the consequences involved in these alternative approaches cut far less deeply, for a far shorter time, into the institutional fabric of the police department than those engendered by the quota solution.

This brings me directly to my understanding of the meaning of "affirmative action." A numerical quota is most certainly not affirmative action. If anything, as I have implied, it represents a failure to take affirmative action.

I understand affirmative action in the police context to consist first and foremost of a basic commitment. I refer to a genuine, good faith, unqualified commitment by the police administrator to seek to reshape those elements of the current police experience which so frequently function to make the environment, if not outrightly hostile, then subtly inhospitable to the minority group individual.

Given that commitment and the resources and executive energy which that implies, the series of programs conventionally grouped under the rubric of affirmative action would accomplish their tasks. In an environment which both reflects the image and seeks the substance of equal opportunity, the problems presently associated with recruitment and promotion would become merely technical problems—susceptible to the imagination of ingenuity and the effort of hard work. In these circumstances, the potential dividends would be of incalculable benefit in terms not only of the department's internal operations but also of the impact of those operations on the nature of police-community relations and on the capacity of the police organization to control crime effectively.

Source: Samuel L. Williams, "Law Enforcement and Affirmative Action," *The Police Chief* 42, no. 2 (February 1975): 72–73.

DOCUMENT 73: Patrick V. Murphy (1977)

Patrick V. Murphy, who took over as police commissioner of New York City after Howard R. Leary resigned amid a corruption scandal in 1970 (see Document 69), was largely responsible for turning the police department around. On the day Murphy resigned in 1973, Mayor John V. Lindsay asserted, "The Police Department is now at its strongest point in history" (Murphy and Plate 1977:16).

Prior to accepting the position as commissioner of the New York City police, Murphy, who had begun his career in law enforcement as a New York City patrolman after World War II, had served as head of police in Syracuse, New York, Detroit, Michigan, and Washington, D.C. After retiring as New York's police commissioner, he became president of the Police Foundation (also see Document 74), a Washington, D.C.–based nonprofit police research organization established by the Ford Foundation in 1970.

Among his many contributions to policing, Murphy is known for instigating "neighborhood policing" in New York City during his tenure as police commissioner (Deakin 1988:261), and also for placing restrictions on police use of deadly force in New York that allowed officers to shoot only in "defense of life" (Walker 1998:232–233).

Following is an excerpt from his 1977 book, *Commissioner* (with Thomas Plate), in which he argued that the modern problems experienced by the police were in part related to both the public's and government's failure to take police work seriously and to their misunderstanding—and/or inability to agree upon—what the role of police was and/or should be.

* * *

I now *know* [about policing] from experience, but there are not that many people in America who do. Partly this is because policing has been almost a clandestine activity; the public has just not been permitted to know what has been going on. But perhaps an even more important reason for the state of our ignorance is that for too long we have simply taken our police forces for granted or romanticized them beyond recognition in our television and movies; and this may be because some of us do not take our cops seriously. Like the orangutan in the city zoo, the American police officer, with his sirens and flashing lights, .38 Police Special, official shield, and quaint way of talking (e.g., "poip-a-trait-uh"), is viewed by some as a spectacle of entertainment. Whereas, in truth, the police officer, in his mission to help secure observance of the law, is in fact, as the noted Scottish scholar Charles Reith has put it, "the primary essential to the existence of all communities."

Yet another reason for the current state of policing (and for our failure to take it seriously) is that federal and state governments, evidenced by their behavior, themselves do not take the problem seriously. The states have not, as they should, coordinated policing within their respective boundaries as an antidote to the decentralized chaos which makes law enforcement more a matter of chance than the functioning of a logical system. By adopting what is virtually a laissez-faire attitude toward our seventeen thousand police departments, the states have managed to do little more than witness the deepening chaos. The federal government has also neglected the problem, perhaps fearing to raise the specter of a national police force. But when it hasn't been inept, its involvement has been pernicious and destructive. Federal law enforcement institutions like the Federal Bureau of Investigation and the U.S. Law Enforcement Assistance Administration—potentially, in my view, key elements of the overall answer—have more often than not been part of the problem. But without proper overall guidance and example at the federal level, and detailed standards and planning at the state level, policing at the local level simply has no chance at all; and in the war on crime, not only will more battles be lost but in the hasty retreat from the front lines of our streets and our communities the very style of our lives may be on the line.

But a final thought to be considered comes even closer to home. It concerns the citizen's appropriate demands on his police. The question even goes beyond the matter of asking cops to eliminate crime; it goes to a deeper understanding of what police do, what they should do, and what they cannot do.

On the simplest level, it involves understanding the sheer mechanics of policing, and the mores and styles of the police world. It involves being taken on a tour of headquarters, and sitting behind the cluttered desk of the police commissioner. It takes in a clear and unsentimental examination of the terrible problem of police corruption, and the even more difficult and essential problem of managing police departments. It means looking at the whole problem of crime from the level of the lowliest beat officer to the heights of the most powerful police commissioner.

But more than this, it involves a better understanding of the role of the police in the context of our lives. Do we ask too much of our police, or too little—or some of both? Do we ask them simply to be keepers of our gates, or also custodians of our morals? What are the offensive and societally destructive behaviors which we ask them to regulate, and which ones are susceptible to actual regulation?

In short, as we look at our police, do we see the red or the black? Do we see them for what they are or should be—professionals providing a vital public service? Like my mother, who wanted me to be a priest, can we be satisfied to permit them to be just cops? For if we ask them to do too much, in the confusion of what they are we may find that they are doing too little.

Source: Patrick V. Murphy and Thomas Plate, *Commissioner: A View from the Top of American Law Enforcement* (New York: Simon and Schuster, 1977), 27–29.

DOCUMENT 74: *The Quality of Police Education* (Lawrence W. Sherman et al., 1978)

In 1976, prompted by criticisms of the quality of the vast number of new criminal justice and law enforcement programs being offered by universities nationwide (Sherman et al. 1978:x); controversy over federal funding for police higher education, which had reached approximately $40 million per year through the Law Enforcement Assistance Administration's Law Enforcement Education Program (Sherman et al. 1978:ix); and reduced public concerns about crime, which threatened Congressional support for such funding (Deakin 1988:281); the Washington, D.C.–based Police Foundation sponsored a report on police education.

The report, *The Quality of Police Education*, was prepared by the National Commission on Higher Education for Police Officers, a twelve-member group assembled by the Police Foundation. Executive director of the commission and lead author of its report was Lawrence W. Sherman, then an assistant professor in the Graduate School of Criminal Justice at the State University of New York (SUNY) at Albany.

After a lengthy investigation that included soliciting and reviewing the opinions of state and national law enforcement and higher education organizations, police officers, city administrators, police union leaders, college administrators, academics, consultants, students, and others, the commission issued its report in 1978. The report included a review of the historical development and purpose of police education, recommendations for improving the quality of police education, and recommendations for changes in both police and educational policies that could lead higher education to have a greater impact on policing (Sherman et al. 1978:xiii).

One of the commission's most important recommendations was that the scope of police education programs be broadened to include greater emphasis on such courses as urban planning, family relations, and psychology, all of which have important implications for law enforcement (Sherman et al. 1978:3).

Moreover, while it found no conclusive evidence that higher education leads to improved police performance, the commission maintained the premise that "[m]ore and better higher education may be the key to producing the personal qualities necessary for police officers to create a new role for the police institution" (see document below).

Indeed, although Congress pulled the plug on the LEAA and LEEP in 1982, subsequent research on the role of police education has indicated that the efforts of these programs to increase and improve police education made important progress toward producing "more responsive, more comprehensive, and more insightful police service" (Barker et al. 1994:304).

* * *

Part One: Purposes

This report addresses one of the most important objectives of police education, one that in recent years has received too little attention: fostering basic change in policing. Higher education for police officers was first proposed fifty years ago as a strategy for changing the police role in society, and the same objective was implicit in the federal legislation enacted ten years ago to support police education. Yet the present structure of police education often results in little more than tacking credentials on to police personnel, serving the status quo in policing rather than stimulating change. Police education will have to do much more if it is to help the police find new methods, new organizational structure, and a more effective role in society for coping with crime and providing social justice.

The commission believes that the best way to educate the police institution for change is to develop the capacity of the police to use knowledge to solve problems. The art of using knowledge includes the habits of working with written and spoken ideas, computational tools, and information gathered from many sources to produce and test new conclusions. Much of the college education that present and future police officers now receive develops those essential habits. But much of it— particularly the courses offered in specialized police education programs—does not. In order to improve the quality of many of these programs, major changes must be made in their curriculums, the level of resource support they receive from their colleges, the qualifications of their faculty, and the nature of their students' educational experiences.

The commission's recommendations rest on the premise that more and better higher education may be the key to producing the personal qualities necessary for police officers to create a new role for the police institution. Our review of the scant empirical evidence about this premise was inconclusive, but it did suggest that the recent dramatic increase in the educational levels of police personnel has had little impact on police performance. Given the many complex factors shaping police behavior, as well as the often poor quality of police education, the absence of any impact—if true—is not surprising. No matter how high the quality of police education, education alone cannot change the police. New organizational designs, better management, and community leadership are also necessary conditions of change. The potential contribution of higher education to police work will not be realized until police department policies generally treat education as a resource rather than a threat.

Source: Lawrence W. Sherman and the National Advisory Commission on Higher Education for Police Officers, *The Quality of Police Education* (San Francisco: Jossey-Bass, 1978), 1–2.

NOTES

1. Parker didn't resign. However, he died suddenly of a heart attack on July 16, 1966.

2. However, Regoli and Hewitt (1996:291) note that Miranda was not released as a result of the Supreme Court's decision. He was retried for his crime in 1967 and again found guilty, this time largely due to the testimony of his common-law wife, to whom he had confessed. He was paroled in 1972 and was stabbed to death in a bar fight four years later.

3. Terry and Chilton were tried and convicted together, and appealed their case to the U.S. Supreme Court together. However, Chilton died before the case made it to the Court, and therefore only Terry's conviction was reviewed by the Court (392 U.S. 1:5n2).

4. Wilson, long considered one of the most prominent researchers in the field of crime and public policy, today is the James A. Collins Professor of Management in the Anderson School of Management at the University of California, Los Angeles.

5. Serpico's story eventually was told in the 1973 book *Serpico*, by Peter Maas, and in a 1981 movie by the same name, which starred Al Pacino in the title role.

Part VI

Reexamining and Redefining the Role of the Police, 1979–1989

RESULTS-ORIENTED POLICING

In the 1980s the United States shifted away from the introspection and philosophical turmoil of the 1960s and 1970s. A major theme in the resurgent conservative ideology associated with the administrations of Presidents Ronald Reagan and George Bush during that era was the belief that government should become more businesslike. Like their counterparts in other government agencies, influential police executives and scholars increasingly began to focus on "the bottom line" during this decade.

In contrast to the previous fifty years' preoccupation with who should become a police officer and how police organizations should be administered, attention now shifted toward what the police should be expected to accomplish. Although there had been some discussion during the early twentieth century about policing goals (e.g., Documents 33, 42, and 44), it was overwhelmed by the conception of police as fighters in a "war against crime" (e.g., Document 39). Crime statistics became the measure of police performance, and the role of law enforcer often was seen as more pressing and important than that of peace officer or police officer—particularly in the large urban police departments that dominated public policy debates and scholarly interest. Of course, these trends away from intimate police ties to the communities they served were reinforced by technological innovations such as the radio-dispatched squad car, which took more and more police officers out of direct routine contact with the average citizens in their communities. Increasingly, officers' contacts with "civilians" (as they came to characterize non–law enforcement personnel) were limited to criminals, their victims, and dysfunctional people who were unable to handle personal relations, alcohol, or drugs. This was a far cry from the constable and the beat cop who knew *all* the people on their beats and routinely interacted with them during the course of their rounds.

Herman Goldstein's recommendation in 1979 that police seek long-term solutions for community problems—especially crime-related problems (Document 75)—was a major step away from the status quo. Instead of responding to robberies, burglaries, or spousal assaults, Goldstein argued that police should work with others in their communities to identify the underlying causes of these problems and try to solve them.

The "broken windows" approach to policing advocated by James Q. Wilson and George L. Kelling (Document 78) broadened police goals even more. Instead of focusing just on serious crime, they argued that police should be responsible for maintaining public order and helping people feel safe in public places. This meant having officers take an active part in improving the quality of public life by discouraging panhandlers, prostitutes, addicts, and drunks from controlling streets, parks, and sidewalks. It also meant working to help people clean up their communities and make them appear less inviting for criminals.

However, the idea of increasing the role of police in American society did have its detractors. Donald Black and M. P. Baumgartner (Document 77) contended that our goal should be to gradually diminish reliance on police to resolve disputes and assure public safety. Increased dependence on police, Black and Baumgartner argued, makes people less inclined to help themselves or their neighbors. Because the ability of police to actually control crime is very limited, this loss of self-reliance will tend over the long term to make communities less safe.

The eminent police scholar David H. Bayley also urged caution in the move toward community-oriented policing (Document 83), but his rationale was less esoteric than Black and Baumgartner's. In the midst of a growing consensus about the value of results-oriented policing, Bayley pointed out that broader, more intimate, and autonomous relations between officers and people in their communities would increase opportunities for misconduct and make it more difficult for managers to control subordinates' conduct. Good managers, Bayley seemed to say, still needed to pay attention to how the job got done and who did it.

Although the role and goals of police were shifting rapidly during the 1980s, a number of important administrative and tactical issues still needed to be resolved. Many of them revolved around the individual officers themselves. Although policing still was a predominantly blue-collar occupation, the professionalization movement (e.g., Documents 52 and 53) had had a profound effect on the way officers perceived their jobs and themselves. For many, police work was a profession, a warrior's calling, an identity—not just a job.

ADMINISTRATIVE ISSUES

One of the more difficult personal issues for many male police officers and managers to deal with in the last decades of the twentieth century was the irreversible entry of women into full-time patrol work. Male officers, especially those who saw their job as pursuing a war against crime, challenged—and continue to challenge—the idea that a woman can do the job. Yet in order for women to have equal career opportunities in police work, they also had to acquire equivalent experience. Policing in the United States is a bottom-up occupation; almost all of the nation's police supervisors, managers, and executives climbed the promotional ladder from the rank of officer, deputy, or trooper. Despite the skepticism and hostility of male counterparts, women gradually established that, overall, they could perform the job as well as men (Document 79).

Another issue with important implications for how police perceived their role in society was raised by James Fyfe (Document 76). By the 1980s, almost all officers were either allowed or required to carry firearms while off duty. As a matter of official policy and/or subcultural belief, officers considered themselves to be on duty twenty-four hours a day. This affected their ability to deal with job stress and tended to increase their alienation from non-police. It also sometimes exposed them to greater hazards when they tried to confront criminals while off duty and out of uniform.

Off-duty concerns also were raised by Albert J. Reiss, Jr. (Document 82), who questioned the wisdom of the common practice of allowing off-duty officers to work as police officers for private organizations. Aside from potential problems with officer fatigue and conflicts of interest, Reiss raised concerns about whether the police would tend to become a private, rather than public, good. That is, would this practice tend to increase differences between levels of police service provided for poor versus well-to-do communities? Would businesses and individuals who could afford to hire off-duty officers receive adequate police protection while those that could not would not?

REFINING CONSTITUTIONAL CONSTRAINTS ON POLICE BEHAVIOR

During the 1980s the Supreme Court continued to refine the constitutional boundaries of acceptable police behavior. The 1980 case of *Payton v. New York* reemphasized the sanctity of the home, holding that warrantless searches of people's homes by police would be acceptable only under the most pressing circumstances. However, other court decisions in 1984 appeared to signal a slightly more flexible interpretation of the High Court's bulwark against police misconduct, the exclusionary rule. For example, *Nix v. Williams* established that evidence obtained as the result of a statement obtained improperly from a suspect still could be admissible in court if police could establish that the evidence would have been discovered inevitably. And in *United States v. Leon et al.*, the Court established a "good faith" exception to the exclusionary rule that allowed evidence obtained unconstitutionally by officers to be used in court if the officers believed they were acting within the confines of the Fourth Amendment.

In contrast to this slight loosening of constitutional constraints on police behavior, however, during this period the Court also substantially narrowed the circumstances under which officers could use deadly force. In the 1985 case of *Tennessee v. Garner et al.* (Document 80) the Court unequivocally renounced the common policy of shooting at fleeing felons, ruling that deadly force may be used only in defense of life. Further, in the 1986 case of *Malley et al. v. Briggs* (Document 81), the Court ruled that officers could be held responsible for acting on unconstitutional warrants even though the warrants had been issued by a magistrate. After decades of talk about professionalism, the justices were holding police accountable for errors that a reasonably competent officer could be expected to avoid. They also were reinforcing the oft-overlooked role of the police as defenders of the Constitution.

DOCUMENT 75: "Improving Policing: A Problem-Oriented Approach" (Herman Goldstein, 1979)

For many years, attempts to improve the quality of policing in the United States focused on administrative and personnel issues—such as updating equipment and operating procedures and improving the quality of police personnel through higher education and better training programs (Goldstein 1979:238).

While many of these efforts were commendable, by the end of the 1970s it had become apparent to at least one police researcher that too much emphasis was being placed on the "means" of police work, rather than on the end results. As Herman Goldstein, professor of law at the University of Wisconsin, Madison, put it, "If the police are to realize a greater return on the investment made in improving their operations, and if they are to mature as a profession, they must concern themselves more directly with the end product of their efforts" (1979: 236).

Goldstein, who introduced the concept of problem-oriented policing in his 1979 article, "Improving Policing: A Problem-Oriented Approach" (see document below), argued that the role of the police should focus more directly on identifying, defining, analyzing, and solving specific and persistent problems in the community—such as street robberies, residential burglaries, spouse abuse, vandalism, etc.— rather than simply responding to these same types of incidents over and over again (242). Such problem-solving efforts, which attempt to get at the underlying causes of problems, often might involve not only the patrol officer, but the police department as a whole, as well as other public and private agencies and/or members of the local community, all working together to plan and implement a solution to the problem (Barker et al. 1994:141–142; Palmiotto 1997:166; Walker 1998:238).

Goldstein's problem-oriented policing approach typically is considered akin to the more general concept of community policing, which seeks to bring the police and the community—including schools, businesses, associations, government agencies, and individuals—together to address the problem of crime and create a safer environment (Peak 1997:161; Regoli and Hewitt 1996:231).

* * *

WHAT IS THE END PRODUCT OF POLICING?

To urge a more direct focus on the primary objectives of a police agency requires spelling out these objectives more clearly. But this is no easy task, given the conglomeration of unrelated, ill-defined, and often inseparable jobs that the police are expected to handle.

The task is complicated further because so many people believe that the job of the police is, first and foremost, to enforce the law: to regulate conduct by applying the criminal law of the jurisdiction. One commentator on the police recently claimed: "We do not say to the police: 'Here is the problem. Deal with it.' We say: 'Here is a detailed code. Enforce it.' " In reality, the police job is perhaps most accurately described as dealing with problems. Moreover, enforcing the criminal code is itself only a means to an end—one of several that the police employ in getting their job done. The emphasis on law enforcement, therefore, is nothing more than a continuing preoccupation with means.

Considerable effort has been invested in recent years in attempting to define the police function: inventorying the wide range of police responsibilities, categorizing various aspects of policing, and identifying some of the characteristics common to all police tasks. This work will be of great value in refocusing attention on the end product of policing, but the fact that it is still going on is not cause to delay giving greater attention to substantive matters. It is sufficient, for our purposes here, simply to acknowledge that the police job requires that they deal with a wide range of behavioral and social problems that arise in a community—that the end product of policing consists of dealing with these *problems*.

By problems, I mean the incredibly broad range of troublesome situations that prompt citizens to turn to the police, such as street robberies, residential burglaries, battered wives, vandalism, speeding cars, runaway children, accidents, acts of terrorism, even fear. These and other similar problems are the essence of police work. They are the reason for having a police agency. . . .

IMPLEMENTING THE PROCESS

. . .

How does a police agency make the shift to problem-oriented policing? Ideally, the initiative will come from police administrators. What is needed is not a single decision implementing a specific program or a single memorandum announcing a unique way of running the organization. The concept represents a new way of looking at the process of improving police functioning. It is a way of thinking about the police and their function that, carried out over an extended period, would be reflected in all that the administrator does: in the relationship with personnel, in the priorities he sets in his own work schedule, in what he focuses on in addressing community groups, in the choice of training curriculums, and in the questions raised with local and state legislators. Once introduced, this orientation would affect subordinates, gradually filter through the rest of the organization, and reach other administrators and agencies as well. . . .

EFFECT ON THE ORGANIZATION

. . .

Those who have been strongly committed to improving policing through better administration and organization may be disturbed by any move to subordinate their interests to a broader concern with the end product of policing. However, a problem-oriented approach to police improvement may actually contribute in several important ways to achieving their objectives.

The approach calls for the police to take greater initiative in attempting to deal with problems rather than resign themselves to living with them. It calls for tapping police expertise. It calls for the police to be more aggressive partners with other public agencies. These changes, which would place the police in a much more positive light in the community, would also contribute significantly to improving the working environment within a police agency—an environment that suffers much from the tendency of the police to assume responsibility for problems which are insolvable or ignored by others. And an improved working environment increases, in turn, the potential for recruiting and keeping qualified personnel and for bringing about needed organizational change.

Focusing on problems, because it is a practical and concrete approach, is attractive to both citizens and the police. By contrast, some of the most frequent proposals for improving police operations, because they do not produce immediate and specifically identifiable results, have no such attraction. A problem-oriented approach, with its greater appeal, has the potential for becoming a vehicle through which long-sought organizational change might be more effectively and more rapidly achieved.

Source: Herman Goldstein, "Improving Policing: A Problem-Oriented Approach," *Crime and Delinquency* 25, no. 2 (April 1979): 241–243, 256–257 (footnotes omitted).

DOCUMENT 76: "Always Prepared: Police Off-Duty Guns" (James J. Fyfe, 1980)

Most American police officers take the job home with them each day—not just figuratively, but literally. In fact, a 1978 Police Foundation survey (Heaphy 1978:item 20) reported that 49 percent of the forty-nine police departments surveyed required their officers to carry their guns while off duty, while 51 percent allowed but did not require them to do so. Hence, as James J. Fyfe pointed out in his 1980 article, "Always Prepared: Police Off-Duty Guns" (excerpted below), even when relaxing with family and friends, most police officers are "expected to be armed and ready for action" (282).

However, while there may be some additional protection benefits to requiring or encouraging police officers to carry their weapons while off duty, Fyfe, then an associate professor at the American University in Washington, D.C., who spent sixteen years as a New York City police officer prior to becoming an academic, argued that these benefits actually might be outweighed by the drawbacks.

For example, Fyfe noted that in New York City, 681 police officers fired their weapons while off duty between 1971 and 1975. Of these weapons discharges, about 75 percent were for law enforcement purposes, such as self-defense, defense of others, crime prevention or intervention, or destruction of a dangerous animal. However, the remaining quarter of off-duty weapons discharges involved officer suicides or suicide attempts, accidents, and other events ranging from venting frustration to murder of family members (Fyfe 1980:288–289).

Such incidents, perhaps resulting in part from the psychological stress experienced by many police officers, led Fyfe to question the wisdom of encouraging police officers to have such ready access to guns while off duty. Moreover, Fyfe notes that when intervening during law enforcement situations while off duty, police officers are at a distinct disadvantage—without advance warning, radio communications, backup assistance, or uniform identification (see document below).

* * *

American police are citizens and police officers. Considerable effort has been expended to eliminate distinctions between them and the communities they serve. Some distinctions, however, are both desirable and necessary and thus are not subject to these efforts. It is desirable and necessary that on-duty police fulfill the role of active intervenor in threatening situations. It is also necessary, therefore, that they be distinguishable from most citizens by being armed during that time.

It is less clear that it is desirable and necessary for police to attempt to fulfill the active intervenor role while off duty. To do so, they must continue to be armed and therefore distinguishable from other citizens. Thus it may be difficult for police to relate their own life experiences to those of the unarmed citizens for whom they work. Further, this distinction may be less than desirable because police may be even more vulnerable than most citizens to the forces that lead to gun abuse.

Before police practice their craft, they are usually screened, tested, and trained. While they practice their craft, they are subject to stresses far more psychologically demanding than are most citizens. The combination of these job stresses and ready access to off-duty guns sometimes ends tragically. Many laudable efforts to avert such tragedies have focused on eliminating or neutralizing the stresses which precede them, but little or no attention has been given to the desirability or necessity of access to the off-duty guns which complete the tragedies.

The question of desirability or necessity of off-duty guns does not involve only intentional and accidental misuse. When off-duty police do use their guns in well-intended interventions, it is not at all clear that they reduce violence. Conversely, their actions in threatening situations may even create actual violence where only potential violence exists.

This negative effect is often due to important qualitative distinctions between the situations in which on-duty and off-duty police typically intervene. On-duty police are usually advised by their radio dispatchers of potential violence. Since this usually occurs while they are at a distance from the scene, they have the opportunity to plan their approach to it and to coordinate their efforts with colleagues. On-duty police are also usually in uniform and are clearly identifiable to other officers.

Off-duty police who intervene in potential violence rarely enjoy such luxuries. They are typically not given any warning of impending events, but rather, are suddenly confronted by suspects whose guns are already drawn. Off-duty police are not typically in the company of colleagues, but are alone or with friends or family. They do not usually have instant access to police communications systems. They are usually in civilian clothes and are thus easily mistaken for armed suspects by arriving police. Finally, they are far more likely than on-duty officers to have judgment and reflexes dulled by liquor.

In such circumstances, it is rarely desirable or necessary that off-duty police distinguish themselves from other citizens by attempting to actively intervene nor is it fair to them or other citizens. Indeed, it may be most fair to require off-duty police to leave their guns in their lockers with the rest of their uniforms.

Source: James J. Fyfe, "Always Prepared: Police Off-Duty Guns," *The Annals of the American Academy of Political and Social Science* 452 (November 1980): 72–81. Reprinted in James J. Fyfe, ed., *Readings on Police Use of Deadly Force* (Washington, D.C.: Police Foundation, 1982), 282–296.

DOCUMENT 77: The Concept of "Depolicing" (Donald Black and M. P. Baumgartner, 1980)

While most police departments in America have expanded significantly in response to growing population and crime rates during the past few decades, some researchers argue that we actually would be better served by having fewer rather than more police officers. In their article, "On Self-Help in Modern Society," Donald Black, then a Harvard Law School professor, and his graduate student, M. P. Baumgartner, explained that the greater the level of police protection in a community, the more dependent people become on the state for their security and law enforcement needs, and the less likely they are to help themselves and others (see document below).

Black and Baumgartner argued that the overall level of protection in the community could be increased by gradually reducing (but not eliminating) police protection. As the police role diminished, they argued, people eventually would tend to take more responsibility for their own safety and conflict settlement, and also would be more likely to help others in need.

* * *

Most people concerned with crime and law enforcement take for granted that more police, with more power, will mean less crime. Increases of this kind are claimed to work preventively against crime through the greater surveillance they entail. They are also asserted to work remedially, by allowing more speedy and certain apprehension of offenders.

While these ideas undoubtedly have some validity, especially in the short term, strengthening the police presence is not a sure means of crime reduction, . . . and it has its own disadvantages as well. Since the relationship between law and self-help is inverse, it follows that the larger and more intrusive a police force is, the weaker self-help will be, a pattern that could in the long term exacerbate the problem of crime. With the growth of law and the police—an evolutionary process involving many variables . . . —the citizenry becomes increasingly dependent upon the state to define and maintain order. As this happens, people increasingly cease to take responsibility for their own security and dispute settlement, and hesitate to help others with matters of this kind. Waiting for the police to arrive, they may even stand by passively as an assault or other victimization takes place. Each expansion of police and other legal protection thus results in a new and higher level of need for these very services, leading to their ever-escalating proliferation. . . . It is partly this dependence that explains why an increase in the number and power of police is usually seen as the solution to problems of public order. Cutting back on the police—or depolicing—is almost never considered as a way to ameliorate these problems.

If police protection were reduced, however, the volume and intensity of self-help would be expected to rise correspondingly, reversing the trend toward ever greater dependence upon law. This too follows from the inverse relationship between law and self-help. Everywhere, people would undertake more preventive surveillance on their own, would work out more informal settlements of their disputes with other parties involved, and would lend assistance to those in need of help more readily. There is already experimental evidence to show that people are generally most helpful when the need for their assistance seems most apparent—that is, when alternatives to their participation are most clearly lacking. . . . In light of this, it would seem that making the police conspicuous by their absence would lead citizens to draw upon their own resources and to assist one another in solving their problems.

Given the currently high level of reliance upon police, it would seem advisable to begin a transition to self-help with small cutbacks and, from there, to proceed gradually. Indeed, in a society in which people have become conditioned to depend upon the government for public order, a sudden and complete removal of officials could well precipitate a Hobbesian "war of all against all." . . . There have already been, in fact, a number of cases in which a drastic decrease of police service has resulted in widespread rioting, looting, and assault. . . . Nevertheless, extensive disruptions of police service often produce self-help smoothly and quickly. In the wake of disasters such as earthquakes, tornadoes, and floods, for example, routine operations by the police and other authorities frequently break down, while the demand for their services increases sharply. At such times, individuals in the stricken communities typically take command of the situation and willingly lend assistance to one another. Informal social control exercised by the citizens themselves virtually always maintains order; plundering and fighting are rare. . . . Even a sudden breakdown of police control, then, may give rise to self-help without large-scale disorder, and a program of gradual depolicing should encourage this all the more.

Once depolicing has begun, for whatever reason, the self-help that arises tends to feed upon itself. Just as self-help atrophies when law grows, with law continually creating conditions that make itself necessary, so the reverse is true: Self-help engenders more self-help. The more people come to rely upon themselves for dispute settlement and other social control, the more established does their self-reliance become. The more people help each other in any way, the more their mutual aid flourishes. . . . Moreover, it is likely that if people were more dependent upon self-help they would come to expect this service from each other and would hold in disrepute those not doing their part. This process, a system of social control in its own right, is believed to have occurred in earlier societies that had no law at all. . . .

In sum, a body of theory and research suggests that depolicing would contribute to the growth of self-help in modern society. Depolicing would in and of itself produce self-help to some degree, and this self-help would in turn produce still more.

Source: Donald Black and M. P. Baumgartner, "On Self-Help in Modern Society," in Donald Black, *The Manners and Customs of the Police* (New York: Academic Press, 1980), 195–199 (footnotes omitted).

DOCUMENT 78: "Broken Windows" (James Q. Wilson and George L. Kelling, 1982)

As the 1980s progressed, the concepts of problem-oriented (see Document 75) and community policing continued to grow, as more and more researchers began to look at the police role in a new light. For example, in a well-received article published in the March 1982 issue of the *Atlantic*, James Q. Wilson (also see Document 65), then the Shattuck Professor of Government at Harvard University, and George Kelling, then a research fellow at Harvard's John F. Kennedy School of Government, argued that the police role should be expanded beyond law enforcement to include active participation in maintaining and/or improving the quality of community life through an increased focus on order maintenance.

Wilson and Kelling based their recommendations in part on the results of a Police Foundation study of the effects of police foot patrol conducted in Newark, New Jersey, during the mid-1970s. The study found that while foot patrol did not actually lead to reduced crime in a neighborhood, it did lead to increased public order in the community. The foot patrol officers kept an eye on strangers, and also helped to keep "disreputable regulars" such as drunks, drug addicts, prostitutes, panhandlers, loiterers, rowdy teenagers, and others under control. As a result, people's fears of being "bothered by disorderly people" decreased, and their perceptions of public safety increased, despite the fact that crime levels had not actually gone down (Wilson and Kelling 1982:29–30).

Although the Newark foot patrol experiment did not result in a decrease in crime, Wilson and Kelling noted that there is a strong link between the type of increased order maintenance it promoted and crime prevention. They termed this link the "broken windows" theory. Summarized briefly, this means that evidence of community deterioration—ranging from broken windows left unfixed, graffiti, and rubbish to public drunks, beggars, and prostitutes—is a sign that no one in the community cares. Left unchecked, these outward signs of public disorder often lead to further community deterioration and increased potential for "criminal invasion," as residents become more fearful and therefore tend to stay off the streets or move away altogether (Wilson and Kelling 1982:32–34).

Hence, in contrast to the concept of "depolicing" advocated by their Harvard colleagues Donald Black and M. P. Baumgartner (see Document 77), Wilson and Kelling saw a need for a greater police presence, particularly in neighborhoods on the brink of deterioration (Wilson and Kelling 1982:38).

* * *

From the earliest days of the nation, the police function was seen primarily as that of a night watchman: to maintain order against the chief threats to order—fire, wild animals, and disreputable behavior. Solving crimes was viewed not as a police responsibility but as a private one. In the March, 1969, *Atlantic*, one of us (Wilson) wrote a brief account of how the police role had slowly changed from maintaining order to fighting crimes. The change began with the creation of private detectives (often ex-criminals), who worked on a contingency-fee basis for individuals who had suffered losses. In time, the detectives were absorbed into municipal police agencies and paid a regular salary; simultaneously, the responsibility for prosecuting thieves was shifted from the aggrieved private citizen to the professional prosecutor. This process was not complete in most places until the twentieth century.

In the 1960s, when urban riots were a major problem, social scientists began to explore carefully the order-maintenance function of the police, and to suggest ways of improving it—not to make streets safer (its original function) but to reduce the incidence of mass violence. Order-maintenance became, to a degree, coterminous with "community relations." But, as the crime wave that began in the early 1960s continued without abatement throughout the decade and into the 1970s, attention shifted to the role of the police as crime-fighters. Studies of police behavior ceased, by and large, to be accounts of the order-maintenance function and became, instead, efforts to propose and test ways whereby the police could solve more crimes, make more arrests, and gather better evidence. If these things could be done, social scientists assumed, citizens would be less fearful.

A great deal was accomplished during this transition, as both police chiefs and outside experts emphasized the crime-fighting function in their plans, in the allocation of resources, and in deployment of personnel. The police may well have become better crime-fighters as a result. And doubtless they remained aware of their responsibility for order. But the link between order-maintenance and crime-prevention, so obvious to earlier generations, was forgotten.

That link is similar to the process whereby one broken window becomes many. The citizen who fears the ill-smelling drunk, the rowdy teenager, or the importuning beggar is not merely expressing his distaste for unseemly behavior; he is also giving voice to a bit of folk wisdom that happens to be a correct generalization—namely, that serious street crime flourishes in areas in which disorderly behavior goes unchecked. The unchecked panhandler is, in effect, the first broken window. Muggers and robbers, whether opportunistic or professional, believe they reduce their chances of being caught or even identified if they operate on streets where potential victims are already intimidated by prevailing conditions. If the neighborhood cannot keep a bothersome panhandler from annoying passersby, the thief may reason, it is even less likely to call the police to identify a potential mugger or to interfere if the mugging actually takes place. . . .

Though citizens can do a great deal, the police are plainly the key to order-maintenance. For one thing, many communities . . . cannot do the job by themselves. For another, no citizen in a neighborhood, even an organized one, is likely to feel the sense of responsibility that wearing a badge confers. . . .

But the police forces of America are losing, not gaining, members. Some cities have suffered substantial cuts in the number of officers available for duty. These cuts are not likely to be reversed in the near future. Therefore, each department must assign its existing officers with great care. Some neighborhoods are so demoralized and crime-ridden as to make foot patrol useless; the best the police can do with limited resources is respond to the enormous number of calls for service. Other neighborhoods are so stable and serene as to make foot patrol unnecessary. The key is to identify neighborhoods at the tipping point—where the public order is deteriorating but not unreclaimable, where the streets are used frequently but by apprehensive people, where a window is likely to be broken at any time, and must quickly be fixed if all are not to be shattered.

Most police departments do not have ways of systematically identifying such areas and assigning officers to them. Officers are assigned on the basis of crime rates (meaning that marginally threatened areas are often stripped so that police can investigate crimes in areas where the situation is hopeless) or on the basis of calls for service (despite the fact that most citizens do not call the police when they are merely frightened or annoyed). To allocate patrol wisely, the department must look at the neighborhoods and decide, from first-hand evidence, where an additional officer will make the greatest difference in promoting a sense of safety.

One way to stretch limited police resources is being tried in some public-housing projects. Tenant organizations hire off-duty police officers for patrol work in their buildings. The costs are not high (at least not per resident), the officer likes the additional income, and the residents feel safer. Such arrangements are probably more successful than hiring private watchmen, and the Newark experiment helps us understand why. A private security guard may deter crime or misconduct by his presence, and he may go to the aid of persons needing help, but he may well not intervene—that is, control or drive away—someone challenging community standards. Being a sworn officer—a "real cop"—seems to give one the confidence, the sense of duty, and the aura of authority necessary to perform this difficult task.

Patrol officers might be encouraged to go to and from duty stations on public transportation and, while on the bus or subway car, enforce rules about smoking, drinking, disorderly conduct, and the like. The enforcement need involve nothing more than ejecting the offender (the offense, after all, is not one with which a booking officer or a judge wishes to be bothered). Perhaps the random but relentless maintenance of standards on buses would lead to conditions on buses that approximate the level of civility we now take for granted on airplanes.

But the most important requirement is to think that to maintain order in precarious situations is a vital job. The police know this is one of their functions, and they also believe, correctly, that it cannot be done to the exclusion of criminal investigation and responding to calls. We may have encouraged them to suppose, however, on the basis of our oft-repeated concerns about serious, violent crime, that they will be judged exclusively on their capacity as crime-fighters. To the extent that this is the case, police administrators will continue to concentrate police personnel in the highest-crime areas (though not necessarily in the areas most vulnerable to criminal invasion), emphasize their training in the law and criminal apprehension (and not their training in managing street life), and join too quickly in campaigns to decriminalize "harmless" behavior (though public drunkenness, street prostitution, and pornographic displays can destroy a community more quickly than any team of professional burglars).

Above all, we must return to our long-abandoned view that the police ought to protect communities as well as individuals. Our crime statistics and victimization surveys measure individual losses, but they do not measure communal losses. Just as physicians now recognize the importance of fostering health rather than simply treating illness, so the police—and the rest of us—ought to recognize the importance of maintaining, intact, communities without broken windows.

Source: James Q. Wilson and George L. Kelling, "Broken Windows." *The Atlantic* 249, no. 3 (March 1982): 33–35, 37–38.

DOCUMENT 79: "The Evolving Role of Women in American Policing" (Edith Linn and Barbara Raffel Price, 1985)

The role of women in American policing changed significantly between the late nineteenth century, when women first became involved in policing as matrons (see Document 19), and the late twentieth century. Most of the changes occurred as a result of the civil rights and women's rights movements of the 1960s and 1970s, as women fought for, and gradually won, more and more equal status with men.

Yet while women police—who first began working routine patrol duty in 1968—were no longer restricted to serving as matrons in jails, in clerical roles, or working solely with women and children, they still remained highly underrepresented in the field. As Edith Linn and Barbara Raffel Price pointed out in their 1985 article, "The Evolving Role of Women in American Policing," despite the fact that women made up more than half of the American population as of 1981, only 5.5 percent of all sworn police officers (and 4 percent in urban departments) were women (1985:69, 76). While this was a marked increase since 1972, when only 1.5 percent of all police officers were women, these figures are quite low when compared to the percentage of women in other traditionally male fields such as higher education, law, and the federal judiciary (Linn and Price 1985:76).

One reason for this, said Linn and Price, was that despite the fact that women consistently had demonstrated their ability to perform well at all types of regular police duties, they still were "not yet fully accepted in the majority of American police departments" (1985:70).

Another reason for the small gains made in the number of women police officers in the United States, they said, was shrinking municipal budgets, which had resulted in an overall reduction in the number of police in many departments in recent years, and hence made it more difficult for women to break into the field (see document below).

* * *

THE PRESENT SITUATION

Women officers are making significant inroads into all aspects of police work and in all types and sizes of police jurisdictions—municipal, state, and federal. The number of policewomen employed in the ten largest urban police departments in the United States in 1974 . . . as compared to the female police complement in 1982 . . . documents this gain. And nationwide, women police officers have increased in ranks from 1.5 percent in 1972 to 5.5 percent in 1981. However, while the major city departments have moved ahead of the law enforcement national average, they still rank well below the percentage of women employed in other fields. For example, among college faculty, women comprise 23 percent, with 9 percent full professors. In law, 32 percent of the students are female. Even the prestigious federal judiciary positions have more women proportionately than policing has. Women make up 6.7 percent of all federal judges. In addition, they hold 6.7 percent of all top level federal government positions. By comparison, law enforcement agencies have neither hired nor promoted women in proportion to other professions.

The most promising indicator of progress in the sexual integration of law enforcement is to be found in the changes in officer deployment from 1974 to 1982. . . . The percentage of women assigned to the patrol function has greatly increased in recent years although the actual numbers are still low; hence the visibility of women police remains limited. However, the fact that about half of the women in large city police forces are now assigned to patrol (Houston reported the lowest percentage with 32 percent of its women out on the street and Boston the highest with 93 percent) suggests a policy commitment in these departments to the fuller utilization and involvement of women.

In the 1960s, when women began to seek remedies for the inferior status they held as members of women's bureaus in police departments, they pressed for promotions commensurate with their years of experience and performance. In response, police administrators maintained that women could only be promoted within their own bureaus because they had not had the full "police experience" of being on the street, i.e., patrol duty. Of course, women had been systematically denied opportunities in the past for general patrol assignments. Energetic women fought to turn this situation around by gaining the right to be assigned to patrol and to work in the same capacity as male officers in order to earn the same pay and the same promotion opportunities. Therefore, the percentage of women in patrol assignments is one critical indicator of the integration of women in policing. . . .

Achieving sexually integrated police forces has been made more difficult recently by the fiscal difficulties of many cities. Municipal budgetary problems have forced many departments to reduce their total number of officers. The problem has been most severe in the Northeast but few areas of the country have remained untouched by reduced revenues. . . .

The reduction in total officer numbers means that male officers will be competing for even more limited promotion opportunities than in the past and will be less sympathetic to personnel reform measures being pressed by women's groups, minorities, and civil rights commissions. . . .

It may be that the constriction of police departments is a temporary situation which future recovery of the national economy will reverse. If so, we can anticipate the slow but steady gains of sexual integration in law enforcement to continue in the coming decade. And we can conclude with confidence that women have forged a permanent place for themselves in American policing.

Source: Edith Linn and Barbara Raffel Price, "The Evolving Role of Women in American Policing," in Abraham S. Blumberg and Elaine Niederhoffer, *The Ambivalent Force: Perspectives on the Police*, third edition (Fort Worth: Harcourt Brace College Publishers, 1985), 76–78 (footnotes omitted).

DOCUMENT 80: *Tennessee v. Garner et al.* (1985)

Despite growing public concern during the 1970s and early 1980s about the police use of deadly force, many states at that time still followed an old common law rule that permitted police officers to use deadly force if necessary to apprehend *any* fleeing felon, regardless of whether he or she posed a threat to the officers or others.

This "fleeing felon" rule was first established in England during the Middle Ages. It made more sense at the time, when all felonies were punishable by death anyway, and apprehending fleeing criminals was much more difficult once they were out of sight due to limited weapons and communications technology. However, at a time when police had many more options available to them for capturing criminals, especially those who did not appear to be armed or dangerous, the rule was "condemned by many commentators and scholars" (Reid 1990: 246).

The issue came before the United States Supreme Court in 1985, in the case of *Tennessee v. Garner*. The case involved the police shooting and killing of Edward Garner, a 15-year-old, unarmed boy, as he fled from an empty house that he apparently had broken into and burgled (ten dollars and a stolen purse were later found in his possession). The boy's father subsequently sought damages in a federal district court, on the grounds that his son's constitutional rights had been violated. However, the court concluded that the officer's actions had been authorized by a Tennessee statute permitting the use of deadly force to stop a fleeing felon, and that the statute was constitutional. The court of appeals upheld the lower court's decision with regard to the officer, who had been acting within the law, but it eventually reversed that court's ruling that the statute was constitutional, explaining that the killing of a fleeing suspect constitutes seizure under the Fourth Amendment, and therefore is constitutional only if "reasonable" (471 U.S. 1:6).

The state of Tennessee appealed to the U.S. Supreme Court to defend its fleeing-felon statute, but the Court affirmed the ruling of the court of appeals, explaining that under the reasonableness standard of the Fourth Amendment, the use of deadly force against an unarmed suspect who does not appear to pose a threat to police officers or others is unconstitutional (see document below). The Court's decision established the "defense of life" standard for the police use of deadly force, meaning that if the suspect is armed and threatens police officers or others, or if there is probable cause to believe the suspect has committed a crime involving the infliction of serious physical harm, then the police may use deadly force if necessary to prevent his or her escape. This ruling compelled many states to alter their common-law based fleeing-felon statutes (Champion and Rush 1997:223–224; Regoli and Hewitt 1996:348).

* * *

A. OPINION OF THE COURT

Justice White delivered the opinion of the Court. . . .

II

Whenever an officer restrains the freedom of a person to walk away, he has seized that person. . . . While it is not always clear just when minimal police interference becomes a seizure . . . there can be no question that apprehension by the use of deadly force is a seizure subject to the reasonableness requirement of the Fourth Amendment. . . .

B

. . .

The use of deadly force to prevent the escape of all felony suspects, whatever the circumstances, is constitutionally unreasonable. It is not better that all felony suspects die than that they escape. Where the suspect poses no immediate threat to the officer and no threat to others, the harm resulting from failing to apprehend him does not justify the use of deadly force to do so. It is no doubt unfortunate when a suspect who is in sight escapes, but the fact that the police arrive a little late or are a little slower afoot does not always justify killing the suspect. A police officer may not seize an unarmed, nondangerous suspect by shooting him dead. The Tennessee statute is unconstitutional insofar as it authorizes the use of deadly force against such fleeing suspects.

It is not, however, unconstitutional on its face. Where the officer has probable cause to believe that the suspect poses a threat of serious physical harm, either to the officer or to others, it is not constitutionally unreasonable to prevent escape by using deadly force. Thus, if the suspect threatens the officer with a weapon or there is probable cause to believe that he has committed a crime involving the infliction or threatened infliction of serious physical harm, deadly force may be used if necessary to prevent escape, and if, where feasible, some warning has been given. As applied in such circumstances, the Tennessee statute would pass constitutional muster. . . .

V

We wish to make clear what our holding means in the context of this case. The complaint has been dismissed as to all the individual defendants. The State is a party only by virtue of 28 U.S.C. §2403(b) and is not subject to liability. The possible liability of the remaining defendants—the Police Department and the city of Memphis . . . is left for remand. We hold that the statute is invalid insofar as it purported to give Hymon the authority to act as he did. As for the policy of the Police Department, the absence of any discussion of this issue by the courts below, and the uncertain state of the record, preclude any consideration of its validity.

The judgment of the Court of Appeals is affirmed, and the case is remanded for further proceedings consistent with this opinion.

B. DISSENTING OPINION

JUSTICE O'CONNOR, with whom THE CHIEF JUSTICE and JUSTICE REHNQUIST join, dissenting. . . .

IV

The Court's opinion sweeps broadly to adopt an entirely new standard for the constitutionality of the use of deadly force to apprehend fleeing felons. Thus, the Court "lightly brushe[s] aside," *Payton* v. *New York* . . . a longstanding police practice that predates the Fourth Amendment and continues to receive the approval of nearly half of the state legislatures. I cannot accept the majority's creation of a constitutional right to flight for burglary suspects seeking to avoid capture at the scene of the crime. Whatever the constitutional limits on police use of deadly force in order to apprehend a fleeing felon, I do not believe they are exceeded in a case in which a police officer has probable cause to arrest a suspect at the scene of a residential burglary, orders the suspect to halt, and then fires his weapon as a last resort to prevent the suspect's escape into the night. I respectfully dissent.

Source: 471 U.S. 1 (1985), 3–33.

DOCUMENT 81: *Malley et al. v. Briggs* (1986)

The decision-oriented and action-oriented nature of the police role make it likely that most police officers will, at some point, make a mistake, such as arresting a person who is later found to be innocent. It is equally likely that some guilty persons arrested by the police will be acquitted of the charges in court. In most such cases, the arresting officer cannot be held liable for damages associated with "wrongful arrest," as long as he or she had reasonable grounds—that is, probable cause—for making the arrest.

However, the U.S. Supreme Court established in 1986 that should it be determined that the officer did *not* have probable cause to make an arrest, he or she may be held liable for damages by the arrested person or persons. This ruling holds true even if the officer obtained an arrest warrant prior to making the arrest.

The precedent-setting case, *Malley et al. v. Briggs*, involved a prominent Rhode Island couple, James and Louisa Briggs, who were arrested for possession of marijuana based on telephone conversations between a male friend of their daughter's, whose phone was legally being tapped, and an unknown person who called himself "Dr. Shogun." In these conversations, the two men discussed a party at the Briggs' home in which the Briggses allegedly participated in smoking marijuana (475 U.S. 335:337–338).

The grand jury did not indict the Briggses, and the charges were subsequently dropped, but not until after local and statewide newspapers had published the news of their arrest. They then brought an action against Edward Malley, the state trooper who had arrested them, charging that he, "in applying for warrants for their arrest, violated their rights under the Fourth and Fourteenth Amendments" (475 U.S. 335: 338). The district court ruled against them, but the Court of Appeals for the First Circuit reversed the decision, ruling that "an officer who seeks an arrest warrant by submitting a complaint and supporting affidavit to a judge is not entitled to immunity unless the officer has an objectively reasonable basis for believing that the facts alleged in his affidavit are sufficient to establish probable cause" (in 475 U.S. 335: 339).

The U.S. Supreme Court affirmed the decision of the court of appeals, noting that "an officer who knows that objectively unreasonable decisions will be actionable may be motivated to reflect, before submitting a request for a warrant, upon whether he has a reasonable basis for believing that his affidavit establishes probable cause" (475 U.S. 335: 343).

* * *

A. OPINION OF THE COURT

Justice White delivered the opinion of the Court. . . .

II

. . .

B

Although we have previously held that police officers sued under §1983 for false arrest are qualifiedly immune . . . petitioner urges that he should be absolutely immune because his function in seeking an arrest warrant was similar to that of a complaining witness. The difficulty with this submission is that complaining witnesses were not absolutely immune at common law. In 1871, the generally accepted rule was that one who procured the issuance of an arrest warrant by submitting a complaint could be held liable if the complaint was made maliciously and without probable cause. Given malice and the lack of probable cause, the complainant enjoyed no immunity. The common law thus affords no support for petitioner.

Nor are we moved by petitioner's argument that policy considerations require absolute immunity for the officer applying for a warrant. As the qualified immunity defense has evolved, it provides ample protection to all but the plainly incompetent or those who knowingly violate the law. At common law, in cases where probable cause to arrest was lacking, a complaining witness' immunity turned on the issue of malice, which was a jury question. Under the *Harlow* standard, on the other hand, an allegation of malice is not sufficient to defeat immunity if the defendant acted in an objectively reasonable manner. The *Harlow* standard is specifically designed to "avoid excessive disruption of government and permit the resolution of many insubstantial claims on summary judgment," and we believe it sufficiently serves this goal. Defendants will not be immune if, on an objective basis, it is obvious that no reasonably competent officer would have concluded that a warrant should issue; but if officers of reasonable competence could disagree on this issue, immunity should be recognized. . . .

C

. . .

In the case of the officer applying for a warrant, it is our judgment that the judicial process will on the whole benefit from a rule of qualified rather than absolute immunity. We do not believe that the *Harlow* standard, which gives ample room for mistaken judgments, will frequently deter an officer from submitting an affidavit when probable cause to make an arrest is present. True, an officer who knows that objectively unreasonable decisions will be actionable may be motivated to reflect, before submitting a request for a warrant, upon whether he has a reasonable basis for believing that his affidavit establishes probable cause. But such reflection is desirable, because it reduces the likelihood that the officer's request for a warrant will be premature. Premature requests for warrants are at best a waste of judicial resources; at worst, they lead to premature arrests, which may injure the innocent or, by giving the basis for a suppression motion, benefit the guilty. . . .

III

We also reject petitioner's argument that if an officer is entitled to only qualified immunity in cases like this, he is nevertheless shielded from damages liability because the act of applying for a warrant is *per se* objectively reasonable, provided that the officer believes that the facts alleged in his affidavit are true. Petitioner insists that he is entitled to rely on the judgment of a judicial officer in finding that probable cause exists and hence issuing the warrant. This view of objective reasonableness is at odds with our development of that concept in *Harlow* and *Leon*. In *Leon*, we stated that "our good-faith inquiry is confined to the objectively ascertainable question whether a reasonably well-trained officer would have known that the search was illegal despite the magistrate's authorization." . . . The analogous question in this case is whether a reasonably well-trained officer in petitioner's position would have known that his affidavit failed to establish probable cause and that he should not have applied for the warrant. If such was the case, the officer's application for a warrant was not objectively reasonable, because it created the unnecessary danger of an unlawful arrest. It is true that in an ideal system an unreasonable request for a warrant would be harmless, because no judge would approve it. But ours is not an ideal system, and it is possible that a magistrate, working under docket pressures, will fail to perform as a magistrate should. We find it reasonable to require the officer applying for the warrant to minimize this danger by exercising reasonable professional judgment.

B. DISSENTING OPINION

JUSTICE POWELL, with whom JUSTICE REHNQUIST joins, . . . dissenting in part. . . .

II

. . .

The police, where they have reason to believe probable cause exists, should be encouraged to submit affidavits to judicial officers. I therefore believe that in a suit such as this, the Court should expressly hold that the decision by the magistrate is entitled to substantial evidentiary weight. A more restrictive standard will discourage police officers from seeking warrants out of fear of litigation and possible personal liability. The specter of personal liability for a mistake in judgment may cause a prudent police officer to close his eyes to facts that should at least be brought to the attention of the judicial officer authorized to make the decision whether a warrant should issue. Law enforcement is ill-served by this *in terrorem* restraint.

III

This Court has long sought to divide the functions of law enforcement to impose on the magistrate the primary responsibility for determining whether a warrant will issue. It is inconsistent with this jurisprudence to imply or hold that the magistrate's determination of probable cause is irrelevant in this suit. A judicial officer's "judgment call" in determining probable cause, although not conclusive, is entitled to substantial evidentiary weight in suits seeking to impose personal liability on the police officer. In this case, in the light of the judge's determination and the evidence of illegal activity, I would hold that petitioner is immune from damages.

Source: 475 U.S. 335 (1986), 337–354 (footnotes omitted).

DOCUMENT 82: *Private Employment of Public Police* (Albert J. Reiss, Jr., 1988)

The role of the police officer is a demanding one—yet many officers can't seem to get enough of it. In fact, in recent years, more and more public police officers have begun moonlighting in the private sector—as police officers. Partly in response to growing demand from the private sector, most police departments today allow their officers to accept "extra-duty" policing assignments—such as traffic control, crowd control, and private security (see document below)—during their off-duty hours.

Officers may contract with private employers independently, through their unions, or through their departments (Reiss 1988:9). However, assignments must be approved by the department to ensure that they don't interfere with the officer's regular work, and that they meet the department's "standards for conduct becoming a police officer" (Reiss 1988:13).

While such employment provides a valuable service to the private sector, and also provides police officers with an additional source of income, many people have raised concerns that extra-duty police work may interfere with the officers' regular police duty and performance. For example, the long work hours, sleep disruption, and subsequent fatigue that may result from frequent extra-duty assignments may affect officers' driving performance, interactions with the public, decision-making abilities, and other important job-related activities (Peak 1997: 65; Reiss 1988:69; Vila 1996).

* * *

As citizens go about their daily routines, they encounter uniformed police officers performing duties ordinarily associated with foot or traffic patrol or with guard or private security duty. They see them directing traffic around construction sites and at places of business. They encounter them patrolling or standing guard in shopping malls, stores, and banks. They note them at public events such as rock concerts, sporting contests, or political gatherings and at private ceremonies. Although in most communities citizens have become used to seeing their public police in these roles, many also seem puzzled by it—wondering why, with so many serious demands for police service, the police department would assign officers to these jobs.

What the public is unaware of is that in many instances these officers are privately employed—that they are working on their off-duty time for a private employer or a public agency other than the police department. Citizens' confusion is understandable. They aren't able to distinguish who is paying for the officer's services. The officer is fully uniformed, armed, and usually equipped with a two-way radio. Moreover, the officer, to all appearances, is performing police duties of surveillance, control, and patrol.

Even when aware that police officers are employed off duty as uniformed officers with full police powers, members of the public are unable to distinguish when officers are on the department's payroll and when they are not. The public correctly assumes that whatever the source of the officer's pay, the officer is fully empowered with authority to enforce the law.

The public is experiencing a growing awareness that public police officers are increasingly found serving private interests. A growing industry is emerging in which public police officers are employed off duty by private employers—what some dub a "rent-a-cop" industry.

At the same time, members of the public are aware of a private security industry whose employees are similarly found in these private settings—at banks, supermarkets, sports events, and a host of other places. They are familiar with names of security firms such as Burns, Ogden, Pinkerton's, and Wells-Fargo, and they are becoming familiar with newer or local ones—names like Allsafe, Ace, Danza's, Marston's, United, and Wackenhut. The public has no doubt that some private corporation or interest is employing these officers to provide protection and security.

Despite an inability to determine who is paying the public police officer for work in private or other settings, the public perceives that private security personnel are there to protect private interests rather than to serve as their moral protectors. They are likely to regard security officers as "low level, inept persons" in contrast with a higher regard for the public police officers in those same settings. Although we know too little about the public's comparative judgments about the value of a public police officer or a private security agent in such settings, it is abundantly clear that public police are accorded higher prestige and efficacy in those settings—even when performing routine protection or security functions.

Private security has outstripped the growth of the public police in recent decades. Their numbers now exceed those of the public police. Yet, those relative magnitudes of number of employees fail to take into account the substantial growth in the off-duty employment of public police officers by private employers. What we are witnessing is a growing sector of secondary employment of public police officers—one . . . which has emerged from the status of moonlighting to department contract employment.

Source: Albert J. Reiss, Jr., *Private Employment of Public Police*, U.S. Department of Justice, National Institute of Justice (Washington, D.C.: U.S. Government Printing Office, 1988), 1–2 (endnotes omitted).

DOCUMENT 83: "Community Policing: A Report from the Devil's Advocate" (David H. Bayley, 1988)

By 1988, the concept of community policing had been put into practice in cities and towns across the United States. Based in part on the problem-oriented policing concepts of Herman Goldstein (see Document 75), and on the work of James Q. Wilson and George L. Kelling (see Document 78), community policing took many different forms—such as establishing police foot patrols, improving communication between the police and the public, setting up shopfront police stations in communities, rescaling patrol beats, creating liaisons between minority groups and the police, establishing Neighborhood Watch programs, and door-to-door visits by the police (Bayley 1988:225).

However, in the preface to their edited volume, *Community Policing: Rhetoric or Reality*, Jack R. Greene, then associate professor of criminal justice at Temple University, and Stephen D. Mastrofski, then assistant professor of administration of justice at Pennsylvania State University, noted, "While many programs are currently under way, there has yet to be a systematic look at the new police strategies and tactics. Many questions remain unanswered. Is this a new form of policing, or is it 'old wine in new bottles'? Is this reform substantive or theoretical?" (Greene and Mastrofski 1988:xii).

According to one of the contributors to the book, David H. Bayley, a professor in the School of Criminal Justice at the State University of New York at Albany and a leading police scholar, "It is probably fair to say that community policing in 1988 is more rhetoric than reality. It is a trendy phrase spread thinly over customary reality" (Bayley 1988: 225–226).

From the position of devil's advocate, Bayley pointed out twelve potential problems with community policing. However, despite these potential problems, he concluded that community policing should not be abandoned, but rather monitored and evaluated systematically, and implemented fairly and carefully (see document below).

* * *

[I]f community policing truly becomes the wave of the future, what sort of problems might it engender that should be anticipated? Progress is never entirely unmixed, and the police have been reformed before. From the perspective of 1998, ten years hence, what sort of problems might it have been well to foresee? What might be the unanticipated consequences of community policing? Drawing upon growing experience with community policing in Europe, Asia, and North America, I shall discuss 12 problems that might be anticipated.

PROBLEMS WITH COMMUNITY POLICING

One: Public safety may decline. Community policing is based on the notion that the police cannot protect the public by their own unaided efforts. Successful crime prevention requires public participation as watchdogs and as less-vulnerable victims; successful apprehension and prosecution of criminals requires identification of suspects by the public and willing testimony. Yet the efficacy of the public as co-producers of public safety is untested. . . .

Two: The police may lose the will, and perhaps the capacity, to maintain public order. Community policing emphasizes the development of close relations with the public. The achievement of this goal, which is likely to be determined impressionistically, may undermine the determination of the police to take strong enforcement action when it is needed. . . .

Three: Community policing provides a new and less demanding rationale for the police at the very moment when the traditional justification is failing. Massive research on the efficacy of the police undertaken during the past 20 years has been singularly unsuccessful in demonstrating any connection between public safety and the numbers of police. . . .

Community policing, however, creates a new role for police with new criteria for performance. If police can not reduce crime and apprehend more offenders, they can at least decrease fear of crime, make the public feel less powerless, lessen distrust between minority groups and the police, mediate quarrels, overcome the isolation of marginal groups, organize social services, and generally assist in developing "community." These are certainly worthwhile objectives. But are they what the police should be doing? . . .

Four: Community policing makes the public an interest group for the police. A key feature of community policing is the redeployment of police personnel so as to encourage regular, routine, nonemergency interaction with the public. . . .

Community policing provides a rationale for the systematic organization of communities at the grass roots in favor of the police. If police budgets tended to be untouchable in the past due to the public's fear of crime, they may become much more so in the future as community policing transforms communities into police interest groups.

Five: Community policing will increase the power of the police relatively among government agencies. This will occur in two ways. First, crime prevention, unlike crime response, is open-ended. For example, if the police develop their capacity to diagnose circumstances that lead to crime, as fire departments have done with respect to fires, the police will have a consultative role in planning educational programs, public health, building design, street layout, public housing, municipal services, and welfare and employment policies. . . . Second, community policing places officers in a position to act as advocates for the public vis-à-vis other governmental agencies. . . .

Six: Community policing legitimates the penetration of communities by forceful enforcement agents of government. . . .

Traditionally the police deterred, arrested, constrained, warned, and did so almost exclusively in public places. Now they advise, mediate, lecture, organize, participate, cooperate, communicate, reach out, solicit, and encourage as much in private places as public. . . .

Western political theory as well as practice has tried, increasingly vainly, to separate public from private domains. Community policing seeks to make that division indistinguishable. It tries to enlist the public in the state's maintenance of order just as it tries to insinuate police officers into private spheres of activity. . . .

Seven: Community policing may weaken the rule of law in the sense of equal protection and evenhanded enforcement. An axiom of community policing is that police operations should adapt to local circumstances. . . .

Community policing makes a virtue of command discretion with respect to priorities and operations and hopes to make it responsible. The problem is that enforcement of law is rarely altogether popular. Community policing can easily be read as bending the law so as not to offend. Local commanders may begin to think it is more important not to alienate loud voices than to protect quiet ones. . . .

Eight: Community policing may lessen the protection afforded by law to unpopular persons. It may even encourage vigilantism. Community policing mobilizes the populace for crime prevention, including systematic surveillance and informing. In many U.S. cities, for example, mobile civilian-band radio patrols have been informed [sic]. . . . Members of

Neighborhood Watch are encouraged to report suspicious persons and activity. Under community policing, local commanders are judged by their ability to develop such activities. In these circumstances, the line between community protection and harassment may become blurred. . . .

Nine: Community policing may exacerbate a growing dualism in the structure of policing in modern industrial societies. Police officers report greater difficulty in organizing crime prevention efforts, eliciting responsible community feedback, and obtaining reliable information among people who are poor and uneducated than people who are affluent and professional. Evaluations of Neighborhood Watch show greater success in ethnically homogenous, relatively affluent, middle-class communities. . . . This suggests that the vitality of community policing may depend on social structure. Community policing over a period of years may become unevenly distributed socially and hence geographically. It could become the mode for the affluent, educated middle class, while traditional reactive policing remained the mode for the poor and uneducated underclass. . . .

Ten: Community policing makes supervision within police organizations ends, rather than means, based. . . .

To the extent that community policing magnifies command responsibility at all subordinate levels, encourages initiative and adaptation, and stresses the achievement of objectives over adherence to formal rules, community policing requires more successful internalization of norms of conduct. The training of community police officers must be done with unusual care and thoroughness. If this new sort of police officer is not created, community policing may lead to increased slackness, time-wasting, inattention, and mismanagement.

Eleven: Police organizations may be less accountable for the character of operations because community police officers will have greater freedom of action. . . .

As long as the conduct of community police officers is exemplary, their independent power base is not a cause for concern. But if they should mismanage funds, take bribes, abuse authority, or wink at violations of the law, they may be able to defy disciplinary action. . . .

Twelve: Community policing may undermine professionalism. . . .

Community policing . . . rests on the assumption that law enforcement and the maintenance of order are not so complex or "scientific" that the public cannot play a major role both intellectually and physically. Policing is not a profession with principles of operation understandable only by trained practitioners and supervision best accomplished by peers. The problem with this view is that while scientific pretensions of police professionalism have probably been overdone, community policing may forfeit the distance necessary for taking unpopular actions. Policing may not be like the practice of medicine, but it may be like the practice of public health. Concern for the wishes of the patient must be combined with authority to require compliance. Public health, unlike private medical treatment, cannot be refused. Like public health, policing cannot always be popular and must always be equitable.

CONCLUSION

The problems I anticipate arising out of community policing are not yet social fact. They are implications of the theory of community policing supported by scattered observations on the ground where community policing is currently being practiced. Community policing is not yet so well entrenched that [it] is a problem in itself. It would be unfortunate, therefore, if criticism at this stage discouraged further rethinking of police practices and retarded deserved change. Evidence about the shortcomings of customary policing is much greater than evidence about community policing's failings. I certainly do not believe that community policing should be abandoned. Its goals are worthwhile and its practice responsive to defects in current police performance.

However, because the problems enumerated touch profound questions of morality and politics, responsible policy making should take them into account before they arise. Community policing does not represent a small, technical shift in policing; it is a paradigmatic change in the way police operate. It is the most fundamental change in policing since the rise of police professionalism early in this century. Because community policing is serious and fateful, we must be open minded about its potential infirmities as well as its promise.

Source: David H. Bayley, "Community Policing: A Report from the Devil's Advocate." In Jack R. Greene and Stephen D. Mastrofski, eds., *Community Policing: Rhetoric or Reality* (New York: Praeger, 1988), 226–236.

Part VII

The Role of the Police in the 1990s

FROM TURMOIL, A CONSENSUS EMERGES

For the first time in decades, a consensus began to emerge in the 1990s about which duties and responsibilities should be included in the police role. Also for the first time, Americans began to confront the complexities of police work and the conflicting demands being placed on officers.

The gradual shift toward variants of community-oriented policing became a sudden surge early in the 1990s after a citizen's videotape of white Los Angeles police officers beating a black man at the end of a lengthy car chase brought the brutal, stroke-by-stroke reality of police misconduct into millions of homes night after night (Document 87). In spite of the suspect's extensive criminal background, most of the public—and many police officers across the nation—were appalled by the beating. Concerns were raised further when a riot tore through Los Angeles after an all-white jury acquitted officers involved in the beating of all criminal charges (Document 88).

In the aftermath of the beating, the riots, and the fact-finding commissions appointed to study them, it seemed clear that the LAPD's militaristic, aggressive, and aloof approach to policing, which once had been a national model (Document 53), was outdated.

THE ROLE AND CONDUCT OF POLICE

The documents in this section all deal with the conduct and role of police in American society. In a discussion of police ethics and integrity, philosopher Stephen J. Vicchio develops a list of virtues required of a police officer (Document 93) and recommends a course of ethics training for police recruits. His list of virtues is more direct and less dramatic than the revised codes of ethics and conduct promulgated by the International Association of Chiefs of Police in 1991, yet quite consistent with them (Document 86).

Another series of documents explores the sources of police misconduct and approaches to discouraging it. Aside from predictable problems arising from greedy or brutal people who should be weeded out in the selection process, tensions and frustrations arising from conflicting demands placed on officers and our unrealistic expectations of them are discussed from several perspectives in Documents 84, 85, and 89. Yet the approach to dealing with these conflicting expectations recommended by several renowned experts is to accept the complexity of the job and to develop the ability of officers and agencies to deal with that complexity in a professional manner (Documents 90 and 91).

Policing, especially contemporary urban community policing, requires that officers meet the high expectations of August Vollmer (Document 33) but in a far more challenging and diverse environment than he could have imagined. The documents in this section indicate that policing must make another transition in order for the goals of community policing to be met; it must evolve from a largely blue-collar occupation with pretensions of professionalism to a true profession that takes responsibility for self-regulation and requires that its members be skilled in conflict resolution and community problem solving as well as enforcing the law.

DOCUMENT 84: *The Police Mystique* (Anthony V. Bouza, 1990)

Should the police officer's role extend beyond fighting crime and violence to helping to solve the underlying social and economic causes of these problems? According to retired Minneapolis Police Chief Anthony V. Bouza, police officers, and particularly their chiefs, are in a unique position to "advise Americans on the sources and causes of urban violence, and they have a moral obligation to inform the nation of what is happening on their battlegrounds and why" (see document below).

Bouza, who spent thirty-six years in policing, including twenty-four years with the New York City Police Department, is a well-known and outspoken advocate of police involvement in social welfare issues.

Many of his views are somewhat controversial, particularly among more traditional police leaders. However, according to Norval Morris, professor of law and criminology at the University of Chicago:

Over the past ten or fifteen years there has gradually been emerging, in administrative positions in the city police forces of this country, a group of younger though experienced police leaders, impatient with traditional ways, willing to take seriously the important roles that police should play in social welfare, and willing to resist vigorously the long tradition of improper political meddling in their work. To them, Bouza is somewhat of a hero. (In Bouza 1990:vii)

Following is an excerpt from Bouza's 1990 book, *The Police Mystique: An Insider's Look at Cops, Crime, and the Criminal Justice System*, in which he discusses America's social and economic problems, and the police officer's potential role in drawing greater public attention to them.

* * *

The future is headed somewhere and the direction may be discerned in the trends evident today. These are shaped by alterable human decisions. There is nothing immutable or inevitable about the choices made. We seem to have opted for a widening of the chasm between the haves and the have-nots. We seem to feel perfectly comfortable with the economic, social, and cultural walls we've erected to keep the underclass out. We seem to have decided to grow ever more unequal. And we seem to have lost our appetite for service or a sense of joy in doing something useful with our lives.

It is easy to see the ever-present bitterness when a spark strikes the kindling of resentments in the ghetto. A white cop shoots a black youth and a riot starts. A black prisoner dies in police custody and chaos breaks loose. The incident is the variable. In the ghetto, anger, resentment, frustration, and defeat are the constants.

Rising levels of technology create walls against the entrance of the uneducated into the work force. The jobs created in recent years are at the ends of the spectrum—either highly skilled or absurdly low-level.

Health and welfare policies are in such wide disrepute that few serious initiatives for reform that would reintegrate the family or assist in getting clients a salary find any significant support. Issues of contraception, sex education, birthweight, maternal care, abortion, treatment programs for adults, or even programs intended to encourage a male's presence get swept aside with derisive comments about foggy liberalism. But today's abused child is tomorrow's rapist.

Educational policies are following the bankrupt notion of educating the overclass, while suffering appalling dropout rates among black male high-schoolers. Urban school systems have been abandoned to the poor, where the blacks and Hispanics compete for the crumbs a failing system provides.

The plight of the homeless adds to the present and future problems of the cities, and the situation is deteriorating rapidly.

The war on drugs is being lost. The oppression of the underclass will continue to produce crime and violence. These will fan the flames of fear licking at the overclass.

The overclass is purchasing its own security and services and abandoning the underclass.

There is a trend toward harsher sentences and greater numbers of people sent to prisons already bursting at the seams. Our jails are our Maginot Line against crime and violence. They will prove just as effective as their namesake.

The street criminal exists against a backdrop of corporate and governmental morality that has in recent years, produced shocking scandals—of the sort that raise troubling questions about the fate of the republic. The overclass mugs with phone, computers, high-tech devices, and fountain pens. Armies of lawyers are enlisted in the fray. The hypocrisy is only too evident to the blacks and Hispanics flooding our prisons.

The irony lies in the fact that civilizations save themselves through altruism, not hedonism.

Addressing the problems reflected in the rising tides of crime and violence in America actually holds out the best hope for reinvigorating the nation, cleansing its soul, and moving forward energetically to the American Dream of equality, justice, and peace.

The future, given our inattention to the urgent problems in our cities, is bleak precisely because the festering sores are not being lanced and cured. They are being papered over and ignored.

Oh for a muse of fire that would touch the public conscience like Rachel Carson's *Silent Spring* and awaken the nation to the danger of neglecting the fateful problems of its cities.

The cops generally, and the chief in particular, might be the muses needed. Like the Vietnam generals, police chiefs are the daily witnesses to the problems of crime and to the social and economic sources fueling the violence. Fighting that war is the chief's principal assignment, but is it the only one? Hasn't the chief a responsibility to report to the people on the complex, underlying forces at work? Police chiefs are uniquely positioned to advise Americans on the sources and causes of urban violence, and they have a moral obligation to inform the nation of what is happening on their battlegrounds and why.

Source: Anthony V. Bouza, *The Police Mystique* (New York: Plenum, 1990), 280–282.

DOCUMENT 85: Police Role Strain and Role Conflict (A. Daniel Yarmey, 1990)

Modern definitions of the role of police typically center around three separate functions: peacekeeping (order maintenance), crime fighting (law enforcement), and community service (for example, Barker et al. 1994:100–108; Folley 1989:557–558; Johnson 1970; Rubin 1972:23; and Yarmey 1990:64). Juggling these three roles—and the public's inconsistent expectations—is not always easy for police officers. As James S. Campbell, Joseph R. Sahid, and David P. Stang, directors of the Task Force on Law and Law Enforcement to the National Commission on the Causes and Prevention of Violence, explained:

[P]erhaps the most important source of police frustration, and the most severe limitation under which they operate, is the conflicting roles and demands involved in the order maintenance, community service, and crime-fighting responsibilities of the police. Here both the individual police officer and the police community as a whole find not only inconsistent public expectations and public reactions, but also inner conflict growing out of the interaction of the policeman's values, customs, and traditions with his intimate experience with the criminal element of the population. The policeman lives on the grinding edge of social conflict, without a well-defined, well-understood notion of what he is supposed to be doing there. (1970:291)

As an example of the type of role conflict described by Campbell et al., Rubin (1972:25) noted that many police officers consider crime fighting to be their primary role, despite the fact that most of their work revolves around community service and maintenance of order.

More recently, A. Daniel Yarmey, professor of psychology at the University of Guelph in Ontario, Canada, identified five different conditions or situations that are likely to lead to police role conflicts: the quasi-military structure of many police organizations; dealing with a sometimes hostile and/or disrespectful public; juggling competing expectations; coping with competing values; and attempting to maintain perspective during undercover operations.

In the following excerpt from his 1990 book, *Understanding Police and Police Work: Psychosocial Issues*, Yarmey discusses these five types of conflict-producing situations in detail and offers recommendations for resolving police role strain.

* * *

POLICE ROLE STRAIN AND ROLE CONFLICT

All individuals typically play many roles in their everyday behavior such as husband, father, wife, mother, neighbor, friend. Some of these roles evoke competing expectations that cannot be fulfilled. Furthermore, even a single role, such as that of police officer, has within it conflicting and varied expectations. Consequently, officers may experience role strain when expectations from one of their roles are incompatible with the demands arising from another. The strain from role conflicts produce feelings of dissatisfaction, inadequacy, tension, anxiety, and frustration. These reactions make it difficult for officers to relate with their partners, which further weakens the interpersonal relationships and the trust, confidence, and respect so necessary for police work. Persistent conflict between citizens and police and between police and fellow officers can be reflected in communication failures, social isolation, and increased hostility.

Role strain and conflict result from three major sources. First, if the expectations that make up the role are ill-defined, correct role performance is difficult. Second, contradictory role expectations, resulting from incompatibilities in the role itself, produce strain. Finally, if there are ambiguities or disagreements among participants over goals and values, relationships among role partners can be strained.

Five types of role strain and conflict in police work are described below.

Quasi-Military Organizations Versus Social Work

. . .

It is increasingly apparent to social scientists that the use of traditional quasi-military criteria to assess police performance is inappropriate when applied to sensitive interpersonal conflict situations. . . . In fact, the paramilitary police model as an objective for all police is inappropriate. . . . It is worth emphasizing that most calls for police assistance are requests for help from people in distress. These calls require tact and assistance, not force and muscle. . . .

Although the police are not social workers and dislike being labeled as such, their roles are similar in some respects. . . .

Deference to Versus Disrespect for Police

If respect for their occupation is not forthcoming, officers "put heavy emphasis on not taking any crap" (Richardson 1974). Officers are faced with a conflict between trying to do their duty and finding the public uncertain about their value or, at worst, hostile to them. The lack of respect and criticism often shown by the press also leads to tension and insecurity. Society does not know what it wants from police and often acts inconsistently toward its law enforcement officers. The consequence is further police uncertainty, discouragement, and resentment. . . .

Competing Expectations

Police are expected to be: (1) the "guardians of society," which gives them the legitimate right to use coercion to prevent crime; (2) the "peace-keepers of society," meaning that they are supposed to maintain public order, arbitrate disputes, and settle conflicts; and (3) "public servants," that is, responsible to community needs. . . . Society tends to rely on the police to solve a wide variety of problems that other agencies cannot or are unwilling to manage, such as looking for runaway teenagers or evacuating towns in emergency situations. . . . However, as mentioned earlier, police administrators have failed to provide clear and consistent guidelines of what is expected of a "good police officer." Police officers often discover that their perceptions of their job are not consistent with their supervisors' perceptions of their roles. . . .

Conflicting Values

Police generally subscribe to a value system that reflects the institution's authoritarian, quasimilitary structure. Consistent with this view, several social scientists . . . have noted that the police consider themselves morally superior. They feel that they themselves are best suited to judge right from wrong or good guys from bad guys, and they are committed to defending this moral position.

When their authority is challenged, officers are placed in a conflict. They can attack the offender, swallow their pride and forget the incident, or compromise their morality and manufacture a false excuse to arrest the individual. . . .When the police believe that they are in the best position to judge the culpability of an offender, especially for an offence that violates their moral sensibilities, "street justice," such as harassment or physical force, may be handed out quickly and self-righteously. . . . These moral actions, however, violate the basic civil rights of all citizens. . . .

"Real" Role-Playing: Undercover Police

One of the best examples of role conflict can be found in the work of undercover agents. . . .Undercover police officers working in drug enforcement have to learn to physically, intellectually, and emotionally play the role of criminals. This type of activity is exciting and brings tangible rewards of accomplishment and achievement that boost feelings of self-esteem. High emotional and intellectual investment in this work, however, often accounts for an agent's high vulnerability to conflict and emotional distress both during and after an operation. Sometimes losing perspective, undercover police can fail to "turn off" their roles outside of the operational situation when, for example, interacting with the cover team, peers, and family. Operators may begin to lead the life of the role and cover story. High attachment and loyalty to their "new friends" and the life-style provided by this role may result. When undercover work finally concludes, some officers have difficulty in making the transition to more mundane police work.

RESOLVING ROLE STRAIN

Individuals in any role category cannot be all things to all people. Some interests have to be set aside or relegated to a secondary level of importance, whereas other expectations must be given priority. One way for individuals to resolve role strain is to reestablish or rearrange priorities. If individuals cannot do so, institutions may impose a hierarchy of role expectations. . . .

One proposed solution to resolving role conflicts is professionalization of the police occupation. . . . *Professionalization*, according to Filley, House, and Kerr (1976), entails specialized training in a body of abstract knowledge; a code of ethics concerning an obligation to render services to the public; the exercise of autonomy or self-control over work decisions, methods, and activities; collegial maintenance of standards to best assure quality of service, a deep sense of commitment to occupation or calling; and close identification with the chosen profession and use of fellow professionals and professional organizations as important referents. While policing as an occupation has not yet become professionalized and individual police officers cannot claim to be professional . . . , this is not to say that police officers do not share or are not striving toward these attributes already. A commitment to professionalization is known to reduce role conflict among police. . . .

Source: A. Daniel Yarmey, *Understanding Police and Police Work: Psychosocial Issues* (New York: New York University Press, 1990), 61–68.

DOCUMENT 86: The "Law Enforcement Code of Ethics" (revised version, 1991) and the "Police Code of Conduct" (1991)

In 1989, the Executive Committee of the International Association of Chiefs of Police replaced the IACP's 32-year-old "Law Enforcement Code of Ethics" (see Document 54) with an entirely new code. The goal of the Executive Committee in adopting the new code was "to increase the code's relevance to modern policing" (*Police Chief* 1992: 14).

However, many IACP members, who had not been given the opportunity to vote on this change (*Police Chief* 1992:14), were not pleased with the new code, which was "longer, less idealistic and more pragmatic" (Kleinig with Zhang 1993:115) than the 1957 code. A main concern was that the new code was too long to be used as an oath of office at police academy graduation ceremonies (*Police Chief* 1992: 14).

The controversy over the new code was resolved at the 1991 meeting of the IACP in Minneapolis, Minnesota. By unanimous approval of the IACP membership, the 1957 version of the "Law Enforcement Code of Ethics" was reinstated, with some minor revisions and additions. At the same time, the 1989 code which had briefly replaced the 1957 code was renamed the "Police Code of Conduct" (Kleinig with Zhang 1993: 91; *Police Chief* 1992:14). Both codes are reprinted below.

* * *

A. "LAW ENFORCEMENT CODE OF ETHICS" (1991 REVISED VERSION)

As a law enforcement officer, my fundamental duty is to serve the community; to safeguard lives and property; to protect the innocent against deception, the weak against oppression or intimidation and the peaceful against violence or disorder; and to respect the constitutional rights of all to liberty, equality and justice.

I will keep my private life unsullied as an example to all, and will behave in a manner that does not bring discredit to me or my agency. I will maintain courageous calm in the face of danger, scorn or ridicule; develop self-restraint; and be constantly mindful of the welfare of others. Honest in thought and deed both in my personal and official life, I will be exemplary in obeying the law and the regulations of my department. Whatever I see or hear of a confidential nature or that is confided to me in my official capacity will be kept ever secret unless revelation is necessary in the performance of my duty.

I will never act officiously or permit personal feelings, prejudices, political beliefs, aspirations, animosities or friendships to influence my decisions. With no compromise for crime and with relentless prosecution of criminals, I will enforce the law courteously and appropriately without fear or favor, malice or ill will, never employing unnecessary force or violence and never accepting gratuities.

I recognize the badge of my office as a symbol of public faith, and I accept it as a public trust to be held so long as I am true to the ethics of police service. I will never engage in acts of corruption or bribery, nor will I condone such acts by other police officers. I will cooperate with all legally authorized agencies and their representatives in the pursuit of justice.

I know that I alone am responsible for my own standard of professional performance and will take every reasonable opportunity to enhance and improve my level of knowledge and competence.

I will constantly strive to achieve these objectives and ideals, dedicating myself before God to my chosen profession . . . law enforcement.

Source: International Association of Chiefs of Police, "Law Enforcement Code of Ethics" (1991 version), reprinted in John Kleinig with Yurong Zhang, *Professional Law Enforcement Codes: A Documentary Collection* (Westport, Conn.: Greenwood Press, 1993), 92–93.

B. "POLICE CODE OF CONDUCT" (1991)

All law enforcement officers must be fully aware of the ethical responsibilities of their position and must strive constantly to live up to the highest possible standards of professional policing.

The International Association of Chiefs of Police believes it is important that police officers have clear advice and counsel available to assist them in performing their duties consistent with these standards, and has adopted the following ethical mandates as guidelines to meet these ends.

Primary Responsibilities of a Police Officer

A police officer acts as an official representative of government who is required and trusted to work within the law. The officer's powers and duties are conferred by statute. The fundamental duties of a police officer include serving the community; safeguarding lives and property; protecting the innocent; keeping the peace; and ensuring the rights of all to liberty, equality and justice.

Performance of the Duties of a Police Officer

A police officer shall perform all duties impartially, without favor or affection or ill will and without regard to status, sex, race, religion, political belief or aspiration. All citizens will be treated equally with courtesy, consideration and dignity.

Officers will never allow personal feelings, animosities or friendships to influence official conduct. Laws will be enforced appropriately and courteously and, in carrying out their responsibilities, officers will strive to obtain maximum cooperation from the public. They will conduct themselves in appearance and deportment in such a manner as to inspire confidence and respect for the position of public trust they hold.

Discretion

A police officer will use responsibly the discretion vested in the position and exercise it within the law. The principle of reasonableness will guide the officer's determinations and the officer will consider all surrounding circumstances in determining whether any legal action shall be taken.

Consistent and wise use of discretion, based on professional policing competence, will do much to preserve good relationships and retain the confidence of the public. There can be difficulty in choosing between conflicting courses of action. It is important to remember that a timely word of advice rather than arrest—which may be correct in appropriate circumstances—can be a more effective means of achieving a desired end.

Use of Force

A police officer will never employ unnecessary force or violence and will use only such force in the discharge of duty as is reasonable in all circumstances.

Force should be used only with the greatest restraint and only after discussion, negotiation and persuasion have been found to be inappropriate or ineffective. While the use of force is occasionally unavoidable, every police officer will refrain from applying the unnecessary infliction of pain or suffering and will never engage in cruel, degrading or inhuman treatment of any person.

Confidentiality

Whatever a police officer sees, hears or learns of, which is of a confidential nature, will be kept secret unless the performance of duty or legal provision requires otherwise.

Members of the public have a right to security and privacy, and information obtained about them must not be improperly divulged.

Integrity

A police officer will not engage in acts of corruption or bribery, nor will an officer condone such acts by other police officers.

The public demands that the integrity of police officers be above reproach. Police officers must, therefore, avoid any conduct that might compromise integrity and thus undercut the public confidence in a law enforcement agency. Officers will refuse to accept any gifts, presents, subscriptions, favors, gratuities or promises that could be interpreted as seeking to cause the officer to refrain from performing official responsibilities honestly and within the law. Police officers must not receive private or special advantage from their official status. Respect from the public cannot be bought; it can only be earned and cultivated.

Cooperation with Other Police Officers and Agencies

Police officers will cooperate with all legally authorized agencies and their representatives in the pursuit of justice.

An officer or agency may be one among many organizations that may provide law enforcement services to a jurisdiction. It is imperative that a police officer assist colleagues fully and completely with respect and consideration at all times.

Personal-Professional Capabilities

Police officers will be responsible for their own standard of professional performance and will take every reasonable opportunity to enhance and improve their level of knowledge and competence.

Through study and experience, a police officer can acquire the high level of knowledge and competence that is essential for the efficient and effective performance of duty. The acquisition of knowledge is a never-ending process of personal and professional development that should be pursued constantly.

Private Life

Police officers will behave in a manner that does not bring discredit to their agencies or themselves.

A police officer's character and conduct while off duty must always be exemplary, thus maintaining a position of respect in the community in which he or she lives and serves. The officer's personal behavior must be beyond reproach.

Source: International Association of Chiefs of Police, "Police Code of Conduct" (1989, 1991), reprinted in John Kleinig with Yurong Zhang, *Professional Law Enforcement Codes: A Documentary Collection* (Westport, Conn.: Greenwood Press, 1993), 115–117.

DOCUMENT 87: The Rodney King Beating and the Christopher Commission Report (1991)

The videotaped beating of Rodney King by Los Angeles Police Department (LAPD) officers is perhaps the most widely publicized incident involving the use of excessive force by police officers in modern history. The incident took place early in the morning of March 3, 1991, following a high-speed chase that began when California Highway Patrol officers observed King driving at speeds reportedly in excess of 100 miles per hour on a San Fernando Valley freeway, and attempted to pull him over. LAPD officers joined the pursuit after King exited the freeway, still speeding, and reportedly ran a stop sign and a red light (Independent Commission on the Los Angeles Police Department 1991:4).

King finally stopped his vehicle near the corner of Osborne Street and Foothill Boulevard. In addition to the CHP and LAPD officers initially involved in the chase, twenty-one other LAPD officers eventually arrived at the scene in ten police cars and one helicopter. The LAPD told the CHP officers that they would handle the arrest from there, and although it remains unclear whether King initially obeyed police orders to lie down on the ground, it is evident from the videotape made by local resident George Holliday that what occurred next went far beyond the use of force necessary to make the arrest. Over an eighty-one-second period, several officers struck King a total of fifty-six times with their batons as other officers at the scene looked on (Independent Commission on the Los Angeles Police Department 1991:5–7, 11).

Holliday took his videotape public after his attempt to report the incident to the police was met with apparent disinterest by the desk officer who took his call (Independent Commission on the Los Angeles Police Department 1991:11). The incident, so vividly captured on videotape for millions to see, not only revived the issue of police brutality, which long has been a problem among police departments (Inciardi 1993:274; also see Documents 36, 45, 46, 63, 66, and 89), but also rekindled allegations of racism within the LAPD,[1] which had been a prominent issue during the investigation following the Watts riots (see Document 59).

Moreover, the King incident raised a number of questions related to the police role, model, and mission. For example, was the King beating an aberration, as Los Angeles Police Chief Daryl Gates characterized it (Independent Commission on the Los Angeles Police Department 1991:12), or was it the result of an outdated style of policing still used by the LAPD?

Since the 1950s, when William H. Parker was named police chief in the wake of a corruption scandal (see Document 53), Los Angeles had become known nationwide for its professional style of policing, which emphasized high recruitment standards, discipline, and efficiency via a militaristic, "war on crime" style (Deakin 1988:228–229; Walker 1998:174). Forty years later, under Gates' leadership, the LAPD maintained this professional policing style, in which crime fighting was a key objective and officers often saw themselves as the "thin blue line" between order and chaos.

While this style of policing produces results in terms of violent crime arrests per sworn officer, rapid response times to calls for service, and other measurable statistics, it has a tendency to alienate officers from the community they serve (Independent Commission on the Los Angeles Police Department 1991:98–99). Such alienation—characterized in part by a "them" and "us" attitude—is likely to contribute to harsher treatment of citizens by police officers.

Acknowledging these and other problems associated with this policing style, the Independent Commission on the Los Angeles Police Department, created by Los Angeles Mayor Tom Bradley in the aftermath of the King incident and chaired by Warren Christopher, recommended in its July 1991 report that the LAPD abandon the professional model of policing in favor of a community policing approach (see document below).

* * *

During the past century, the purposes and methods of policing have evolved as different philosophies or models have dominated police behavior. The LAPD's current approach is the product of a reform era that emphasized creation of professionalism within the force. A "professional" model of policing is primarily concerned with maintaining a well-disciplined, highly trained, and technically sophisticated force insulated from improper political influence. Crime-fighting is seen as the principal objective of policing.

A competing model of community-based policing has developed and gained increased acceptance in the 1980's and is seen by many as the preferred policing style of the future. The community policing model treats service to the public and prevention of crime as the primary function of police in society. Proponents believe that the police, the public, and other government agencies must form a working partnership to have a meaningful impact on crime. Officers at the patrol level are required to spend less time in their cars communicating with other officers and more time on the street communicating with the public.

Evidence from all sources—senior LAPD officials, rank-and-file patrol officers, community leaders, and members of the public—describes the LAPD as having a "professional" organizational culture that has emphasized crime control over crime prevention and isolated the police from the communities and the people they serve. To the applause of many, the LAPD insists on aggressive detection of major crimes—murder, burglary, automobile theft—and a rapid, seven-minute response time to calls for service. Patrol officers are evaluated by statistical measures (for example, the number of calls handled and arrests made) and are rewarded for being "hardnosed." This style of policing produces results (the LAPD consistently outperforms other major city police departments in the number of violent crime arrests per sworn officer), but it does so at the risk of creating a siege ("we/they") mentality that alienates the officer from the community. . . .

A number of commanding officers share the opinion that too many LAPD patrol officers view the public with resentment and hostility. One recently promoted lieutenant, who is currently a watch commander, testified that LAPD training emphasizes "command presence" that can lead to inappropriate confrontations on the street. He also testified that, in his view, too many LAPD officers fail to treat the public with the necessary courtesy and respect. That opinion was also expressed by former Assistant Chief Brewer, who testified that he has believed for several years that officers' conduct is "out of control" in terms of rude and disrespectful treatment of the public.

William Rathburn, Chief of Police of Dallas, Texas, and former Deputy Chief of the LAPD, testified that many techniques and procedures used by the LAPD tend to exacerbate, rather than calm, potentially volatile situations. Chief Rathburn specifically noted that the "prone-out" position as used in minority neighborhoods generates substantial hostility against the LAPD in those communities. While acknowledging the need for officer safety, Chief Rathburn expressed the view that the prone-out tactic was used by many LAPD officers in an indiscriminate and offensive manner.

The LAPD, in turn, is viewed, in the words of one minister of an African-American and Latino congregation, with "a grave mistrust." Another minister who is a former police officer, expressed the view that the "problem transcends cultural differences. The police department divides everybody into two categories: blue and everyone else." . . .

"COMMUNITY POLICING" AS AN ALTERNATIVE TO TRADITIONAL METHODS OF CRIME CONTROL

The Commission heard from several experts in police administration who urged adoption of the community policing model as a means of combatting excessive use of force and improving relations between the LAPD and the people it serves. . . .

Community policing emphasizes a department-wide philosophy oriented toward problem solving, rather than arrest statistics. The concept also relies heavily on the articulation of policing values that incorporate community involvement in matters that directly affect the safety and quality of neighborhood life. To acquire an understanding of the particular concerns and priorities of different neighborhoods, officers must interact with residents on a routine basis and keep them informed of police efforts to prevent neighborhood crime. Community policing proponents believe that, as this communication continues, a cooperative and mutually beneficial relationship will develop between the police and the community that will ensure police accountability to the community, as well as to the Department, and will promote a better understanding by the community of the realities of police work.

To be effective, a department adopting community policing principles must decentralize managerial control and provide officers greater autonomy to approach and solve the underlying causes of crime and other neighborhood problems. Proponents of this style of policing insist that addressing the causes of crime makes police officers more effective crime-fighters, and at the same time enhances the quality of life in the neighborhood.

Source: Independent Commission on the Los Angeles Police Department (Warren Christopher, Chair), *Report of the Independent Commission on the Los Angeles Police Department* (Los Angeles: The Commission, July 9, 1991), 97–101.

DOCUMENT 88: The Los Angeles Riot and Its Impact on Police-Community Relations (Karen Grigsby Bates, 1992)

When the four white police officers arrested and charged with excessive use of force in the Rodney King beating (see Document 87) were acquitted by a mostly white jury on April 29, 1992, the city of Los Angeles erupted into a riot reminiscent of the 1965 Watts riot (see Document 59). Like the Watts riot, the 1992 riot continued for six days, and assistance from outside law enforcement personnel was needed before it was over. Overall, 52 people were killed, compared to 34 in 1965; 16,000 were arrested, compared to about 4,000 in 1965; and almost $1 billion worth of property had been damaged or destroyed, compared to $40 million in 1965.

In addition to this massive physical destruction, outrage over the King beating and jury verdicts also contributed to further erosion of trust between the police and minority communities in Los Angeles (see document below).

* * *

Growing up in the 1950s, most elementary school children of all races were taught to respect authority, to salute the flag when it was presented to us, and to always know that if we found ourselves in trouble, if there was an emergency, "the policeman is your friend."

Policemen, in the '50s, at least, in my Connecticut hometown, were presented as benign, avuncular figures; they were guys who shepherded lost dogs home, patted little kids on the head and cheerfully told you which way to go to get to the public library.

I don't know many black people who stop policemen and ask for directions anymore. Mostly they give a wide berth, and, after yesterday's verdict in the Rodney King trial, that berth will get wider still.

I watched the verdict come in as I bounced my 8-month-old son on my knee. My mouth tightened in grim disbelief as verdict after "not guilty" verdict from a jury with no African-Americans came back. My mind's eye flashed back to tales of trials in the segregated Deep South, trials where—when they occurred at all—smirking white defendants who had assaulted or killed black people walked away, acquitted by a jury of what was indeed their peers.

Listening to the television's drone, one part of me grunted in resignation—same ol' same ol'—and the other part just couldn't grasp it. The verdicts defied logic. Had not the jury seen the same tape I did, the one that showed the officers in question pounding away at Rodney King? Had they read—and dismissed—the computer transcripts describing we black people as animals (specifically gorillas)? Could they ignore the testimony of emergency room personnel about one officer's menacing jocularity as King lay bleeding from the injuries administered by the same officer? Obviously, they could and did. So I learned some things from the King trial:

—Southern California needn't be so smug about how far it's come in race relations. Simi Valley is thousands of physical miles away from Johannesburg. But some similarities are disturbingly familiar, and the suburban hostility directed toward Los Angeles, with its multiracial population and its urban challenges, would look right at home on "World News Tonight."

—The policeman, at least for the moment, is *not* my friend. Many people feel the Simi Valley jury's verdict has handed the LAPD an open season, a license to hunt its minority citizenry. African-Americans and Latinos felt beleaguered enough by the police before Rodney King. It doesn't take a rocket scientist to envision a worst-case scenario: angry young men of color who will do anything to keep from being stopped because they don't want to turn into another notch on some cop's baton.

As I write this, elected officials, civic leaders and, yes, the police department are preparing for what they fear may be massive urban unrest. Isolated incidents of violent anger were already occurring. But I hope that, for the most part, the anger from the King trial can be channeled into specific actions. Instead of trashing our own neighborhoods from a feeling of hopeless impotence, we should take stock of our numbers, coalesce with other minority groups and work for a little home improvement.

—Vote for Charter Amendment F, which provides specific recommendations for police reform, on June 2.

—Lobby to further change the city charter so that residence in the city is mandatory for LAPD officers. It's easy to wreak havoc in one neighborhood and drive several miles away to live in another. Perhaps if they were truly local residents, LAPD officers who aren't now living in the city would understand it in a different, better way.

I'm well aware that the job of policing a city as huge and as diverse as Los Angeles is gigantic, that the advent of drug-related violence and crime has increased exponentially and that the police are the first vanguard against it. Often their lives are on the line.

But there's a considerable distance between collaring criminals and the practice of harassing citizens because they happen to be black and male and thus automatically suspect. I hope, when he's sworn in, that Willie L. Williams will get the support and cooperation he needs, so that the tension between much of the LAPD and Los Angeles' minority communities will lessen. I hope he makes enough progress that, by the time my 8-month-old is ready to go to school, I can tell him what my parents told me: If something happens, if there's an emergency, find a policeman. That policeman (or, today, woman) is your friend. Till that day comes, especially considering Wednesday's verdict, I can't say a thing.

Source: Karen Grigsby Bates, "Perspective on the Rodney King Verdict: Dashing the Possibility of Trust," *Los Angeles Times*, April 30, 1992, B7.

DOCUMENT 89: "The Cops' Code of Silence" (Bryan Vila, 1992)

The Rodney King beating (Document 87), the Los Angeles riot of 1992, and the Christopher Commission's findings provided a graphic reminder that, despite the professional ideals articulated in codes of ethics and conduct (Document 86), officer misconduct still was a major problem. Something else that became increasingly clear was that a great deal of misconduct was able to persist only because an informal "code of silence"—the aversion of police officers to reporting each other—made it very difficult to police the police.

One of the assumptions of the police professionalization movement was that careful recruit screening, training, and supervision would be sufficient for controlling police misconduct. However, in spite of drastic improvements in these areas, officer misconduct continued to plague American police departments. The city of Los Angeles, for example, paid more than $20 million in legal judgments, settlements, and verdicts for excessive use of force from 1986 to 1990 (Independent Commission on the Los Angeles Police Department 1991:56). Los Angeles County paid $15.5 million from January 1989 to May 1992 (Kolts et al. 1992:26). New York City paid $44 million from 1987 to 1991 to settle police misconduct cases (Staff 1992, in Kappeler 1993:7). Why?

Critics of the police have suggested that policing institutions attract bullies or that the true role of police is to perpetuate the domination of the underclass by oppressive elites. A very different causal pattern was suggested by Bryan Vila, a University of California professor and former police officer. He argued that the code of silence and persistent problems with improper use of force usually were not due to selecting the wrong people; the intensive screening and training procedures used by most large police departments in the United States are quite thorough. Rather, Vila pointed to our unrealistic expectations as the sustaining force behind the police code of silence. Specifically, institutional cultures that portray police as crusaders against crime and the unrealistic physical and emotional demands of the job create a setting where understandable, yet illegal, mistakes are inevitable. When such mistakes occur, they are covered up to avoid severe penalties. And once an officer has been "covered for" by peers, he or she owes them the same favor in return.

* * *

The police "code of silence" may well be the year's most cited and least understood problem. Recent news articles, editorials, and commission reports concerned with police misconduct—especially misuse of force—in poor urban neighborhoods mistakenly treat the term as though it describes some immutable artifact of contemporary policing.

This error has led them to ignore the fact that the code of silence must itself be substantially weakened before the changes in police training, supervision, policies, procedures, and discipline they recommend can be effective.

The tendency of police to protect one another is a natural response by people who routinely try to meet unrealistic demands in extraordinarily difficult situations. But this tendency need not become the exaggerated code of silence often found among police in high-crime urban slums. These communities already suffer concentrated poverty, racism, and crime. Their burden is compounded when police are perceived as yet another potential source of danger.

If we could control the unreasonable expectations that allow officers to justify their failure to police one another, we might eliminate much of the actual and perceived police misconduct that cripples our ability to control crime in many urban slums.

Several factors enable the code to infect even the most well-intentioned officers. The way a law enforcement organization describes its mission can influence how much misbehavior officers will tolerate from peers.

Many police managers and politicians portray officers as a thin line of warriors standing between civilization and the barbarian hordes.

This unrealistic expectation that cops, rather than communities, control crime increases the zeal with which many officers approach their job. When one participates in a crusade, it is easy to rationalize extreme measures.

The patrol environment is also important. We often have unrealistic expectations of patrol officers in high-crime areas, who regularly handle several adrenaline-pumping incidents a shift. Moreover, they often do so while exhausted from overtime assignments, off-duty court appearances, and job-related activities such as attending college. This combination of environmental stressors and fatigue magnifies perceptions of threats, degrades decisionmaking, and increases the tendency to overreact.

We limit the amount of time pilots, truck drivers, and medical interns work, yet tolerate chronically fatigued cops.

Repeated exposure to stressful and dangerous situations obviously increases the likelihood that patrol officers will eventually act improperly. Most officers spend from five to 15 years in patrol. For enthusiastic officers in high-crime areas, this can translate into thousands of arrests and tens of thousands of contacts with people who are intoxicated, belligerent, or irrational. Yet when the courts make their leisurely and meticulous assessment of an officer's use of force, each incident is evaluated in isolation.

Combining institutionally fostered zealousness with unrealistic physical and emotional expectations is a recipe for misconduct.

Take the case of a normally diligent and professional officer who erupts and strikes that one person too many who screams in his face at the end of an arduous night. Acting out of anger rather than fear for his safety, he has committed a felony. If he is truthful, the career that defines him is over. He could go to prison. If he chooses to lie, he must obtain his partner's complicity. They both know he was wrong, but they also know that any person who repeatedly dealt with the same situation would blow it eventually. Recognizing that the system makes impossible demands and offers impossible choices, they choose to submit a false report and, if necessary, perjure themselves.

The code of silence is reborn each time this decision is made.

Later, when his partner uses excessive force, our officer reciprocates. Eventually, even the most idealistic officers can be infected by the code. As this erodes an officer's moral fiber, self-interest and continued stress make future compromises easier. Since police agencies promote mostly from within, many supervisors and managers are tainted by past misdeeds. This hardly leaves them in a position to control the behavior of subordinates.

The code of silence can undermine even determined attempts at police reform. If we want to control the conduct of our police and strengthen their ability to work with communities to control crime, we need to inhibit the code. How? First, we should debunk the demagoguery of the "thin blue line" myth. Our inner cities need calm professional officers, not exhausted crusaders.

More fundamentally, we must ensure that officers are emotionally and physically fit for duty each time they hit the streets, just as the military must ensure the reliability of those who control nuclear weapons. For decades, the military has accomplished this via personnel reliability programs combining cooperative self-regulation with active monitoring by health-care professionals.

Exhausted or otherwise debilitated cops should be encouraged to excuse themselves from duty. Good cops protect one another. Supervisors and peers need to learn that protection includes convincing unfit officers to stay off the streets. As a final safety check, a trained professional should have the authority to immediately remove unfit officers from duty. Personnel reliability program costs would be offset by fewer lawsuits and accidents.

Steps such as these would neither condone nor excuse police misbehavior. But they would attack the source of the awful silence that allows it to persist.

Source: Bryan Vila, "The Cops' Code of Silence," *Christian Science Monitor*, August 31, 1992, 18.

DOCUMENT 90: "The New Policing: Confronting Complexity" (Herman Goldstein, 1993)

By the 1990s, community policing programs in one form or another were being implemented at police departments throughout the country. The term had practically become a household word, and yet, with so many different programs and activities now being included under its umbrella, it was becoming more and more unclear to some practitioners just what community policing encompassed (Goldstein 1993: 95–96).

To some, the solution appeared to be the development of a simple, clear definition of community policing. However, as Herman Goldstein (also see Document 75) cautioned, oversimplification of the concept of community policing could be just as problematic, and "a deadly enemy to progress in policing" (Goldstein 1993:96). Instead, he argued, "[w]e need to better understand the complicated rather than search for the simple" (see document below).

* * *

RETHINKING THE POLICE ROLE

The policing of a free, diverse, and vibrant society is an awesome and complex task. The police are called upon to deal with a wide array of quite different behavioral problems, each perplexing in its own way. The police have tremendous power—to deny freedom and to use force, even to take a life. Individual officers exercise enormous discretion in using their authority and in making decisions that affect our lives. The very quality of life in this country and the equilibrium of our cities depend on the way in which the police function is carried out.

Given the awesome and complex nature of the police function, it follows that designing the arrangements and the organization to carry it out is equally complex. We are now in a period in which more attention is being given to the police function than at any prior time, a period in which we are rethinking, in all of its multiple dimensions, the arrangement for the policing of our society. We should not, therefore, lose patience because we have not yet come up with the perfect model; we should not get stalled trying to simplify change just to give uniform meaning to a single, catchy, and politically attractive term. We need to open up explorations rather than close them down. We need to better understand the complicated rather than search for the simple.

Some of the most common changes associated with community policing are already being implemented; for example, the permanent assignment of officers to specific beats with a mandate to get to know and relate to the community. There is now growing and persuasive support for decentralization, permanent assignments, and the development of "partnerships" between the police and the community. But these changes represent only a fragment of the larger picture.

Policing in the United States is much like a large, intricate, complex apparatus with many parts. Change of any part requires changes in many others and in the way the parts fit and work together. For example, altering the way officers are assigned and how they patrol may be easy. But to gain full value from such changes, and to sustain them, changes are also necessary in the organization and leadership of the police department—in its staffing, supervision, training, and recruitment; and in its internal working environment. Thus, a change in direction requires more than tinkering. It requires, if it is to be effective, simultaneous changes in many areas affecting the enterprise. This, in turn, requires careful planning and coordination. And perhaps more important, it requires time, patience, and learning from experience.

Moreover, to succeed in improving policing, we need to move beyond the exclusive focus on the police *agency*. There is an urgent need to alter the public's expectations of the police. And we need to revise the fundamental provisions that we as a society make for carrying out the police function. For example:

- Refine the authority granted the police (curtail it in some areas and expand it in others).
- Recognize the discretion exercised by the police and provide a means for its review and control.
- Provide the police with the resources that will enable them to get their job done.

We need, in other words, without compromising our commitment to democratic values, to [bring] expectations and capacity more into harmony so that a job increasingly labeled as "impossible" can be carried out. . . .

CONCLUSION

Dwelling on complexity is risky, for it can be overwhelming and intimidating. It is difficult. It turns many people off. But for those who get involved, the results can be very rewarding.

There have been extraordinary accomplishments in policing in the past two decades by police agencies that have taken on some of these difficult tasks. There is an enormous reservoir of ability and commitment in police agencies, especially among rank and file officers, and a willingness on the part of individual citizens and community groups at the grass roots level to engage with the police and support change. Viewed collectively, these achievements should be a source of optimism and confidence. By building on past progress and capitalizing on current momentum, change that is deeper and more lasting can be achieved.

But there is an even more compelling overriding incentive to struggle with these complexities. We are being challenged today to commit ourselves anew to our unique character as a democracy, to the high value we as a nation place on diversity, ensuring equality, protecting individual rights, and guaranteeing that all citizens can move about freely and enjoy tranquil lives. The social problems that threaten the character of the Nation are increasing, not decreasing. It will take major changes—apart from those in the police—to reduce these problems. In this turbulent period it is more important than ever that we have a police capacity that is sensitive, effective, and responsive to the country's unique

reducing crime.

needs, and that, above all else, is committed to protecting and extending democratic values. That is a high calling indeed.

Source: Herman Goldstein, "The New Policing: Confronting Complexity," National Institute of Justice, *Research in Brief* (Washington, D.C.: U.S. Department of Justice, December 1993). Reprinted in Paul F. Cromwell and Roger G. Dunham, eds., *Crime and Justice in America* (Upper Saddle River, N.J.: Prentice-Hall, 1997), 96–97, 103.

DOCUMENT 91: *Police for the Future* (David H. Bayley, 1994)

From the establishment of the first modern American police force in New York City in 1845 (see Document 11), crime prevention typically has been considered an important part of the police role. However, as David H. Bayley (also see Document 83) pointed out in his 1994 book, *Police for the Future*, a large body of evidence indicates that the police do not, in fact, prevent crime (3–5).

Bayley, who has conducted numerous studies on the effectiveness of police practices, noted that research "has consistently failed to find any connection between the number of police officers and crime rates" and that "the primary strategies adopted by modern police have been shown to have little or no effect on crime" (1994:3).

However, this does not mean that Bayley advocates eliminating our police forces, nor does he believe that the burden of crime prevention should be transferred to some other institution or institutions. Rather, Bayley recommends expanding and redefining the police role so that finding and implementing ways to prevent crime truly is one of the main responsibilities of the police (see document below).

* * *

All in all, I believe it would be easier, safer, and more effective to broaden the functions of the police to include the activities of crime prevention than to create new institutions to mobilize and direct society's resources against the menace of crime. This does not mean that efforts should not also be made to develop and invigorate other institutions for the same purpose. But it does mean that the police should be told that crime prevention is their primary responsibility. Unless this is done, I fear it will not happen in ways that we will find acceptable.

There is a dilemma here. The police cannot be relied upon to prevent crime, but they cannot be excused from the responsibility either. The solution is to recognize that there are two questions here, not one. What should societies do to prevent crime? What should the police do? We cannot rely upon the police, even when they are dedicated to preventing crime, to save society from crime. No single institution can do that. At the same time, we must charge them with taking the lead in exploring what must be done. In institutional terms, they are best for the purpose.

If this reasoning is sound, then the challenge is to find ways of using the police for crime prevention without (1) losing other important functions that they perform, (2) discouraging the strengthening of other social processes that are critical to the enterprise, and (3) creating an omnicompetent police that combines coercion with consultation, amelioration, and coordination.

Can this be done? I think so. It will require policing to be demilitarized. Policing must no longer be viewed as a war, dominated by the use of force devised by senior ranks and carried out by "troops" whose primary duty is obedience. Policing will need to be stood on its head. In conventional policing, the assessment of needs and the development of strategies are done at the top, by senior staff. Lower echelons carry out the plans that headquarters formulate. In order for crime to be prevented effectively, responsibility for diagnosing needs and formulating action plans must be given to frontline personnel. Higher echelons should act in a supporting role, either by delivering the necessary resources or managing the organization in a facilitating way. In other words, the roles of staff and line personnel must be reversed. This can be accomplished through a three-tiered system.

1. Neighborhood police officers (NPOs), whose exclusive responsibility is to deliver crime prevention.
2. Basic police units (BPUs), which would be full-service command units responsible for delivering police services as needed.
3. Police forces, which would provide resources, manage the organization, and evaluate effectiveness.

. . .

Level 1: The Neighborhood Police Officer

The only way crime prevention can be made a core function of policing is by assigning a large number of frontline officers to it. In order for crime prevention to become important in policing, it must be staffed. A new line of work must be created, with personnel assigned to it who are deployed as extensively in communities as are conventional patrol officers. Crime prevention will not take place if it is tacked onto the existing duties of patrol officers and detectives. . . .

Therefore, the front line of policing should consist of mature, experienced, and carefully selected NPOs with the responsibility of designing policing in relatively small areas. The NPOs would assess all of the security needs of their areas and determine corrective courses of action. Such measures might involve law enforcement but would also include referral to other agencies and mobilization of the self-help capacity of each community. Each area should be small enough so that one officer, or perhaps two, would be able to consult continually with individuals and institutions about crime and disorder problems. The NPO in a community must become known to all the residents as "our police officer." NPOs would be encouraged to create local crime-prevention councils, along the lines of London's sector working groups or Edmonton's community advisory panels. Since the entire jurisdiction of any police force would be checkerboarded in this way, similar to the current beat system, the corps of NPOs would become the largest uniformed specialization within policing.

The primary function of NPOs would be the diagnosis of security needs and the formulation of plans to meet recurring needs before they become law-enforcement emergencies. It would be unrealistic for NPOs to try to prevent all crime. Rather, they would focus on incidents caused by visible circumstances within local communities. NPOs cannot be expected to reform society, but they can be expected to address local circumstances that lead to crime and disorder....

Level 2: The Basic Police Unit

. . .

... A BPU would be the smallest full-service territorial command unit of a police force. Similar to precincts in large U.S. cities, subdivisions in Britain, and police stations in Japan, BPUs would be responsible for delivering all but the most specialized police services. Their essential function would be to determine local needs and to devise strategies to meet those needs....

Level 3: The Police Force

BPUs look very much like miniature police forces, but with one vital difference. They cannot provide several crucial ingredients that are required for effective operation. These are support, organization, and evaluation. These needs must be met by a higher level of organization—namely, the police force.

First, police forces must supply the physical, technical, financial, and human resources that frontline operations require, and they need to do so in a timely way. They need to recruit, train, equip, build, maintain, and generally administer the housekeeping functions of policing.

Second, police forces should be responsible for creating an organization that operates in the decentralized, prevention-focused fashion recommended here....

Third, police forces must evaluate the performance of constituent units and personnel.... Police forces must provide the feedback that allows

BPUs to determine whether what they are doing should be changed. They must also monitor the nonnegotiable aspects of policing—justice, equity, and discipline.

The distinct function of police forces is organizational management. They do not command operations, and they do not diagnose or develop strategies. They provide the infrastructure that effective crime prevention requires.

Source: David H. Bayley, *Police for the Future* (New York: Oxford University Press, 1994), 145–147, 151–152, 155–156 (footnotes omitted).

DOCUMENT 92: "A Theory of Excessive Force and Its Control" (Carl B. Klockars, 1996)

Despite repeated public outcry and scrutiny by various commissions, academics, and practitioners, the problem of police use of excessive force continues. One reason the problem has been so difficult to resolve, according to Carl B. Klockars, professor of sociology and criminal justice at the University of Delaware, may be the lack of an adequate definition of what is meant specifically by "excessive use of force." In his 1996 article, "A Theory of Excessive Force and Its Control," Klockars proposed that rather than relying on definitions based on criminal law, civil liability, and avoidance of public scandal, "Excessive force should be defined as the use of more force than a highly skilled police officer would find necessary to use in that particular situation" (8).

Klockars went on to examine the implications this definition would have on the way police excessive use of force is identified, evaluated, and ultimately controlled, noting, "The breakthrough in controlling excessive use of force by police will come about only when skilled officers are willing to apply their knowledge and expertise to identifying uses of excessive force and specifying alternatives that would minimize its use" (16). Klockars' article is excerpted below.

* * *

Toward a Definition of Excessive Force

. . .

The enormous range of the legitimate authority of the police to use force is at the heart of the problem of defining and controlling its excessive use. At present, three of the major mechanisms that appear to do so are *criminal law*, which says that an officer's use of force shall not be so excessive as to constitute a crime; *civil liability*, which says that an officer's use of force shall not cause such an injury to a person that the person or heirs should be awarded compensation for the officer's misconduct; and *fear of scandal*, which says that an officer's behavior shall not be of such nature as to embarrass his employer. Each of these mechanisms for controlling excessive force by police embodies a form of definition of it. . . .

Beyond Crimes, Civil Penalties, and Scandals

It is necessary to move beyond the impasse of these three defining standards in order to make practical progress in controlling the excessive use of force by police. If policing is to move beyond these three standards, it must go to the same source where every other profession finds standards: within the skills of policing itself, as exemplified in the work of its most highly skilled practitioners. . . . *Excessive force should be defined as the use of more force than a highly skilled police officer would find necessary to use in that particular situation.* . . .

Controlling Excessive Force: An Administrative Agenda

. . .

EVALUATING POLICE SKILL. . . . The only individuals who have the detailed knowledge necessary to distinguish good policing from that which is merely not criminal, civilly liable, or scandalous are highly skilled police officers.

The breakthrough in controlling excessive use of force by police will come about only when skilled officers are willing to apply their knowledge and expertise to identifying uses of excessive force and specifying alternatives that would minimize its use. That must be the engine of any second-generation effort to control the use of excessive force. Three obstacles stand in the way. The first is "the code," the usually unspoken agreement among police officers which calls upon them to go to extreme lengths to protect one another from punishment. . . . The second is the "cover your ass" syndrome. Endemic in police agencies, "CYA" calls upon all police to behave in ways that will not expose them to criticism. The third is the view, widely held among line officers and among many supervisors, that the "good" supervisor is the one who will "back up" an officer when he or she makes a mistake. . . .

Each of these obstacles springs from a single source: the fundamentally punitive orientation of the quasi-military administrative apparatus of American police agencies. . . .

In the face of the occupational culture and punitive administrative environment of police agencies, under what conditions might police supervisors become willing to apply their skills and knowledge to the identification of excessive force and teach alternatives to it? Some supervisors, for reasons ranging from their own lack of skill to opposition to reducing the use of force on people who they believe deserve it to categorical refusal to second guess the field decisions of a fellow police officer, will refuse to do so under virtually any conditions. Others may be made willing to apply their skills and knowledge under three conditions. They are:

1. They be clearly and specifically required to do so.
2. They be held accountable for doing so by having their evaluation of each use-of-force incident reviewed by persons who are equally expert.
3. They be permitted to offer their evaluation under circumstances in which the normal punitive and disciplinary orientation of police administration is suspended. . . .

After the review is complete, and it should normally be completed within forty-eight hours of the use-of-force incident, the use-of-force report and evaluation by three supervisors should be returned to the officer. A finding that the use of force was necessary and appropriate requires no further comment, but a letter complimenting the officer for handling the incident with a high level of police skill would not be out of order. A reference to internal affairs will inform an officer that the incident is under further investigation and punishment of some form may follow, pending its outcome. But a finding that the officer's behavior was legitimate (i.e., that it did not constitute criminal, civil, or scandalous misconduct) but that an alternative approach might have made it unnecessary should prompt an occasion in which a senior skilled and experienced police officer explains to a fellow officer in detail how that officer might have conducted himself in a way that might have avoided the need to use force or minimized its actual use. No discipline or punishment should follow such an advisory session, but supervisors must make clear that the officer will be expected to work in ways that minimize the use of force in the future.

EDUCATING POLICE OFFICERS IN THE SKILLS OF MINIMIZING THE USE OF FORCE. This analysis of the concept of excessive force and the consequences that spring from alternative constructions of it concludes that *only* from such instruction, from skilled supervisors taking seriously their obligation to supervise and to teach the skills of good police work, will real progress be made in controlling excessive use of force by police. To some unknown degree such teaching already takes place in many police agencies. It is done by some field training officers, by some senior police officers who mentor young officers, and by some skilled supervisors. It happens for the most part sub rosa because identifying publicly a use of excessive force triggers almost automatically an assumption on the part of someone that it should be punished. Willful, malicious, sadistic, conscience-shocking, unreasonable uses of force certainly should be reprimanded. However, the just outrage that such violence provokes has had the effect of suppressing the identification, discussion, and development of alternatives to everyday uses of excessive force that are often the product of nothing more malevolent than a lack of skill. The irony in defining excessive force at a point which merits punishment is that all sorts of unnecessary force will be deemed acceptable up to that point and police behavior will continue to flirt with legal liability and scandal. As long as that lack of skill is denied, tolerated, hidden, or otherwise removed from administrative control in sympathetic efforts to shield well-meaning officers from punishment, no real progress will be made in controlling the police use of excessive force.

Not all uses of excessive force by police should be punished. Understanding excessive force in the way I have argued that it should be understood, most uses of excessive force should not be punished, any more than should all mistakes in diagnosis or unsuccessful treatment by doctors. Every trial lawyer of experience has lost cases that a more skilled attorney might have won. Engineers continually develop approaches to solving problems that reveal defects in previously accepted engineering strategies and render them unacceptable. Progress in medicine, law, and engineering and the development of skilled physicians, lawyers, and engineers have occurred largely when their mistakes are identified by fellow professionals of the highest skills and are reviewed candidly, and when efforts are made to avoid them in the future. Progress will come in control of excessive force when the same can be said of police.

Source: Carl B. Klockars, "A Theory of Excessive Force and Its Control," in William A. Geller and Hans Toch, eds., *Police Violence* (New Haven, Conn.: Yale University Press, 1996), 2, 8, 15–18.

DOCUMENT 93: "Ethics and Police Integrity: Some Definitions and Questions for Study" (Stephen J. Vicchio, 1996)

The highly publicized beating of Rodney King by Los Angeles police officers (see Document 87) and a number of other incidents[2] that occurred during the 1990s not only focused national attention on the issue of police use of excessive force (Documents 88 and 89), but also led the public and many law enforcement experts to question the ethics and integrity of the police.

In response, the Office of Community Oriented Policing Services (COPS) and the National Institute of Justice (NIJ) sponsored a National

Symposium on Police Integrity, held July 14–16, 1996, in Washington, D.C. The goal of the symposium, which brought together approximately two hundred law enforcement executives, researchers, police officers, labor organizations, and community and political leaders, was to examine police integrity and develop a plan for fostering and maintaining integrity within police departments (U.S. Department of Justice 1997:7, 9).

Keynote speakers at the symposium were U.S. Attorney General Janet Reno, who presented the federal perspective on police integrity, and Stephen J. Vicchio, professor of philosophy at the College of Notre Dame in Baltimore, Maryland. Vicchio, a nationally respected ethicist, presented a definition of police integrity as well as a list of seven core virtues required for police integrity (see document below).

* * *

The Concept of Integrity

. . .

. . . [I]ntegrity in the context of police work should amount to the sum of the virtues required to bring about the general goals of protection and service to the public. In short, professional virtue should always bring about the moral goals of the professional organization in question. A list of the virtues of a good cop, then, ought to tell us something important about why police departments exist. Professional integrity, then, in any professional context, is the integrated collection of virtues that brings about the goals of the profession. Presumably, in police organizations those major goals are connected to protection of and service to the public.

A List of Core Virtues

. . .

- **Prudence**. Practical wisdom, the virtue of deliberation and discernment. The ability to unscramble apparent conflicts between virtues while deciding what action (or refraining from action) is best in a given situation.

- **Trust**. This virtue is entailed by the three primary relationships of the police officer: the citizen-officer relationship, the officer-officer relationship, and the officer-supervisor relationship. Trust ought to engender loyalty and truthfulness in these three contexts.

- **Effacement of self-interests**. Given the "exploitability" of citizens, self-effacement is important. Without it, citizens can become a means to advance the police officer's power, prestige, or profit, or a means for advancing goals of the department other than those to protect and to serve.

- **Courage**. As Aristotle suggests, this virtue is a golden mean between two extremes: cowardice and foolhardiness. There are many professions—surgery and police work, to name two—where the difference between courage and fool-hardiness is extremely important.

- **Intellectual honesty**. Acknowledging when one does not know something and being humble enough to admit ignorance is an important virtue in any professional context. The lack of this virtue in police work can be very dangerous.

- **Justice**. We normally think of justice as giving the individual what he or she is due. But taking the virtue of justice in a police context sometimes requires the removal of justice's blindfold and adjusting what is owed to a particular citizen, even when those needs do not fit the definition of what is strictly owed.

- **Responsibility**. Again, Aristotle suggests that a person who exhibits responsibility is one who intends to do the right thing, has a clear understanding of what the right thing is, and is fully cognizant of other alternatives that might be taken. More importantly, a person of integrity is one who does not attempt to evade responsibility by finding excuses for poor performance or bad judgment.

At a minimum, then, these seven virtues are required for integrity because they are required as well by the general goals of police organizations. . . . In short, a police officer who exhibits integrity is a person who has successfully integrated these seven virtues so that they become a whole greater than the parts.

Source: Stephen J. Vicchio, "Ethics and Police Integrity: Some Definitions and Questions for Study," speech presented at the National Symposium on Police Integrity, July 14–16, 1996, Washington, D.C. Reprinted in U.S. Department of Justice, *Police Integrity: Public Service with Honor* (Washington, D.C.: U.S. Government Printing Office, 1997), 14–15.

DOCUMENT 94: "The Thin Blue and Pink Line" (Lisa Shores, 1997)

There were no regularly appointed female officers at the start of the twentieth century. Even when women grudgingly were allowed into police work, their roles largely were limited to the kinds of preventive work that now is the vital core of contemporary community policing. When pioneering policewoman Alice Stebbins Wells received her commission as a Los Angeles police officer in 1910, Chief of Police Galloway apologized for offering a woman "so plain an insignia of office," stating that "when he had a squad of Amazons he would ask the police commission to design a star edged with lace ruffles" (Document 28B).

By the 1920s, many departments had hired policewomen to handle clerical duties and juvenile and female victims and prisoners, and to act as "municipal mothers" (Document 28). In the Wickersham Commission's 1931 *Report on Police* (Document 44), one of August Vollmer's ten conclusions was that qualified women should be hired to handle these types of cases. The restriction of women's roles in policing to these sorts of activities still was the norm as late as the 1960s (Document 56), but by the 1980s women had begun to move into all aspects of police work (Document 79).

In this document Sgt. Lisa Shores of the Charlotte-Mecklenburg, North Carolina, police department provides a fitting counter to Chief Galloway's offer of a lace-trimmed badge, arguing that badges come in silver or gold, not blue or pink. Sgt. Shores shows how much progress women had made in policing by the end of the twentieth century, and how much room for improvement still existed. This document also is important because, unlike other documents in this book, it provides a direct glimpse into how contemporary rank-and-file officers—regardless of gender—view policing.

* * *

Why Are *They* Here?

Why do women want to be cops anyway? Are there some women who join the force because they feel they have something to prove? Probably. (Thank God that is never the case with men.) As shocking as it may seem, many women are drawn to this line of work because they want to help the good guys and put the bad guys away. Others join the ranks because they feel a spiritual calling of sorts (you know? . . . that unexplainable tug on your heart in the middle of the night). Some are seeking a profession that is exciting and personally challenging, others feel a sense of civic duty and, for some, it is a family affair.

The things that draw people to police work are not gender-biased. Most cops—male and female—took up the challenge of law enforcement with pure motives. People look for jobs that they think they will like. If they are lucky—as I have been—it won't dawn on them that their gender may have predetermined their marketability and they will, therefore, feel free to pursue whatever line of work best suits them. Novel idea, huh?

What Do *They* Want?

Inclusion. Women should be included in every aspect of the organization. Are there any women on the Honor Guard in your department? Do women in your agency work in homicide or armed robbery? Are any of your operational command-level employees women? How many women recruit or are allowed to train in your agency? When a work group is formed, are women included in the solicitation of ideas?

"They" want to be a part of "We." Police proudly boast of this big family of ours. Only in dysfunctional families are members ostracized on the basis of gender alone. The hands of the clock are not turning back. With time, education and enlightenment, women in the police ranks will be gender-representative of the communities we serve. Won't that best serve the interests of our customers and, by extension, our police family?

Standardization. Mother Nature predetermined physical distinctions between men and women that should be reflected in physical fitness standards. There is no such distinction in intellectual areas and, therefore, none should be made. Avoid adjusting (lowering) entrance and promotional test scores in an effort to hire and/or promote women. Consider qualifications, not gender. There is no victory in a "token" promotion or assignment. Recent promotions in my own department have shown that if the playing field is leveled, women do well irrespective of gender.

With the exception of those officers who are injured or pregnant, special "light" duty assignments (desk duty, etc.) should not be made available to police employees who cannot successfully perform at the street policing level. If the established standard of performance has not been maintained, do not extend probationary periods or bend the rules beyond what has traditionally been done for all employees. In policing, those who have not "paid their dues" on the street lack credibility with operational level employees in the organization. The agency does a disservice to the individual and to the organization when exceptions are made and standards are softened because of gender. . . .

Who Are *They*?

We represent every race, religion and socioeconomic background. We are citizens, homeowners, spouses and parents. We worry about schools, taxes, the environment and community safety. While off-duty, some of us like to wear pretty dresses, make-up and jewelry. On-duty we like to catch the bad guys. There should be no contradiction between the ability of a woman to be strong and feminine.

We are your canine handlers, beat cops, field training officers, detectives, mentors, firearms trainers and chiefs. Like our male counterparts, we have been assaulted and tragically killed for the honor of serving our communities. Many of us are motivated, some are not. Many of us are professional law enforcement officers, some are not.

So you see? Police officers who happen to be women are not alien creatures after all. We are cops—just like most of you. So if there is to be a distinction between badges, let that distinction be that badges come in gold or silver—not pink or blue.

Source: Lisa Shores, "The Thin Blue and Pink Line," *Subject to Debate* 11, no. 11 (November 1997): 3–4.

DOCUMENT 95: "A Time to Remember" (Darrell L. Sanders, 1997)

No book about the role of police would be complete without acknowledging the very real sacrifices made by the men and women who every day don uniforms in our thousands of police agencies. Officers often sacrifice a large part of their family and personal lives because of the irregular hours that have been part of American policing since the mid-1800s. They pay with a piece of their hearts each time they hold a broken child or advise a family of the death of a loved one. And they daily test their integrity dealing with the corrosive cynicism and malevolence of people at their worst. In performing these duties, they relieve each of us of unpleasant social responsibilities and make us feel more safe (Documents 77 and 78).

Policing can be a dangerous occupation, but not necessarily the most dangerous. Workers in a number of other jobs (e.g., farm workers, firemen, and a number of construction specialties) have higher mortality and injury rates. But only the police consciously prepare every day to kill or be killed. The gun on the hip, the chafe of body armor, the litany of hazard crackling from the radio—all are constant reminders that malevolent death may be the outcome of each shift.

This book is dedicated to the memory of Deputy George R. Barthel of the Los Angeles County Sheriff's Department, who was ambushed and killed in the line of duty in 1979. What made George special was not the honorable manner in which he died. Rather, it was the way that he embodied the virtues of police integrity (Document 93) throughout his career. George was as aggressive, diligent, and "hard-charging" as any street cop working in any urban slum. But he treated people with respect. Everyone, from the most wretched winos, prostitutes, and junkies to grandmothers and young children, was treated courteously and with compassion. He saw himself as their protector.

Even more remarkable, given the time and place in which one of us (Bryan Vila) had the honor of working with George, was his sense of fairness. In the 1970s all the world often seemed adrift from its moral anchor, especially in South Central Los Angeles' slums. Yet George knew what was right and did what was right. He fought hard and well when it was called for. But he also was the first person who, in the midst of a melee, would wade in, saying, "All right. That's enough. We've got him cuffed now." If George had been there, there never would have been a Rodney King incident (Document 87).

* * *

During the week of May 12th—National Police Week—people across the country will be honoring police officers who have died in the line of duty. Although this is a difficult and emotional time, it is also a time to remember. . . .

Death is a subject that few in our society are willing or able to talk about openly or honestly. In the event of an officer's death in the line of duty, however, we must be prepared to direct the agency in providing proper support for his or her family and co-workers. While the loss to the agency and the community is serious, each police death leaves family, friends and co-workers with the emotional trauma of a devastating loss.

There is a bond joining those in the "police family" that is formed by the experiences they have faced together. A police death hits hard within that family as others are reminded of their own vulnerability. When police departments establish systematic policies for dealing with a departmental death, they are better able to respond to the needs of the survivors in a prompt, organized manner and remain sensitive to the profound human emotions they must confront. . . .

As we all know, police officers face difficult challenges every day. Our jobs can be dangerous, frustrating, even tedious, but law enforcement is a tremendously rewarding career. In today's society, police officers can significantly improve the quality of life for the citizens of their community by keeping the peace despite sometimes overwhelming odds. It's important that police officers everywhere receive appropriate recognition, support and respect for the work they do.

One of any agency's greatest strengths is the depth of pride and commitment its personnel bring to the job. The strength of the agency's personnel is often reflected in the commitment of the administrators who lead them.

We have the opportunity to demonstrate this leadership this month as we honor the memory and valor of the officers we have lost. Let us take fullest advantage of this opportunity to celebrate the lives of the men and women in blue whose hard work, dedication and sacrifice remain as an inspiration to us all. Our challenge today and in the future can best be summarized by a very moving quote from Vivian Eney, a survivor and IACP employee, which appears on the National Law Enforcement Officers' Memorial: "It is not how these officers died that made them heroes; it is how they lived."

Source: Darrell L. Sanders, "A Time to Remember," *Police Chief* 64, no. 5 (May 1997): 6.

NOTES

1. As is widely known, King is African American and the officers who beat him are white.

2. These included the events at Ruby Ridge and Waco; a recent corruption investigation in the New York Police Department; an assault on immigrant laborers by law enforcement officers in Riverside, California; testimony at the O. J. Simpson murder trial of retired police officer Mark Fuhrman, who spoke of routine acts of police brutality; and numerous other incidents at smaller police departments in Florida, New York, California, Alaska, and Virginia (U.S. Department of Justice 1997:7).

Glossary

Amerciament (also *amercement*). A fine or other monetary penalty imposed by a court.

Bertillon system. A time-consuming method for identifying criminals by systematically recording measurements of various parts of their bodies as well as any abnormalities.

Community policing. A policing philosophy emphasizing proactive and decentralized approaches to reducing crime, disorder, and fear of crime in communities. It involves long-term personal involvement by officers with residents and community groups.

Frankpledge system. In old English law, a system where adult male members of a *tithing* group were responsible for one another's good behavior and for assuring that any member who broke the law would be brought forward.

Militia. A military force similar to contemporary National Guard units that is raised from the civilian populace and that may be used by a governor in emergencies.

Prima facie. Presumed to be true unless proven otherwise.

Problem-oriented policing. A policing strategy in which citizens help define community crime problems and suggest solutions for them.

Public house. An inn serving alcoholic drinks for consumption on the premises.

Rattel wacht. A citizens' night watch in Dutch New Amsterdam (later New York City). Watchmen used rattles to communicate with one another and to announce their presence.

Roundsmen. Police line supervisors who made the rounds among officers walking foot-patrol beats and standing fixed posts.

Schout fiscal. A Dutch colonial official in New Netherlands (later New York State) whose duties combined those of a sheriff and attorney general.

Shire reeve. The senior law enforcement officer in early English shires or counties; forerunner of the contemporary sheriff.

Sweat box. A small and very hot room near the furnace in some early police stations where suspects were held and interrogated in order to coerce statements from them.

Temperance societies. Groups formed to combat widespread alcoholism that were especially active in the nineteenth and early twentieth centuries.

Third degree. The use of prolonged questioning, threats, or actual violence to coerce a confession or other information from a prisoner or criminal suspect.

Tithing. An old English civil division composed of ten freeholders and their families who were bound to the king for one another's peaceable behavior.

Volstead Act. A federal law prohibiting the manufacture, transportation, or sale of liquor. It was passed under the Eighteenth Amendment and later repealed under the Twenty-first Amendment.

APPENDIX A

Selected U.S. Supreme Court Cases

U.S. Supreme Court cases excerpted in this book:

Hopt v. Utah, 110 U.S. 574 (1884) [Document 16]

Weeks v. United States, 232 U.S. 383 (1914) [Document 31]

Carroll et al. v. United States, 267 U.S. 132 (1925) [Document 38]

Brown et al. v. Mississippi, 297 U.S. 278 (1936) [Document 47]

Chambers et al. v. Florida, 309 U.S. 227 (1940) [Document 50]

Mapp v. Ohio, 367 U.S. 643 (1961) [Document 55]

Miranda v. Arizona, 384 U.S. 436 (1966) [Document 60]

Terry v. Ohio, 392 U.S. 1 (1968) [Document 62]

Tennessee v. Garner et al., 471 U.S. 1 (1985) [Document 80]

Malley et al. v. Briggs, 475 U.S. 335 (1986) [Document 81]

For further reading on U.S. Supreme Court cases related to police issues:

Wilson v. United States, 162 U.S. 613 (1896)

Silverthorne Lumber Co., Inc., et al. v. United States, 251 U.S. 385 (1920)

Hester v. United States, 265 U.S. 57 (1924)

Ashcraft et al. v. Tennessee, 322 U.S. 143 (1944)

Spano v. New York, 360 U.S. 315 (1959)

Escobedo v. Illinois, 378 U.S. 478 (1964)

Schmerber v. California, 384 U.S. 757 (1966)

Katz v. United States, 389 U.S. 347 (1967)

Harris v. United States, 390 U.S. 234 (1968)

Bumper v. North Carolina, 391 U.S. 543 (1968)

Chimel v. California, 395 U.S. 752 (1969)

Payton v. New York, 445 U.S. 573 (1980)

Illinois v. Gates, 462 U.S. 213 (1983)

Nix v. Williams, 467 U.S. 431 (1984)

United States v. Leon et al., 468 U.S. 897 (1984)

APPENDIX B

Selected Police-Related Groups, Organizations, and Web Sites

Following is a partial list of national organizations, groups, and Web sites related to policing in the United States.

Community Policing Consortium
1726 M St., NW, Suite 801
Washington, DC 20036
800–833–3085
http://www.communitypolicing.org/

Federal Bureau of Investigation (FBI)
J. Edgar Hoover Building
935 Pennsylvania Avenue, NW
Washington, DC 20535
202–324–3000
http://www.fbi.gov/

International Association of Chiefs of Police (IACP)
5154 North Washington Street
Alexandria, VA 22314–2357
800–843–4227
http://www.theiacp.org/index.html/

International Police Association
United States Section
1203 Edgewood Road
Redwood City, CA 94062
650–364–5966
http://www.ipa-usa.org/main.htm

International Union of Police Associations (IUPA)
1421 Prince Street, Suite 330
Alexandria, VA 22314–2805
800–247–4872
http://www.iupa.org/iupa/

Law Enforcement Statistics
Bureau of Justice Statistics
Office of Justice Programs
U.S. Department of Justice
810 Seventh Street, NW
Washington, DC 20531
202–307–0703
http://www.ojp.usdoj.gov/bjs/lawenf.htm

National Center for Women & Policing (NCWP)
8105 West Third Street
Los Angeles, CA 90048
213–651–2532
http://www.feminist.org/police/ncwp.html

National Organization of Black Law Enforcement Executives (NOBLE)
4609 Pinecrest Office Park Drive, Suite F
Alexandria, VA· 22312–1442
703–658–1529
fax: 703–658–9479
http://www.noblenatl.org/

National Sheriffs' Association (NSA)
1450 Duke Street
Alexandria, VA 22314–3490
703–836–7827
http://www.sheriffs.org/

Police Executive Research Forum (PERF)
1120 Connecticut Avenue, NW, Suite 930
Washington, DC 20036
202–466–7820
fax: 202–466–7826
http://www.PoliceForum.org/

Police Foundation
1201 Connecticut Avenue, NW, Suite 200
Washington, DC 20036
202–833–1460
fax: 202–659–9149

Additional Internet search link sites:

Law Enforcement Links: http://www.leolinks.com/
CopNet: http://www.cop.net/

Select Bibliography

GENERAL WORKS

"An Act for Improving the Police in and near the Metropolis." In *Parliamentary Papers*, vol. 2, Bills, N.P., 10° GEORGII IV., Cap. 44. (June 19, 1829).

"Adding Policemen to the List of Those Who Know How to Shoot." *American Rifleman* 71, no. 7 (September 1, 1923): 14.

Allinson, Edward P., and Boies Penrose. *Philadelphia 1681–1887: A History of Municipal Development*. Philadelphia: Allen, Lane & Scott, 1887.

Astor, George. *The New York Cops*. New York: Charles Scribner's Sons, 1971.

Ayres, Richard M. "Police Unions: A Step Toward Professionalism?" *Journal of Police Science and Administration* 3 (1975): 4.

Bailey, Victor, ed. *Policing and Punishment in Nineteenth Century Britain*. New Brunswick, N.J.: Rutgers University Press, 1981.

Bailey, William G., ed. *The Encyclopedia of Police Science*. New York: Garland Publishing, 1989.

Baldassare, Mark, ed. *The Los Angeles Riots: Lessons for the Urban Future*. Boulder, Colo.: Westview Press, 1994.

Ball, Larry D. *The United States Marshals of New Mexico and Arizona Territories, 1846–1912*. Albuquerque: University of New Mexico Press, 1978.

Barker, Thomas, Ronald D. Hunter, and Jeffery P. Rush, eds. *Police Systems and Practices*. Englewood Cliffs, N.J.: Prentice-Hall, 1994.

Bates, Karen Grigsby. "Dashing the Possibility of Trust." *Los Angeles Times*, April 30, 1992, B7.

Bayley, David H. "Community Policing: A Report from the Devil's Advocate." In Jack R. Greene and Stephen D. Mastrofski, eds., *Community Policing: Rhetoric or Reality*. New York: Praeger, 1988.

———. *Police for the Future*. New York: Oxford University Press, 1994.

Bechtel, Kenneth H. *State Police in the United States: A Socio-Historical Analysis*. Westport, Conn.: Greenwood Press, 1995.

Berman, Jay Stuart. *Police Administration and Progressive Reform: Theodore Roosevelt as Police Commissioner of New York*. New York: Greenwood Press, 1987.

Bittner, Egon. *The Functions of the Police in Modern Society*. Chevy Chase, Md.: National Institute of Mental Health, Center for Studies of Crime and Delinquency, 1970.

Black, Donald. *The Manners and Customs of the Police*. New York: Academic Press, 1980.

Blumberg, Abraham S., and Elaine Niederhoffer. *The Ambivalent Force: Perspectives on the Police*. Third edition. Fort Worth: Harcourt Brace College Publishers, 1985.

Boone, Nicholas. *The Constables Pocket-Book*. Boston: Nicholas Boone, 1710.

Bopp, William J. *"O. W.": O. W. Wilson and the Search for a Police Profession*. Port Washington, N.Y.: Kennikat Press, 1977.

Bopp, William J., and Donald O. Schultz. *Principles of American Law Enforcement and Criminal Justice*. Springfield, Ill.: Charles C Thomas, 1972a.

————. *A Short History of American Law Enforcement*. Springfield, Ill.: Charles C Thomas, 1972b.

Bouza, Anthony V. *The Police Mystique*. New York: Plenum, 1990.

Boyer, Paul. *Urban Masses and Moral Order in America, 1820–1920*. Cambridge, Mass.: Harvard University Press, 1978.

Bridenbaugh, Carl. *Cities in the Wilderness: The First Century of Urban Life in America, 1625–1742*. New York: Ronald Press, 1938.

Brown, Richard Maxwell. *The South Carolina Regulators*. Cambridge, Mass.: Belknap Press of Harvard University Press, 1963.

Buraker, Carroll D. "The Educated Police Officer: Asset or Liability?" *The Police Chief* 44, no. 8 (September 1977): 37–39.

Bureau of Investigation. *Uniform Crime Reporting: A Booklet Published for the Information of Law Enforcement Officials and Agencies*. Washington, D.C.: U.S. Government Printing Office, 1930.

Burnham, David. "Graft Paid to Police Here Said to Run into Millions." *New York Times*, April 25, 1970, 1, 18.

Burpo, John H. *The Police Labor Movement: Problems and Perspectives*. Springfield, Ill.: Charles C Thomas, 1971.

Cahalane, Cornelius F. "Police Training." *Annals of the American Academy of Political and Social Science* 146 (November 1929): 167–168.

Caldwell, Harry M., and Paul G. Flynn. "Search and Seizure." In William G. Bailey, ed., *The Encyclopedia of Police Science*. New York: Garland Publishing, 1989, 569–577.

Calhoun, Frederick S. *The Lawmen: United States Marshals and Their Deputies, 1789–1989*. Washington, D.C.: Smithsonian Institution Press, 1989.

Campbell, James S., et al. *Law and Order Reconsidered: Report of the Task Force on Law and Law Enforcement to the National Commission on the Causes and Prevention of Violence*. New York: Bantam Books, 1970.

Capeci, Dominic Joseph, Jr. *The Harlem Riot of 1943*. Philadelphia: Temple University Press, 1977.

Carte, Gene, and Elaine H. Carte. *Police Reform in the United States: The Era of August Vollmer, 1905–1932*. Berkeley: University of California Press, 1975.

Carter, David I., Allen D. Sapp, and Darrel W. Stephens. *The State of Police Education: Policy Direction for the Twenty-First Century*. Washington, D.C.: Police Executive Research Forum, 1988.

Chafee, Zechariah, Jr. Foreword to *Our Lawless Police: A Study of the Unlawful Enforcement of the Law*, by Jerome Ernest Hopkins. New York: Viking Press, 1931, vii–xiii.

Champion, Dean J., and George E. Rush. *Policing in the Community*. Upper Saddle River, N.J.: Prentice-Hall, 1997.

Chapman, Samuel G. Introduction to the reprint edition of *Police Administration: A Critical Study of Police Organisations in the United States and Abroad*, by Leonhard Felix Fuld. New York: G. P. Putnam's Sons, 1909. [Montclair, N.J.: Patterson Smith, 1971.]

Chevigny, Paul. *Police Power: Police Abuses in New York City*. New York: Vintage Books, 1969.

Chicago Commission on Race Relations. *The Negro in Chicago: A Study of Race Relations and a Race Riot*. Chicago: University of Chicago Press, 1922.

"Chicago's Police Scandal." *Literary Digest* 54, no. 4 (January 27, 1917): 179.

Christian, Charles. *A Brief Treatise on the Police of New York*. New York: Southwick & Pelsue, 1812.

Citizens' Police Committee. *Chicago Police Problems*. Chicago: Leonard D. White, 1931. [Montclair, N.J.: Patterson Smith, 1969.]

Clarke, Lewis G. *Narratives of Suffering*. 1846. Available on Library of American Civilization microfiche #12812.

Clum, John P. "The San Carlos Apache Police." *New Mexico Historical Review* 4, no. 3 (July 1929): 203–219.

The Colonial Laws of New York from the Year 1664 to the Revolution, Vol. 1. Albany: James B. Lyon, State Printer, 1894.

Commission to Investigate Allegations of Police Corruption. *The Knapp Commission Report on Police Corruption*. New York: George Braziller, 1973.

Committee on Uniform Crime Records, International Association of Chiefs of Police. *Uniform Crime Reporting: A Complete Manual for Police*. Second edition. New York: J. J. Little and Ives, 1930.

Conley, John A. "Police History: The Police in Urban America, 1860–1920." In William G. Bailey, ed., *The Encyclopedia of Police Science*. New York: Garland Publishing, 1989, 439–447.

Conover, Milton. "State Police." *American Political Science Review* 15 (February 1921): 82–93.

Cromwell, Paul F., and Roger G. Dunham, eds. *Crime and Justice in America*. Upper Saddle River, N.J.: Prentice-Hall, 1997.

Cunliffe, Marcus. "Testing a Union: 1788–1865." In Arthur M. Schlesinger, Jr., ed., *The Almanac of American History*. New York: Barnes and Noble, 1993, 146–297.

Dantzker, Mark L. "Being a Police Officer: Part of a Profession?" In M. L. Dantzker, ed., *Contemporary Policing: Personnel, Issues, and Trends*. Boston: Butterworth-Heinemann, 1997, 127–140.

Dawson, Edgar. "New York State Police." *American Political Science Review* 11 (August 1917): 539–541.

Deakin, Thomas J. *Police Professionalism: The Renaissance of American Law Enforcement*. Springfield, Ill.: Charles C Thomas, 1988.

Deutsch, Albert. *The Trouble with Cops*. New York: Crown, 1955.

Domanick, Joe. *To Protect and Serve*. New York: Pocket Books, 1994.

Donner, Frank. *Protectors of Privilege*. Berkeley: University of California Press, 1990.

Dowling, Jerry L. "Supreme Court Decisions Affecting American Policing." In William G. Bailey, ed., *The Encyclopedia of Police Science*. New York: Garland Publishing, 1989, 603–610.

The Duke of York's Laws, 1665–75. In *The Colonial Laws of New York from the Year 1664 to the Revolution*, Vol. I. Albany: James B. Lyon, State Printer, 1894.

Easterlin, Richard A. *Birth and Fortune: The Impact of Numbers on Personal Welfare*, Second edition. Chicago: University of Chicago Press, 1987.

Elliott, J. F. *The "New" Police*. Springfield, Ill.: Charles C Thomas, 1973.

Elliston, Frederick A., and Michael Feldberg, eds. *Moral Issues in Police Work*. Totowa, N.J.: Rowman & Allanheld, 1985.

Emsley, Clive. *The English Police: A Political and Social History*. New York: St. Martin's Press, 1991.

"The Evolution of the Law Enforcement Code of Ethics." *Police Chief* 59, no. 1 (January 1992): 14.

"Exercises Marking Termination of First FBI Police Training School." *FBI Law Enforcement Bulletin* 4 (1935): 11.

"The FBI Pledge for Law Enforcement Officers." *FBI Law Enforcement Bulletin* 6, no. 12 (December 1937): 2.

Fink, Joseph, and Lloyd G. Sealy. *The Community and the Police—Conflict or Cooperation?* New York: John Wiley & Sons, 1974.

"First Woman 'Policeman.' " *Los Angeles Times*, September 13, 1910, 9.

Fleek, T. A., and T. J. Newnam, "The Role of the Police in Modern Society," *Police*, March–April 1969, 21–27. Reprinted in Harry W. More, Jr., ed., *Critical Issues in Law Enforcement*. Cincinnati: W. H. Anderson, 1972.

Flinn, John J., and John E. Wilkie. *History of the Chicago Police*. Chicago: Police Book Fund, 1887. [New York: Arno Press and the New York Times, 1971.]

Fogelson, Robert M. *Big-City Police*. Cambridge, Mass.: Harvard University Press, 1977.

Folley, Vern L. "Role of the Police." In William G. Bailey, ed., *The Encyclopedia of Police Science*. New York: Garland Publishing, 1989, 556–560.

Fosdick, Raymond B. *American Police Systems*. New York: Century Co., 1920.

Franklin, Benjamin. *Memoirs* (circa 1789). [*The Autobiography of Benjamin Franklin*. New York: Heritage Press, 1951.]

Fuld, Leonhard Felix. *Police Administration*. New York: G. P. Putnam's Sons, 1909. [Montclair, N.J.: Patterson Smith, 1971.]

Fyfe, James J. "Always Prepared: Police Off-Duty Guns." *Annals of the American Academy of Political and Social Science* 452 (November 1980): 72–81. [Reprinted in James J. Fyfe, ed., *Readings on Police Use of Deadly Force*. Washington, D.C.: Police Foundation, 1988, 282–296.]

———. "Deadly Force." In William G. Bailey, ed. *The Encyclopedia of Police Science*. New York: Garland Publishing, 1989, 133–136.

———. "Police Use of Deadly Force." *Justice Quarterly* 5 (1988): 165–205.

———, ed. *Contemporary Issues in Law Enforcement*. Beverly Hills: Sage, 1981.

———, ed. *Readings on Police Use of Deadly Force*. Washington, D.C: Police Foundation, 1982.

Gallup Opinion Index, No. 27 (September 1967). Princeton, N.J.: American Institute of Public Opinion.

Gallup Opinion Index, No. 157 (1978). Princeton, N.J.: American Institute of Public Opinion.

Gallup Political Index, No. 5 (October 1965). American Institute of Public Opinion.

The Gallup Poll Monthly, No. 306 (March 1991). Princeton, N.J.: The Gallup Poll.

The Gallup Report, No. 279 (December 1988). Princeton, N.J.: Gallup Poll.

The Gallup Report, No. 285 (June 1989). Princeton, N.J.: Gallup Poll.

Gammage, Allen Z., and Stanley L. Sachs. *Police Unions*. Springfield, Ill.: Charles C Thomas, 1972.

Gash, Norman. *Sir Robert Peel: The Life of Sir Robert Peel after 1830*. Totowa, N.J.: Rowman and Littlefield, 1972.

Geller, William A., and Hans Toch, eds. *Police Violence: Understanding and Controlling Police Abuse of Force*. New Haven, Conn.: Yale University Press, 1996.

Gillett, James B. *Six Years with the Texas Rangers*. New Haven, Conn.: Yale University Press, 1925.

Goldstein, Herman. "Improving Policing: A Problem-Oriented Approach." *Crime and Delinquency* 25, no. 2 (April 1979).

———. "The New Policing: Confronting Complexity." National Institute of Justice, *Research in Brief*. Washington, D.C.: United States Department of Justice, December 1993. Reprinted in Paul F. Cromwell and Roger G. Dunham, eds., *Crime and Justice in America*. Upper Saddle River, N.J.: Prentice-Hall, 1997.

———. *Problem-Oriented Policing*. Philadelphia: Temple University Press, 1990.

Governor's Commission on the Los Angeles Riots. *Violence in the City—An End or a Beginning?* Sacramento: California State Government, 1965.

Grano, Joseph D. *Confessions, Truth, and the Law*. Ann Arbor: University of Michigan Press, 1993.

Greenberg, Douglas. *Crime and Law Enforcement in the Colony of New York, 1691–1776*. Ithaca, N.Y.: Cornell University Press, 1976.

Greene, Jack R., and Stephen D. Mastrofski, eds. *Community Policing: Rhetoric or Reality*. New York: Praeger, 1988.

Griffin, James S. "African Americans in Policing." In Kenneth J. Peak, *Policing America: Methods, Issues, Challenges*. Second edition. Upper Saddle River, N.J.: Prentice-Hall, 1997.

Haager, J. H. "The Automobile as a Police Department Adjunct." In *International Association of Chiefs of Police: Sixteenth Annual Session*, Buffalo, N.Y., June 15–18, 1909. [*Proceeedings of the Annual Conventions of the International Association of Chiefs of Police*: 1906–1912, Vol. 2. New York: Arno Press and the New York Times, 1971.]

Hafen, LeRoy R., and Carl Coke Rister. *Western America*. Second edition. New York: Prentice-Hall, 1950.

Hagan, William T. *Indian Police and Judges*. New Haven, Conn.: Yale University Press, 1966. [Lincoln: University of Nebraska Press, 1980.]

Hall, Kermit L., ed. *Police, Prison, and Punishment*. New York: Garland Publishing, 1987.

Harring, Sidney L. *Policing a Class Society*. New Brunswick, N.J.: Rutgers University Press, 1983.

Harris, Fred R. Preface to the 1988 edition of *The Kerner Report: The 1968 Report of the National Advisory Commission on Civil Disorders*, by the National Advisory Commission on Civil Disorders. New York: Pantheon, 1988.

Hawke, David. *The Colonial Experience*. Indianapolis: Bobbs-Merrill, 1966.

Heaphy, John F., ed. *Police Practices: The General Administrative Survey*. Washington, D.C.: Police Foundation, 1978.

Higgins, Lois Lundell. *Policewoman's Manual*. Springfield, Ill.: Charles C Thomas, 1961.

Hindus, Michael Stephen. *Prison and Plantation: Crime, Justice, and Authority in Massachusetts and South Carolina, 1767–1878*. Chapel Hill: University of North Carolina Press, 1980.

Hoover, John Edgar. *Present-Day Police Problems*. Address before the Convention of the International Association of Chiefs of Police, Baltimore, Md., Oct. 4, 1937. Washington, D.C.: U.S. Department of Justice, Federal Bureau of Investigation, 1937.

Hoover, Larry T., and Ronald G. DeLord. "Unionization." In William G. Bailey ed., *The Encyclopedia of Police Science*. New York: Garland Publishing, 1989, 639–644.

Hopkins, Ernest Jerome. *Our Lawless Police: A Study of the Unlawful Enforcement of the Law*. New York: Viking, 1931.

Hutzel, Eleanore L. "The Policewoman." *Annals of the American Academy of Political and Social Science* 146 (November 1929): 104–114.

Inciardi, James A. *Criminal Justice*. Fourth edition. Fort Worth: Harcourt Brace, 1993.

———. *Elements of Criminal Justice*. Fort Worth: Harcourt Brace, 1997.

Independent Commission on the Los Angeles Police Department (Warren Christopher, Chair). *Report of the Independent Commission on the Los Angeles Police Department*. Los Angeles: The Commission, July 9, 1991, i–v.

International Association of Chiefs of Police. "Law Enforcement Code of Ethics and Canons of Police Ethics." *The Police Chief* 24, no. 12 (December 1957): 4–6.

———. "Police Code of Conduct." *The Police Chief* 59, no. 1 (January 1992), 17. Reprinted in John Kleinig with Yurong Zhang, *Professional Law Enforcement Codes: A Documentary Collection*. Westport, Conn.: Greenwood Press, 1993.

———. *Police Unions and Other Police Organizations*. Washington, D.C.: IACP, 1944. [New York: Arno Press and The New York Times, 1971.]

———. "Law Enforcement Code of Ethics," *The Police Chief* 59, no. 1 (January 1992): 15.

———. Sixteenth Annual Session, Buffalo, N.Y., June 15–18, 1909. [*Proceedings of the Annual Conventions of the International Association of Chiefs of Police: 1906–1912*, Vol. II. New York: Arno Press and the New York Times, 1971.]

International City Managers' Association. *Municipal Police Administration* Third edition. Chicago: ICMA, 1950.

"The Investigation of a Videotaped Beating." *Los Angeles Times*, March 7, 1991, B6.

Jeffers, H. Paul. *Commissioner Roosevelt: The Story of Theodore Roosevelt and the New York City Police, 1895–1897*. New York: John Wiley & Sons, 1994.

Johnson, David R. *American Law Enforcement: A History.* St. Louis: Forum Press, 1981.

―――. *Policing the Urban Underworld.* Philadelphia: Temple University Press, 1979.

Johnson, Elmer. "Police: An Analysis of Role Conflict." *Police* 14 (1970): 47–52.

Juris, Hervey A., and Peter Feuille. *Police Unionism.* Lexington, Mass.: Lexington Books, 1973.

Kamisar, Yale. *Police Interrogation and Confessions: Essays in Laws and Policy.* Ann Arbor: University of Michigan Press, 1980.

Kappeler, V. E. *Critical Issues in Police Civil Liability.* Prospect Heights, Ill.: Waveland, 1993.

Keith, Elmer. "The Police at Perry." *American Rifleman* (October 15, 1925): 11, 23.

Kelling, George L., Tony Pate, Duane Dieckman, and Charles E. Brown. *The Kansas City Preventive Patrol Experiment: A Summary Report.* Washington, D.C.: Police Foundation, 1974.

Kirkham, George L. "A Professor's 'Street Lessons.'" *FBI Law Enforcement Bulletin* 43, no. 3 (March 1974): 14–22.

Kleinig, John. *The Ethics of Policing.* Cambridge, U.K.: Cambridge University Press, 1996.

Kleinig, John, with Yurong Zhang, eds. *Professional Law Enforcement Codes: A Documentary Collection.* Westport, Conn.: Greenwood Press, 1993.

Klockars, Carl B. "The Dirty Harry Problem." *Annals of the American Academy of Political and Social Science* 452 (November 1980): 33–47.

―――. "A Theory of Excessive Force and Its Control." In William A. Geller and Hans Toch, eds., *Police Violence.* New Haven, Conn.: Yale University Press, 1996.

Kolts, James G., et al. *The Los Angeles County Sheriff's Department.* Los Angeles: Los Angeles County, July 1992, 351–354.

Lane, Roger. *Policing the City: Boston, 1822–1885.* Cambridge, Mass.: Harvard University Press, 1967.

―――. *Violent Death in the City.* Cambridge, Mass.: Harvard University Press, 1979.

Lane, Roger, and John J. Turner, Jr., eds. *Riot, Rout and Tumult: Readings in American Social and Political Violence.* Westport Conn.: Greenwood Press, 1978.

Lanks, George A. "How Should We Educate the Police?" *Journal of Criminal Law, Criminology, and Police Science* 61 (1971): 4.

The Law Enforcement Assistance Administration (LEAA): The Title I Program of the Omnibus Crime Control and Safe Streets Act of 1968, as Amended. Washington, D.C.: U.S. Government Printing Office, 1968.

Lee, Henry J., ed. *Eagle Police Manual: A Handbook for Peace Officers.* New York: Eagle Library Publications, 1933.

Linn, Edith, and Barbara Raffel Price. "The Evolving Role of Women in American Policing." In Abraham S. Blumberg and Elaine Niederhoffer, *The Ambivalent Force: Perspectives on the Police.* Third edition. Fort Worth: Harcourt Brace College Publishers, 1985, 76–78.

Lipsky, Michael, ed. *Law and Order: Police Encounters.* Chicago: Aldine, 1970.

Lord, Lesli Kay. "Policewomen." In William G. Bailey, ed., *The Encyclopedia of Police Science.* New York: Garland Publishing, 1989, 491–502.

Louis, Paul. "New York City Police Department." In William G. Bailey, ed., *The Encyclopedia of Police Science*. New York: Garland Publishing, 1989, 346–352.

Maas, Peter. *Serpico*. New York: Viking Press, 1973.

MacNamara, Donal E. J. "August Vollmer." In William G. Bailey, ed., *The Encyclopedia of Police Science*. New York: Garland Publishing, 1989, 657–659.

Mantz, Charles A. "Introductory Address," *Official Proceedings of the National Police Convention*. St. Louis: R. & T. A. Ennis, 1871. [New York: Arno Press and the New York Times, 1971, 9–11.]

Martin, Susan Ehrlich. *Breaking and Entering: Policewomen on Patrol*. Berkeley: University of California Press, 1980.

Mayer, S. L. "Forging a Nation: 1866–1900." In Arthur M. Schlesinger, Jr., *The Almanac of American History*. New York: Barnes and Noble, 1993.

Mayo, Katherine. "Demobilization and State Police." *North American Review* 209 (June 1919): 786–794.

McLellan, Howard. "Our Inefficient Police." *North American Review* 227, no. 2 (February 1929): 219–228.

Miller, Wilbur R. *Cops and Bobbies*. Chicago: University of Chicago Press, 1977.

Mishkin, Barry D. "Female Police in the United States." *Police Journal* 54 (January 1981): 22–25.

More, Harry W., Jr., ed. *Critical Issues in Law Enforcement*. Cincinnati: W. H. Anderson, 1972.

Morn, Frank. "Allan Pinkerton." In William G. Bailey, ed., *The Encyclopedia of Police Science*. New York: Garland Publishing, 1989.

Morrison, Gregory Boyce. *A Critical History and Evaluation of American Police Firearms Training to 1945*. Ann Arbor, Mich.: UMI, 1995.

Morrison, Gregory B., and Bryan J. Vila. "Police Handgun Qualification: Practical Measure or Aimless Activity?" *Policing: An International Journal of Police Strategies & Management* 21, no. 3 (1988): 510–533.

Morrison, Patt, et al. "Frustrated Officers Try to Sort Out the Crisis." *Los Angeles Times*, May 11, 1992, A1, A6.

Mosse, George L., ed. *Police Forces in History*. London: Sage, 1975.

Murphy, Patrick V. "John Edgar Hoover: The Federal Influence in American Policing." In Philip John Stead, ed., *Pioneers in Policing*. Montclair, N.J.: Patterson Smith, 1977, 262–279.

Murphy, Patrick V., and Thomas Plate. *Commissioner: A View from the Top of American Law Enforcement*. New York: Simon and Schuster, 1977.

Murray, Edmund P. "Should the Police Unionize?" *The Nation* (June 14, 1959): 530–533.

Myers, Gloria E. *A Municipal Mother*. Corvallis: Oregon State University Press, 1995.

Myren, Richard A. "The Role of the Police." Reference document submitted to the President's Commission on Law Enforcement and Administration of Justice, 1967. Reprinted in Harry W. More, Jr., ed., *Critical Issues in Law Enforcement*. Cincinnati: W. H. Anderson, 1972.

National Advisory Commission on Civil Disorders. *Report of the National Advisory Commission on Civil Disorders*. Washington, D.C.: U.S. Government Printing Office, 1968.

National Commission on Law Observance and Enforcement. *Report on Police*. Washington, D.C.: U.S. Government Printing Office, 1931. [New York: Arno Press and the New York Times, 1971.]

"A Needed Police Reform: The Movement for the Employment of Matrons." *New York Times*, March 23, 1890, 20.

"New Police Instructions." *London Times*, September 25, 1829, 3.

New York (City). *The Complete Report of Mayor LaGuardia's Commission on the Harlem Riot of March 19, 1935*. (Originally published by the *New York Amsterdam News*, July 18, 1936.) [Reprinted in *Mass Violence in America: The Harlem Riot of 1935*. New York: Arno Press and the New York Times, 1969.]

Norton, William J. "Chief Kohler of Cleveland and His Golden Rule Policy." *The Outlook* 93 (November 6, 1909): 537–542.

Palmer, Milton R. "The State Police as an Asset." *American Industries* 23 (August 1922): 19–23.

Palmiotto, Michael J. *Policing: Concepts, Strategies, and Current Issues in American Police Forces*. Durham, N.C.: Carolina Academic Press, 1997.

Parker, Alfred E. *The Berkeley Police Story*. Springfield, Ill.: Charles C Thomas, 1972.

Parker, William H. "The Police Challenge in Our Great Cities." *Annals of the American Academy of Political and Social Science* (January 1954). Reprinted in O. W. Wilson, ed., *Parker on Police*. Springfield, Ill.: Charles C Thomas, 1957.

Peak, Kenneth J. *Policing America*. Second edition. Upper Saddle River, N.J.: Prentice-Hall, 1997.

Peak, Kenneth J., and Ronald W. Glensor. *Community Policing and Problem Solving*. Upper Saddle River, N.J.: Prentice-Hall, 1996.

Pfuhl, Erdwin H., Jr. "Strikes and Job Actions." In William G. Bailey, ed., *The Encyclopedia of Police Science*. New York: Garland Publishing, 1989, 596–602.

Pinkerton, Allan. *General Principles of Pinkerton's National Police Agency*. Chicago: George H. Fergus, 1867.

"The Police Commission—Uniforming the Police." *The Public Ledger*, August 3, 1860, 1.

Police Gazette, January 31, August 22, September 26, September 5, 1846.

"The Police Uniform." *New-York Daily Times (New York Times)*, June 30, 1854.

Prassel, Frank Richard. *The Western Peace Officer: A Legacy of Law and Order*. Norman: University of Oklahoma Press, 1972.

Preiss, Jack J., and Howard J. Ehrlich. *An Examination of Role Theory: The Case of the State Police*. Lincoln: University of Nebraska Press, 1966.

President's Commission on Law Enforcement and Administration of Justice. *Task Force Report: The Police*. Washington, D.C.: U.S. Government Printing Office, 1967.

Proceedings of the Annual Conventions of the International Association of Chiefs of Police: 1893–1905. Vol. 1. New York: Arno Press & the New York Times, 1971.

Proceedings of the Annual Conventions of the International Association of Chiefs of

Police: 1906–1912. Vol. 2. New York: Arno Press and the New York Times, 1971.

Proceedings of the Annual Conventions of the International Association of Chiefs of Police: 1913–1920. Vol. 3. New York: Arno Press and the New York Times, 1971.

Proceedings of the Annual Conventions of the International Association of Chiefs of Police: 1921–1925. Vol. 4. New York: Arno Press and the New York Times, 1971.

Proceedings of the Annual Conventions of the International Association of Chiefs of Police: 1926–1930. Vol. 5. New York: Arno Press and the New York Times, 1971.

Raffel Price, Barbara. *Police Professionalism.* Lexington, Mass.: Lexington Books, 1977.

Regoli, Robert M., and John D. Hewitt. *Criminal Justice.* Englewood Cliffs, N.J.: Prentice-Hall, 1996.

Reichel, Philip L. "The Misplaced Emphasis on Urbanization in Police Development." *Policing and Society* 3 (1992): 1–12.

———. "Southern Slave Patrols as a Transitional Police Type." *American Journal of Police* 7, no. 2 (1988): 51–77.

Reid, Sue Titus. *Criminal Justice.* Second edition. New York: Macmillan, 1990.

Reiss, Albert J. Jr., "Controlling Police Use of Deadly Force." *Annals of the American Academy of Political and Social Science* 452 (November 1980): 122–134.

———. *The Police and the Public.* New Haven, Conn.: Yale University Press, 1971.

———. "Police Brutality . . . Answers to Key Questions." In Michael Lipsky, ed., *Law and Order: Police Encounters.* Chicago: Aldine, 1970.

———. *Private Employment of Public Police.* Washington, D.C.: U.S. Government Printing Office, 1988.

Reppetto, Thomas A. "Bruce Smith: Police Reform in the United States." In Philip John Stead, ed., *Pioneers in Policing.* Montclair, N.J.: Patterson Smith, 1977, 191–206.

Richardson, James F. Introduction to the reprint edition of *Recollections of a New York Chief of Police*, by George W. Walling. New York: Caxton Book Concern, 1887. [Montclair, N.J.: Patterson Smith, 1972.]

———. *The New York Police: Colonial Times to 1901.* New York: Oxford University Press, 1970.

———. *Urban Police in the United States.* Port Washington, N.Y.: Kennikat Press, 1974.

Roberg, Roy R., and Jack Kuykendall. *Police Organization and Management: Behavior, Theory, and Processes.* Pacific Grove, Calif.: Brooks-Cole, 1990.

Roe, George M., ed. *Our Police: A History of the Cincinnati Police Force, from the Earliest Period until the Present Day.* Cincinnati: N.P. 1890. [New York: AMS Press, 1976.]

Romier, Lucien. *History of France.* New York: St. Martin's Press, 1966.

Roosevelt, Theodore. *American Ideals and Other Essays Social and Political.* New York: G. P. Putnam's Sons, 1897.

———. "The Lawlessness of the Police." In *The Works of Theodore Roosevelt*, Vol. 14. New York: Charles Scribner's Sons, 1926.

Rubin, Jesse. "Police Identity and the Police Role." In Robert F. Steadman, ed., *The Police and the Community*. Baltimore: Johns Hopkins University Press, 1972.

Russell, Francis. *A City in Terror: 1919, the Boston Police Strike*. New York: Viking Press, 1975.

Rutledge, William P. "Radio in Police Work." In *International Association of Chiefs of Police: Proceedings Thirty-Sixth Convention*, Atlanta, Ga., June 3–6, 1929. [*Proceedings of the Annual Conventions of the International Association of Chiefs of Police: 1926–1930*, Vol. 5. New York: Arno Press and the New York Times, 1971.]

Rutman, Darrett B. *Winthrop's Boston: Portrait of a Puritan Town, 1630–1649*. Chapel Hill: University of North Carolina Press, 1965.

Sanders, Darrell L. "A Time to Remember." *Police Chief* 64, no. 5 (May 1997): 6.

Savage, Edward H. *Police Records and Recollections, or Boston by Daylight and Gaslight for Two Hundred and Forty Years*. Boston: John P. Dale & Co. 1873. [Montclair, N.J.: Patterson Smith, 1971.]

Scharf, Peter, and Arnold Binder. *The Badge and the Bullet: Police Use of Deadly Force*. New York: Praeger, 1983.

Schlesinger, Arthur M., Jr. ed. *The Almanac of American History*. New York: Barnes and Noble, 1993.

Schmalleger, Frank. *Criminal Justice Today: An Introductory Text for the Twenty-First Century*. Englewood Cliffs, N.J.: Prentice-Hall, 1995.

Schulz, Dorothy Moses. *From Social Worker to Crimefighter: Women in United States Municipal Policing*. Westport, Conn.: Praeger, 1995.

Sears, David O. "Urban Rioting in Los Angeles: A Comparison of 1965 with 1992." In Mark Baldassare, ed., *The Los Angeles Riots: Lessons for the Urban Future*. Boulder, Colo.: Westview Press, 1994, 237–254.

Sebold, Philip. "The Conduct of a Policeman." In Henry J. Lee, ed., *Eagle Police Manual: A Handbook for Peace Officers*. New York: Eagle Library Publications, 1933.

Segrave, Kerry. *Policewomen: A History*. Jefferson, N.C.: McFarland & Co., 1995.

Shearing, C., and P. Stenning. "Modern Private Security: Its Growth and Implications." In M. Tonry and N. Morris, eds., *Crime and Justice—An Annual Review of Research, Vol. 3*. Chicago: University of Chicago Press, 1981.

———. *Private Policing*. Newbury Park, Calif.: Sage, 1987.

Sherman, Lawrence W., and the National Advisory Commission on Higher Education for Police Officers. *The Quality of Police Education*. San Francisco: Jossey-Bass, 1978.

Shores, Lisa. "The Thin Blue and Pink Line." *Subject to Debate* 11, no. 11 (November 1997): 1–4.

Skolnick, Jerome H. "It's Not Just a Few Rotten Apples." *Los Angeles Times*, March 7, 1992, B7.

Skolnick, Jerome H., and David H. Bayley. *The New Blue Line*. New York: The Free Press, 1986.

Skolnick, Jerome H., and Thomas C. Gray, eds. *Police in America*. Boston: Little, Brown, 1975.

Smith, Bertha H. "The Policewoman." *Good Housekeeping* 52 (February 1911): 296–298.

Smith, Bruce. "Municipal Police Administration." *Annals of the American Academy of Political and Social Science* 146 (November 1929): 1–27.

———. *The State Police.* New York: Macmillan, 1925.

Sparrow, Malcolm K., Mark H. Moore, and David M. Kennedy. *Beyond 911: A New Era for Policing.* New York: Basic Books, 1990.

Stead, Philip John, ed. *Pioneers in Policing.* Montclair, N.J.: Patterson Smith, 1977.

Steadman, Robert F., ed. *The Police and the Community.* Baltimore: Johns Hopkins University Press, 1972.

Stephens, Otis H., Jr. *The Supreme Court and Confessions of Guilt.* Knoxville: University of Tennessee Press, 1973.

Swanson, C. R., L. Territo, and R. W. Taylor. *Police Administration.* Third edition. New York: Macmillan, 1993.

Sylvester, Richard. "A History of the 'Sweat Box' and 'Third Degree.' " In *International Association of Chiefs of Police: Seventeenth Annual Session,* Birmingham, Ala., May 10–13, 1910. [*Proceedings of the Annual Conventions of the International Association of Chiefs of Police: 1906–1912,* Vol. 2. New York: Arno Press and the New York Times, 1971.]

"This Isn't News." *American Rifleman,* 74, no. 11, December 1926, 10.

Thursfield, James R. *Peel.* London: Macmillan, 1893.

Towler, Juby E. *The Police Role in Racial Conflicts.* Springfield, Ill.: Charles C Thomas, 1964.

"Troubles of a Black Policeman." *Literary Digest* 44, no. 4 (January 27, 1912): 177–179.

U.S. Bureau of the Census. *Historical Statistics of the United States: Colonial Times to 1970.* Washington, D.C.: U.S. Government Printing Office, 1975.

U.S. Department of Justice. *Police Integrity: Public Service with Honor.* Washington, D.C.: U.S. Government Printing Office, January 1997.

U.S. Department of Justice, Attorney General's Office. *Instructions to United States Marshals, Attorneys, Clerks, and Commissioners.* Washington, D.C.: U.S. Government Printing Office, 1898.

U.S. Department of Justice, Office of Academic Assistance, Law Enforcement Assistance Administration. *Law Enforcement Education Program Manual.* Washington, D.C.: U.S. Government Printing Office, 1969, 1–3.

Vaughn, Joseph B. "Law Enforcement Assistance Administration." In William G. Bailey, ed., *The Encyclopedia of Police Science.* New York: Garland Publishing, 1989a, 308–309.

———. "Uniform Crime Reporting System." In William G. Bailey, ed., *The Encyclopedia of Police Science.* New York: Garland Publishing, 1989b, 635–638.

Vicchio, Stephen J. "Ethics and Police Integrity: Some Definitions and Questions for Study." Reprinted in U.S. Department of Justice, *Police Integrity: Public Service with Honor.* Washington, D.C.: U.S. Government Printing Office, January 1997, 11–16.

Vila, Bryan. "The Cops' Code of Silence." *Christian Science Monitor,* August 31, 1992, 18.

———. "Tired Cops: Probable Connections Between Fatigue and the Performance, Health and Safety of Patrol Officers." *American Journal of Police* 15, no. 2 (1996): 51–92.

Vila, Bryan, and Cynthia Morris, eds. *Capital Punishment in the United States: A Documentary History.* Westport, Conn.: Greenwood Press, 1997.

Vollmer, August. "Aims and Ideals of the Police." *Journal of the American Institute of Criminal Law and Criminology* 13 (1922): 251–257. A reprint of Vollmer's address as president of the IACP for 1922.

———. *The Police and Modern Society.* Berkeley, Calif.: Regents of the University of California, 1936. [College Park, Md.: McGrath, 1969.]

———. "Police Progress in the Past Twenty-Five Years." *Journal of Criminal Law and Criminology* 24 (May 1933).

Vollmer, August, John P. Peper, and Frank M. Boolsen. *Police Organization and Administration.* Sacramento: California State Department of Education, 1951.

Wade, Richard C. "Expanding Resources: 1901–1945." In Arthur M. Schlesinger, Jr., ed., *The Almanac of American History.* New York: Barnes and Noble, 1993, 400–503.

Walker, Samuel. *A Critical History of Police Reform.* Lexington, Mass.: Lexington Books, 1977.

———. *Popular Justice: A History of American Criminal Justice.* Second edition. New York: Oxford University Press, 1998.

Walling, George W. *Recollections of a New York Chief of Police.* New York: Caxton Book Concern, 1887. [Montclair, N.J.: Patterson Smith, 1972.]

Wambaugh, Joseph. *The Blue Knight.* Boston: Little, Brown, 1972.

———. *The Choirboys.* New York: Delacorte, 1975.

———. *The New Centurions.* New York: Dell, 1972.

Weinbaum, Paul O. *Mobs and Demagogues: The New York Response to Collective Violence in the Early Nineteenth Century.* Ann Arbor, Mich.: UMI Research Press, 1979.

Weisburd, David, and Craig Uchida, eds. *Police Innovation and Control of the Police.* New York: Springer-Verlag, 1993.

Willemse, Cornelius W. *A Cop Remembers.* New York: E. P. Dutton, 1933.

Williams, Samuel L. "Law Enforcement and Affirmative Action." *Police Chief* 42, no. 2 (February 1975): 72–73.

Wilson, James Q. *Varieties of Police Behavior.* Cambridge, Mass.: Harvard University Press, 1968.

Wilson, James Q., and George L. Kelling. "Broken Windows." *The Atlantic* 249, no. 3 (March 1982): 29–38.

Wilson, O. W. *Police Administration.* First edition. New York: McGraw-Hill, 1950.

———, ed. *Parker on Police.* Springfield, Ill.: Charles C Thomas, 1957.

Winsor, Justin, ed. *The Memorial History of Boston.* Boston: James R. Osgood and Co., 1880.

Woodiwiss, Michael. *Crime, Crusades and Corruption: Prohibitions in the United States, 1900–1987.* London: Pinter, 1981.

Woods, Arthur. *Policeman and Public.* New Haven, Conn.: Yale University Press, 1919. [New York: Arno Press and the New York Times, 1971.]

Woods, Gerald. *The Police in Los Angeles.* New York: Garland Publishing, 1993.

Yarmey, A. Daniel. *Understanding Police and Police Work: Psychosocial Issues*. New York: New York University Press, 1990.

Zinn, Howard. *A People's History of the United States*. New York: Harper Colophon Books, 1980.

Index

About the Editors

BRYAN VILA is Associate Professor of Political Science and Administration of Justice at the University of Wyoming. Prior to joining the University of Wyoming, he was Associate Professor of Criminology, Law, and Society in the School of Social Ecology at the University of California, Irvine. Dr. Vila currently is co-principal investigator on two large-scale research studies; one assesses the effects of fatigue on police officer performance, health, and safety; the other is attempting to identify causes and potential solutions to street gang problems in Orange County, California. His research specialties include criminology theory, crime control policy, the police, and human ecology. Prior to becoming an academic, Dr. Vila spent seventeen years in local, national, and international law enforcement, including nine years with the Los Angeles County Sheriff's Department. He is co-editor (with Cynthia Morris) of *Capital Punishment in the United States: A Documentary History* (Greenwood, 1997).

CYNTHIA MORRIS is a writer and editor living in Laramie, Wyoming. She is co-editor (with Bryan Vila) of *Capital Punishment in the United States: A Documentary History* (Greenwood, 1997). From 1985 to 1995, she worked as a research and science writer at the University of California, Irvine. She currently is writing a fact-based novel, *Micronesian Blues*.